MANUSCRIPT VERSE COLLECTORS AND THE POLITICS OF ANTI-COURTLY LOVE POETRY

Manuscript Verse Collectors and the Politics of Anti-Courtly Love Poetry

JOSHUA ECKHARDT

OXFORD
UNIVERSITY PRESS

OXFORD
UNIVERSITY PRESS

Great Clarendon Street, Oxford OX2 6DP

Oxford University Press is a department of the University of Oxford.
It furthers the University's objective of excellence in research, scholarship,
and education by publishing worldwide in

Oxford New York

Auckland Cape Town Dar es Salaam Hong Kong Karachi
Kuala Lumpur Madrid Melbourne Mexico City Nairobi
New Delhi Shanghai Taipei Toronto

With offices in

Argentina Austria Brazil Chile Czech Republic France Greece
Guatemala Hungary Italy Japan Poland Portugal Singapore
South Korea Switzerland Thailand Turkey Ukraine Vietnam

Published in the United States
by Oxford University Press Inc., New York

First published 2009

British Library Cataloguing in Publication Data
Data available

Library of Congress Cataloging in Publication Data
Library of Congress Control Number: 2009921239

Typeset by SPI Publisher Services, Pondicherry, India
Printed in Great Britain
on acid-free paper by
the MPG Books Group, Bodmin and King's Lynn

ISBN 978–0–19–955950–3

1 3 5 7 9 10 8 6 4 2

For Slim

Acknowledgements

Anyone who works on early modern English manuscripts owes a great debt to the scholars who have made them navigable, and to the institutions that keep them available. I spread out my thanks for their invaluable, necessary help throughout the footnotes and endmatter of this book. Yet my gratitude to a number of individuals exceeds the bounds of such bibliographical citations. Achsah Guibbory gave me the distinct advantage of beginning work on this book under the direction of the most encouraging graduate advisor I have ever even heard of, and she continues to offer support and advice with characteristic grace. Zachary Lesser read multiple drafts of the entire typescript, each time improving it with his detailed and incisive comments. Peter Beal and Henry Woudhuysen generously shared their time and expertise over a year's fellowship in London, effectively providing the finest training in Renaissance manuscript studies that I can imagine; moreover, they have since offered the direction necessary to get the book into its present form, for which I remain immensely grateful. Adam Smyth and Curtis Perry each showed me how to reconceptualize the book at a crucial stage. Brian Vickers also offered timely encouragement. Andrew McRae bravely extended an invitation to his conference on libels based only on a chance meeting at the Huntington, and subsequently published an early incarnation of my third chapter in *Huntington Library Quarterly*. Ania Loomba and Tim Dean read the dissertation version, and helped put me on track to turn it into a proper book. Dayton Haskin, Lara Crowley, Tom Cogswell, and Charlotte Morse also took on entire drafts. Alun, together with Carol, Ford has supported the project as librarian, manuscript expert, neighbor, host, and friend. Simon Healy gave me a parliament man's perspective on libels, and sponsored a jolly trip to the Leicestershire Record Office. Chris and Anne Muskopf routinely provided a home away from home within walking distance of the Houghton; Chris has influenced my intellectual development since before preschool, not least by spending hours reading poetry with me and Ladd Suydam in high school. Finally, the literature editors at OUP have forced me to reconsider my disbelief in ideal readers, for they located two of them.

Two department chairs, Marcel Cornis-Pope and Terry Oggel, generously arranged for me to devote my second year at Virginia Commonwealth University to writing the book. Marcel also read and commented on a complete draft, while Terry and Nick Sharp exhibited the understanding that perhaps only bibliographers could provide for this project. The College of Humanities and Sciences at VCU supplied research travel funds, some of them in the form of a 'career scholarship enhancement award.' The Andrew W. Mellon Foundation and the Institute of Historical Research at the University of London supported a formative year of dissertation research. The Graduate College of the University of Illinois funded my first whirlwind tour of archives. And the Illinois Program for Research in the Humanities gave me the time, space, and resources to begin work on the project during a graduate fellowship. The Huntington Library and University of California Press have allowed me to reprint a revised version of '"Love-song weeds, and Satyrique thornes": Anti-Courtly Love Poems and Somerset Libels,' *Huntington Library Quarterly*, 69/1 (2006), 47–66. While these institutions and people have greatly improved the quality of this book, working on manuscripts multiplies the opportunities for error, and any remaining mistakes are nobody's fault but mine.

Most importantly, I thank the people at home who have provided the resources, time, and peace to get an education: first my parents and especially recently my mom, who seems to be watching Silas, and now helping with Ira, at every major phase of this book's completion; and ultimately Sarah, who has been supporting my work on a daily basis for years, and doing so by the uncommon means available only to a genuine researcher, a tough critic, a firm believer, an exquisite beauty, and a devotee of peace and mercy.

Contents

List of Abbreviations and Conventions x

1. The Literary and Political Activity of Manuscript Verse Collectors 1
2. The Politics of Courtly and Anti-Courtly Love Poetry in the Hands of Collectors 33
3. 'Love-song weeds, and Satyrique thornes': Anti-Courtly Love Poetry and Somerset Libels 67
4. The Spanish Match and the History of Sexuality 93
5. Verse Collectors and Buckingham's Assassination 132

Epilogue: Redeploying Anti-Courtly Love Poetry Against the Protectorate 162

Appendix 1: Selected Verse Texts 173

Appendix 2: Manuscript Descriptions 207

Index of Manuscripts Cited 281

List of Printed Works Cited 287

General Index 301

Abbreviations and Conventions

Beal, *Index*	Peter Beal, *Index of English Literary Manuscripts*, vols 1–2 (London: Mansell, 1980–93)
JEGP	*Journal of English and Germanic Philology*
MS	Manuscript
ODNB	*Oxford Dictionary of National Biography*, eds. H. C. G. Matthew and Brian Harrison (Oxford: Oxford University Press, 2004); online edn, Lawrence Goldman, May 2006
STC	A. W. Pollard and G. R. Redgrave, *A Short-Title Catalogue of Books Printed in England, Scotland, and Ireland and of English Books Printed Abroad 1475–1640*, 2nd edn, rev. W. A. Jackson, F. S. Ferguson, and Katharine F. Pantzer, 3 vols. (London: Bibliographical Society, 1976–91)
TLS	*Times Literary Supplement*
Wing	Donald Wing, *Short-Title Catalogue of Books Printed in England, Scotland, Ireland, Wales, and British America and of English Books Printed in Other Countries 1641–1700*, 2nd edn rev., 4 vols. (New York: MLA, 1982–98)

In quotations from sixteenth and seventeenth-century manuscripts, I have generally retained original spelling, including the early modern uses of i/j and u/v, the majuscule *ff*, and superscript abbreviations. Yet I have expanded, in square brackets, those abbreviations indicated by a macron, a tilde, or the letter *p* with a cross-stroke. In addition, the modern computer keyboard has imposed uniformity on the various forms that scribes employed for several letters, especially *e* and *s*. Occasionally a book's page or folio number is followed by a superscript *b*, indicating that this is the second instance of that number in a given volume.

1

The Literary and Political Activity of Manuscript Verse Collectors

When he copied poems into his notebook, a student of St. John's College, Cambridge preserved a wealth of texts that have come to characterize the English Renaissance. He also, however, collected verses that make this famous literary period appear strange. In only the first few surviving leaves of his anthology, for instance, he offered an unfamiliar account of Elizabethan love poetry, in which lyrics from the royal court sharply contrast, even as they resonate with, erotic verse. In the first remaining text that he transcribed, Queen Elizabeth I regrets that she scorned her many suitors when she 'was fayre and younge and fauour graced' her.[1] The series of Nicholas Breton's pastoral works that immediately follows the queen's poem features a song that was actually sung for her on progress, and which she liked so well that she ordered a repeat performance.[2] In Breton's lyric, the shepherdess Phillida at first

1 Bodleian MS Rawl. poet. 85, fol. 1r ('~~Verses made by the queine when she was/ supposed to be in loue wth mountsyre~~.//When I was fayre and younge and fauour graced me'). Transcribed in Laurence Cummings, 'John Finet's Miscellany' (PhD diss., Washington University, 1960), 79. Steven May finds Queen Elizabeth I the most likely, yet not the certain, author of the poem, judging from this attribution and another to her in British Library MS Harley 7392, pt. 2, fol. 21v. The only other early modern ascription, in Folger MS V.a.89, p. 12, assigns it to Edward de Vere, seventeenth earl of Oxford. *Queen Elizabeth I: Selected Works* (New York: Washington Square Press, 2004), 26–27.

2 The printed account of the entertainment describes its performance:

> On Wednesday morning, about nine of the clock, as her Maiestie opened a casement of her gallerie window, ther were three excellent Musitians, who being disguised in auncient countrey attire, did greet her with a pleasant song of Coridon and Phyllida, made in three parts of purpose. The song, as well for the worth of the Dittie, as for the aptnes of the note thereto applied, it pleased her Highnesse, after it had beene once sung, to command it againe, and highly to grace it with her chearefull acceptance and commendation.

The Honorable Entertainement gieuen to the Queenes Maiestie in Progresse, at Eluetham in Hampshire (London: Iohn Wolfe, 1591; STC 7583), sig. D2v.

resists Corridon's advances ('He woulde loue and she woulde not'), recalling the coyness of the 'fayre and younge' Elizabeth who likewise denied her admirers. Phillida, however, avoids the mistake for which the queen repents just two leaves earlier in the manuscript, by finally acquiesing: 'Loue that had bene longe deluded/Was with kisses sweet concluded.'[3] By placing these complementary poems written by and for Elizabeth in such proximity, this manuscript verse collector exhibited love poetry that she approved. He also established, at the outset of his miscellany, the initial theme of the coy mistress.

He then varied or countered this theme by featuring, on the very next leaf, a poem about another initially resistant, but ultimately compliant, woman, who nevertheless proves quite distinct from the coy mistresses of court literature. The female speaker of this poem employs diction that recalls Breton's pastoral characters (who say, 'Yea, and nay, and faythe and trouthe'), as she responds in graphic detail to a man while he coerces her to have sex. She begins the poem by protesting:

> Naye, phewe nay pishe? nay faythe and will ye, fye.
> A gentlman deale thus? in truthe ille crye.
> Gods bodye, what means this? naye fye for shame
> Nay, Nay, come, come, nay faythe yow are to blame.
> Harcke sombodye comes, leaue of I praye

When such verbal resistance fails, the speaker threatens to resist physically: 'Ile pinche, ille spurne, Ile scratche.' Yet she soon turns attention from her own actions to those of the man:

> You ~~hurt~~ marr my ruffs, you hurte my back, my nose will bleed
> Looke, looke the doore is open some bodye sees,
> What will they saye? nay fye you hurt my knees
> Your buttons scratche, o god ⸮ what coyle is heere?
> You make me sweate, in faythe here is goodly geare
> Nay faythe let me intreat leue if you lyste
> Yow marr the bedd, you teare my smock, but had I wist,
> So muche before I woulde haue kepte you oute.

After completing the couplet with another line in the present tense ('It is a very proper thinge indeed you goo aboute'), the speaker changes tense

[3] Bodleian MS Rawl. poet. 85, fol. 3r ('In the merye monthe of Maye'); Cummings, 'John Finet's Miscellany,' 95.

to place the sexual encounter in the past: 'I did not thinke you woulde haue vsed me this./But nowe I see to late I tooke my marke amysse.' She concludes the monologue tending to the man and to the future of her relationship with him:

> A lytle thinge woulde mak vs two not to be freends.
> You vse me well, I hope yow will make me amends.
> Houlde still Ile wype your face: you sweat amayne
> You have got a goodlye thinge wth all this payne.
> O god how ~~w~~hott I am come will you drincke
> Ife^{we} goe sweatinge downe what will they thinke
> Remmember I praye howe you haue vsde me nowe
> Doubte not ere longe I will be quite with you.
> Ife any one but you shoulde vse me so
> Woulde I put vp this wronge? in faythe sir no
> Nay goe not yet: staye supper here with me
> Come goe to cardes I hope we shall agree.[4]

Like the courtly mistresses who came literally before her in this manuscript verse miscellany, the speaker of the monologue first denies her suitor. And like Corridon, the speaker's silent but active lover eventually has his way. Despite these similarities, however, most would have considered this sexually explicit poem inappropriate for either the pen or the ear of the virgin queen.

Almost as if to indicate that he was not arranging his selections haphazardly, the collector placed next a poem that continues this series of increasingly submissive women. In it, a chaste nun falls in love with a falconer and wishes that she would become a falcon so that she could remain with him. The gods smile and decree that it shall be so. And the falconer agrees to perform the transformation. Yet his methods, and the narrator's description, develop sexual overtones, and a series of double entendres eventually makes clear that the metamorphosis under way is that of a maid becoming sexually experienced.

> And bothe her armes he bid her clipp for profe of prety thinges
> Whiche thoughe at firste she nylde to doe yet needes she must haue (winges
> Her legges lykwyse he layes aparte her feete he gann to frame,
> Wherat she softlye cride (alas) in faythe you are to blame

[4] Bodleian MS Rawl. poet. 85, fol. 4r; Cummings, 'John Finet's Miscellany,' 107–8. In an appendix, I provide the full text of the poem.

The woman's exclamation, 'in faythe you are to blame,' could have come from the speaker of the previous text (who indeed says, 'nay faythe yow are to blame'). Also like her, the nun objects to her lover's first moves. Although the falconer replies verbally ('Be still sweet gui^{r}lle and haue no dreade of me your man'), he comes to resemble the silent lover of 'Naye, phewe nay pishe' when he prevails and 'tricks her vp agayne, and agayne wth greate delyghte.'[5] The maid finally transforms not so much into a falcon as into a knowing, willing lover.

Within the span of just five leaves, this manuscript verse collector laid out for himself, and for any readers of his miscellany, a remarkable progression of verses on women variously refusing and submitting to men, proceeding from the chaste queen to the nun turned into a sexually active bird. Like virtually all other early modern manuscript verse collectors, this St. John's student produced a unique book of poems. In balancing polite love lyrics with bawdy verse, however, he was also engaging a practice that would become enormously popular over the next several decades, particularly among young men at the universities and Inns of Court. Together these manuscript verse collectors offer a history of early modern English poetry that differs considerably from those recorded in print, whether in their own time or since. For instance, they circulated several examples of the English Petrarchism well known to students of the period; but they gave especial emphasis to its counterdiscourses, to use Heather Dubrow's term.[6] Indeed, they showed that the literary game of resisting or rejecting the conventions of Petrarchan verse had become much more widespread and spirited than modern readers have realized. While they exhibited a taste for the Petrarchan idealizations of female figures that experts on gender and sexuality have criticized, they also anticipated modern scholars in demystifying such lofty mistresses. Yet they tended to do so by surrounding the Petrarchan figures with representations of women too misogynist or sexually explicit for their contemporaries to print and,

[5] Bodleian MS Rawl. poet. 85, fols 4v–5r ('In Libia lande as storyes tell was bredd and borne'); Cummings, 'John Finet's Miscellany,' 112–14. This poem blends the two styles of literature for which Ovid had become famous in late Elizabethan England—metamorphosis narratives and sexually explicit verse—even as it does away with any classicist pretension.

[6] Heather Dubrow, *Echoes of Desire: English Petrarchism and its Counterdiscourses* (Ithaca: Cornell University Press, 1995).

therefore, too obscure for many modern readers to access. In short, they tended to collect courtly love poems among parodies of courtly love.

By routinely countering or complementing love poetry with erotic or obscene verse, manuscript verse collectors arguably formed an unrecognized poetic genre, which I call *anti-courtly love poetry*. They organized this genre by methods that distinguish them from other literary agents, and that indeed demonstrate their own equally unnoticed literary agency. While their copies of canonical texts have attracted considerable scholarly attention, verse collectors' broader contributions to literary history have received little. This has remained the case even as early modernists have cultivated interest in an expanding array of literary agents, beyond the authors generally regarded as the preeminent and, in some accounts, only producers of literature. Early twentieth-century bibliographers, working in particular on English Renaissance drama, prioritized the work of printers and publishers.[7] More recent scholars of such drama have renewed interest in acting companies, while historians of the book have fostered the emergence of the early modern reader.[8]

[7] See, for instance, Alfred W. Pollard, *Shakespeare Folios and Quartos: A Study in the Bibliography of Shakespeare's Plays, 1594–1685* (London: Methuen, 1909); ___, *Shakespeare's Fight with the Pirates and the Problems of the Transmission of his Text* (London: A. Moring, 1917); W. W. Greg, *Dramatic Documents from the Elizabethan Playhouses* (Oxford: Clarendon, 1931); ___, *Bibliography of the English Printed Drama to the Restoration*, 4 vols. (London: Bibliographical Society at the University Press, Oxford, 1939–59); ___, *The Shakespeare First Folio, Its Bibliographical and Textual History* (Oxford: Clarendon, 1955); F. P. Wilson, 'Shakespeare and the "New Bibliography,"' *The Bibliographical Society, 1892–1942: Studies in Retrospect* (London: Bibliographical Society, 1954), 76–135.

[8] Regarding theatrical companies, see especially Mary Bly, *Queer Virgins and Virgin Queans on the Early Modern Stage* (Oxford: Oxford University Press, 2000) and Scott McMillin and Sally-Beth MacLean, *The Queen's Men and Their Plays* (Cambridge: Cambridge University Press, 1998).

For some of the most traceable early modern English readers, see A. H. Tricomi, 'Philip, Earl of Pembroke, and the Analogical Way of Reading Political Tragedy,' *JEGP*, 85 (1986), 332–45; Lisa Jardine and Anthony Grafton, '"Studied for Action": How Gabriel Harvey Read His Livy,' *Past and Present*, 129 (November 1990), 30–78; Anthony Grafton, '"Discitur ut agatur": How Gabriel Harvey Read His Livy,' in Stephen A. Barney, ed., *Annotation and Its Texts* (New York: Oxford University Press, 1991), 108–29; ___, 'Gabriel Harvey's Marginalia: New Light on the Cultural History of Elizabethan England,' *Princeton University Library Chronicle*, 52/1 (Autumn 1990), 21–24; William H. Sherman, *John Dee: The Politics of Reading and Writing in the English Renaissance* (Amherst: University of Massachusetts Press, 1995); James A. Riddell and Stanley Stewart, *Jonson's Spenser: Evidence and Historical Criticism* (Pittsburgh: Duquesne University Press, 1995); Kevin Sharpe, *Reading Revolutions: The Politics of Reading in Early Modern England* (New Haven: Yale University Press, 2000).

For their part, manuscript experts have turned attention to professional and amateur scribes, usually including manuscript verse miscellanies in surveys including wide ranges of other documents.[9] While these manuscript studies have clearly informed my work, this book proposes a new approach to verse miscellanies, one that investigates the exceptional, and remarkably consequential, activity of manuscript verse collectors.

Their manuscript miscellanies, in other words, distinguish verse collectors from the authors, stationers, and readers who animate most literary histories. For, while many collectors surely also composed, printed, and read verse, they were not necessarily doing any of these things when they copied or bound together poems in manuscript. When they operated as collectors, they did not necessarily transform themselves into authors by rewriting poems; into stationers by prefacing or publishing them; or into the uncommon sort of Renaissance readers who recorded their interpretations of texts. Instead, verse collectors put texts in new contexts, changing their frames of reference and, so, their referential capabilities. They precluded certain interpretations of poems and facilitated others. And they fostered new relationships between verses, associating originally unrelated works and consolidating the genre of anti-courtly love poetry.

Collectors of John Donne's poems played a major role in forming this genre, and so this book devotes considerable attention to their reception of Donne's influential examples of this style of verse. His collectors made Donne the most popular poet in early modern literary manuscripts, by preserving over 5,000 extant copies of his individual works.[10] Of all

[9] Harold Love, *Scribal Publication in Seventeenth-Century England* (Oxford: Clarendon, 1993), esp. 231–83; Arthur F. Marotti, *Manuscript, Print, and the English Renaissance Lyric* (Ithaca: Cornell University Press, 1995), esp. 17–25, 30–73; H. R. Woudhuysen, *Sir Philip Sidney and the Circulation of Manuscripts, 1558–1640* (Oxford: Clarendon, 1996), esp. 134–73; Peter Beal, *In Praise of Scribes: Manuscripts and their Makers in Seventeenth-Century England* (Oxford: Clarendon, 1998), esp. 104, 242, 257. Only Mary Hobbs has devoted a book exclusively to early modern manuscript verse miscellanies: *Early Seventeenth-Century Verse Miscellany Manuscripts* (Aldershot, Hants: Scolar, 1992). In addition to focusing on different authors, poems, and manuscripts than I do here, Hobbs valued miscellanies primarily for the authorial texts that they provide editors, whereas I emphasize the authority of their compilers—that is, the capacity of verse collectors to relate texts to one another and to new contexts without the knowledge or approval of authors.

[10] Beal, *Index*, 1:1:342–564, 566–68; John Donne, *The Variorum Edition of the Poetry of John Donne*, gen. ed. Gary A. Stringer, vol. 2 (Bloomington: Indiana University Press, 2000), xxxii–xxxvii, xlix.

Donne's poems, these collectors most often reproduced his anti-courtly love poems such as 'To his Mistress going to bed' and 'The Anagram.'[11] Yet they tended to gather these sexually explicit Donne texts among more or less related poems by Christopher Marlowe, Thomas Nashe, Sir John Davies, Francis Beaumont, and a number of anonymous poets, including the unknown author or authors of 'Naye, phewe nay pishe.' In the hands and anthologies of verse collectors, such licentious poems begin to look like a coherent poetic mode—one that Donne had mastered but which other poets had certainly engaged as well. For, by gathering them together, collectors emphasized the fact that each of these poems mocks, opposes, or rejects the Petrarchan conventions of late Elizabethan courtly love poetry.

Following the emergence of courtly love poetry at the late Elizabethan court (signaled in particular by Sir Philip Sidney's *Astrophil and Stella* and Sir Walter Ralegh's lyrics), poets began to mock the Petrarchan conventions of such courtier verse. William Shakespeare, in surely the most well known example, playfully refused to apply the standard Petrarchan metaphors to the subject of Sonnet 130: 'My mistress' eyes are nothing like the sun.' Likewise in 'The Anagram,' Donne rejected the terms that courtly lovers used in describing their mistresses. Yet, whereas Shakespeare's speaker ultimately honors his unconventionally beautiful mistress as 'rare,' Donne's poem renders its female subject unrealistically disgusting. Donne's Flavia models all of the requisite qualities of a Petrarchan mistress, but attached to the wrong features. Rather than fair skin and red lips, she has yellow cheeks and black teeth, along with small eyes, a big mouth, rough skin, and red hair. She thus features 'an Anagram of a good face.'[12] While Shakespeare playfully resisted courtly love conventions in realistically describing an alluring woman, Donne assaulted them in order to rail against an unbelievably ugly woman. Moreover, while manuscript verse collectors demonstrated little interest in Shakespeare's sonnets, they turned 'The Anagram' into a central example of a genre that they were fashioning themselves.

[11] The Donne Variorum editors record 62 copies of 'The Anagram,' 63 of 'The Bracelet,' and 67 of 'To his Mistress going to bed' (*Donne Variorum*, 2:8, 165, 219).

[12] William Shakespeare, *The Complete Sonnets and Poems*, ed. Colin Burrow (Oxford: Oxford University Press, 2002), 641 ('Sonnet 130,' 1, 13). *Donne Variorum*, 2:217 ('The Anagram,' 16).

Manuscript Verse Collectors and the Politics of Anti-Courtly Love Poetry focuses on this genre as the quintessential example of collectors' distinctive ability to cultivate relationships between texts. They demonstrated this capacity by relating anti-courtly love poems not only to one another, but also to literature that originally shared little or nothing in common with these salacious verses. For, while my novel generic term accommodates a number of the collectors' favorite poems, their manuscript miscellanies do indeed feature miscellaneous contents. Among the diverse array of literature in their anthologies, they placed poems on affairs of state, or poetic libels, in particularly compelling relationships with anti-courtly love poems, variously relating the genre to a range of political scandals.[13] The St. John's compiler, for instance, interrupted his introductory sequence of amatory and erotic verses with a Latin poem celebrating the death of Sir Thomas Gresham, and later included two libels in English: the 'Libell agaynst Bashe,' criticizing the Henrician and Elizabethan victualler of the Navy, and 'The Libell of Oxenforde,' mocking Oxford academics.[14] Since almost no one printed such slanderous verses at the time, manuscript collectors deserve the credit (or blame) for preserving nearly all of those that survive.[15] They helped to define the genre of verse libel as well, for instance by exhibiting the aesthetic and historical continuities between poems on the court scandals and royal favorites of early modern England.[16] Yet, when they juxtaposed libels to anti-courtly love poems, collectors allowed clearly distinct poetic genres to resonate. They simultaneously immersed the poetry of Donne and others in a political culture defined and even

[13] On libels, see Andew McRae, *Literature, Satire and the Early Stuart State* (Cambridge: Cambridge University Press, 2004). On the abundance of sexual and political literature in miscellanies, see Ian Frederick Moulton, *Before Pornography: Erotic Writing in Early Modern England* (Oxford: Oxford University Press, 2000) and Marotti, *Manuscript, Print, and the English Renaissance Lyric*, 75–133.

[14] Bodleian MS Rawl. poet. 85, fols 2v, 66r–75v; Cummings, 'John Finet's Miscellany,' 92–94, 513–61.

[15] For a rare printed libel, see William Goddard, *A Neaste of Waspes* (Dort: n.p., 1615; STC 11929), sig. F4r. Cited in McRae, *Literature, Satire and the Early Stuart State*, 28. McRae introduces early Stuart verse libels as an 'unauthorized' genre, which writers engaged under 'an undeniable fear of repression' (1, 7).

[16] On royal favorites throughout early modern English culture and especially the theater, see Curtis Perry, *Literature and Favoritism in Early Modern England* (Cambridge: Cambridge University Press, 2006). On early Stuart court scandal, see Alastair Bellany, *The Politics of Court Scandal in Early Modern England: News Culture and the Overbury Affair, 1603–1660* (Cambridge: Cambridge University Press, 2002).

shaped by the topical libels nearby in their miscellanies. Moreover, they introduced a political element to anti-courtly love poetry, and proceeded to modify and tranform the genre's politics as times changed.

Having established such a relationship between libels and anti-courtly love poems in their miscellanies, manuscript verse collectors pose a valuable challenge to dominant distinctions between poetry and politics, literature and history. For, when they copied or bound examples of these two particular genres in their anthologies, collectors did something that literary and political historians have since tended to undo. Editors of Renaissance poetry, for instance, have thoroughly searched these miscellanies, but primarily for more or less authoritative versions of texts attributable to major authors.[17] The political historians who have turned recently to some of the same manuscript books that interest literary editors have proven to be just as selective, choosing anthologies' most overtly political texts to the exclusion of their more aesthetically complicated ones.[18] Thus the division of academic labor imposes

[17] Editors of John Donne's poetry, in particular, have established an impressive tradition of manuscript scholarship—from the Oxford editors (*The Poems of John Donne*, ed. Herbert J. C. Grierson, 2 vols. (Oxford: Clarendon, 1912); *The Divine Poems*, ed. Helen Gardner (Oxford: Clarendon, 1952); *The Elegies and The Songs and Sonnets*, ed. Helen Gardner (Oxford: Clarendon, 1965); *The Satires, Epigrams and Verse Letters*, ed. Wesley Milgate (Oxford: Clarendon, 1967); *The Epithalamions, Anniversaries and Epicedes*, ed. Wesley Milgate (Oxford: Clarendon, 1978)) to John Shawcross and the Donne Variorum committee (*The Complete Poetry of John Donne*, ed. John T. Shawcross (Garden City NY: Anchor, 1967); *Donne Variorum*). For a pertinent critique of particularly the Variorum committee's interest in authorial texts, see Marotti, *Manuscript, Print, and the English Renaissance Lyric*, 147–59.

[18] Exemplary historical work on poetic libels includes Bellany, *The Politics of Court Scandal*; ___, 'Libels in Action: Ritual, Subversion and the English Literary Underground, 1603–42,' in Tim Harris, ed., *The Politics of the Excluded, 1500–1850* (Basingbroke: Palgrave, 2001), 99–124; ___, 'A Poem on the Archbishop's Hearse: Puritanism, Libel, and Sedition after the Hampton Court Conference,' *Journal of British Studies*, 34/2 (1995), 137–64; ___, ' "Rayling Rymes and Vaunting Verse": Libellous Politics in Early Stuart England,' in Kevin Sharpe and Peter Lake, eds., *Culture and Politics in Early Stuart England* (Stanford: Stanford University Press, 1993), 285–310; Thomas Cogswell, 'Underground verse and the transformation of early Stuart political culture,' in Susan D. Amussen and Mark A. Kishlansky, eds., *Political Culture and Cultural Politics in Early Modern England: Essays Presented to David Underdown* (Manchester: Manchester University Press, 1995), 277–300; Pauline Croft, 'Libels, Popular Literacy and Public Opinion in Early Modern England,' *Historical Research*, 68/167 (October 1995), 266–85; ___, 'The Reputation of Robert Cecil: Libels, Political Opinion and Popular Awareness in the Early Seventeenth Century,' *Transactions of the Royal Historical Society*, 6th ser., 1 (1991), 43–69; Adam Fox, 'Ballads, Libels and Popular Ridicule in Jacobean England,' *Past and Present*, 145 (November 1994), 47–83.

generic distinctions on miscellanies that their compilers evidently viewed differently. Whereas early modern verse collectors gathered diverse texts together, modern disciplinary conventions pry them apart: literary critics get the good poetry, historians get the bad.

This book puts some of the miscellanies' now-canonical and political poems back together, and recognizes relationships between texts and genres that their compilers regularly juxtaposed. Authors first established some of these generic associations. But verse collectors initiated others of their own. For example, those who copied epigrams among short libels on political figures were acknowledging a formal connection that poets had made.[19] Yet those who gathered anti-courtly love poems among libels were affiliating originally distinct genres in ways that the authors of the older texts involved could not have imagined and, in some cases, would not have appreciated. In this, manuscript verse collectors assumed roles somewhat similar to those of stationers who printed texts without their authors' knowledge or permission.[20] Manuscript collectors, however, effectively specialized in texts that their contemporaries virtually never printed, like libels, or only rarely published, such as anti-courtly love poems.

In other words, manuscript verse collectors operated somewhat like editors of unprintable poetry anthologies: the successors of Richard Tottel without licenses from the Stationers' Company. Tottel's miscellany, widely considered the first printed anthology of lyric poems in English, differs markedly, for instance, with a nevertheless textually related manuscript verse miscellany such as the Arundel Harington manuscript. The family of the courtier poet Sir John Harington copied

[19] On the relationship between the epigram and the libel, see James Doelman, 'Epigrams and Political Satire in Early Stuart England,' *Huntington Library Quarterly*, 69:1 (March 2006), 31–45.

[20] Of particular relevance to the present book, scholars have recently demonstrated how performers, stationers, and readers transformed the politics of relatively old, early modern English literature, especially drama. See Zachary Lesser, *Renaissance Drama and the Politics of Publication* (Cambridge: Cambridge University Press, 2004); Marta Straznicky, *Privacy, Playreading, and Women's Closet Drama, 1550–1700* (Cambridge: Cambridge University Press, 2004); ___, ed., *The Book of the Play: Playwrights, Stationers, and Readers in Early Modern England* (Amherst: University of Massachusetts Press, 2006); Paul Whitfield White and Suzanne R. Westfall, eds., *Shakespeare and Theatrical Patronage in Early Modern England* (Cambridge: Cambridge University Press, 2002); McMillin and MacLean, *The Queen's Men and their Plays*.

into this manuscript miscellany many of the same poems that Tottel printed, but alongside others that he could not, or would not, publish. Scholars have suggested that Tottel, and whoever else contributed to the compilation and organization of the volume, subdued its political connotations, deemphasizing the revolutionary associations of Sir Thomas Wyatt's family name by printing the poet's verse relatively late in the first edition; and deleting from the second edition Nicholas Grimald's verses honoring the protestant predecessors of the Catholic Queen Mary I.[21] By contrast, the Haringtons had no reason to depoliticize their manuscript miscellany. In addition to many of Tottel's texts they transcribed the libels on Edward Bashe and Oxford academics that the St. John's student also collected.[22] This book investigates the editorial decisions that manuscript verse collectors such as the Haringtons made outside of the regime of prepublication licensing.

In the editorial decisions most relevant to this study, manuscript collectors politicized and recontextualized anti-courtly love poetry with topical libels. Yet, to be sure, they recontextualized other texts as well, even libels themselves. As others have shown, the collectors of the poetic libel known as 'The Parliament Fart' developed and ultimately reversed its political associations over the course of its circulation in the first half of the seventeenth century. The poem originally celebrated a timely fart by a member of James VI and I's first English parliament, Henry Ludlow, immediately following the reading of a message from the House of Lords regarding the naturalization of the Scots, a central issue in James' design to unite Scotland and England. Thus, in its earliest contexts, the libel enacted a gesture of defiance toward the Lords and possibly even the crown on behalf of the Commons and, most likely, certain MPs who also belonged to Donne's coterie: Sir John Hoskyns, Christopher Brooke, Richard Martin, and Edward Jones. Yet few collectors of 'The Parliament Fart' reproduced the poem without modifying, amending, or

21 *Songes and Sonettes* (London: Apud Richardum Tottel, 1557; STC 13861); *Songes and Sonettes* (London: Apud Richardum Tottel, 1557; STC 13862); Hyder E. Rollins, ed., *Tottel's Miscellany* (Cambridge: Harvard University Press, 1928); Paul A. Marquis, 'Politics and print: The curious revisions to Tottel's *Songes and Sonettes*,' *Studies in Philology*, 97/2 (Spring 2000), 145–64.

22 Arundel Castle (The Duke of Norfolk), Arundel Harington MS, fols 136r–39r; Ruth Hughey, ed., *The Arundel Harington Manuscript of Tudor Poetry*, 2 vols. (Columbus: Ohio State University Press, 1960), 1:223–33, 2:276–301.

recontextualizing it. Indeed, in the middle of the seventeenth century, its royalist collectors ironically used this originally Commons libel to signal their distrust of parliament altogether.[23] They did so, in no small part, by collecting 'The Parliament Fart' among explicitly royalist texts.

Verse collectors also repoliticized several poems by another of Donne's close friends, Sir Henry Wotton. Over time they applied Wotton's libel on the fall of James' royal favorite Sir Robert Carr, earl of Somerset, to other political figures: Sir Walter Ralegh, Sir Francis Bacon, George Villiers duke of Buckingham, and 'Secretarye Dauison,' presumably the Elizabethan secretary of state William Davison.[24] Likewise, they reassigned Wotton's poem on James' daughter, Elizabeth, to other royal women. Some copyists redirected the poem to the princess' mother, Queen Anne.[25] Others provocatively reapplied Wotton's high praise of Elizabeth to the Spanish Infanta, Donna Maria Anna, whom James proposed to marry to Prince Charles.[26] In this remarkable example of appropriation, collectors completely overturned the poem's religious and political affiliations. For whereas Princess Elizabeth and her husband, the Elector Palatine, embodied English protestants' hope for an international alliance against Catholicism, the Spanish Infanta

[23] Michelle O'Callaghan, 'Performing Politics: The Circulation of the "Parliament Fart,"' *Huntington Library Quarterly*, 69/1 (March 2006), 121–38. Marotti, *Manuscript, Print, and the English Renaissance Lyric*, 113–15.

[24] Ted-Larry Pebworth, 'Sir Henry Wotton's "Dazel'd Thus, with Height of Place" and the Appropriation of Political Poetry in the Earlier Seventeenth Century,' *Papers of the Bibliographical Society of America*, 71 (1977), 151–69. *The Poems of Sir Walter Ralegh: A Historical Edition*, ed. Michael Rudick (Tempe: Arizona Center for Medieval and Renaissance Studies, 1999), lxvii–lxviii, 122, 223–24. Rudick notes that British Library MS Lansdowne 777, fols 63r–66r, features 'a string of poems with Ralegh connections,' including Wotton's poem attributed correctly and headed 'To a favorite': 'The context there appears to be poems applied to Ralegh.' The Yorkshire antiquary John Hopkinson headed the poem 'On Secretarye Dauison fall' in his late-seventeenth-century miscellany: West Yorkshire Archive Service, Bradford MS 32D86/17, fol. 123v. See Simon Adams, 'Davison, William (*d.* 1608),' *ODNB*.

[25] British Library MS Add. 30982, fol. 145v rev.; Folger MSS V.a.170, pp. 43–44; V.a.245, fol. 42v.

[26] Bodleian MS Malone 19, pp. 37–38; Folger MS V.a.162, fol. 79r–v; Houghton MS Eng. 686, fols 9v–10r. C. F. Main first pointed out two of these appropriations in the concluding footnote to his 'Wotton's "The Character of a Happy Life,"' *The Library: Transactions of the Bibliographical Society*, 5th ser., 10/4 (1955), 270–74. For the fullest discussion on the development of the text of the poem throughout its transmission, see J. B. Leishman, '"You Meaner Beauties of the Night": A Study in Transmission and Transmogrification,' *The Library*, 4th ser., 26/2–3 (September, December 1945), 99–121.

represented James' apparent threat to dissolve any such alliance by marrying the Prince of Wales to a Spanish Catholic. Wotton collectors appropriated his poems both by providing them with new headings and by surrounding them with texts on later political events and figures.

In the middle of the seventeenth century, Robert Overton, an officer in the Parliamentary army, appropriated other manuscript verses. He dedicated a compilation of excerpts of love poems by Donne and Katherine Philips to his deceased wife, Ann. As a pious Independent and supporter of the Parliamentary cause, Overton makes for a surprising reader of the avowed royalist Philips. Moreover, as a mourning husband who turned the love poems of Donne and Philips into a memorial befitting a devout puritan woman, Overton demonstrates how completely manuscript verse collectors could assimilate texts to their own contexts.[27] Yet relatively few collectors appropriated literature in the dramatic fashion that Overton did. Many more collectors recontextualized the literature in their miscellanies simply by surrounding less topical texts with more topical ones. In addition to libels, their miscellanies typically feature several occasional genres that regularly identify individuals or events and, so, tend to relate nearby texts to new contexts: verse letters; prose epistles; funeral elegies; laudatory and mock epitaphs; verses on figures and events at the universities and Inns of Court; and reports of legal trials. On the other hand, early modern verse collectors also filled their miscellanies with genres that, like anti-courtly love poems, regularly leave their original contexts rather unclear and, so, remain particularly open to recontextualization: epigrams that are too reserved to count as libels; love lyrics that are more polite than anti-courtly love poems; devotional verse and prose; texts on religious difference, most of them directed against unspecified Catholics or puritans; 'characters' that represent a cross-section of early modern English society in caricature; verses on the *querrelle des femmes,* or battle over women, including a number of poems on choosing a wife; and many others. Verse collectors tended to recontextualize texts such as these with topical or political literature, if only by gathering them together.

By attending to the effects of such collection practices, this book then presumes that poetic meaning need not be limited to what a poet puts

[27] David Norbrook, '"This blushing tribute of a borrowed muse": Robert Overton and his overturning of the poetic canon,' *English Manuscript Studies, 1100–1700,* 4 (1993), 220–66; Princeton MS C0199 (no. 812).

into a poem, what a reader gets out of it, or what a critic finds in it alone. A poem's full significance, rather, may extend beyond its text to the affiliations and resonances that it develops among other texts and in its various contexts, no matter how local or even physical. Both its historical contexts and its manuscript contexts, in other words, influence what a poem comes to signify, or at least what it comes to suggest. This book thus takes contextual reading to a certain extreme, not only because it proceeds to contexts well beyond those of composition and initial reception but also because it reasons that, if a poem's context determines its meaning, then variations in even its physical, manuscript context may change the poem's meaning.

In attributing meaning to the activity of verse collectors, though, my argument does not require presuming that they intended to generate all of these associations and connotations. Given the thorough criticism of authorial intention in literary studies, I would not reduce the significance of collectors' literary contributions to their intentions any more than I would that of authors'. Some anthologists may have intended to do no more than collect poems that they happened to like, or happened to encounter. Yet even such casual collectors recorded invaluable information regarding their access to texts; their tastes; their working definitions of literary genres, or lack thereof; and their perspectives on recent politics. Without necessarily realizing the ramifications of their actions, many of these anthologists effectively formed, mixed, and politicized certain literary genres. On the other hand, collectors such as those introduced in the following chapter, who attempted to reconstruct the politics of anti-courtly love poetry, inadvertently introduced factual errors and other incongruities to their accounts of literary and political history. *Manuscript Verse Collectors and the Politics of Anti-Courtly Love Poetry* focuses on the ironies, as well as the continuities, of the genre's shifting political affiliations in the changing political contexts of early seventeenth-century England.

By attending to the politics of both libels and anti-courtly love poems, this study also engages the different kinds of politics prioritized in the disciplines of English and history. While historians have assessed the politics of libels, and literary critics have discerned those of Donne's Ovidian elegies, they have not always shared the same conception of politics. The post-revisionist historians who have analyzed libels have expanded their discipline's 'definition of the political' to include the construction and perception of court scandals.[28] Literary critics, on the other hand, have opened up their working notion of politics even more, by positing the politics of a range of cultural phenomena that have little or nothing to do with the state—such as, in the case of Donne's elegies, representations of power relations between men and women. Manuscript verse collectors require an interdisciplinary approach that engages both state and cultural politics and considers their relationship to one another. For, when they gathered together libels and anti-courtly love poems, they likewise forced these two kinds of politics together. One could say that the authors of libels did as much on their own, given how many of them attacked court figures specifically by mocking their gender, sexuality, religion, class origins, or nationality. Yet, by surrounding such libels with Donne's and others' anti-courtly love poems, collectors effectively challenged their readers to recognize and negotiate the relationship between these two conceptions of politics. This book enthusiastically takes up the challenge.

The theoretical developments outlined here proceed directly from the material practices of manuscript verse collectors. Such ambitious claims on behalf of collectors require a careful consideration of how they made their manuscripts, and of who most likely selected and arranged the texts within these rare books. The next section of the chapter turns to such a consideration by briefly surveying some of the ways in which they constructed and compiled their miscellanies, and by endeavoring to assign agency as precisely as possible.

THE MEANS OF REPRODUCTION AND RECONTEXTUALIZATION

The St. John's student with which this study began exhibited one ordinary method of compiling a manuscript verse miscellany. He copied poems into a bound, blank book. Before he starting writing in it, the book had been fully constructed, the margins ruled, and the leaves foliated. He could have purchased such a blank book ready-made but, having purchased paper and a few other supplies instead, he also could have made his book by himself, or with the help of others: perhaps a

[28] Bellany, *Politics of Court Scandal*, 14.

professional bookbinder, or a friend or family member. Whoever contributed to the production of the codex completed the physical book before the compiler filled it in. Whether professional or volunteer, the labor of book construction was complete before the amateur work of transcription began.[29]

His miscellany thus represents one of a variety of ways that people produced manuscript verse miscellanies in early modern England. Others made anthologies in a reverse fashion, by simply binding together verses (often along with other types of writing) that were already written on loose papers; on individual sheets folded once, twice, or three times (resulting in a bifolium, quarto, or octavo, respectively); or in larger gatherings or booklets made of several sheets or half-sheets of paper. Verse regularly circulated in small booklets like these. The St. John's student probably transcribed texts from several such documents into his blank book. Verse collectors could also copy their contents onto other loose leaves or into other small gatherings. Or they could simply keep the little manuscripts that they acquired. Rather few small, individual poetry manuscripts survive unbound. Most of these booklets have been bound together with other documents (if not by their original owners then by a descendant, a rare book collector, or a librarian). Binding together several manuscripts in this fashion results in a composite manuscript. Composite manuscripts commonly feature a wide range of papers and scripts, and so visibly contrast with a book that, like the manuscript of the St. John's student, was constructed all at once and filled in by one hand. The compiler of the St. John's miscellany acted as both its editor and its scribe, but may not have engaged in the construction of his book. A verse collector responsible for a composite manuscript, on the other hand, could have contributed to certain stages of his miscellany's physical production (when he collected his papers, and especially if he ordered them and arranged for them to be bound); but he may have done none of the writing therein.

After collecting or copying manuscripts themselves, people could also have their papers professionally copied. Successful men customarily did this when they prepared their wills. Sir John Finet did so long after he attended St. John's, Cambridge and either befriended the compiler of the miscellany considered at the start of this chapter or compiled it

[29] Cummings, 'John Finet's Miscellany,' 56.

himself, as the manuscript's editor, Laurence Cummings, has suggested.[30] A scribe likewise copied the papers of the judge Sir Christopher Yelverton near the time of his death in 1612, resulting in a thick quarto of verse and mostly political prose.[31] Although Yelverton collected texts composed at various dates throughout his long Elizabethan career, a professional transcribed them all at once, and in no apparent order. The scribe who did so might have served as a personal secretary to Yelverton. Or a clerk or a full-fledged scrivener could have copied a judge's papers, as each worked primarily on legal documents.[32] Yet judges and lawyers surely could look beyond the legal community for scribes, just as scribes could work both within and without the Inns of Court. Indeed, sometime after 1634, a scribe who regularly worked for the theater produced a verse miscellany that was owned by the family of the lawyer Chaloner Chute.[33] Chute may have collected the texts for his miscellany and contracted the playhouse scribe to make a fair copy of them. Yet it is also possible (although impossible to prove) that this scribe provided or even chose texts for his client.

[30] Sir John Finet, *Ceremonies of Charles I: The Note Books of John Finet, 1628–1641*, ed. A. J. Loomie (New York: Fordham University Press, 1987); Roderick Clayton, 'Finet, Sir John (1570/71–1641),' *ODNB*; Cummings, 'John Finet's Miscellany,' 27–32. Randall Anderson doubts Cummings' identification of Finet as the copyist of the manuscript in '"The Merit of a Manuscript Poem": The Case for Bodleian MS Rawlinson Poet. 85,' in Arthur F. Marotti and Michael D. Bristol, eds., *Print, Manuscript and Performance: The Changing Relations of Media in Early Modern England* (Columbus: Ohio State University Press, 2000), 127–71, esp. 168–69 n.77.

[31] All Souls, Oxford MS 155. I discuss this manuscript at greater length in '"From a seruant of Diana" to the Libellers of Robert Cecil: the Transmission of Songs Written for Queen Elizabeth I,' in Peter Beal and Grace Ioppolo, eds., *Elizabeth I and the Culture of Writing* (London: British Library, 2006), 115–31.

[32] A scribe generally apprenticed under a scrivener before becoming a clerk. Love, *Scribal Publication*, 92–101, esp. 94.

[33] British Library MS Add. 33998. The other known manuscripts in the hand of this scribe are each theatrical: British Library MS Egerton 1994, fols 30–51 (Thomas Heywood, *Dick of Devonshire*, post-1626); Folger, Printed Books, STC 17876 (MS addition to Thomas Dekker (or Thomas Middleton?), *Blurt, Master-Constable* (London, 1602)); Worcester College, Oxford, Printed books, Plays.2.5 (George Chapman, *May-Day*, 1611). I thank Peter Beal for this information. See his *Index* 1:2, HyT (Thomas Heywood) 5; MiT (Thomas Middleton) 6. For a summary of the evidence, see Beal, 'The Folger Manuscript Collection: A Personal View,' in Heather Wolfe, ed., *'The Pen's Excellencie': Treasures from the Manuscript Collection of the Folger Shakespeare Library* (Washington DC: Folger, 2002), 16–17. Chute, incidentally, would eventually succeed Yelverton as speaker of the House of Commons, in Richard Cromwell's parliament of 1659. Christopher W. Brooks, 'Chute, Chaloner (c.1595–1659),' *ODNB*.

Regardless of who selected the texts in his miscellany, the presentable hand of the theatrical scribe suggests that Chute purchased the manuscript, possibly as a finished product. Chute's manuscript thus qualifies as one of rather few evidently professional early seventeenth-century verse miscellanies. The so-called Feathery Scribe also produced a verse miscellany, which is unique among the more than 100 manuscripts that Peter Beal has attributed to this law clerk and professional scribe, most of which consist of political, historical, legal, or religious prose.[34] Because it presents such an anomaly in the scribe's extant body of work, and since the miscellany shows 'Feathery in full showcase mode,' Beal convincingly suggests that a client commissioned the anthology. Again, Feathery may have offered texts or editorial suggestions to his client. Yet the customer surely helped to determine the content of his miscellany.

If scribes received commissions for complete manuscript verse miscellanies such as these, one wonders whether they also produced finished anthologies speculatively, for expected yet uncommitted customers, in more or less the same way that stationers printed books. Scribes evidently did this in the late seventeenth century: scholars of this later period have attributed several anthologies of political and erotic poems to networks of professional scribes called scriptoria (regardless of whether the scribes worked at a communal space or in their separate homes).[35] Acknowledging that few 'entrepreneurially published' miscellanies predate 1680, Harold Love has recognized that the professional miscellanies surviving from the late seventeenth century nevertheless resemble their Elizabethan and early Stuart predecessors.[36] Could a professional scribe have made one of these earlier miscellanies without knowing who would buy it? This is possible, but far from certain. Several late sixteenth and early seventeenth-century miscellanies feature signs of professionally trained labor: virtuosic penmanship; uniform gatherings made from a single stock of paper; attractive contemporary bindings. Yet an early modern Englishman surely could have employed a 'professional hand' even when he did not expect payment for the manuscript at hand. Amateurs, like professionals, would have had occasion and incentive to work with a single stock of paper. And, again, bookbinders bound blank books, loose papers, and collections

[34] Bodleian MS Rawl. Poet. 31. Beal, *In Praise of Scribes*, 72, 104, 257.

[35] Love, *Scribal Publication*, 232, 124–26.

[36] Love, *Scribal Publication*, 75, 79.

of small manuscripts, so a professional binding by no means indicates that a finished miscellany was produced for a speculative market.

Furthermore, while professional scribes have left little evidence that they sold manuscript miscellanies like printed books in the early seventeenth century, an extensive record of amateur involvement remains in such volumes. Sloppy, and thus clearly unprofessional, writing abounds in many of these books. Irregular gatherings, each featuring a different number of leaves, can be found even in manuscripts made primarily with a single stock of paper. In the absence of any clear indication that professional scribes produced verse miscellanies for a speculative market before the end of the seventeenth century, such obvious signs of unpaid labor indicate that the editorial work of selecting and arranging their texts regularly fell to amateurs: to the people who enjoyed, or at least prized and preserved, early modern English poetry. These verse collectors thus were acting more like consumers than businessmen when they made their anthologies. Indeed, they would have been consumers at virtually every other stage of their books' production: when they purchased the raw materials (such as paper, or a blank book); if they paid for any small, unbound manuscripts; if they contracted a scribe to make a fair copy; and if they had a bookbinder sew everything together. While amateur verse collectors then did not produce every aspect of all early modern manuscript miscellanies, the editorial stage of obtaining, selecting, and arranging texts nevertheless commonly involved the work of individuals who could expect no payment for their labor: the readers, consumers, and users of literature.

Like the St. John's compiler, many of these relatively private collectors circulated verse at one of the universities. After university, many of them proceeded to another center for verse collection, the Inns of Court, where Chute and Yelverton doubtless acquired some of their texts. Verse collectors also operated at the royal court and certain family households, especially those privileged with a secretary, a tutor, or literary patronage clients.[37] Perhaps ironically, professional scribes may have participated in the editorial stages of making a poetry anthology at such domestic sites more often than anywhere else. Perhaps while employed as a secretary to Francis Fane, first earl of Westmoreland, Rowland Woodward

[37] Woudhuysen, *Sir Philip Sidney*, 163–73. Marotti, *Manuscript, Print, and the English Renaissance Lyric*, 30–48.

transcribed one of the most authoritative collections of the poems of his friend, John Donne.[38] John Rolleston, the personal secretary of William Cavendish, earl (and later duke) of Newcastle, produced one of the most visually striking miscellanies of the early seventeenth century.[39] Hilton Kelliher has shown that, in addition to managing the earl's correspondence, Rolleston amended and copied Newcastle's own literary compositions, and transcribed the whole of the Cavendish family verse miscellany in a beguiling range of distinct scripts.[40] Newcastle may have taken the dominant role in acquiring and selecting texts for this manuscript, given his literary interests and impressive patronage network (which included Ben Jonson and the poet and doctor Richard Andrews, each of whom, along with Donne, composed great numbers of the poems in the Newcastle manuscript). For, after all, even if such editorial duties fell to Rolleston, the secretary worked for the earl and would have tried to please him. Yet a personal secretary like Rolleston played a much more significant part in his master's affairs than did a clerk or scrivener in those of his clients. In a contemporary formulation, a secretary was 'in one degree in place of a *servant*... in another degree in place of a *friend*.' Unlike a mere hired hand, a secretary needed to be capable of using 'the *Pen*, the *Wit* and *Inuention* together.'[41] It is difficult to tell, but tempting to wonder, to what extent Rolleston applied his wit and invention, in addition to his pen, to the impressive Newcastle manuscript.

Other early modern households left verse collection to other servants. Henry Stanford, for example, compiled an important late Elizabethan miscellany while he served as a tutor at a couple of aristocratic houses.[42] His anthology features court poems among verse by himself and his students. Although Stanford was acting in a professional capacity when he had his students compose verse, he seems to have written and collected poems in his leisure. In general, families that produced miscellanies, like the Haringtons, must have done so in their leisure hours as

[38] New York Public Library, Berg Collection, Westmoreland MS.

[39] British Library MS Harley 4955.

[40] Hilton Kelliher, 'Donne, Jonson, Richard Andrews and The Newcastle Manuscript,' *English Manuscript Studies, 1100–1700*, 4 (1993), 134–73.

[41] Love, *Scribal Publication*, 97. Quotes Angel Day, *The English secretary*, ed. Robert O. Evans (Gainesville FL: Scholars', 1967), 106^{b}, 129^{b}.

[42] Cambridge University Library MS Dd. 5.75; Steven W. May, *Henry Stanford's Anthology: An Edition of Cambridge University Library Manuscript Dd.5.75* (New York: Garland, 1988).

well. Probably throughout the 1620s and '30s, the Skipwith family of Cotes, Leicestershire put together a composite manuscript, beginning with poems by Donne that they could have acquired from Donne's friend, and their own relative by marriage, Sir Henry Goodyer.[43] To these quires they added other distinct gatherings in several different hands with poems by Donne, Goodyer, Beaumont, Wotton, Sir Nicholas Hare, and a few members of their own family. Finally, a possibly seventeenth-century hand filled in the manuscript's blank spaces with additional verse. Although they made their miscellany in such a piecemeal fashion, the Skipwiths generally collected poems that were related to one another by theme or social context. In a family, as in a coterie of like-minded students or friends, a collective effort of anthologizing could thus maintain some consistency.

On the other hand, the Skipwiths' method of verse collection did lead to a few interesting juxtapositions, especially when they grouped topical verses with well-known poems by Donne and Beaumont. In Chapters 3 and 4, I return to the Skipwith manuscript to demonstrate the difference that such recontextualizations made to the political and religious associations of Donne's and Beaumont's anti-courtly love poems. From the current section's perspective on the means of producing miscellanies, though, it is worth acknowledging that, given how verse collectors made these books, the fact that they recontextualized literature should not surprise modern readers. When people collected poems from different sources, added to anthologies over a period of time, or bound different manuscripts together, recontextualizations necessarily occurred. Yet this material observation hardly accounts for the content and historical significance of particular recontextualizations, which offer plenty of surprises to students and scholars of early modern English literature, and to which the remainder of this book turns.

THE FORMATION AND POLITICIZATION OF A GENRE

When he went to St. John's in the late sixteenth century, the manuscript verse collector introduced at the beginning of this study arrived at a

[43] British Library MS Add. 25707.

particularly good place to find erotic poetry. Several of the texts that he transcribed indicate that he belonged to a social circle of St. John's students who evidently appreciated such verse, including John Finet, James Reshoulde, and Robert Mills. Indeed, one of these young men probably compiled the manuscript. Finet would go on to gain a reputation at the court of King James for composing bawdy songs to the delight (and once, apparently, to the extreme displeasure) of the king.[44] Reshoulde demonstrated his interest in such literature when he wrote a 'ribald ballad.'[45] And Robert Mills translated Ovid's *Amores* I.5, as did another contemporary Cambridge student, Christopher Marlowe, who Englished all of Ovid's elegies.[46] In addition, Mills collaborated with yet another St. John's student, Thomas Nashe, on an entertainment that seems to have resulted in Mills being 'expelled the Colledge' and Nashe departing for London without his master's degree.[47] Whoever compiled this miscellany collected poems among several authors and readers of Ovidian and otherwise sexually explicit literature in Cambridge.

Indeed, in the days of Marlowe and Nashe, Cambridge must have offered the best place in England to find anti-courtly love poems.[48] Each

[44] Finet, *Ceremonies of Charles I*. In a libel on James I's court ('Listen jolly gentlemen'), Finet (referred to as 'Jacke Finnett') is numbered among the king's 'merry boys . . . with masks and toys.' Bodleian MS Malone 23, pp. 19–22, as transcribed in Alastair Bellany and Andrew McRae, ed., 'Early Stuart Libels: An edition of poetry from manuscript sources,' *Early Modern Literary Studies*, Text Series 1 (2005), L5. http://purl.oclc.org/emls/texts/libels/ accessed 22 June 2005. The editors note that, according to Anthony Weldon, Finet composed the 'bawdy songs' that Sir Edward Zouche, Knight Marshall, would perform for the king, and that John Chamberlain reported the performance in which Finet went too far. In January 1618, at James' palace at Theobald's, he sang 'a certain song . . . of such scurrilous and base stuffe that it put the King out of his good humor, and all the rest that heard it.' Anthony Weldon, *The Court and Character of King James* (London: R.I. and are to be sold by John Wright, 1650; Wing W1273), 91–92; John Chamberlain, *The Letters of John Chamberlain*, ed. Norman Egbert McClure, vol. 2 (Philadelphia: American Philosophical Society, 1939), 131. See also Clayton, 'Finet.'

[45] Cummings, 'John Finet's Miscellany,' 33, 497–500; Bodleian MS Rawl. poet. 85, fol. 64r–65r.

[46] Bodleian MS Rawl. poet. 85, fol. 81r–v; Cummings, 'John Finet's Miscellany,' 585–89. See Woudhuysen, *Sir Philip Sidney*, 259–60; Hilton Kelliher, 'Unrecorded Extracts from Shakespeare, Sidney and Dyer,' *English Manuscript Studies*, 2 (1990), 163–87.

[47] Gabriel Harvey, *The Trimming of Thomas Nashe Gentleman* (London: for Philip Scarlet, 1597; STC 12906), sig. G3r–v. Cummings, 'John Finet's Miscellany,' 575, also 34–39, 570–76.

[48] Consider John Carey, 'The Ovidian Love Elegy in England,' (DPhil diss., Oxford University, 1960), 154–55.

of the earliest examples of the genre that recur in seventeenth-century manuscript verse miscellanies has links to the university: Marlowe's translations of Ovid's elegies; Nashe's 'The choise of valentines'; and the anonymous 'Naye, phewe nay pishe,' which at least circulated at St. John's. The vogue for erotic verse likely spread from Cambridge via the influence of Marlowe. Like so many early modern English writers, most of the other prolific anti-courtly love poets drew on Marlovian models. Shakespeare, like many writers connected to the Inns of Court, wrote epyllia based on Ovid's *Metamorphosis* that looked to Marlowe's *Hero and Leander*. Sir John Davies' most popular anti-courtly love poems first appeared in print with Marlowe's translations of Ovid's elegies.[49] And Donne, who would master the anti-courtly love style among several other poetic genres, most clearly indicated his engagement with Marlowe in 'The Bait,' which takes its first line from Marlowe: 'Come live with mee, and be my love.'[50] Given Marlowe's fame and his reputation as a translator of Ovid, Donne must have written his own Ovidian love elegies and other anti-courtly love poems with Marlowe in mind as well.

Another late sixteenth-century verse collector gave Cambridge University wits a prominent place in his account of English poetry, and emphasized their anti-courtly love poetry in particular. He included in his miscellany, now at the Rosenbach Library, Marlowe's 'If thou wilt liue and be my loue' with another 'answeare' to his famous lyric, this one beginning in a woman's voice, 'If that the world & loue weare young.'[51] Moreover, he collected several anti-courtly love poems from Cambridge: the only other Elizabethan copy of 'Nay pish: nay pue'; a short version of Nashe's 'The choise of valentines' that ends before the prostitute in other copies famously resorts to a dildo; and Marlowe's

[49] Sir John Davies and Christopher Marlowe, *Epigrammes and Elegies. By I.D. and C. M.* (Middleborough[?]: n.p., n.d.[1599?]; STC 6350).

[50] Christopher Marlowe, *The Complete Works of Christopher Marlowe*, ed. Fredson Bowers, 2nd edn, vol. 2 (Cambridge: Cambridge University Press, 1973, 1981), 536–37.

[51] Rosenbach MS 1083/15, pp. 57 ('If thou wilt liue and be my loue'), 57–58 ('Her answeare.//If that the world & loue weare young'); James L. Sanderson, 'An Edition of an Early Seventeenth-Century Manuscript Collection of Poems (Rosenbach MS. 186)' (PhD diss., University of Pennsylvania, 1960), lxix–lxxxi, 288–301. I thank Greg Giuliano for providing me with timely photographs of this manuscript, in addition to his hospitality at the Rosenbach.

translation of Ovid's sexual encounter with Corinna.[52] Rather than balance these erotic verses with courtly lyrics, as did the collector from St. John's, the initial compiler of this Rosenbach manuscript accentuated their style with similarly direct epigrams and crude sexual verse. For instance, he placed first in his miscellany a poem full of sexual innuendo on a pair of lovers playing card games named 'maw' and 'Ruff.' This introductory poem thus resonates with the collector's copy of 'Nay pish: nay pue' on the very next leaf, especially where its speaker complains 'you marr my ruffe' and finally invites her lover to 'come goe to cardes.'[53] The collector fit in between these texts a poem aligning women with roses and men with thorns, or 'prickles,' and a verse graphically detailing the physical characteristics 'required' for a woman to be considered 'faire.'[54] While the St. John's compiler distinguished the female monologue from court poetry, this anthologist featured his copy of 'Nay pish: nay pue' in a block of similarly unpretentious erotica.

Likewise, this manuscript verse collector surrounded Nashe's account of a trip to a brothel with appropriate companion pieces. He introduced it with a short verse 'Of Brothell houses.' Then, after Nashe's prostitute made his speaker's 'Priapus as stiffe as steele,' he copied an epigram that likens the 'pricke' of one Grunnus to 'Paulsteeple.'[55] He similarly followed Marlowe's translation of Ovid with short verses that emphasize its speaker's single-minded focus on sex. Marlowe's Ovidian persona does nothing more to woo Corinna than lie on a bed and tear off her gown as she passes. Immediately below this scene in the Rosenbach manuscript, its compiler inscribed a three-line apostrophe beckoning 'noble Tarse loues slaue' to rise out of his 'codpiece' and 'dig thy selfe a

[52] Rosenbach MS 1083/15, pp. 3 ('Nay pish: nay pue: nay faith [ ] will you fie'), 18–22 ('ffaire was the morne & brightsome was the day'), 43 ('In som[m]ers heat at midtyme of the day'); Sanderson, 'An Edition of an Early Seventeenth-Century Manuscript Collection of Poems,' 9–12, 91–100, 209–12. Sir John Davies, *The Poems of Sir John Davies*, ed. Robert Krueger (Oxford: Clarendon, 1975), 443–44.

[53] Rosenbach MS 1083/15, pp. 1 ('On Holy euen when w[inter]s nightes waxe longe'), 3; Sanderson, 'An Edition of an Early Seventeenth-Century Manuscript Collection of Poems,' 1–3, 9–12.

[54] Rosenbach MS 1083/15, p. 2 ('Your Rose [is sw]eet & woma[n]like in smell'; 'In choice of faire are thirty thinges required'); Sanderson, 'An Edition of an Early Seventeenth-Century Manuscript Collection of Poems,' 5–6.

[55] Rosenbach MS 1083/15, pp. 21, 22 ('In Grunnu[m]//Grunnus his pricke is like Paulsteeple turnd'); Sanderson, 'An Edition of an Early Seventeenth-Century Manuscript Collection of Poems,' 89–101.

graue betweene my m^{es} thyghes.'[56] On the verso of the leaf that features this crude piece, he offered yet another especially direct lover: a 'cuntry swadd,' whose unadorned method of courting contrasts with the behavior of 'a courtier.' In the brief poem by Sir John Davies, both characters attempt to woo the same 'Lady Faire.'

> The Courtier first came lepping in
> & tooke the Lady by the chin
> the cuntry swadd as he was blunt
> came tooke the lady by the elbow.
>
> I D[57]

Once the reader instinctively replaces the last word with one that rhymes, the leaping courtier appears ridiculously indirect as compared to the carnally minded lovers whom this manuscript verse collector, like so many others, showcased in his miscellany.

With these poems, the compiler of the Rosenbach manuscript organized a fine exhibition of late Elizabethan anti-courtly love poetry. He brought together some of the most canonical, most popular, and most obscure examples of the genre available to manuscript verse collectors in the late sixteenth century, in particular at the Inns of Court. The unknown individual responsible for beginning this miscellany must have had at least social, if not official, connections to the Middle Temple. For, in addition to a fine collection of the poetry of the Middle Templar Sir John Davies, he acquired the extremely rare epigrams of Benjamin Rudyard, who belonged to the same Inn of Court.[58]

In addition to helping to locate the initial compiler of the Rosenbach miscellany, the Davies poems that he collected demonstrate how he began to politicize his collection of anti-courtly love poetry. With the

[56] Rosenbach MS 1083/15, p. 43 ('O noble Tarse loues slaue out of my codpeece rise'); Sanderson, 'An Edition of an Early Seventeenth-Century Manuscript Collection of Poems,' 213.

[57] Rosenbach MS 1083/15, p. 44 ('A Lady faire two suiters had'); Sanderson, 'An Edition of an Early Seventeenth-Century Manuscript Collection of Poems,' 215. See *Poems of Sir John Davies*, 181, 402.

[58] Rosenbach MS 1083/15, pp. 48–56; Sanderson, 'An Edition of an Early Seventeenth-Century Manuscript Collection of Poems,' 237–87; *Poems of Sir John Davies*, 443–44. Incidentally, Sir Benjamin Rudyard would also be one of the executors of John Finet's will, along with Sir Thomas Roe, both poets and members of Donne's coterie. Clayton, 'Finet.'

help of a collaborator, he added to his miscellany several late sixteenth-century verse libels, most notably some of Davies' satirical poems on the second marriages of both Richard Fletcher, Bishop of London, and Edward Coke, Attorney General.[59] Moreover, the sixteenth-century compilers of the Rosenbach miscellany interspersed among Davies' libels crude verses on genitals, which extend the collectors' presentation of erotic poetry into the midst of such slanderous satirical verse. In fact, they effectively introduced the libels' critical accounts of the Fletcher marriage with an exchange of obvious riddles on genitals, one in the hand of the initial compiler and the voice of a man named Robin, and the next in the second hand and a female persona named Rachel.[60] Rachel concludes her final couplet with the obscene word that Davies omitted from his poem on the courtier and the 'cuntry swadd.' Then, on the verso of the same leaf and in the hand of the primary compiler, Davies begins to mock 'Byshope Fletcher & my lady Baker': Mary Gifford, the widow of Sir Richard Baker. Davies gave the newly-weds the names of one of Shakespeare's Ovidian couples: 'the Romaine Tarquine' and 'Lucres.' Yet he also gave the bride the name of 'Lais,' after a Corinthian courtesan (in addition to repeatedly calling her a 'whore'). Juxtaposed as they are in this miscellany, the riddles on genitals emphasize the sexual misconduct alleged in the libels, and the libels in turn apply the sexual content of the erotic poems to the scandalous second marriage of a public figure.

Decades after he collected anti-courtly love poems at the Inns and consolidated them in his miscellany, another verse collector repoliticized these very same texts by adding to the Rosenbach manuscript early

[59] Rosenbach MS 1083/15, pp. 67–73 ('A Libell against m^{r} Bash//I know not how it comes to passé'), 76–77 ('Byshope Fletcher & my lady Baker.//The pride of Prelacy wch now longe since'), 79 ('Cæcus the pleader hath a Lady wedd'), 79–80 ('Vppon the Astinian hilles the mountaine mare'), 80 ('ffollow the law & let Primero goe'), 80–81 ('Maddam Olimpia rydeth in her coach'), 81 ('Holla my Muse leaue Cæcus in his greife'), 82–89 ('And doe you thinke I haue naught abode'); Sanderson, 'An Edition of an Early Seventeenth-Century Manuscript Collection of Poems,' 347–71, 377–82, 389–433. See *Poems of Sir John Davies*, 171–79, 395–99.

[60] Rosenbach MS 1083/15, pp. 74 ('Riddle me Rachell whats this/that a ma[n] handles when he does pisse//It is a kind of pleasing sting'), 75 ('Now riddle me Robin & tell me thus much/Quid significant a Cut in Dutch//It is a wound y^{t} nature giues'); Sanderson, 'An Edition of an Early Seventeenth-Century Manuscript Collection of Poems,' lx, 372–76. As Sanderson notes, the second of these obviously related verses is in a second hand.

Stuart libels on another celebrity wedding. When the third collector to work on the manuscript added verse libels on this later high-profile marriage, he brought up to date the miscellany's account of political satire, and complicated the political associations of this manuscript's display of anti-courtly love poetry. This seventeenth-century verse collector copied some of the poems that attack the union of the Jacobean royal favorite Robert Carr, earl of Somerset, to, in the words of the copyist, 'ye diuorced Lady of ye E. of Essex y^{t}/went for a mayd still his present wife,' which I analyze in Chapter 3.[61] If the initial compilers of this Rosenbach manuscript politicized anti-courtly love poetry with late Elizabethan satires, the verse collector responsible for the Somerset libels repoliticized the genre and assimilated it to new contexts, shaped by unprecedented court scandal and corresponding developments in political verse. When he added these Somerset libels to the miscellany, he extended into the early Stuart period the manuscript's consistent objection to the second marriages of the rich and famous. He updated the political context of the volume's erotic verse. And he constructed a tense relationship between such poetry and at least certain members of the early Stuart court, making the anthology's anti-courtly love poetry look more anti-courtly than it ever had before.

Another verse collector politicized 'Nay pish, nay pewe' when he copied the poem in a miscellany now at the Folger Shakespeare Library and affiliated with one Joseph Hall (but not the famous satirist and bishop of Norwich). In the left margin beside the poem, he wrote: 'Against M$^{rs:}$/Ioseph.'[62] While it is possible that the copyist recorded the name of the poem's original subject in this heading, the probable date of his transcript casts some doubt on the compiler's reliability in this

[61] Rosenbach MS 1083/15, pp. 139 ('Of Sr Robert Carr Earl of Somerset/& y^{e} diuorced Lady of ye E. of Essex y^{t}/went for a mayd still his present wife.//Lady chaynd to Venus Doue'; 'plants enow thence may ensue'), 140 ('On the late Earle of Somersett// ICVR, good monseir Carr'); Sanderson, 'An Edition of an Early Seventeenth-Century Manuscript Collection of Poems,' 698–702, 711–13.

[62] Folger MS V.a.339, fol. 188v ('Against M$^{rs:}$/Ioseph://Nay pish, nay pewe, nay fayth, & will you? fie'). In his great study of the manuscript, Giles Dawson insisted that the Joseph Hall who signed his name of the flyleaf was 'not the Bishop of Norwich,' adding that 'the appearance of the signature does not suggest that Hall wrote anything else in the book and does suggest that it was written as late perhaps as 1700' ('John Payne Collier's Great Forgery,' *Studies in Bibliography*, 24 (1971), 3). Arthur Freeman and Janet Ing Freeman have most recently concurred (*John Payne Collier: Scholarship and Forgery in the Nineteenth Century* (New Haven: Yale University Press, 2004), 502).

matter. He entered the poem just a few pages before two much later libels on the earl and countess of Somerset.[63] Probably collecting and transcribing poems well into the seventeenth century then, this verse collector was more likely redeploying the poem against a woman whom the author had not intended to offend. Although it may offer little or no credible information regarding the poem's original context, this copy of 'Nay pish, nay pewe' uniquely exemplifies the interplay that developed between anti-courtly love poems and libels in miscellanies. For its transcriber's brief marginal note shows how little one needed to do to certain poems in order to exploit their libelous potential, which Chapters 3 and 4 demonstrate in regards to epigrams and a masque song that poets turned into libels. While this collector may not have quite turned 'Nay pish, nay pewe' into a libel, he did shame its sexualized speaker who, before he named her, endured no more shame than Marlowe's attractive Corinna. Furthermore, he politicized the poem by placing it where it resonates with the libels directed against the earl and especially the countess of Somerset. Rather like the libel on the countess that he transcribed, this unique copy of 'Nay pish, nay pewe' sexualizes and defames a specific woman. In this Folger miscellany, and like so many of the other mistresses of anti-courtly love poems, the mysterious Mrs. Joseph came to develop a relationship with the sexualized and publicly shamed target of an early Stuart libel.

In the first sustained study of early Stuart libels as literature (as opposed to straightforward political statements), Andrew McRae introduces the genre with a quotation from one of John Donne's weekly letters to his friend Sir Henry Goodyer, in which Donne addresses the 'multitude of libells' on the death of Sir Robert Cecil, earl of Salisbury. Donne wrote this letter while traveling on the continent, yet even there his party received a number of Cecil libels. He proposed, somewhat facetiously, that these libels on Cecil 'are so tastelesse and flat, that I protest to you, I think they were made by his friends.' For, he added:

> when there are witty and sharp libels made which not onely for the liberty of speaking, but for the elegancie, and composition, would take deep root, and make durable impressions in the memory, no other way hath been thought so fit to suppresse them, as to divulge some course, and railing one: for when the

[63] Folger MS V.a.339, fol. 193v ('Letchery [con]sulte wth witchery howe to cause frigidety'; 'Some ar sett on mischeife soe, that they care not w they doe').

noise is risen, that libels are abroad, mens curiositie must be served with something: and it is better for the honour of the person traduced, that some blunt downright railings be vented, of which everybody is soon weary, then other pieces, which entertain us long with a delight, and love to the things themselves.[64]

Bad libels, Donne joked, actually benefited their traduced subject, for these forgettable poems quickly satisfied the curiosity of readers and kept them from seeking out better libels whose 'elegancie, and composition' would entertain and delight them. Donne considered the libels that succeeded his own classicist verse satires worthy of his attention; he admired the poetic qualities of some and acknowledged the political function of even the others. He did not embrace the new culture of libeling without qualification, however. He continued his letter to Goodyer by admitting, 'there may be cases, where one may do his Countrey good service, by libelling against a live man.' But, because their subject had died, he found the latest libels on Cecil 'unexcusable.'[65] The compiler of Joseph Hall's Folger miscellany seems not to have shared Donne's objection to slandering the deceased; he copied two libelous epitaphs on Cecil.[66]

As McRae suggests, Donne's aesthetic appreciation of libels articulates the sentiments of the manuscript verse collectors who gathered so many of these political verses among now-canonical poems in their miscellanies. Collectors preserved far more copies of libels in verse miscellanies than in manuscript books of exclusively topical or political documents; in other words, they deemed libels worthy of sharing space with the most exemplary lyric poetry of the English Renaissance. So they evidently considered libels more than mere records of political events or sentiments. The recent recognition of libels' place in literary culture has led scholars to engage the poetics, in addition to the politics, of these verses—an endeavor that tends to complicate their political significance.[67] I propose that the acknowledgement of libels' popularity

[64] John Donne, *Letters to Severall Persons of Honour* (London: J. Flesher for Richard Marriot, 1651; Wing D1864), 89–90.

[65] Donne, *Letters*, 90–91.

[66] Folger MS V.a.339, fol. 265r ('vpon Cicells death//Here lies Hobbinoll o^{r} Shepherd whileare'; 'Here lyeth inrolled for wormes meate').

[67] See '"Railing Rhymes": Politics and Poetry in Early Stuart England,' ed. Andrew McRae, *Huntington Library Quarterly*, 69/1 (March 2006).

in verse miscellanies calls also for a corresponding reconsideration of the politics of the canonical poems that surround them, starting with anti-courtly love poetry.

The next chapter begins this investigation in earnest by introducing the work of an anonymous seventeenth-century verse collector who related John Donne's most popular anti-courtly love poem, 'To his Mistress going to bed,' to a libel on, and a love lyric by, Sir Walter Ralegh. In order to explain the significance of his arrangement of these texts, I survey a series of answer-poems to Ralegh's love poems, as well as the work of scholars who have suggested that Donne was actually mocking Ralegh with his Ovidian love elegy. This verse collector offers some support for such a political reading of Donne's poem, but he also requires revising it. For he presented Donne's elegy as a parody not simply of Ralegh, but specifically of the love lyrics that Ralegh had employed for political purposes at the Elizabethan court. This verse collector joined others in establishing a striking relationship between Ralegh and Donne. Yet, as the chapter ultimately demonstrates, no two collectors constructed this relationship in the same way. The compilers of certain miscellanies presented Donne's Ovidian love elegy as something of an answer-poem to Ralegh. In the manuscript environments that they produced, Donne seems to mock Ralegh's poetry and politics. A collector responsible for other manuscripts, however, found poems by Ralegh and Donne to be perfectly compatible, and presented the two poets as exemplary authors of complementary love poems.

Chapter 3 deals in detail with a historical event that intensified the early Stuart vogue for the verse libel, and that dramatically recontextualized anti-courtly love poetry: the Overbury affair. This major Jacobean court scandal involved the 1613 divorce of a Catholic noblewoman, Frances Howard, from the son of a legendary militant protestant, Robert Devereux, third earl of Essex, on the grounds of impotence; Howard's prompt remarriage to King James' royal favorite Robert Carr, the new earl of Somerset; and the Somersets' 1616 conviction for conspiring to murder Carr's mentor, Sir Thomas Overbury, who had opposed their marriage. For reasons explored in the chapter, this explosive episode coincided with, and may have contributed to, an early wave of the dissemination of Donne's poetry beyond the tight circle of his coterie. Probably at the earl's request, Donne reluctantly considered dedicating a limited print edition of his poems to Somerset, after the poet aquired the secretary position that Overbury had vacated under duress. While Donne apparently avoided publishing his poems for Somerset, verse collectors soon intensified the scribal publication of Donne's poems. Moreover, they included his poems in books quite unlike the one that Donne contemplated presenting to Somerset, and placed them in relationships to the royal favorite that the author could not have approved. In their miscellanies, many of these collectors gathered Donne's poems among libels attacking the countess of Somerset—libels that, needless to say, Donne would not have included in his collection for her second husband. By associating Somerset libels with Donne's poems, the compilers of these miscellanies effectively turned Donne against his own patron. In this way the Overbury affair radically recontextualized Donne's poetry—as it did Overbury's own poem, 'A Wife,' and one of Francis Beaumont's anti-courtly love poems, 'Ad Comitissam Rutlandiæ.'

Chapter 4 proceeds to a scandal surrounding another Catholic woman: Prince Charles' proposed bride, Donna Maria Anna of Spain. By adding to their miscellanies libels on the marriage negotiations, otherwise known as the Spanish match, collectors of anti-courtly love poetry continued to assimilate the genre to a manuscript culture that disrespected prominent Catholic women. Yet Spanish match libels also began a new chapter in the history of early Stuart libels by introducing issues of *male* sexuality, through the figure of George Villiers, first duke of Buckingham. Like Somerset, Buckingham served as James' royal favorite, and had an emotionally intense, and possibly sexual, relationship with the king. Yet, unlike Somerset, Buckingham came under harsh censure for this purportedly erotic relationship in libels. By documenting this shift in the way that libelers criticized royal favorites, verse collectors marked a significant moment in both political history and the history of sexuality. One early Buckingham libel turned Ben Jonson's blessing of King James' senses (from the Buckingham-sponsored masque *Gypsies Metamorphosed*) into a provocative prayer that God keep those senses free from Buckingham's sexual advances. Several verse collectors juxtaposed this libelous representation of the royal bedchamber to Donne's 'To his Mistress going to bed.' In doing so, collectors hinted ironically at the love elegy's resonance with Ralegh, even as they associated Donne's poem with the libel's harsh censure of a more recent favorite.

Chapter 5 continues to focus on Buckingham, turning to his assassination, which most late Buckingham libels celebrate. By surrounding them with verses on the murdered duke and his assassin, collectors effectively completed the recontextualization of anti-courtly love poems with early Stuart politics. The chapter begins with collectors who sketched a progression of erotic royal favoritism from Ralegh to Buckingham, and who correspondingly positioned Donne's 'To his Mistress going to bed' as a tame predecessor to poetic criticisms of the later royal favorites. After opening with a professional miscellany featuring a decidedly radical political perspective, the chapter concludes with a future royalist collector who astonishingly misattributed a Buckingham libel to Donne, thereby associating its radical politics with the religious, satirical, and erotic poems that he also ascribed to Donne in his miscellany. This chapter also shows how collectors immersed other anti-courtly love poems by Donne, Beaumont, Carew, and Davies in the context of Buckingham's assassination. In the hands and books of these collectors, anti-courtly love poetry became caught up in the religious and political polarization that would ultimately constitute an early step toward the English civil wars.

After the civil wars, verse collectors would transform the politics of anti-courtly love poetry yet again, when critics of the protectorate put the genre to completely new purposes in printed miscellanies. The epilogue studies the first printed books to include the anti-courtly love poems that the Stationer's Company had prohibited the publisher of Donne's collected poems to print in 1633. In his 1654 anthology, *The Harmony of the Muses*, Robert Chamberlain claimed for the royalist cause all three of Donne's banned anti-courtly love poems: 'To his Mistress going to bed,' 'Loues Progresse,' and 'Loves War.' Chamberlain helped to make the printed miscellany of bawdy verse such an effective mode of announcing discontent with the protectorate that soon even nonroyalists adopted his model. In particular, Milton's nephew John Phillips and the publisher Nathaniel Brook, who had recently printed books in support of Cromwell, criticized recent developments in the protectorate when they included anti-courtly love poems in the two miscellanies that they printed in 1656. And the government responded by banning at least one of these miscellanies and fining its producers. Despite their innovativeness, these critics of the protectorate were extending what was by now a long tradition of verse collectors politicizing anti-courtly love poetry for their own purposes. Together, these collectors defined a literary genre that proved particularly adaptable while remaining pointedly political.

2

The Politics of Courtly and Anti-Courtly Love Poetry in the Hands of Collectors

The scribe responsible for the majority of a verse miscellany in the Stowe collection at the British Library produced a remarkable reconstruction of the politics of one of John Donne's anti-courtly love poems. In a thick quarto largely given over to Donne's verse and prose, he chose the leaves immediately following 'To his Mistress going to bed' for two poems that he affiliated with Sir Walter Ralegh: a libel attacking the courtier and a love lyric attributed to him.[1] He thus showed that he was willing to entertain, and to facilitate, a critical interpretation of Ralegh's love poem, which begins 'Callinge to minde mine eye went longe about.' For the libel that he placed immediately before Ralegh's song criticizes the courtier for writing lyrics like it. Thomas Rogers, a distant relation to Donne by marriage, probably composed the libel in the second half of 1603, celebrating and moralizing Ralegh's fall after the failures of the Bye Plot to kidnap and imprison King James and the Main Plot to replace James with Arabella Stuart.[2] Accordingly, the scribe gave to the

[1] British Library MS Stowe 962, fols 82v–83r ('An Elegie•or/vndressinge of ons/ mistresse.//Come madame, come, all rest my powers defie'), 84r–85v ('Vppon sir Walter Rayleigh Treason wth Lo: Gray S$^{r:}$//Watt, well I wott thy ouerweaninge witt'), 85v ('Callinge to minde mine eye went longe about//Sir Walter Rawlyegh'). I hypothesize that the scribe copied Donne's elegy on the final two facing pages of a gathering, turned a leaf, and began transcribing the Ralegh texts at the start of the next quire—leaving blank space below Donne's poem that either he or another hand filled in later. Yet the fact that Donne's poem and the pair of Ralegh texts appear on distinct gatherings leaves open the possibility that the binder, and not the scribe, juxtaposed them.

[2] For a complete edition of the poem, based on Folger MS X.d.241, fols 1v–3r (the only attributed copy), see *Poems of Sir Walter Ralegh*, 182–85. For biographical information on the libeler, see John Craig, 'Rogers, Thomas (c. 1553–1616),' *ODNB*; Thomas Rogers, *Leicester's Ghost*, ed. Franklin B. Williams, Jr. (Chicago: University of Chicago Press, 1972), xvi–xvii. For context, see Bellany and McRae, 'Early Stuart Libels,' B4.

poem the heading: 'Vppon sir Walter Rayleigh Treason wth Lo: Gray S$^{r:}$.'[3] The libel begins by directly addressing Ralegh after his fall: 'Watt, well I wott thy ouerweaninge witt/led by ambition now hath wrought thy fall.' To heighten the tragedy of Ralegh's fall, Rogers recalls that Queen Elizabeth I, figured conventionally here as Cynthia, once showed the courtier great favor.

> I pittie y^{t} the sum[m]ers nightingall
> (Im[m]ortall Cinthias somtimes deare delight)
> that vsd to singe soe sweete a madrigall
> should like an owle goe ma^{u}ndringe in ye night
>   hated of all, and pittied of none,
>   though swan[n]like now hee makes his dijnge mone[4]

The libel represents Ralegh as Elizabeth's former 'deare delight'; as a nightingale who 'vsd to singe soe sweet a madrigall' to his queen; or, in other words, as a royal favorite who once wrote songs for her like the very next one in the Stowe manuscript. When he composed these lines, Rogers may not have been referring precisely to 'Callinge to minde mine eye went longe about.' Regardless of their author's intentions, however, the copyist of these lines explicitly connected them to the Ralegh poem that he placed next in his miscellany. With his copy of Rogers' libel, the compiler of the Stowe manuscript identified Ralegh as a Jacobean traitor, fallen from the favor that Elizabeth had shown him when he 'vsd to singe' for her. He then supplied a representative example of the sort of songs that Ralegh wrote for the queen. By effectively introducing it with a lengthy libel on the author, this verse collector provided an ironic, critical setting for Ralegh's poem.

In Steven May's judgment, Ralegh may have indeed used this poem 'to maintain and promote his rapport with Elizabeth.'[5] The song shares a number of characteristics with lyrics that the courtier is known to have addressed to the queen. Most importantly, it models a courtly lover's devotion to his mistress in terms that could also apply to a courtier's dependence on his queen. Love so consumes and torments Ralegh's speaker that he considers plucking out his eye for seeing his mistress and

[3] 'Thomas, Lord Grey of Wilton, participant in the Bye Plot' (Bellany and McRae, 'Early Stuart Libels,' B4 n.18).

[4] British Library MS Stowe 962, fol. 84r.

[5] May, *Elizabethan Courtier Poets*, 119.

misleading his heart; slaying his heart for becoming her property; and even killing himself. His anguish lifts, however, at the end of the poem. He explains that, once he recognized his own honorable devotion to his mistress, 'I loued my selfe, because my selfe loued you.'[6] Acknowledging his love for a singularly worthy mistress, the speaker's self-loathing instantly turns to self-love. As this chapter will demonstrate, when Ralegh started writing poems like this, he was reviving the short-lived practice of elite courtiers composing Petrarchan love lyrics for Queen Elizabeth. He was also changing the tradition by exploiting the potential of courtly love poems to further his own career at the expense, he vainly hoped, of a rival courtier.

Both Rogers and the compiler of the Stowe manuscript attributed a political function to Ralegh's courtly love poetry. Whereas Rogers wrote critically about his use of songs at court, the verse collector reconstructed the politics of Ralegh's lyric by thoughtfully arranging texts. Juxtaposing poems by and about Ralegh, the collector glossed the royal favorite's Petrarchan devotion as political ambition, which led to treason. And by placing these poems near Donne's 'To his Mistress going to bed,' he anticipated arguments that scholars have made about possible, uncomplimentary references to Ralegh in Donne's Ovidian elegy. Without drawing on the support that certain early modern verse collectors offer their arguments, these critics have shown that Donne's poem looks critical of Ralegh when placed in the context of the courtier's career at the late Elizabethan court. This is precisely what the compiler of the Stowe manuscript did with Donne's elegy: he placed it in the context of Ralegh's political love poetry, and invited criticism of the fallen courtier. In the manuscript context that this verse collector devised, 'To his Mistress going to bed' begins to resemble poems that others wrote in response to Ralegh, and scholars' political interpretations of the poem become difficult to dismiss, but also difficult to accept without revision. In order to explain how an early modern collector could have related Donne's poem to Ralegh, this chapter initially surveys a number of answer-poems to the courtier, as well as the work of the literary critics who have argued that Donne wrote the poem with Ralegh in mind. I then return to the poem's place in the Stowe manuscript, as well as other manuscript verse miscellanies. The compilers of each of these

[6] British Library MS Stowe 962, fol. 85v.

miscellanies gathered sexually explicit elegies by Donne among love lyrics that they attributed to Ralegh. Some of these verse collectors presented Ralegh's courtly and Donne's anti-courtly love poetry as one another's aesthetic and ideological antithesis. Another verse collector, however, evidently saw no tension between these poems and regarded them as entirely compatible examples of love poetry. While they recorded and facilitated such divergent interpretations, all of these early modern verse collectors demonstrated their capacity to reconstruct the politics of courtly and anti-courtly love poetry.

ANSWERING RALEGH

If Donne was indeed criticizing Ralegh in 'To his Mistress going to bed,' he was engaging a specialized literary practice that Elizabethan courtier poets had begun when he was only a boy. In the early 1580s, Sir Thomas Heneage, long-time gentleman and treasurer of the Privy Chamber, answered Ralegh's 'Farwell falce Love thow oracle of lies' with his only love poem, 'Most welcome love, thow mortall foe to lies.'[7] In order to counter Ralegh's rising prominence, Heneage had recently formed an alliance with another former royal favorite who likewise maintained important positions at court, Sir Christopher Hatton.[8] Although their companion poems show Ralegh bidding farewell to, and Heneage welcoming, love, both poets implicitly agreed that a courtier owed love to his sovereign. They disagreed, however, regarding what kind of love was appropriate to her court. In this and several other amorous complaints, Ralegh insisted on a neo-Petrarchan mode of courtly love, characterized by the same sort of relentless suffering on display in his 'Callinge to minde mine eye went longe about.' In welcoming love, Heneage was by no means welcoming this sort of consuming, discontented love. Indeed, where Ralegh characterized love as 'An envious boye from whome all cares arise,' Heneage honored love as 'An Impe of heaven, that troth to vertue ties.' Where Ralegh represented love as

[7] *Poems of Sir Walter Ralegh*, 11–12 (10A.25, 1).

[8] Steven W. May, 'Companion Poems in the Ralegh Canon,' *English Literary Renaissance*, 13/3 (1983), 260–73.

'a bastard vile, a beast with rage possest,' Heneage's chaste love 'bastard lustes doth hate.'[9] Thus objecting to every line of Ralegh's poem, Heneage redefined love in direct opposition to the new royal favorite's impassioned, dispairing iteration of courtly love.

After Heneage, others at court responded to Ralegh's courtly love poetry, most importantly Robert Devereux, second earl of Essex, and Queen Elizabeth herself. Despite the efforts of senior courtiers such as Heneage, Ralegh maintained and solidified his status as royal favorite until, early in 1587, he encountered his first serious challenger in Essex. After Robert Dudley, earl of Leicester, established his stepson, Essex, at court, Elizabeth's newest two favorites endorsed opposing foreign policies and engaged in a poetic contest that would continue intermittently until Essex's 1601 rebellion and execution.[10] Ralegh initiated the poetic exchange when, to offset Essex's mounting favor with the queen, he raised the political stakes of his poetry by addressing Elizabeth as his 'love' and casting Essex in the relatively unconventional role of 'fortune.' 'Fortune hath taken away my love' protests the loss of the courtly speaker's 'love/my lyves joy and my soules heaven,' 'my princes/my worldes joy and my true fantasies misteris.'[11] If some of Ralegh's other verses referred obliquely to his beloved or addressed lesser women at court in bawdy terms, he made clear that the courtly 'misteris' of this love poem was also his 'princes[s].' Likewise, he indicated that his version of the figure of 'fortune' is no mere abstraction, having 'taken thee away from mee,' having 'becomme my fantasies foe,' and having 'Conquer[ed] kinges.'[12] As Steven May and Leonard Tennenhouse have claimed, 'fortune' refers here not simply to fate but also to a person of

9 *Poems of Sir Walter Ralegh*, 11–12 (10A.28, 4).

10 On the Essex–Ralegh rivalry, which began in earnest during Leicester's 1587 absence from court, resumed after his death in 1588, and subsided in 1592, see Paul E. J. Hammer, *The Polarisation of Elizabethan Politics: The Political Career of Robert Devereux, 2nd Earl of Essex, 1585–1597* (Cambridge: Cambridge University Press, 1999), 54–70, 83–87, 115–16. For a conflicting date, see Walter Bouchier Devereux, *Lives and Letters of the Devereux, Earls of Essex, in the Reigns of Elizabeth, James I., and Charles I. 1540–1646*, vol. 1 (London: L. Murray, 1853), 172: 'he entered that fatal circle [court] in 1584, being then in his seventeenth year.'

11 *Poems of Sir Walter Ralegh*, 19 (15A.1–4).

12 *Poems of Sir Walter Ralegh*, 19 (15A.5, 4, 17). Similarly, in Ralegh's 'Farewell to the Court,' he laments his 'life in fortune's hand' (17.7).

superior social standing whose privilege is allegedly only an accident of fate: 'undoubtedly' Essex.[13]

Elizabeth responded to Ralegh with a poem of her own—'Ah silly pugge wert thou so sore afraid'—that both signaled an acceptance of his use of lyric poetry at court and refused, or ignored, certain implications of his poem. Elizabeth's poem must have indicated to Essex as well that she condoned the use of at least intimate, if not love, poetry at court, for the earl took to writing poems for the queen after this episode. Yet, more maternal than amorous in tone, Elizabeth's answer poem resists describing her relationship with Ralegh in terms of courtly love.[14] Likewise, and more to the point that concerned Ralegh and Essex, the queen refused to acknowledge that her relationship with Essex is at issue in Ralegh's poem at all, for she did not endorse Ralegh's identification of Essex as Fortune. Instead Elizabeth insisted on a more traditional and explicitly feminine characterization of Fortune who, she assures her 'Wat,' cannot 'force my harte to thinke thee any ill.'[15]

Essex, however, did recognize the role that Ralegh had assigned him in what he tellingly described as Ralegh's 'competition of Love.' In a July 1587 conversation with the queen, which Essex reported to Sir Edward Dyer in a letter, he 'did let her see, whether I had cause to disdain his competition of Love; or whether I could have Comfort to give myself over to the Service of a Mistress, that was in Aw of such a Man.'[16] If Elizabeth resisted seeing her court in terms of Ralegh's 'competition of Love,' Essex acknowledged and 'did let her see' the challenge that Ralegh posed in his poem. In this conversation and letter, Essex implicitly accepted the terms of Ralegh's 'competition,' going so far as to call Elizabeth his 'Mistress.' In the same breath, he also may have let Ralegh know that he was prepared to fight his rival: according to Essex, Ralegh 'standing at the door, might very well hear the worst that I spoke of himself.'[17] If 'Ah silly pug' shows Elizabeth resisting her favorites' political use of courtly love, this episode demonstrates how she

[13] Leonard Tennenhouse, 'Sir Walter Ralegh and the Literature of Clientage,' in Guy Fitch Lytle and Stephen Orgel, eds., *Patronage in the Renaissance* (Princeton: Princeton University Press, 1981), 235–58, esp. 240. May, *Elizabethan Courtier Poets*, 120.

[14] May, *Elizabethan Courtier Poets*, 122.

[15] *Poems of Sir Walter Ralegh*, 20 (15B.2, 4).

[16] Bodleian MS Tanner 75, fol. 84v. Quoted in May, *Elizabethan Courtier Poets*, 122.

[17] Bodleian MS Tanner 75, fol. 84v. Quoted in Devereux, *Lives and Letters of the Devereux*, 1:188.

nevertheless allowed those courtiers to enact a politicized version of the love triangle conventional to the literary style right in her chamber.

As Essex recognized, Ralegh's 'Fortune hath taken away my love' represents Elizabethan courtier love poetry at its most audacious: engaged with courtly love conventions, addressed and indeed sent to the queen, intended for polemical purposes at court, and disseminated in a variety of texts. Within two and a half years of its composition, quotations from Ralegh's poem and the queen's answer appeared in print and, by approximately the same time, verse collectors had made at least two manuscript copies of Ralegh's poem and one of Elizabeth's reply.[18] On 13 June 1590, William Wright registered the first of several ballads based on the poems ('Fortune hath taken thee away my love, beinge the true dittie thereof') with the Company of Stationers.[19] Potentially facilitating their dissemination, both Ralegh's and the queen's poems could have been sung to William Byrd's tune, 'Fortune.'[20] By the early 1590s then, people in and potentially around court could have noticed, in any of a variety of media, Ralegh's bold, political love poetry. Many who did encounter it would no doubt have recognized, as did Heneage and Essex, that Ralegh's openly political use of courtly love poetry at court was unprecedented.

When Essex finally responded to Ralegh in verse, he appropriated the diction of poems that Ralegh published more widely than 'Fortune hath taken away my love.' Indeed, Ralegh's commendatory verses for Edmund Spenser's *The Faerie Queene* must have done more than his exchange with the queen to publicize his use of courtly love poetry at

[18] George Puttenham, *The Arte of English Poesie* (London: Richard Field, 1589; STC 20519.5). The earliest manuscript copies of Ralegh's poem are British Library MS Add. 63742, fol. 116r and Marsh's MS Z3.5.21, fol. 30v; neither is attributed to Ralegh. The earliest manuscript of Elizabeth's reply is Inner Temple Library MS Petyt 538, vol. 10, fol. 3r, which is headed 'per Reginam/Waltero Rawly' (*Poems of Sir Walter Ralegh*, xxxix–xl, 19–21).

[19] May, *Elizabethan Courtier Poets*, 320. Cites Edward Arber, ed., *A Transcript of the Registers of the Company of Stationers, 1554–1640*, vol. 2 (Gloucester MA: P. Smith, 1967), 550; L. G. Black, 'A Lost Poem by Queen Elizabeth I,' *Times Literary Supplement* (23 May 1968), 535; Gerald Abraham, letter, *TLS* (30 May 1968), 553; Hyder Edward Rollins, *Analytical Index to the Ballad-Entries (1557–1709) in the Registers of the Company of Stationers of London* (University of North Carolina Press, 1924; repr. Hatboro PA: Tradition, 1967), nos. 911, 2569; William Chappell and Joseph W. Ebsworth, eds., *The Roxburghe Ballads*, vol. 3 (Hertford: Ballad Society, 1871–99), 192–93.

[20] Gerald Abraham, letter, *TLS* (30 May 1968), 553. May, *Elizabethan Courtier Poets*, 132.

court. Spenser's epic engagement with the fuller courtly love tradition appeared in print in 1590, after Ralegh had introduced Spenser to court in the previous winter. Ralegh's prefatory poem, 'A Vision upon this conceit of the Faery Queene,' explicitly associates the quintessential courtly mistress, Petrarch's Laura, with Spenser's fairy queen and, so, with Queen Elizabeth. It opens with a dream vision of Laura's grave in Venus' temple that is 'All suddeinly' eclipsed by 'the Faery Queene.'[21] Thus Spenser's *The Faerie Queene* supersedes Petrarch's *Rime sparse*, just as Spenser's queen transcends the model courtly mistress, Laura. Before this queen, even Petrarch himself forgets about Laura: the graces attend, stones bleed, and ghosts groan—including that of Homer, come again to curse both Spenser for stealing his fame and the queen for stealing Laura's.

Whereas 'A Vision' used courtly love literature to flatter the queen, Ralegh's second sonnet for *The Faerie Queene* deployed it for polemical purposes. In this second poem, Ralegh attacked the 'meaner wits' who have apparently criticized or insufficiently praised *The Faerie Queen*, comparing them to 'the Cuckoes' who dare to sing over 'Philumena' and insisting that only 'Vertue her selfe' is qualified to judge Spenser's epic.[22] Ralegh very well may have considered Essex one of these 'meaner wits.' In any event, Essex must have felt implicated by this poem, for he redeployed its diction against Ralegh when he had reason to resort to polemical verse of his own. Suffering from the queen's displeasure over his secret marriage to Frances Sidney, and so denied his usual means of influencing her, Essex adopted, and turned against his rival, Ralegh's style of political love poetry. Just as Ralegh had identified the unjust figure of 'Fortune' with Essex, Essex blamed 'fortune' for treading the muses' 'favours under feete.' Appropriating Ralegh's dichotomy of '*Cuckoes*' and 'Philumena,' Essex complained that 'sweete Philomela's note' has been 'crost' by 'that cursed cuckowe's throate.'[23] In this way Essex inverted and reassigned the values of Ralegh's poetics, associating himself with the muses and Philomena, and Ralegh with unjust Fortune and the carping 'cuckowe.' Not content to associate his rival with so abstractly negative a character as Fortune, Essex elaborated by specifying

[21] *Poems of Sir Walter Ralegh*, 2 (2.6). May mentions as precedents Oxford's poem 8 and Sidney's *Old Arcadia*, 73 (*Elizabethan Courtier Poets*, 123).

[22] *Poems of Sir Walter Ralegh*, 2 (3.2, 4).

[23] *Poems of Sir Walter Ralegh*, 2 (3.2); May, *Elizabethan Courtier Poets*, 250–51 (Essex 1.4, 2, 5–6).

'that byrde,/That parratelike can never cease to prate'—'a crowe'—and by evoking Ralegh's first name in the phrases 'filthy water' and 'puddle water.'[24] Essex's poem juxtaposes such negative metaphors to positive counterparts which clearly identify the queen: he likens her to a 'phoenix' incongruously looking upon a 'crowe' and a 'pure... mouth' sadly drinking 'puddle water.'[25] With Ralegh enjoying, and Essex denied, the royal presence, 'the world is in such a wofull state,' 'the sunne is in a cloud,/And darksome mists doe overrunne the day.'[26] But all will be right in the world if Elizabeth simply denies Ralegh: 'Let not a horse be meated with an Asse.'[27]

> So shall the world comend a sweet conceite,
> And humble fayth on heavenly favour waite.[28]

Far from rejecting Ralegh's audacious conflation of the queen with the courtly mistress—Elizabeth with Laura—as did Heneage, Essex begged Elizabeth to let him replace Ralegh as her courtly lover.

In redeploying against Ralegh his own polemical diction, Essex was acknowledging and helping to establish 'a consistent language of poetic competition at court.'[29] And in complaining that his unworthy rival had usurped the queen's 'heavenly favour' (as Ralegh had charged in 'fortune hath taken away my love'), Essex made clear that this poetic competition was the very same 'competition of Love' that Ralegh had initiated. Essex thus answered Ralegh both by adopting a style of literature suitable only for a royal favorite, and by promoting the increasingly popular literary practice of mocking Ralegh.[30] Essex must have encouraged, even if

[24] May, *Elizabethan Courtier Poets*, 250–51 (Essex 1.7–8, 19, 24, 36).

[25] May, *Elizabethan Courtier Poets*, 250–51 (Essex 1.19, 36).

[26] May, *Elizabethan Courtier Poets*, 250–51 (Essex 1.10, 13, 25–6).

[27] May, *Elizabethan Courtier Poets*, 250–51 (Essex 1.38–9).

[28] May, *Elizabethan Courtier Poets*, 250–51 (Essex 1.41–2).

[29] May has shown that Essex's and Ralegh's subsequent Elizabethan poetry was 'utilitarian,' adapted to 'self-serving, political ends': 'For these rivals, the muse had become an ally in their campaigns for self-promotion at court' (*Elizabethan Courtier Poets*, 124–25).

[30] The only other courtier who could have addressed such poems to Elizabeth in the 1590s was Sir Robert Cecil. For the only such poem of Cecil's that survives, see Katherine Duncan-Jones, '"Preserved Dainties": Late Elizabethan Poems by Sir Robert Cecil and the Earl of Clanricarde,' *Bodleian Library Record*, 14/2 (April 1992), 136–44; and my '"From a seruant of Diana" to the Libellers of Robert Cecil.' See also May, *Elizabethan Courtier Poets*, 133–34.

unwittingly, the composition and dissemination of libels on Ralegh. Verse collectors attributed some of the most popular Ralegh libels to Essex and to authors with connections to the earl. They credited Essex with the composition of a couple of answer poems to 'The Lie,' which they routinely attributed to or associated with Ralegh.[31] They also ascribed a stanza-for-stanza reply to 'The Lie' to Richard Lateware or Latewar, a chaplain to the Essex partisan, Charles Blount, Lord Mountjoy.[32] Lateware must have responded to Ralegh in verse in part because of his patron's support for the popular Essex. Similarly, in his libel copied in the Stowe manuscript, Thomas Rogers pointedly contrasted Ralegh to 'Renowned Essex,' whose innumerable admirers 'will not cease yet to lament his death.'[33]

Another Essex proponent joined his patron both in mocking Ralegh at court and in leading poets beyond court to do the same. Sir John Harington attacked Ralegh in thirteen epigrams on one 'Paulus.' And Sir John Davies, who lacked a position at court, followed his friend Harington's lead by libeling Ralegh in his own Paulus epigram.[34] Ralegh libelers found much about the favorite to mock without isolating his political use of courtly love poetry, which so bothered Essex. Indeed, Harington's epigrams on Paulus criticize his alleged atheism; his interest in tobacco; his license to plunder Spain. Yet one of Harington's Paulus epigrams satirizes Ralegh's lyric means of self-promotion at court.

Of Paulus, *a Flatterer.*

No man more seruile, no man more submisse,
Then to our Soueraigne Lady *Paulus* is.
He doth extoll her speech, admire her feature,
He calls himselfe her vassall, and her creature.

[31] *Poems of Sir Walter Ralegh*, xliii, 41.

[32] Bodleian MS Rawl. poet. 212, fols 88r–91v. One copy of 'The Lie' itself is attributed to 'Dr Latworthe': Bodleian MS Rawl. poet. 172, fols 12v–15r. *Poems of Sir Walter Ralegh*, xlii–xlvii, 34–41, 220. Paul E. J. Hammer, 'Latewar, Richard (1559/60–1601),' *ODNB*.

[33] *Poems of Sir Walter Ralegh*, 183.

[34] G. C. Moore Smith, 'Sir Walter Raleigh as seen by Sir John Harington,' *TLS* (10 March 1927), 160; V. T. Harlow, 'Harington's Epigrams,' *TLS* (14 July 1927), 488; Carolyn Bishop, 'Raleigh Satirized by Harington and Davies,' *Review of English Studies*, new ser., 23/89 (February 1972), 52–56. As Bishop notes, Harington mentions Davies favorably in epigrams 112, 163, 219, 388. These numbers correspond to those in *The Letters and Epigrams of Sir John Harington*, ed. Norman Egbert McClure (New York: Octagon, 1977).

Thus while he dawbes his speech with flatteries plaster,
And calls himselfe her slaue, he growes our Master,
  Still getting what he list without controle,
  By singing this old song, *re mi fa sol.*[35]

Harington astutely reveals the irony in Ralegh's political use of courtly love poetry: posing as a 'seruile,' 'submiss[iv]e' lover to 'our Soueraigne Lady' for his own political gain, Ralegh paradoxically 'calls himselfe her slaue' and yet 'growes our Master.' And he acquires such power all for a song.

Harington thus advanced a withering critique of the politics of Ralegh's courtly love poetry. In this, he arguably anticipated the critique of Ralegh that scholars have attributed to Donne's 'To his Mistress going to bed.' Donne scholars have given both this Ovidian poem and Ralegh central positions in discussions of the political undertones of Donne's elegies. R. V. Young has shown Donne 'inverting the central conceit' of Ralegh's public campaign to encourage Elizabeth to compete with Spain by colonizing Guyana.[36] Whereas Ralegh printed proposals to colonize

35 McClure, *Letters and Epigrams of Sir John Harington*, 273 (epigram 315).

36 R. V. Young, '"O my America, my new-found-land": Pornography and Imperial Politics in Donne's *Elegies*,' *South Central Review*, 4/2 (Summer 1987), 41, 36. Dennis Flynn has argued that in the summers of 1596 and '97, Donne served under Ralegh on Essex's expeditions to Cadiz and the Azores—and not directly under Essex ('Donne, Henry Wotton, and the Earl of Essex,' *John Donne Journal*, 14 (1995), 185–218). The personal connections and political commitments that Flynn has attributed to Donne suggest how he could have both served and ridiculed Ralegh at the time that he most likely composed 'To his Mistress going to bed.' The Catholic family of Donne's close friend Henry Percy, ninth earl of Northumberland, was preparing for the end of Elizabeth's reign by forging an otherwise unlikely alliance with Ralegh, against the more powerful courtiers Essex and Cecil. Flynn's argument regarding Donne's conditional support for Ralegh at this time is part of his long-term project to demonstrate Donne's family connections to the ancient Catholic nobility (*John Donne and the Ancient Catholic Nobility* (Bloomington: Indiana University Press, 1995)). Even as Donne served Ralegh, he did so out of personal, religious, and political commitments that led him to regard with suspicion and distaste Ralegh's protestant vision of English expansion and martial glory over Spain. Donne's early portrait in miniature, with its Spanish motto ('ANTES MVERTO QUE MVDADO,' which translates, 'sooner dead than changed'), offers a particularly striking illustration of Flynn's thesis (John Donne, *Poems by J.D.* (London: M.F. for John Marriot, 1635; STC 7046), frontispiece). Regarding poetic evidence, M. Thomas Hester has shown that, during or shortly after these voyages, Donne began to criticize Ralegh's colonial ambitions in the epigram 'Cales and Guyana' and certain verse letters ('Donne's Epigrams: A Little World Made Cunningly,' in Ted-Larry Pebworth and Claude Summers, eds., *The Eagle and the Dove: Reassessing John Donne* (Columbia: University of Missouri Press, 1986), 87–89).

a New World figured feminine and sexually available, Donne circulated manuscripts of a love poem about a woman figured as the New World. Whereas Ralegh and crew wanted to rescue America from the Spanish as a damsel in distress, Donne's speaker colonized his mistress as 'my America, my newfound land' in politically sensitive texts that he wisely confined to coteries.[37]

Building on Young's reading, M. Thomas Hester has considered 'To his Mistress going to bed' in relation to the Virginia colony. In turning attention from Guyana to Virginia, named after the virgin queen, Hester came to consider Elizabeth's role in Donne's poetic criticisms of early English colonialism. He pointed out that, whereas Elizabeth had granted Ralegh '*free liberty* and *license*... to *discover* search fynde out and *view* such remote heathen landes Contries and territories,' Donne's speaker asks his mistress to 'License my roaving hands, and let them go,/Before, behind, between, above, below.'[38] And, whereas Elizabeth had named Ralegh '*Lord* and Governor' of the colony that he had named after her, Donne's mock-colonial speaker claims the figurative colony that literally is his mistress: 'Then where my hand is set, my seal shall be.'[39] Donne thus exploited the irony of naming a colony after Elizabeth and a royal favorite lord of that colony. As a result, in Hester's words, the poem becomes a 'sort of wry comment on *what Ralegh said to Elizabeth in the bedroom*.'[40]

Elaborating on the elegies' representations of women and implications regarding Elizabeth, Achsah Guibbory has further detailed the politics of this passage. Guibbory recognized that, between the speaker's request for 'Licence' and his proclamation regarding his seal, 'Donne transfers power from the woman, desired and praised, to the man who hopes to possess her.'[41]

[37] *Donne Variorum*, 2:163 ('Elegy 8. To his Mistress going to bed,' 27).

[38] M. Thomas Hester, 'Donne's (Re)Annunciation of the Virgin(ia Colony) in *Elegy XIX*,' *South Central Review*, 4/2 (Summer 1987), 59. *Donne Variorum*, 2:163 ('To his Mistress going to bed,' 25–26). Hester cites David Beers Quinn, ed., *The Roanoke Voyages 1584–1590: Documents to Illustrate the English Voyages to North America under the Patent Granted to Walter Ralegh in 1584* (London: Hakluyt Society, 1955), 82.

[39] Hester, 'Donne's (Re)Annunciation,' 59–60. *Donne Variorum*, 2:163 ('To his Mistress going to bed,' 32).

[40] Hester, 'Donne's (Re)Annunciation,' 54.

[41] Achsah Guibbory, '"Oh, Let Me Not Serve So": The Politics of Love in Donne's *Elegies*,' *ELH*, 57 (1990), 821.

Licence my roaving hands, and let them go,
Before, behind, between, above, below.
O my America! my new-found-land,
My kingdome, safliest when with one man man'd,
My Myne of precious stones, My Emperie,
How blest am I in this discovering thee!
To enter in these bonds, is to be free;
Then where my hand is set, my seal shall be.[42]

Precisely summarizing the power dynamics of these lines, Guibbory has argued:

> At the beginning of this passage the woman is the monarch, providing a license; but the moment she gives this license she loses her sovereignty.... The man becomes not only explorer but conqueror, and she becomes *his* land and kingdom.... he has now become the monarch, setting his 'seal.'[43]

Donne's speaker honors his mistress as a monarch in order to conquer her like a colony, thereby effectively denying her sovereignty.

Harington's critique of Paulus' flattery of the queen closely parallels the reactionary yet oppositional point that Guibbory has attributed to Donne's 'To his Mistress going to bed.' Yet Harington isolated Ralegh's use of 'song' or verse. If Donne was criticizing Ralegh, I would propose that, like Harington, he was criticizing the politics of Ralegh's courtly love poetry. Arguably, both Harington's epigram and Donne's Ovidian elegy refer to Ralegh and openly mock discourses that he promoted at court and in print. And both do so by pointing to the self-interest that such discourses obscured. Like Ralegh, Harington's Paulus poses as the queen's 'slaue' in order to become 'our Master.' Similarly, Donne's mock-colonialist lover treats his mistress as a queen in order to become *her* master. Of course, the two poems differ. In one, a courtier complained about a royal favorite becoming the master of other courtiers—not of the queen. In the other, a poet without a place at court dramatized a lover becoming the master of his mistress and, only implicitly if at all, a royal favorite becoming that of a queen. The verseforms of the poems further distinguish them. Nevertheless, Harington and Donne each selected a verseform that has traditionally been opposed to courtly

[42] *Donne Variorum*, 2:163 ('To his Mistress going to bed,' 25–32).
[43] Guibbory, '"Oh, Let Me Not Serve So,"' 822.

love. Harington mocked Ralegh's literary style in a genre—the epigram—that he had helped to define against the sugared sonnets of his fellow late Elizabethan courtiers. Indeed, as a prolific writer of unornamented epigrams, Harington offered Elizabeth's court its only consistent poetic alternative to courtly love. Beyond court, Donne turned to another genre, the Ovidian love elegy, to burlesque the courtly style, enthusiastically enacting its obscene and subversive implications. In distinct genres that nevertheless both counter courtly love, Harington and Donne arrived at quite similar critiques of characters who, like Ralegh, pose as submissive lovers in order to gain power.

Long before Donne scholars advanced their political interpretations of 'To his Mistress going to bed,' the compiler of the Stowe manuscript suggested a reading of the poem that both supports and challenges their readings. Rather like the modern scholars, this early modern verse collector placed Donne's poem in a context that makes it look critical of Ralegh. Yet he made it look critical of Ralegh's courtly love poetry, in particular. Again, beginning on the leaf following his copy of 'To his Mistress going to bed,' the scribe responsible for most of the miscellany transcribed Rogers' libel on Ralegh and the royal favorite's lyric 'Callinge to minde mine eye went longe about.' He thus welcomed Rogers' critical perspective on Ralegh's love lyric. Moreover, he facilitated, and may have even endorsed, reading Donne's elegy from this perspective: as yet another poetic response to Ralegh's politically engaged courtly love poetry.

For, in his arrangement of texts, 'To his Mistress going to bed' seems to mock Ralegh and his lyric. That is, Donne's elegy appears both to mimic the courtier and to oppose his verse. Whereas Ralegh's Petrarchan speaker suffers the excruciating absence of his mistress, Donne's Ovidian persona thoroughly enjoys the presence and availability of his. While Ralegh's speaker focuses on himself, deciding which of his own body parts to 'plucke . . . out' or 'slay,' the voice of Donne's poem happily talks his mistress into revealing her body parts: 'Offe wth that girdle. . . . vnpine that spangled breastplate. . . . vnlace yor selfe.'[44] Donne's speaker does consider one of his own body parts. In the twenty-fourth line, the very center, of this 48-line poem, he points to his own erection, or 'flesh vpright.' The speakers of these two poems thus emerge as one another's opposite, especially in the Stowe manuscript. Yet the compiler of the

[44] British Library MS Stowe 962, fols 82v–83r, 85v.

miscellany also showed how early modern collectors could read Donne's poem as if it were spoken by a caricature of Ralegh, rather like Young and Hester have done. Although Donne's poetic persona spends most of the poem dwelling on his mistress, he occasionally mentions other people: the 'buisie fooles' and 'lay=men' who are satisfied with admiring a woman's clothing or jewelry. Donne's speaker, by contrast, will be satisfied with nothing less than 'full nakednes.' In the context of the Stowe manuscript, the speaker of Ralegh's poem emerges as one such fool, content to love an unattainable mistress with patience and long-suffering. Yet the compiler of this miscellany also presented Ralegh himself as a courtier who was no more satisfied with distant longing than was Donne's Ovidian persona. Indeed, with Rogers' libel, this verse collector fashioned Ralegh as a royal favorite who used love lyrics such as 'Callinge to minde mine eye went longe about' in order to gain intimacy with his royal mistress, and so to separate himself from the 'buisie fooles' who could admire Elizabeth only from afar.[45] In his arrangement of texts, the main scribe of the Stowe miscellany suggested reading Donne's poem as the facetious, private version of Ralegh's polite and relatively public courtly love poetry. Moreover, he was not the only early modern verse collector to suggest such a relationship between Donne's Ovidian love elegy and lyrics attributed to Ralegh.

PUTTING WORDS IN RALEGH'S MOUTH

Several manuscript verse collectors included in their miscellanies both 'To his Mistress going to bed' and a conflation of two poems that they apparently misattributed to Ralegh. Michael Rudick has explained that collectors most likely affiliated this composite text with Ralegh in the second quarter of the seventeenth century due to 'popular notions... about Ralegh's rise in Elizabeth's favor.'[46] Thomas Carew probably wrote the first six lines, a single stanza beginning 'Passions are likened to floods & streames,' since the only attributed copy of the sixain on its own assigns it to 'Th: C:'.[47] Sir Robert Ayton must have written the

[45] British Library MS Stowe 962, fols 82v–83r.
[46] *Poems of Sir Walter Ralegh*, lx.
[47] British Library MS Harley 6057, fol. 9r; *Poems of Sir Walter Ralegh*, lx, 223.

eight quatrains that in many copies immediately follow, and begin 'Wronge not deare empresse of my heart.' The poem appears in two collections of Ayton's poems evidently connected to his family.[48] After Ayton's poem started circulating at court, someone incorrectly ascribed it to Lord de Walden and applied it to his courtship of King James's daughter, Princess Elizabeth.[49] In Rudick's words, '[a]t some point in transmission, the Princess Elizabeth mutated to the Queen Elizabeth, and Ralegh's name was supplied as that of her silent admirer, in conformity with prevalent stories about his initial diffidence in paying court to her.'[50] If Rudick's attributions to Carew and Ayton are accurate, it follows that Ralegh did not compose so much as a line of a poem that has long been considered his.

The professional scribe of a beautiful miscellany in the Rawlinson Poetry collection at the Bodleian Library recorded one of these misattributions. He gave the conflation of Carew's and Ayton's verses the heading, 'SIR/Walter Ralegh to/Queene Eliza=/=beth.'[51] Whereas Ayton had written to a strictly metaphorical 'empresse,' this scribe, or possibly a client who supplied his texts, retrospectively turned her into Ralegh's actual, royal mistress. Thus, when he and other verse collectors incorrectly ascribed this composite lyric to Ralegh, they were altering the Elizabethan past even as they reconstructed it. They may have tried to portray Ralegh's relationship with Elizabeth accurately; yet they did so by putting someone else's words into his mouth. These words share certain beguiling features with accepted Ralegh lyrics. Like Ralegh's speaker in 'Callinge to minde mine eye went longe about,' Carew's persona experiences deep passion, and Ayton's speaker endures pain for loving a mistress like none other: 'A Saint of such perfection/As all desire, yet none deserve,/A place in her affection.' The composite voice of this conflated poem would seem to replace Ralegh's lyric complaints with a firm resolve to suffer in silence, explaining, 'He smarteth most y^{t}

48 British Library MSS Add. 10308; Add. 28622; *Poems of Sir Walter Ralegh*, lx.

49 Incidentally, the main scribe of the Stowe manuscript recorded this appropriation in his heading for Ayton's poem: 'The Lord Walden to y^{e} princesse Eliz.//Wronge not deere mistresse of my ~~thoughts~~^{hart}' (British Library MS Stowe 962, fols 185r–v).

50 *Poems of Sir Walter Ralegh*, lxi.

51 Bodleian MS Rawl. Poet. 160, fol. 117r ('SIR/Walter Ralegh to/Queene Eliza=/=beth://Our passions are most like to floods & strea^{mes}'). See also the heading 'Sir Walter Ralegh to Queene Elizabeth' in Britsh Library MS Add. 22602, fols 30v–31r; *Poems of Sir Walter Ralegh*, 106–8.

hides his smart/And sues for noe Compassion.'[52] But of course, with this explanation, the speaker lodges a lover's complaint even as he brags about never complaining.

The scribe responsible for this elaborate Rawlinson Poetry folio joined a number of contemporary verse collectors in establishing a relationship between the Ralegh misattribution and anti-courtly love poetry, especially that of Donne. In addition to including 'To his Mistress going to bed' elsewhere in the volume, he preceded the Ralegh conflation with an unattributed, partial copy of one of Carew's rather gentle attempts at the anti-Petrarchan genre, beginning 'Dearest thie tresses are not threds of gold/thie eyes not Diamonds.' Carew's speaker proceeds with an exemplary contreblazon until explaining that he compares his mistress to 'nothing earthly' because she is 'all devine.'[53] Thus Carew's anti-courtly love gesture turns out to have merely set the stage for conventional, high praise. This poem makes a nice companion piece to the Ralegh conflation in the Rawlinson Poetry manuscript, because it too deifies its addressee. One blank leaf before the fictional Ralegh invokes Elizabeth I as a beloved saint, Carew's speaker aligns his mistress with mythological deities. Before revealing this similarity, however, Carew's poem briefly poses as an anti-courtly love poem. When he exhibited the similarity between these two poems, therefore, the compiler of the Rawlinson Poetry manuscript also juxtaposed the courtly love associated with Ralegh to the anti-courtly love that Carew momentarily adopted, and that this verse collector modeled elsewhere in his manuscript verse miscellany.

Several leaves earlier in the Rawlinson Poetry manuscript, for instance, this scribe conflated two elegies by Donne, 'The Autumnall' and 'The Anagram.'[54] On its own, 'The Autumnall' does not make for much of an anti-courtly love poem. The elegy offers a paradoxical encomium on the beauty of a woman in the autumn of her life, well past her more generally admired spring or summer. It thus praises physical

[52] Bodleian MS Rawl. poet. 160, fol. 117r.

[53] Bodleian MS Rawl. poet. 160, fol. 115r ('TO HIS M^{rs}//Dearest thie tresses are not threds of gold'). Only blank leaves appear between Carew's 'Dearest thie tresses' and his appropriated 'Our passions are most like to floods.'

[54] Bodleian MS Rawl. poet. 160, fols 103v–4r ('AN OT[H]ER//Noe spring nor somer beawty hath such grace'), 104r–v ('Marry and loue thy fflauia for she'), 115r, 117r, 171r–v ('AN ELIGIE//Come madam come, all rest my powers defy').

characteristics that many considered undesirable, and effectively opposes dominant stereotypes of female beauty. Although some of Donne's anti-courtly love poems do the same, several scholars have plausibly read 'The Autumnall' as sincere praise. In any event, the speaker of this elegy does not clearly proceed with his tongue in his cheek—as does the voice of the Donne elegy crammed up against this one in the Rawlinson Poetry manuscript. In this miscellany, Donne's probably genuine adulation for a woman of middle age suddenly turns into his obviously ironic, and ultimately disgusting, representation of the unbelievably ugly Flavia in 'The Anagram.' A poet can apply to Flavia all of the adjectives usually reserved for a conventionally beautiful woman, only not to the usual features. He can invoke the Petrarchan color scheme of red and white, for instance, but not in relation to her lips and skin. Ostensibly encouraging his addressee to 'Marry and loue thy fflauia,' the speaker of 'The Anagram' facetiously explains the advantages of her ugliness. His addressee need not fear Flavia's infidelity since, even though she has spent 'seaven yeares' in 'ye stewes' or brothels, 'A Nunnery' would take her for 'a maid.' Even if she is pregnant, 'Midwiues would sweare, it but a timpanye,' or a distention or swelling. Even if Flavia accuses herself of adultery, the speaker would credit her 'lesse/then witches wch impossibles confesse.' Donne's hyperbole culminates when his speaker makes an impossible charge of his own, claiming that 'dildoes bedstaues & the veluet glasse/would be as loth to touch' Flavia 'as Ioesph was.' In a couplet that sharply distinguishes Donne's anti-courtly love poetry from any sort of literary realism or merely frank representation of sexuality, Donne's speaker states that not even bed-staffs (used for smoothing the sheets on a bed) or Flavia's velvet-backed mirror would 'touch' her. Editors gloss 'Ioseph' as the Joseph from Genesis, who deflected the advances of the wife of his master, Potiphar. Yet the reference may also invoke the Joseph who would not 'touch' the Virgin Mary before, and in some traditions even after, the birth of Christ. With this connotation, 'The Anagram' reaches a roundly offensive conclusion.

In the Rawlinson Poetry manuscript, this conclusion subsumes 'The Autumnall' into an anti-courtly love poem. Although Donne likely composed 'The Autumnall' in genuine appreciation of the beauty and character of a woman of relatively advanced age, the scribe of this miscellany turned the poem into an ambiguous prelude to one of

Donne's most deliberately disgusting anti-courtly love poems. Even a close reader of these conjoined elegies would have to question the instinct to separate them when the composite voice shifts to describing Flavia. For the two poems demonstrate strong similarities. Each exemplifies both epideictic and paradoxical poetry, valuating the female subject of the poem by contrasting her to less desirable women, who nevertheless feature more widely desired qualities. Heightening the confusion, if 'The Autumnall' compliments its subject by contrasting her to women whom most would conisder more beautiful, 'The Anagram' makes fun of Flavia by exactly the same method. For instance, a careful reader of the Rawlinson Poetry manuscript may have interpreted the following lines from 'The Autumnall' as a compliment:

> were her first yeares ye golden age? 'tis true
> But now shees gold oft try'de & ever newe
> that was her torrid & inflaming time
> this is her tollerable tropick Clime.[55]

If the middle-aged woman's youth represented her golden age, she has since emerged as tried and renewed gold. Whereas her youth was hot, she has adapted to a more temperate climate. The paradoxes in these lines do not necessarily make their praise insincere—that is, not until they lead to similar lines in this miscellany's copy of 'The Anagram,' such as these:

> ffor one nights revells silk and gold we chuse
> but in long iournyes cloth and lether vse
> beawty is barren oft best husbands saye
> there is best land where there is foulest way[56]

Like silk and gold clothing, beautiful women remain so for only brief periods; Flavia's looks, by contrast, will last as long as leather. Similarly, farmers know that fair land is often barren, whereas the best land has the 'foulest' appearance, like Flavia. When their epideictic paradoxes become so obviously facetious, the conflated copy of these two elegies in the Rawlinson Poetry manuscript begins to lose the ambiguity that 'The Autumnall' retains on its own. The conclusion of 'The Anagram' dispels any such ambiguity. By turning these two elegies into a single, complex

[55] Bodleian MS Rawl. poet. 160, fol. 104r.
[56] Bodleian MS Rawl. poet. 160, fol. 104v.

anti-courtly love poem, the scribe responsible for this miscellany imposed an ironic, derogatory tone on 'The Autumnall.'

This verse collector provided a number of alternatives to the sort of courtly love poem purportedly sent from 'SIR/Walter Ralegh to/ Queene Eliza=/=beth.' These alternatives range from the gentle, and brief, anti-Petrarchan introduction of Carew's 'Dearest thie tresses are not threds of gold'; to Donne's paradoxical encomium of a middle-aged woman in 'The Autumnall'; to its exaggerated, obscene conclusion in 'The Anagram.' Farther on in the volume, the compiler offered a few erotic alternatives as well, including Donne's 'To his Mistress going to bed' as well as the monologue 'Of a slumbering maid' beginning, 'As I lay slumbering once within my bedd.' Each of these poems contrasts with the Ralegh conflation, whether by refusing, however briefly, to praise a woman in the terms that Ralegh reputedly employed for Elizabeth, or by making a mockery of those terms, as in 'The Anagram.' By gathering these various representations of women in the same miscellany, the compiler of the Rawlinson Poetry manuscript countenanced a measure of disrespect for the sytle of love poetry that he associated with Ralegh. Yet, as later chapters will demonstrate, this verse collector did not allow such disrespect to extend to Elizabeth, and reserved his more direct political criticism for figures from later English courts.

The main copyist of an early seventeenth-century miscellany now in the Rosenbach Library exhibited a sharper contrast between the Ralegh conflation and another pair of Donne's love elegies. He did so by placing 'To his Mistress going to bed' and then a partial copy of Donne's 'Loues Progresse' immediately before the composite text of Carew's and Ayton's verses, headed 'Sr Walter Rawleigh to his M^{ris}.'[57] By arranging these poems in a series, this verse collector made Ralegh represent hopelessly loyal, perpetually suffering courtly love, and used Donne's elegies to offer a sexually explicit alternative bent on satisfaction. Furthermore, he placed 'Loues Progresse' where it accentuates both the water imagery in Carew's introductory lines to the composite

[57] Rosenbach MS 239/27, pp. 47–48 ('Vpon on goeinge to bed to his mistresse.// Come madam come, all rest my powers defye'), 49–50 ('Loues voyage into the Netherlands.//The haire a forrest is of ambushes'), 50 ('Sr Walter Rawleigh to his M^{ris}.// Passions are likened to floods & streames'), 50–51 ('Wronge not deare empresse of my heart').

Ralegh lyric (which begin, 'Passions are likened to floods & streames') and the diction of naval exploration in 'To his Mistress going to bed.' In this, he also emphasized that such imagery and diction had long been associated with Ralegh.

The main compiler of the Rosenbach manuscript began his partial copy of 'Loues Progresse' with the poem's metaphorical voyage across a woman's body. In longer versions of the poem, this journey forms part of the speaker's demonstration of how suitors should not love a woman, or of 'Howe much they stray, that sett out at the face.'[58] The speaker facetiously proceeds to a blazon of a woman's body, beginning with the hair on her head, likening each body part to a potential obstacle for a shipping vessel, or for a hypothetical lover who finds himself making his way across a giantess of sorts. The copy in the Rosenbach manuscript begins with this anti-blazon:

> The haire a forrest is of ambushes
> Of springes, fetters, snares & manacles
> The brow betrayes vs when tis smooth & plaine
> And when tis wrincled, shipwrackes vs againe[59]

For lovers represented as ships or sailors, a woman's hair and brow threaten shipwreck, and a premature end to their voyage. For these features are too beautiful to pass. If lovers do somehow make it past them, they will encounter other dangers at the woman's nose, lips, teeth, tongue, chin, breasts, and so on. Donne's speaker hyperbolically stresses that, if lovers proceed in this way, from the woman's head down, they will never reach their destination. 'Rather sett out belowe,' he advises, where no such obstacles distract lovers from their goal. As if to make its obscenity absolutely clear, the speaker concludes the poem with its most specific genital reference, followed by a patently disgusting simile. 'Rich nature each in women wisely made/Two purses & there mouthes auersely laide.' Any lover who proceeds to the wrong one, 'his error is as great/As who by clysters giues, the stomacke meat' or who, in other words, treats enemas as food.[60]

'Loues Progresse' exhibits a more obscene strain of Donne's anti-courtly love poetry than does 'To his Mistress going to bed,' which

[58] *Donne Variorum*, 2:302 ('Loues Progresse,' 40).
[59] Rosenbach MS 239/27, p. 49.
[60] Rosenbach MS 239/27, p. 50.

plenty of critics have read as a sincere or even edifying portrayal of sex. For obvious reasons, few have regarded 'Loues Progresse' so positively.[61] These two elegies agree, however, in rejecting the suffering, unfulfilled style of love that the main compiler of the Rosenbach manuscript juxtaposed to them, and explicitly associated with Ralegh. Indeed, the poetic persona confused with Ralegh defends silence in love, begging his mistress to recognize that the lover who does not complain or ask for compassion patiently endures the greatest suffering. By contrast, the lover in 'To his Mistress going to bed' tells his mistress precisely what he wants, and objects to even the slightest patience. The speaker of 'Loues Progresse' advises suitors to approach sex even more directly, refusing to pause at any features above a mistress' waist.

The main compiler of the Rosenbach manuscript laid out these Donne poems almost as if a single speaker addressed the first one to his mistress and, afterward, used the second to tell his friends what he had learned from her. Furthermore, despite the distinctions between these two Donne elegies, this verse collector used them to oppose the style of courtly love that he attributed to Ralegh in the composite text following them. By copying these poems together, he highlighted Donne's provocative response to the courtly love associated with Ralegh and, specifically, to the courtier's poetic means of addressing his 'empresse.'

Yet this verse collector was hardly preserving the original politics of anti-courtly love poetry. Even if he was intentionally reconstructing the Elizabethan context of Donne's rejection of Ralegh's courtly love, the main compiler of the Rosenbach manuscript was fabricating it. Indeed, he represented Ralegh's courtier poetry with texts that Ralegh did not even write. So his reconstruction of Ralegh's relationship with Elizabeth misconstrued the Elizabethan past. Regardless of whether he realized what he was suggesting about the politics of these Donne elegies, this anonymous collector was also changing those politics, by immersing the poems in a political culture that had changed a great deal since Ralegh wrote to his 'empresse' and Donne arguably mocked him for doing so. Beyond the few leaves considered here, he surrounded these poems with libels on virtually every seventeenth-century event considered in the

[61] *Donne Variorum*, 2:666–737, 875–911.

following pages of this book, including the death of Elizabeth.[62] In doing so, he joined the host of contemporary verse collectors who together demonstrated their literary agency by recontextualizing and repoliticizing anti-courtly love poetry.

RECONCILING RALEGH AND DONNE

The compiler of a pair of miscellanies, held respecitvely by the Folger Shakespeare Library and the University of Nottingham, established a particularly strong relationship between Ralegh and Donne in both of his extant manuscripts.[63] Yet, whereas some of his fellow verse collectors opposed these two poets, this anthologist consistently represented them as compatible authors. Uniquely, he organized both of his miscellanies under running headers that assign a genre to each section: 'Laudatory Epitaphs,' 'Epitaphs Merry & Satyricall,' 'Love Sonnets,' 'Panegyricks,' 'Satyres,' 'Miscellanea,' and, in the Nottingham manuscript alone, three additional genres.[64] Moreover, he filled the 'Love Sonnets' section of both miscellanies with poems that he attributed to Ralegh and Donne, a few of them incorrectly. Beginning on his first page of love poems, he ascribed each of four consecutive examples of the genre to 'Sr W.R.': 'Calling to mind mine Eies went long about'; two poems 'On his mistress Serena'; and the composite text of Carew and Ayton verses under a title that nicely emphasizes the 'Empres' in the poem: 'To the sole Governes of his affections.'[65] On the leaves following, he attributed

[62] Rosenbach MS 239/27, p. 325 includes three epitaphs for Elizabeth, discussed below.

[63] University of Nottingham MS Portland PwV 37; Folger MS V.a.103.

[64] University of Nottingham MS Portland PwV 37 is divided into the following sections: 'Laudatory Epitaphs' (pp. 1–32); 'Epitaphs Merry & Satyricall' (pp. 37–46); 'Love Sonnets' (pp. 59–79); 'Panegyricks' (pp. 107–117); 'Satyres' (pp. 135–57); 'Miscellanea' (pp. 169–206); 'Serious Poemes' (pp. 225–54); 'Merry Poems' (pp. 307–23); 'Verses on Christ=Church Play' (pp. 363–73).

Folger MS V.a.103 has only the following sections: 'Laudatory Epitaphs' (fols 2r–12r); 'Epitaphs Merry & Satyricall' (fols 20r–23r); 'Love Sonnets' (fols 29r–46r); 'Panegyricks' (fols 52r–62r); 'Satyres' (fols 66r–75v), 'Miscellanea' (fols 76r–77r).

[65] University of Nottingham MS Portland PwV 37, pp. 59 ('Sr W.R./A Lover on his Mistresse.//Calling to mind mine Eies went long about'), 60 ('Sr W.R./On his Mistresse

another sequence of four poems to 'M[r] Dunne.' In another manuscript setting, a couple of these reputed Donne lyrics might sit uneasily next to the Ralegh poems nearby. But the compiler of this pair of miscellanies deemphasized the contrast between these texts by surrounding them with quite complementary love poems that he assigned to the same two poets. He thus represented Ralegh and Donne as exemplary authors of entirely compatible 'Love Sonnets.'

In both of his miscellanies, this collector attributed a poem to Donne that editors have subsequently rejected from his canon: 'To his Scornefull Mistresse' which begins, 'Cruell, since that thou dost not feare the curse.'[66] Right after 'To his Scornefull Mistresse,' the compiler transcribed the accepted Donne poem, 'The Apparition,' with the heading 'To the Same'—that is, to the same 'Scornefull Mistresse' addressed in

Serena.//Nature that washt her hands in milke'), 61 ('S[r] W.R./To the sole Governes of his affections.//Passions are likened best to Flouds and Streames'), 62 ('S[r] W.R./To his love when hee had obtained her.//Now Serena, bee not coy').

Folger MS V.a.103, fols 29r–v ('S[r] W.R:/A Lover to his Mistresse//Calling to minde myne eies wente long about'), 29v ('S. W.R./On his Mistresse Serena.//Nature that washt her hands in milke'), 30r ('S[r] Wa: Ral:/To the sole Governesse of His affections.//Passions are likned best to flouds and streames'), 30v ('S[r] W. Ra:/To his Love When hee had obtained Her//Now Serena, bee not coy').

See *Poems of Sir Walter Ralegh*, lxii, 10 (9B), 106–8 (39A), 113–14 (43B), 115 (44). According to Rudick, collectors attributed only one of these poems to Ralegh during his lifetime: 'Calling to mind.'

66 University of Nottingham MS Portland PwV 37, pp. 64 ('M[r] Dunne./To the Sunne that rise too earely to call/Him and His love from bed.//Busy old Foole, unruly Sunne'), 65 ('M[r] Dunne./To his Scornefull Mistresse.//Cruell, since that thou dost not feare the curse'; 'M[r] Dunne./To the Same.//When by thy Scorne (great Murthres) I am dead'; 'M[r] Dunne./To his Loving Mistres when hee travaild.//Sweetest Love, I do not goe').

Folger MS V.a.103, fols 31v ('M[r] Dunne./To the Sunne that rise too early to call/Him and his Love from bedd.//Busy old foole, unruly Sunne'), 32r ('M[r] Dunne/To his scornefull Mistresse.//Cruell, since that thou dost not feare the curse'; 'D[r] Dunne./To the same.//When by thy Scornes greate Murtheresse I am deade'), 32v ('D[r] Dunne./To his loving Mistres When hee travailed.//Sweetest love I do not goe').

The anonymous poem misattributed to Donne shows up in a couple of important manuscripts of his works: Houghton MSS Eng. 686, fol. 51v; Eng. 966.2, pp. 17–19; Eng. 966.5, fol. 79v; Huntington MS EL 6893, fol. 115r (collated in Grierson, *Poems of John Donne*, 1:446). In the Huntington copy, an annotation astutely relates it to 'The Apparition' ('This hath relation to when by thy/I scorne O Murdresse &c'). As transcribed by Ted-Larry Pebworth, 'First-Line Index to HH1 (The Bridgewater ms., Huntington Library ms. EL 6893),' http://donnevariorum.com/fli/hh1fli.htm accessed 22 June 2005. 'The Apparition' is found on fol. 81r of the Bridgewater MS.

the preceding poem. Indeed, each of these two poems addresses a typically resistant Petrarchan mistress. Each also features a speaker who refuses to tolerate the courtly love arrangement. The persona of 'To his Scornefull Mistresse' has apparently cursed his mistress in the past, and begins the poem explaining that, since she does 'not feare the curse,' he will try a new tack. Counterintuitively, he prays that her beauty 'Bee doubled,' so that 'the whole world' will fall in love with her. Then, like 'great Monarchs,' she will 'Weepe that thy Honours are so limited,' and thus that no potential admirers remain for her to conquer. Her grief, the speaker hopes, will produce 'an unlooked for and wondrous change' (the details of which remain murky), making her desire more from her lovers and somehow turning those lovers against her.[67] The persona of this poem thus exaggerates the Petrarchan characteristics of his mistress in order to subvert her power.

Similarly, the speaker of Donne's 'The Apparition' threatens his mistress with revenge. He warns her that, once her scorn has killed him (in familiar Petrarchan fashion), his ghost will 'come unto Thy Bed' and find her in the arms of another. If, seeing the ghost, she tries to wake her lover, her new partner will think that she is calling 'for more,/And in a feign'd sleepe from Thee shrinke.' While her apparently worn-out lover pretends to be asleep, the woman facing the ghostly speaker of the poem will be 'neglected,' 'Bath'd in a cold quicksilver sweate,' 'A verier Ghost then I.'[68] Donne allowed only one conventional feature of courtly love literature in his poem: the speaker's death by scorn. Rather than submit to such a death, as a good courtly lover should, however, Donne's speaker promises to continue pursuing his mistress from beyond the grave, resulting in a menacing bedroom scene.

By directing 'To his Scornefull Mistresse' and 'The Apparition' to 'the Same' fictional woman, the compiler of the Folger and Nottingham miscellanies accentuated the anti-courtly love poetics that these poems share. But he also balanced their anti-Petrarchanism with additional Donne poems nearby. He surrounded these two lyrics with two others in which Donne by no means parodied courtly love conventions: 'The Sun Rising,' here addressed 'To the Sunne that rise too earely to

[67] University of Nottingham MS Portland PwV 37, p. 65.
[68] University of Nottingham MS Portland PwV 37, p. 65.

call/Him and His love from bed' and another 'To his Loving Mistres when hee travaild' beginning, 'Sweetest Love, I do not goe.' By arranging these poems in a series, the collector compactly represented a range of 'Love Sonnets' attributed to Donne. He showed the poet treating a cruel mistress with cruelty, and a loving mistress accordingly. Moreover, he selected Donne poems that together offer more of a comparison than a contrast to the Ralegh lyrics nearby. He juxtaposed the verses of Ralegh and Donne, in other words, without opposing them. He thus joined a number of his fellow manuscript verse collectors in establishing a relationship between these two poets, but constructed this relationship without the aesthetic and political tension that characterizes it in other miscellanies.

At the end of the 'Love Sonnets' section of the Nottingham manuscript, and at the conclusion of another series of Donne poems, this verse collector juxtaposed two especially complementary poems. At the top of a page, he attributed to 'Sr W.R.' a lyric beginning, 'Thou sentst to mee a heart was crown'd.' Immediately below this, he made an unattributed copy of Donne's 'The Message,' which starts, 'Send home my long straid Eies to mee.'[69] In the lyric ascribed to Ralegh, the speaker receives a heart from his mistress and, upon seeing that it has a wound, realizes that it must be his own heart, damaged by and returned from his mistress. The persona of Donne's poem revives the same conceit immediately below, demanding that his disdainful mistress return his eyes and heart. Typically, Donne responded more harshly to the conventionally aloof beloved than did Ralegh. But here again, the compiler of the Folger and Nottingham manuscripts minimized the distinction between these two poets. Rather than distinguishing their characteristic responses to a cruel mistress, he emphasized that these poems share diction and a common conceit. Ralegh and Donne thus emerge in the Nottingham manuscript as fellow poets who engaged parallel literary pursuits and wrote decidedly compatible 'Love Sonnets.'

This verse collector included the same two poems at the end of the 'Love Sonnets' in the Folger manuscript. But he placed in between them

[69] University of Nottingham MS Portland PwV 37, p. 78 ('Sr W.R. To his M$^{rs.}$//Thou sentst to mee a heart was crown'd'; 'A Lover to his M$^{rs.}$//Send home my long straid Eies to mee').

an attributed copy of Donne's 'To his Mistress going to bed.'[70] This love elegy introduces a certain contrast between Ralegh and Donne that one does not find in the Nottingham manuscript. In the Folger miscellany, the Ovidian persona of 'D.r Donne' concludes verbally undressing his mistress just before a voice identified with 'Sr W.R.' recognizes that his beloved has wounded his heart and sent it back. As in the compilations of other verse collectors, Donne here models sexual satisfaction, while Ralegh poses as the lonely, hurt suitor. Yet the verse collector who admitted the distinction between these two poems also mitigated it. He effectively resolved the tension between the poems by placing them at the conclusion of a section dominated by the complementary 'Love Sonnets' that he attributed to Donne and Ralegh. In the manuscript environment that this collector devised, the contrast between Donne's 'To his Mistress going to bed' and one of Ralegh's reputed love poems lacks the sharpness, and in particular the political edge, that it acquired in the hands of other verse collectors. While some of his contemporaries exhibited poems by Ralegh and Donne as aesthetically and politically opposed, the compiler of the Folger and Nottingham manuscripts represented these poets and their verse as entirely compatible.

In the leaves beyond the 'Love Sonnets' that he copied into the Folger and Nottingham manuscripts, this verse collector made especially clear that he did not see any criticism of Ralegh in Donne's anti-courtly love poetry. In the sequences of epitaphs with which he began his anthologies, he showed such respect for the deceased Elizabethan courtier, and for Elizabeth herself, that he seems not to have been able to imagine that anyone would mock the illustrious representative of Elizabeth's bygone court. Even the one verse on Ralegh that he included in his sections of 'Epitaphs Merry & Satirical' does Ralegh no disservice. Indeed, although the libel identifies Ralegh as its subject, it reserves its satire for another Elizabethan courtier. In this political verse, Ralegh addresses Essex from the grave, after King James finally executed him in 1618, technically for his treason in 1603: 'Essex, thy death's reveng'd; lo here I lie.'[71] Casting doubt on the legality of the charge revived against him,

70 Folger MS V.a.103, fols 38r–v ('D.r Donne./To his Mistresse.//Send home my long straid eies to mee'), 40v–41r ('D.r Donne./Going to bedd.//Come Mistresse; all rest my powers defie'), 41r ('S.r W.R. to his mistresse.//Thou sentst to mee a heart was crown'd').

71 University of Nottingham MS Portland PwV 37, p. 37 ('On Sr Walter Rawley.// Essex, thy death's reveng'd; lo here I lie').

the fictional Ralegh explains to his old rival that he 'died not (as all see)/ So much to satisfy the Law as Thee.' Thus while he complains of injustice, Ralegh admits that he deserved to die for orchestrating the downfall of Essex.[72] Then, in the libel's only slanderous reference, Ralegh tells Essex, 'Thou hadst another foe, Hee went before;/The French undid us both, but Him the Whore.' Ralegh's alleged collusion with the French, in other words, undid him. Yet the 'French' disease of syphillis spelled the end of Essex's other foe, Sir Robert Cecil.[73] This ostensible Ralegh libel thus turns its scurrility on someone else, and effectively maintains the respect for Ralegh that this verse collector indicated with his other epitaphs on the courtier.

In the series of 'Laudatory Epitaphs' with which he began his miscellanies, this verse collector fittingly showed Ralegh great reverence. He did so not only by copying two epitaphs on Ralegh in this section, but also by affiliating the courtier with Elizabeth I, whom he honored with a block of epitaphs on the first page of each of his anthologies. He started each miscellany with an epitaph beginning, 'Kings, Queenes, Mens, Virgins eies/See where your myrrhour lies.'[74] Using Elizabeth as a mirror, 'her Friends haue seene/A Kings state in a Queene,' and 'her Foes survaid/A Kings heart in a Maid.' The epitaph concludes by explaining that 'Heaven' summoned Elizabeth to her death 'least men for her Piety/Should grow to thinke a Deity.' This verse collector thus opened his miscellanies with a queen whom one could understandably mistake for a goddess. He proceeded to epitaphs that effectively

72 Bellany and McRae, 'Early Stuart Libels,' A, D, I4.

73 Bellany and McRae, 'Early Stuart Libels,' D, I4 n.3.

74 University of Nottingham MS Portland PwV 37, p. 1. The only nominee for the poem's authorship is Nicholas Burghe, who subscribed it with his own initials in one of three copies in his miscellany: Bodeian MS Ashmole 38, p. 36 (the additional copies appear on pp. 29 (crossed out) and 167). Including these four, at least 18 early modern manuscript copies of the poem survive: Bodleian MSS Don. d.58, fol. 15r; Eng. poet. c.50, fol. 22v; Eng. poet. e.40, fol. 139r (18th century); Rawl. poet. 26, fol. 88v; British Library MSS Egerton 923, fol. 44v; Egerton 2725, fol. 63v; Clark MS S4975M1, p. 31; Folger MSS V.a.103, fol. 2r; V.a.262, pp. 56–57; V.a.345, p. 110; Rosenbach MS 1083/16, pp. 98–99; Trinity College Dublin MS 877, fol. 248r; University of Edinburgh MS H.-P. Coll. 401, fol. 71v; West Yorkshire Archive Service, Bradford MS SpSt 9/1a, fol. [6r]. In print, the poem appeared first in William Camden, *Remaines Concerning Britaine.... The fift Impression* (London: Thomas Harper, for John Waterson, 1636; STC 4525), 394; and thereafter in *Witts Recreations* (London: for Humph: Blunden at ye Castle in Corn-hill, 1640; STC 25870), sig. Cc5r–v.

prohibited readers of his miscellanies from thinking much less of her, or her former royal favorite.

This anthologist filled the rest of the first page of the Nottingham manuscript by copying three additional epitaphs for Elizabeth from William Camden's *Remaines concerning Britain.*[75] Thomas Dekker had composed the first of these poems, 'On the remooveall of her body from/Richmond to White-Hall.' In Dekker's account of the procession, the oars of the funeral barge, even the fish of the Thames, wept for Elizabeth.

> The Queene was brought by water to Whitehall,
> At every stroke the oares teares let fall;
> More clung about the Barge, Fish under water
> Wept out their eies of Pearle, and swamme blind after.
> I think the Bargemen might with easier thighs,
> Have rowd her thether in her people eies:
> For howsoere thus much my thoughs have scan'd,
> Shee had come by water had shee come by land.[76]

Her subjects' tears so filled the land that Elizabeth's funeral procession would have been conducted by water in any event. Despite its simple,

[75] He annotated each of these three poems with the marginal initials, 'C.R.,' which must refer to 'C[amden's]. R[emaines],' for the epitaphs that bear them appear in the same order in the following editions: William Camden, *Remaines, concerning Britaine* (London: Iohn Legatt for Simon Waterson, 1614; STC 4522), 378–79; ___, *Remaines, Concerning Britaine* (London: Nicholas Okes, for Simon Waterson . . . at the signe of the Crowne in Pauls Churchyard, 1623; STC 4523), 342; ___, *Remaines Concerning Brittaine* (London: A.I. for Symon Waterson . . . at the signe of the Crowne in Pauls Churchyard, 1629; STC 4524), 338.

A version of 'Kings, Queenes, mens judgements, eyes' appeared in the posthumous 1636 edition of *Remaines*, but the compiler of the Nottingham manuscript could not have copied the poem from this printed book. The first line of the poem in *Remaines* differs from the version in the miscellany, replacing the manuscript's 'Virgins' with 'judgements.' Furthermore, the compiler of the Nottingham miscellany did not write 'C.R.' beside this epitaph, strongly suggesting that he copied texts from an earlier version of *Remaines*, and making clear that he was working from a manuscript copy of 'Kings, Queenes, Mens, Virgins eies.' In other manuscript versions, the word 'womens' replaces or precedes 'virgins': Bodleian MS Eng. poet. c.50, fol. 22v ('Kings, Queenes, mens womens virgins, eies'); Folger MS V.a.262, pp. 56–57 ('Kings, Queenes, Mens, Womens eyes').

In the Folger manuscript, this collector did not include the initials 'C.R.' for any of his Elizabeth epitaphs, or for Dekker's 'The Queene was brought by water to Whitehall.'

[76] University of Nottingham MS Portland PwV 37, p. 1.

perhaps facile, sentiment, the poem memorialized a monarch and an occasion of great importance, which manuscript verse collectors recognized by making it the most popular of all epitaphs for the queen.[77]

Following Camden's lead, the compiler of the Nottingham manuscript copied next an epitaph by Camden's pupil, Hugh Holland. In both the *Remaines* and the manuscript, Holland's poem maintains the sequence's focus on the tears that filled the island upon the queen's death.

[77] Dekker first printed the epitaph, along with two others, in *The Wonderfull Yeare. 1603* (London: Thomas Creede, n.d.; STC 6535.3), sig. B4r–v. With this title Dekker was not putting a positive construction on a year characterized by the death of Elizabeth I and a plague that forced the dramatist to turn to the print market. He was drawing, rather, on the negative connotation that the word *wonderful* has since lost, evident for instance in Sir John Smythe's phrase, 'a wonderfull payne in my stomacke,' and that of the traveller William Lithgow: 'a wonderfull massacre of poore afflicted Christians.' The year 1603 was wonderful in this sense: awful, not awesome. 'Wonderful, *a.*,' *The Oxford English Dictionary*, 2nd edn (Oxford: Oxford University Press, 1989) http://dictionary.oed.com/cgi/entry/50286815 accessed 19 August 2007. The *OED* cites a 1596 letter by Sir John Smythe printed in Sir Henry Ellis, ed., *Original Letters of Eminent Literary Men of the Sixteenth, Seventeenth, and Eighteenth Centuries* (London: Camden Society, 1843), 91; William Lithgow, *The Totall Discourse, of the Rare Aduentures, and Painefull Peregrinations of Long Nineteene Yeares Trauayles* (London: Nicholas Okes, and are to be sold by Nicholas Fussell and Humphrey Mosley, 1632; STC 15713), 134.

Dekker's three 'Epigrams' for Elizabeth I focused respectively on the removal of the queen's body from Richmond; the funeral procession by water; and the queen lying 'Dead at White Hall at Westminster,/But liuing at White Hall in Heauen.' While the verseform and occasion of these three epitaphs made them perfect for transcribing and circulating separately, the first of these poems appears in only three known manuscript copies (Bodleian MS Rawl. poet. 117, fol. 163r rev.; British Library MSS Egerton 2877, fol. 16v; Sloane 1489, fol. 57v), and no manuscript verse collector seems to have reproduced the awkward last poem in the series.

Yet collectors made the second of Dekker's funeral poems the most popular of all the epitaphs written for Elizabeth I, transcribing it into 37 surviving early modern manuscripts: Beinecke MSS Osborn b62, p. 42; b208, p. 57; c152, p. 43; Bodleian MSS Add. A.368, fol. 45v; Eng. poet. e.40, fol. 124r (18th century); Eng. poet. f.27, p. 156; Rawl. poet. 117, fol. 163r rev.; Rawl. poet. 153, fol. 8v; British Library MSS Add. 15227, fol. 2v; Add. 27406, fol. 74v; Add. 30982, fols 23v–24r; Add. 33998, fol. 89r; Add. 47111, fols 11v–12r; Egerton 923, fol. 15r; Egerton 2421, fol. 45v rev.; Egerton 2877, fol. 16v; Sloane 1792, fol. 112v; Cambridge University Library MS Add. 7196, fol. [1]; Corpus Christi, Oxford MSS 176, fol. 32; 328, fol. 49v; Folger MSS V.a.97, p. 9; V.a.162, fol. 83r; V.a.262, p. 137; V.a.319, fol. 3r; V.a.322, p. 27; V.a.345, p. 111; Huntington MS HM 116, pp. 37–38; Meisei University MS Crewe, p. 40; Morgan MS MA 1057, p. 2; National Library of Wales MS NLW 12443A, pt. 2, p. 44; Rosenbach MSS 239/18, pp. 60–61; 239/27, p. 325; Shakespeare Birthplace Trust MS ER 93/2, fol. 190; University of Edinburgh MS H.-P. Coll. 401, fol. 72v; University of Nottingham MS Portland PwV 37, p. 1; West Yorkshire Archive Service, Bradford MS SpSt 9/1a, fol. [6v]; West Yorkshire Archive Service, Leeds MS WYL 156/237, fol. 35v.

C.R. On the same.

Weepe greatest Isle, and for thy Mistris death
Swimme in a double sea of brackish water;
Weepe little world for great Elizabeth,
Daughter of Warre, for Mars himselfe begate her:
Mother of Peace, for shee brought forth the later.
Shee was, shee is, (what can there more bee said?)
On Earth the cheife, in Heaven the second Maid.[78]

Once he invokes Elizabeth, Holland's imperative to weep yields to idealizing appellations for the queen: 'Daughter of Warre,' 'Mother of Peace,' the 'second Maid' in heaven, after only the Virgin Mary. The next epitaph that Camden and the collector of the Folger and Nottingham manuscripts recorded adds several more lofty designations for the queen. This anonymous distich shares Holland's emphasis on Elizabeth's military reputation but underlines its protestant character.

C.R. On the same.

Spaines Rodd; Romes Ruine, Netherlands releife,
Earths Ioy, Englands Gemme, Worlds Wonder, Natures Cheife.[79]

Elizabeth threatened Catholic powers with discipline and destruction, and provided fellow protestants with 'releife.'

The reference to Spain connects this first page of verse on Elizabeth to one of the Ralegh epitaphs in the Folger and Nottingham manuscripts,

[78] University of Nottingham MS Portland PwV 37, p. 1. Judging from the seven known manuscript copies of the full poem, Holland's epitaph attracted far fewer collectors than did Dekker's verse on the funeral procession: Beinecke MS Osborn b62, p. 77; Bodleian MS Eng. poet. e.40, fol. 124r (18th century); British Library MSS Egerton 923, fol. 8v; Stowe 962, fol. 167r–v; Corpus Christi, Oxford MS 328, fol. 62r; Rosenbach MS 239/27, p. 324.

Yet Holland's elegant final couplet, with its terse rendering of the complicated relationship between the virgin queen and the Virgin Mary, evidently interested more collectors than did Dekker's odd poem on the earthly and heavenly Whitehall. In addition to the manuscripts of Holland's entire epitaph, at least four other sources feature the poem's concluding couplet on its own (for a total of eleven whole or partial manuscript copies of Holland's poem): Bodleian MSS Ashmole 38, p. 189; Rawl. poet. 153, fol. 8v; Folger MS V.a. 345, p. 75; Victoria & Albert MS Dyce 44, 25.F.39, fol. 70v.

[79] University of Nottingham MS Portland PwV 37, p. 1. This couplet appears in just five early modern manuscripts, regularly among one or more of the other epitaphs for Elizabeth that Camden collected: Bodleian MSS Eng. poet. e.40, fol. 124r (18th century); Rawl. poet. 153, fol. 8v; Rosenbach MS 239/27, p. 325; Rosenbach MS 1083/16, p. 243.

which praises the deceased courtier as 'the Muses Friend, and Spaines Arch Foe.' In the contexts of these particular miscellanies, this poem recalls Elizabeth's role as 'Spaines Rodd,' and points to evidence of Ralegh's friendship with the muses in his 'Love Sonnets.' Ralegh thus emerges in these anthologies as Elizabeth's partner in antagonizing Catholic Spain, and a great poet, even 'Englandes Muse.'[80] With these texts, the compiler of the Folger and Nottingham manuscripts promoted a particularly 'Laudatory' view of Ralegh's poetry and politics. Furthermore, he used these poems to fashion manuscript contexts that do not permit much criticism of Ralegh.

One can most clearly see the respect that this verse collector afforded Ralegh in his copies of a Ralegh libel whose criticism of the courtier he probably overlooked and certainly deemphasized. He included in the 'Satyres' sections of each of his miscellanies the long poem usually called 'The Lie,' and regularly attributed to Ralegh, followed by an answer-poem written by someone who clearly believed that Ralegh had written the poem. Whereas 'The Lie' begins 'Go Soule the Bodies Guest upon a thankless arrant,' the 'Reply to this flying Satyre' answers back, 'Go Eccho of the mind, a careless truth protest,/Make answere that so raw a ly no stomack can digest.' By punning on Ralegh's name with the phrase 'so raw a ly,' the author of these lines made clear to whom he thought that he was 'Mak[ing] answere.' The compiler of the Folger and Nottingham manuscripts, however, obscured the libeler's claim regarding the authorship of 'The Lie,' or indicated that he did not trust it: he attributed 'The Lie' to 'Dr Latewarr of St Iohns.'[81] As this survey of his miscellanies has shown, this collector was keen to extend Ralegh's claims of authorship to a number of poems that he could not possibly have written. Nevertheless he ascribed a possible Ralegh poem to another writer, thereby deemphasizing the politics of the most libelous

[80] Folger MS V.a.103, fol. 6v; Rudick, *Poems of Sir Walter Ralegh*, 200; Bellany and McRae, 'Early Stuart Libels,' I24. The poem also appears in University of Nottingham MS Portland PwV 37, p. 14.

[81] University of Nottingham MS Portland PwV 37, pp. 138–39 ('Dr Latewarr Satyra Volans./Or/A flying Satyre made by Dr Latewarr of St Iohns.//Go Soule the Bodies Guest upon a thankless arrant'), 139 ('A Reply to this flying Satyre.//Go Eccho of the mind, a careless truth protest'); Folger MS V.a.103, fols 67r–v ('Satyra Volans./A flying satyre made by Dr Lateware/St Iohns.//Go Soule the body's Guest upon a thankelesse arrant'), 67v–68r ('A Reply to this flying Satyre.//Goe Eccho of ye mind, a careles truth protest'). See *Poems of Sir Walter Ralegh*, xlii–xlvii, 30–44, 150–54.

representation of Ralegh that he collected and maintaining his positive representation of the courtier.

In the midsts of such positive portrayals of Ralegh, not even Donne's most elaborate anti-courtly love poems appear to oppose Ralegh's courtly love. The collector responsible for the Folger and Nottingham manuscripts made even Donne's flagrantly anti-Petrarchan gesture in 'The Anagram' difficult to discern. He placed Donne's contreblazon on the ugly Flavia in his sections of 'Panegyricks' under the misleading heading 'The praise of an old Woman.'[82] As discussed, Donne laced any praise that he offered Flavia with paradox and facetiousness, and he characterized her not as old but as impossibly disgusting. Yet the verse collector responsible for these copies of the elegy surrounded them with examples of the sort of unambiguous praise generally associated with the panegyric genre.[83] Contrast his presentation of 'The Anagram' and 'The Autumnall,' which he also placed in his section of panegyrics, to that of the professional scribe of the Rawlinson Poetry manuscript, discussed earlier in this chapter. Again, this scribe copied these two elegies continuously, such that 'The Anagram' effectively turned 'The Autumnall' into an anti-courtly love poem. By contrast, the compiler of the Folger and Nottingham manuscripts presented 'The Anagram,' like 'The Autumnall,' as a poem of praise.

To be sure, a close reader of 'The Anagram' in the Folger or Nottingham manuscript would eventually conclude that its 'praise' is ironic. Anyone attending so closely to one of these miscellanies, however, could not miss the epitaphs honoring Ralegh earlier in the manuscript, and especially those praising his queen on the very first page. Such an ideal reader may well have noticed Donne mocking the genre of courtly love poetry, or even that of panegyric. Yet, in the unlikely event that one suspected that Donne was also mocking Ralegh, he or she would have had to ask why anyone would show irreverence to such an honorable courtier, who served so legendary a monarch. For the verse collector who compiled these miscellanies deemphasized the distinguishing characteristics of Donne's anti-courtly love poems, and related them

[82] University of Nottingham MS Portland PwV 37, pp. 112–13; Folger MS V.a.103, fol. 54r–v.

[83] Consider, for instance, Sir Henry Wotton's popular verse 'Yee glorious trifles of the East,' here appropriately headed, 'On the Lady Elizabeth, when/shee was first crowned Queene/of Bohemia' (University of Nottingham MS Portland PwV 37, p. 110).

to the writings of a courtier poet whom he represented with great respect.

When manuscript verse collectors constructed such close relationships between Ralegh's Petrarchan and Donne's anti-Petrarchan verse, they gave these relationships an appearance of intertextuality. In their particular miscellanies, Donne can seem to have responded to Ralegh, whether by complementing or attacking the courtier's Petrarchism. To be sure, none of the verse collectors considered in this chapter qualifies as a dependable witness of Donne's authorial intent, and most of them joined in fabricating Ralegh's courtly love poetry. Nevertheless, these collectors could have been trying to reconstruct plausible relationships between these two poets, suggesting that Donne knew of the courtier's love lyrics and replied to them in his own anti-courtly love poems. When verse collectors related such Donne poems to verses on subsequent courtiers, however, they could not have realistically imagined that Donne wrote them in response to the Jacobean royal favorites considered in the rest of this book. As the next chapter explains, Donne had a brief working relationship with one of these favorites, Robert Carr, earl of Somerset, for whom he both composed an epithalamion and attempted, but apparently failed, to collect his own verse. Yet these professional connections hardly gave more successful collectors of Donne's works reason to believe that the poet authorized their routine practice of gathering his anti-courtly love poems among libels on Somerset and his wife. Without necessarily imagining that Donne had mocked courtly love with such early Stuart courtiers in mind, the collectors surveyed throughout the rest of this book initiated a series of striking relationships between anti-courtly love poetry and the political verse that recognized and encouraged increasing criticism of the English court in the early seventeenth century.

3

'Love-song weeds, and Satyrique thornes': Anti-Courtly Love Poetry and Somerset Libels

Manuscript verse collectors apparently saw in the Overbury affair a political event of great significance. In many of their manuscript verse miscellanies, the explosive episode takes priority as the first early Stuart court scandal of note. Collectors populated these anthologies with the scandal's principal players, and sprinkled libels on them among their other favorite texts, regularly assimilating earlier and originally unrelated poems to the context of the Jacobean court in crisis. The Overbury affair began with the Essex nullity case of 1613, in which Frances Howard divorced Robert Devereux, third earl of Essex, claiming that he could not consummate their marriage (even though she did not doubt his prowess with other women). Scandalous enough at this early stage, the scandal grew more sensational when Frances Howard promptly married James' Scottish-born royal favorite Robert Carr, the new earl of Somerset, and especially, in 1616, when the Somersets were tried and convicted for conspiring to murder Carr's mentor, Sir Thomas Overbury, who had opposed their marriage.

A court scandal of this magnitude could not help but recontextualize older literature, especially when represented by verse libels in books as rich and diverse as manuscript verse miscellanies. In anthologies featuring libels on the earl and countess of Somerset, commonplaces on the depravity of the court resonated anew. Jokes about Scots brought to mind the earl's Scottish roots. And the standard rhetorical attacks on women found new support, however anecdotal, in the sins of the countess. Before considering how manuscript verse collectors effectively used the Overbury affair to recontextualize anti-courtly love poetry, this chapter introduces a few poets and publishers who took the court scandal as an occasion to revive older texts, and to reapply them to the political moment. After these brief examples, the chapter focuses on manuscript verse collectors who featured in their miscellanies both anti-courtly love poems and libels on the earl and countess of Somerset. These collectors and miscellanies, I argue, transformed the political and religious associations of anti-courtly love poems by immersing predominantly late Elizabethan texts in a manuscript culture that became increasingly concerned with early Stuart court scandal and the threats that such scandal posed to the English church and state.

INTERTEXTUAL EPIGRAMS AND LIBELS: DAVIES AND BASTARD

Poetic libels circulated in both news and literary manuscripts, yet collectors preserved far more of these political verses in miscellanies than in collections of exclusively topical or political documents.[1] For instance, Somerset libels appear in only one manuscript reserved for material on the Overbury affair: an elaborately decorated, professional collection of verses and trial reports associated with one Henry Feilde, and now held at Senate House Library.[2] Feilde also owned a large, calligraphic folio of political texts that includes, but is by no means

[1] McRae, *Literature, Satire and the Early Stuart State*, 36. On political miscellanies, see David Colclough, *Freedom of Speech in Early Stuart England* (Cambridge: Cambridge University Press, 2005), 196–250.

[2] The first part of Senate House Library, University of London MS 313 includes only material on the Overbury affair: a short prose text beginning 'Sir Walter Rawleye sent a bible/to Earle Somersett being in the tower' (fol. 15r); verse libels beginning 'ffrom Katherins docke ther launcht A Pincke,' 'Ladie chang'd to venus dove,' 'The som[m]er sunne is sett' (fol. 16r), 'Shee whoe wth troopes of bustuary slaves' (fols 16v–17r), 'Poore Pilat thou art like to loose thy Pincke,' 'Here he lyes that once was poore,' 'A Page a Knight a Vicunt and an Earle' ('murderer' version), 'A Page/ a knight/ a vicunt and an Earle' ('poysoner' version, fol. 17v), 'Some—ar—sett in places highe' (fols 18r–v), 'A Essex bird hath broke the Cage' (fol. 18v), 'There was an old ladd' (fols 19r–v), 'Letcherye consulted wth witcherye,' 'The howse of the Howards,' 'Henrye raysed Brandon, Iames, Carr, vpo[n] my life/' (fol. 20r), 'Whye how now Robbine? what dismounted quite' (fol. 20v); and the arraignments of Sir Thomas Monson (fols 23r–25r), the countess of Somerset (fols 26r–28r), the earl of Somerset (fols 29r–33r), Richard Weston (fols 38r–42v), Anne Turner (fols 43r–46v), Sir Gervase Elwes (fols 47r–53v), and James Franklin (fols 54r–58r). The scribe notes that the trial reports have been bound in the wrong order, and should begin with Weston and end with the earl of Somerset (fol. 2r). The second part of the manuscript, which is

limited to, verse and prose on the Overbury affair.[3] Political miscellanies, such as this privately owned manuscript, feature far more Somerset libels than do tightly focused collections like the Senate House manuscript. Even a collector such as William Davenport of Bramhall, who began his manuscript primarily with Overbury affair literature, later added texts on subsequent scandals and so turned his collection into a miscellany.[4] Yet most collectors of Somerset libels added them to miscellanies full of poetry that initially bore no obvious relation to any political event. And many transcribed these libels years, even decades, after the Overbury affair occurred, indicating that they valued such topical verses well after they had become old news.

A chapter on the role of Somerset libels in literary—as distinct from news—culture may well begin, then, with a libel that gets the news wrong but its literary heritage right. One of the most numerous Somerset libels—the one that recounts Robert Carr's impressive career as 'A page a knight a Vicount, and an Earle'—closes with a complementary description of his wife, Frances Howard, that drew on and varied a rather common phrase in early modern English literature. The earliest versions of the libel identify Howard as 'A mayde, a wyfe, a Countess and A whore,' but a unique copy (in a Bodleian Rawlinson manuscript) reads, 'A mayd a wife a widow and a whore.'[5] Since she had married Somerset promptly after divorcing Essex on the grounds of impotence, one can understand, without condoning, how the authors and collectors of the more numerous early version of the libel called Frances Howard

in a comparatively sloppy script but not necessarily in a distinct hand, features prose on the late Elizabethan trial of the second earl of Essex and Henry Wriothesley, earl of Southampton (fols 59r–73r, 74v–76r). I am grateful to Alun Ford for checking this manuscript for me and for his hospitality and expertise at the Palaeography Room.

[3] New York, Robert S. Pirie MS. I have not seen this privately owned miscellany, but I understand that it includes Overbury trial testimonies and more than a dozen Somerset libels, among a great many other political texts. I am grateful to Peter Beal for sharing his notes on this and Feilde's other books with me.

[4] Cheshire Archives MS ZCR 63/2/19. On Davenport's miscellany, see Bellany, *The Politics of Court Scandal*, esp. 85–111.

[5] The 'countess' version is here transcribed from Bodleian MS Ashmole 38, p. 116. Marotti transcribed the full text from this source in *Manuscript, Print, and the English Renaissance Lyric*, 103. Another copy of the 'countess' version appears in University of Wales, Bangor MS 422, p. 59. The 'widow' line is quoted from Bodleian Rawlinson MS D.1048, fol. 64r, which is variously transcribed in David Lindley, *The Trials of Frances Howard: Fact and Fiction at the Court of King James* (London: Routledge, 1993), 178; and in Beatrice White, *Cast of Ravens: The Strange Case of Sir Thomas Overbury* (New York: Braziller, 1965), 222. At least nineteen additional manuscript copies of the poem are extant (making for a total of 22, listed in the following appendix of verse texts), most of

'A mayde, a wyfe, a Countess and A whore.' But she by no means qualified as a 'widow': Essex remained quite alive when his ex-wife remarried and, for that matter, well after she and her second husband were tried and convicted, along with several accomplices, for Overbury's murder.

Although the libeler who called Howard a widow was not accurately reporting the facts of the scandal, he (or she) did faithfully reproduce a phrase that recurs in the literature of the period—from the Shakespearean stage to the *querelle des femmes* texts printed as the Overbury affair unfolded.[6] Among the numerous variations on this apparently popular expression, only one (to my knowledge) matches the 'widow' version of

which identify Howard as a murderer or murderess. On dating the variants, see Bellany, *The Politics of Court Scandal*, 98, 149.

[6] Such a list appears, for example, at the end of *Measure for Measure* when the Duke tells Mariana that she is 'nothing.... neither maid, widow, nor wife!' Adding the deprecatory fourth term in the list, Lucio suggests that 'she may be a punk,' or prostitute, 'for many of them are neither maide, widow, nor wife' (5.1.176–78; as edited in *The Norton Shakespeare*, gen ed. Stephen Greenblatt (New York: Norton, 1997), 2079). In the formal *querelle des femmes* text printed in the midst of the Overbury murder trials, Joseph Swetnam similarly told 'vnmarried wantons' that 'you haue... made your selues neither maidens, widowes, nor wiues, but more vile then filthy channell durt fit to be swept out of the heart and suburbes of your Countrey.' In one of the three printed replies to Swetnam, the pseudonymous Esther Sowernam subversively identified herself as '*neither Maide, Wife nor Widdowe, yet really all, and therefore experienced to defend all*' (Joseph Swetnam, *The Araignment of Lewde, Idle, Froward, and Vnconstant Women: or the Vanitie of them, choose you whether* (London: Edw: Allde for Thomas Archer, 1615; STC 23533), 27. Esther Sowernam [pseudonym], *Ester Hath Hang'd Haman: or An Answere to a Lewd Pamphlet, entituled, The Arraignment of Women. With the Arraignment of Lewd, Idle, Froward, and Vnconstant Men, and Husbands* (London: for Nicholas Bourne, 1617; STC 22974), sig. A1r. Swetnam and Sowernam are quoted in Linda Woodbridge, *Women and the English Renaissance: Literature and the Nature of Womankind, 1540–1620* (Urbana: University of Illinois Press, 1984), 84, 93). In the second through the sixth editions of Overbury's 'A Wife,' which first appeared a few months after the author's death, John Stephens of Lincoln's Inn asserted that the 'abstract' 'woman' featured in the title poem 'hath no more/Then hath the wife, the widdow, maiden, whore.' (I[ohn] S[tephens], 'A MORNING SACRIFICE to the Author,' 27–28, in Sir Thomas Overbury, *A Wife now the Widdow of Sir Thomas Overbury* (London: T.C. for Laurence Lisle, 1614; STC 18907), sig. A3r). A manuscript poem 'on a french knight' tells the story of 'A Wanton knight borne, wed, & curst in france' who returned to his first wife after marrying a second at the English court, 'Who wife, nor Widdow, Maid, nor whore, doth proue' (Folger MS V.a.162, fol. 4v).

For similar lists of just the first three or fewer categories, see Sir John Harington's 'Against Faustus,' in which Faustus is said to have 'Corrupted neuer Widdow, Wife nor Maid' (McClure, *The Letters and Epigrams of Sir John Harington*, 197); Sir John Davies' 'A Contention between a Wife, a Widowe and a Maide for Precedence at an Offering'

the Somerset libel word for word: Sir John Davies' mid-1590s epigram 'In Librum.'

> Liber doth vaunt how chastely he hath livde
> Since he hath bin in towne, seven yeeres and more,
> For that he sweares he hath foure onely swivde,
> A maide, a wife, a widow and a whoore:
> Then Liber thou hast swivde all women kinde,
> For a fift sort I know thou canst not finde.[7]

Despite its satirical tendency, Davies' poem names no one. Such discretion distinguishes it and the epigram genre from the slanderous libels that are formally indebted to them. Although 'In Librum' begins attacking an individual, a Latin name obscures his identity. (The name, 'Liber,' short for libertine, incidentally provides the etymological root of the word 'libel,' as *liber* refers to the inner bark of a tree, used for writing.[8]) Moreover, after listing Liber's sexual partners, which invites suspicion as to just who these women were, the epigram widens its focus to 'all women kinde.' This directs scrutiny away from Liber and his

(*Poems of Sir John Davies*, 216–224); 'the way of harts,' which consists of three numbered stanzas assigned respectively to 'the wife,' 'widow,' and 'ye maide' (Bodleian MS Eng. poet. c.50, fol. 33v); 'An Epitaph vppon the Ladye Markham//A mayde, a wief, shee liu'd, a wydowe, dyed' (British Library MS Harley 4064, fol. 252r, also found in Bodleian MS Rawl. poet. 31, fol. 30r; Huntington MS HM 198, pt. 2, fol. 10r); 'A wife is like a garment vsed and torne,/A mayd, like one made up, but never worne,/ A widdow is a garment worne thredbare,/Selling at second hand, like broken ware:' (Rosenbach MS 1083/16, p. 27, also found in Bodleian MS Eng. poet. e.14, fol. 33r). The Rosenbach copy is transcribed in David Coleman Redding, 'Robert Bishop's Commonplace Book: An Edition of a Seventeenth-Century Miscellany' (PhD diss., University of Pennsylvania, 1960), 87.

[7] *Poems of Sir John Davies*, 133. Krueger dates the poem to 1595 or earlier, judging from Bodleian MS Add. B.97, fol. 42r (*Poems of Sir John Davies*, 381). The Chaucerian verb *swive* also appears in Thomas Nashe's 'The choise of valentines,' as 'dame Bawde' tells the protagonist, 'As yow desire, so shall yow swive with hir' (David Norbrook and H. R. Woudhuysen, eds., *The Penguin Book of Renaissance Verse, 1509–1659* (London: Penguin, 1992), 255). A manuscript poem, 'Listen jolly gentlemen,' commemorates 'old king harry' in part because he 'would swiue while hee was aliue/ffrom the Queene vnto the begger' (Bodleian MS Malone 23, pp. 19–22; the same poem is found in Bodleian MS Malone 19, p. 87; British Library MS Add. 29879, fol. 26r). The penultimate line of 'In Vxore[m] Cottae' reads: 'bycause he swiud her for him selfe before.' In his dissertation edition of the manuscript, Sanderson glosses the word as '"Swive," to have sexual intercourse' (Rosenbach MS 1083/15, pp. 26–7; 'An edition of an early seventeenth-century manuscript collection of poems,' 134).

[8] I owe this point to Bernard J. Kavanagh.

partners, disrupting the libelous potential of the epigram form by denying its reader identifiable subjects.

The Somerset libel that appropriated and, in its more numerous versions, modified Davies' line does precisely the opposite: it lists what initially appear to be two groups of unspecified people in order to reveal that these are multiple identities of just two individuals, whom the headings of several copies name explicitly.[9]

A Page a kn^{t}- a Vicount & an Earle
did lately mary wth an English Girle
A mayd a wife a widow and a whore
Who ever saw so crosse a match before?[10]

Unlike Davies' epigram, the libel that reproduced his line leaves no doubt as to its target.

Although the 'widow' version of the libel reproduces the exact wording of Davies' poem, the libeler may not have consciously quoted the epigram. The poet responsible for another Somerset libel, however, must have realized that he was appropriating a late Elizabethan epigram. 'When Carre in Court at first a Page began' consists of the full text of Thomas Bastard's epigram 'In Getam,' with only the first line changed. Although Bastard's poem appeared in print in 1598 and so could not have originally referred to Robert Carr, it must have seemed perfectly suited to him during or shortly following his fall nearly two decades later. Bastard had mocked his anonymous target 'Gæta' for the same sort of ambition summed up in 'A page a knight a Vicount, and an Earle.'

[9] Both 'countess' versions feature such headings: 'A libell made on ye earle of Sommerset' (University of Wales, Bangor MS 422, p. 59); 'vppon S. R. C. and the Ladye F. H:' (Bodleian MS Ashmole 38, p. 116). Over the 'murderess'/'murderer' versions, the following headings appear: 'One the Earle of ~~Essex~~ Sum[m]erset' (Bodleian MS Malone 19, p. 38); 'On the Earle of Somerset' (Bodleian MS Tanner 465, fol. 96v); 'vppon Carr l. of Som[m]erset' (University of Edinburgh MS H.-P. Coll. 401, fol. 43^{b}r); 'On the Earle of Sommersett' (Folger MS V.a.162, fol. 62v); 'On Carr' (Folger MS V.a.262, p. 139); 'On the Earle of Sommerset' (Houghton MS Eng. 686, fol. 10r). Although the unique copy of the 'widow' version lacks a heading, the poem occupies a leaf that features only Somerset libels, two of which invoke the name of Carr and two that of Somerset. 'Poore Pylott thou art like to loose thy pinke' is headed 'Carres Ignomynye.' That heading and 'I. C. V. R. good monseur Carre' each play on the name of Carr. The name of Somerset is invoked in 'Our Somer Sun is sett' and the following line of 'ffrom Katherine docke did launch a pinke': 'But Som ar sett to mend her keele' (Bodleian MS Rawl. D.1048, fols 64r–v).

[10] Bodleian MS Rawl. D.1048, fol. 64r.

Bastard had also reminded Gæta of his humble origins—which, fortuitously, could also describe Carr's Scottish roots.

> Epigr. 4. *In Getam.*
> *Gæta* from wooll and weauing first beganne,
> Swelling and swelling to a gentleman.
> When he was gentleman, and brauely dight
> He left not swelling till he was a knight.
> At last, (for getting what he was at furst)
> He swole to be a Lord : and then he burst.[11]

Somerset libelers needed to change virtually nothing beyond the first line in order to turn this epigram to their purpose: 'When Carre in Court at first a Page began,/He sweld, & sweld into a gentleman,' and so on.[12] Intertextual examples such as these demonstrate that many libels differed from epigrams in only one crucial regard: whereas epigrams tended to obscure their subjects with Latin names, libels slanderously identified them in English; whereas epigrams potentially satirized specific targets, libels actually did so.

APPROPRIATION, OVERBURY'S 'A WIFE,' AND ONE OF BEAUMONT'S ANTI-COURTLY LOVE POEMS

These pairs of late Elizabethan epigrams and Somerset libels offer vivid examples of appropriation. Somerset libelers appropriated the exact wording, even the full text, of poems that had been composed decades before the Overbury affair. They recontextualized these verses in ways that their authors could not have foreseen and redeployed them against figures of whom the authors could not have known at the time of

[11] The original six-line version of 'In Getam,' on which the Somerset libel is based, was printed in Thomas Bastard, *Chrestoleros. Seuen Bookes of Epigrames written by T B* (London: Richard Bradocke for I.B., 1598; STC 1559), 107. An eight-line version can be found in W[illiam] B[asse?] and E[dward] P[hillips, or Edward Pond?], *A Helpe to Discovrse* (London: Bernard Alsop for Leonard Becket, 1619; STC 1547), 165. For full texts and manuscript sources of both versions, see the following appendix of verse texts. I have recently learned that, well before me, C. F. Main recognized the intertextual relationship between the Bastard epigram and Somerset libel in 'Ben Jonson and an Unknown Poet on the King's Senses,' *Modern Language Notes*, 74/5 (1959), 392.

[12] Bodleian MS Malone 19, p. 151. A full text of the libel and a list of its manuscript sources follow in the appendix of verse texts.

composition. Sir Thomas Overbury's own poem, 'A Wife,' may offer the perfect example of such appropriation. Early references to the poem certainly date it before 1612; and its most important manuscript source suggests that it was composed by 1608—when it would have been impossible for Overbury, or anyone else, to compose it with Frances Howard in mind.[13] Nevertheless, few readers and collectors had an opportunity to engage the poem without comparing Overbury's fictional 'Wife' to Carr's actual wife, especially in print.[14] The poem's publisher Lawrence Lisle quickly capitalized on the notoriety of the scandal not only by rushing 'A Wife' into print a few months after Overbury's death but also by cornering the market for books related to the Essex divorce and Somerset wedding in the first significant year of his publishing career: his 1614 publications alone include four editions of 'A Wife'; a companion poem entitled 'The Husband'; the masque that Thomas Campion wrote for the Somersets' wedding night; and George Chapman's poem and prose tract defending the Essex divorce.[15] As Alastair Bellany has pointed out, not until 1616, in the seventh edition

[13] British Library MS Lansdowne 740, fol. 79v attributes 'A Wife' to 'Mr. Tho: Overburie,' as opposed to Sir Thomas Overbury, as it probably would have if the ascription (in the source text, if not in this very copy) had been made after the author was knighted in 1608. Among the references that date the poem before 1612 is Ben Jonson's claim to have read the poem to Lady Rutland on Overbury's behalf, which must have occurred before the countess' death in 1612 (Ben Jonson, *Conversations with William Drummond of Hawthornden*, ed. R. F. Patterson (London: Blackie, 1923), 20). Another reference is John Owen's epigram on the poem in a manuscript predating Prince Henry's death in November 1612 (John Considine, 'The Humanist Antecedents of the First English Character-Books' (DPhil diss., Oxford University, 1994), 60. Cited in Sir Thomas Overbury, *Characters*, ed. Donald Beecher (Ottawa: Dovehouse, 2003), 95).

[14] 'A Wife' has continued to give scholars the impression that it was written for the purpose of dissuading Carr from marrying Howard. See J. L. Simmons, 'Diabolical Realism in Middleton's and Rowley's *The Changeling*,' *Renaissance Drama*, new ser., 11 (1980), 163; and Paul Yachnin, 'Scandalous Trades: Middleton's *The Witch*, the "Populuxe" Market and the Politics of Theater,' *Medieval and Renaissance Drama in England*, 12 (1999), 222.

[15] Before 1614, Laurence Lisle appears only as a bookseller, via his shop at the sign of the tiger's head in St. Paul's churchyard, for such works as George Chapman, *The Conspiracie, and Tragedie of Charles Duke of Byron, Marshall of France* (London: G. Eld for Thomas Thorppe, and are to be sold at the Tygers head in Paules Church-yard, 1608; STC 4968); Ben Jonson, *The Characters of Two Royall Masques* (London: for Thomas Thorp, and are to be sold at the signe of the Tigers head in Paules Church-yard, [1608]; STC 14761); Richard West, *Wits A.B.C. or a Centurie of Epigrams* (London: for Thomas Thorp, and are to be sould at the signe of the Tigers head in Paules Church-yard, [1608]; STC 25262); Claude Morillon, *The Fvnerall Pompe and Obseqvies of the Most Mighty and*

of 'A Wife,' did Lisle add elegies that 'dwelled at length on the scandalous circumstances of [Overbury's] death.'[16] Yet the publishing specialty that Lisle had established already in 1614 must have encouraged buyers and readers of even earlier editions to make the unflattering comparison between Overbury's idealized 'Wife' and Somerset's actual wife.

To the nine subsequent editions of the poem that he published between 1614 and 1618, Lisle added texts of a variety of genres that made his book resemble the manuscript miscellanies in which 'A Wife' was simultaneously circulating. In the eleventh edition, printed in 1622, Lisle's successor Henry Seile added a couple of items that demonstrate the sentiment and tone of the anti-courtly love poetry that manuscript verse collectors were making particularly popular in such miscellanies. For instance, Seile included the facetious 'Essay of Valour,' which scholars have cautiously attributed to John Donne, no doubt in part because it shares the irreverent attitude toward courtly love that characterizes some of his most popular poems. The essay ostensibly praises valor as the best quality for attracting women, especially as opposed to the laughable tactics of courtly lovers.

> Whilome before this age of wit, and wearing blacke broke in vpon vs, there was no way knowne to win a Lady, but by Tilting, Tournying, and Riding through Forrests, in which time these slender striplings with little legs, were held but of strength enough to marie their widowes.[17]

Puissant Henry the Fourth, King of France and Nauarre (London: Nicholas Okes, and are to be sold in Pauls Church-yard, at the signe of the Tygers head, 1610; STC 13136). Lisle's 1614 publications include: *The Hvsband. A Poeme Expressed In a Compleat Man* (London: for Lawrence L'isle, dwelling at the Tygres head in Pauls Church-yard, 1614; STC 14008); Thomas Campion, *The Description of a Maske: Presented in the Banqueting Roome at Whitehall, on Saint Stephens Night Last, at the Mariage of the Right Honourable the Earle of Somerset: and the Right Noble the Lady Frances Howard* (London: by E. A. for Laurence Li'sle, dwelling in Paules Church-yard, at the signe of the Tygers head, 1614; STC 4539); George Chapman, *Andromeda Liberata. Or The Nvptials of Persevs and Andromeda* (London: for Lavrence L'isle and are to be sold at his shop in S^t^, Paules-Church-yard, at the signe of the Tigers-head, 1614; STC 4964); ___, *A Free and Offenceles Iustification, of a Lately Pvblisht and Most Maliciously Misinterpreted Poeme: Entitvled Andromeda Liberata* (London: for Lavrence L'isle and are to be sold at his shop in Pauls church-yard at the signe of the Tigers-head, 1614; STC 4977).

16 Bellany, *The Politics of Court Scandal*, 115.

17 Sir Thomas Overbury, *Sir Thomas Ouerbury his Wife* (London: for Laurence Lisle, and are to be sold by Henry Seile at the Tigers-head in Pauls Church-yard, 1622; STC 18913), sig. Q7r–v. The 'Essay of Valour' covers sigs Q6r–R1r.

Thus Donne, or whoever wrote the piece, signaled irreverence for both self-fashioned melancholy and the chivalry denoted by 'Tilting, Tournying, and Riding through Forrests'—in other words, for the courtly love of both Ralegh's forlorn love poems to Elizabeth and Spenser's epic.

To the 1622 edition, Seile also added Francis Beaumont's poem 'Ad Comitissam Rutlandiæ,' which constitutes an exemplary engagement with the genre of anti-courtly love poetry, worthy of extended analysis here.[18] Beaumont's poem to the countess of Rutland shares with Donne's most popular manuscript poems a parodic attitude toward the courtly love poetry that emerged at the late Elizabethan court. Beaumont may at first seem to have made a poor choice of addressee in Lady Rutland, since her father, Sir Philip Sidney, had written just the sort of courtier love lyrics that Beaumont parodies in his poem to the countess. The posthumous print publication of Sidney's *Astrophil and Stella* initiated a brief, yet rather intense, vogue for sonnet sequences in the 1590s. The genre must have gained cultural capital from its association with Sidney and, through him, with the court, to which stationers ostensibly marketed many of the printed sonnet sequences. Given his negative representation of the court in *Astrophil and Stella* and elsewhere, Sidney and his sequence may make for rather ironic representatives of the Elizabethan court. In making fun of love poets in a poem to Sidney's daughter, Beaumont may have actually signaled to her that he recognized this irony. In general, poets must have felt obligated to pronounce their respect for Sidney and his poetry in compositions to or about his daughter, such as Ben Jonson's epigram and verse epistle to her and Beaumont's own elegy on her death.[19] Nevertheless, respect for Sidney by no means required respect for those poets who modeled their work on his. When he mocked love poets, Beaumont may have been making a similar distinction, attacking not the countess' renowned father but those would-be literary inheritors who could not live up to his memory.

[18] Overbury, *Wife* (1622), sigs C4r–C5r.

[19] Writing to or about Lady Rutland definitely put poets in mind of her father. Consider Ben Jonson's epigram and epistle each entitled 'To Elizabeth Countesse of Rutland' (Ben Jonson, *The Complete Poetry of Ben Jonson*, ed. William B. Hunter, Jr. (Garden City NY: Anchor, 1963), 33, 102–5) and Beaumont's 'An Elegie on the Death of the LADY RVTLAND,' which Lisle printed in the tenth and eleventh editions of 'A Wife' (Overbury, *Wife* (1622), sig. C5v–C7v).

Beaumont seems to have expected in Lady Rutland a reader capable of such a distinction and, in any event, one who would have laughed at a conventional love or praise poem from him. He began his poem registering the difficulty of composing verses to her, 'So you may laugh at them and not at me.'[20] Accordingly, his speaker decides to 'auoid the common beaten waies/To Women vsed, which are loue or praise.' In other words, Beaumont distinguished his verse from two kinds of poetry: love and epideictic. 'As for the first' of these two types of verse, love poetry, his speaker opts to leave that genre to poets who are more prolific, and less respectable, than he—in an extended caricature of such writers.[21]

> Let such as in a hopelesse witlesse rage,
> Can sigh a quire, and read it to a Page;
> Such as can make ten Sonnets ere they rest,
> When each is but a great blot at the best;
> Such as doe backes of bookes and windowes fill,
> With their too furious Diamond or quill;
> Such as are well resolu'd to end their daies,
> With a loud laughter blowne beyond the Seas;
> Who are so mortified that they can liue
> Contemn'd of all the world, and yet forgiue.
> Write loue to you:[22]

In short, let poets who can produce great numbers of inferior verses, and who do not mind the shame of doing so, 'Write loue to you.' Beaumont preferred rather to avoid infamy:

> I would not willingly
> Be pointed at in euery company.
> As was that little Taylor, who till death,
> Was hot in loue with *Qu: Elizabeth*.[23]

This reference to Elizabeth claims attention for a number of reasons. For one, it invokes an Elizabethan context in relation to love poetry, and

[20] In the context of Seile's edition of 'A Wife,' I quote from Overbury, *Wife* (1622), sigs C4r–C5r ('Ad Comitissam Rutlandiæ,' 2).

[21] Overbury, *Wife* (London, 1622), sig. C4r ('Ad Comitissam Rutlandiæ,' 2, 5–7).

[22] Overbury, *Wife* (London, 1622), sig. C4r–v ('Ad Comitissam Rutlandiæ,' 11–21).

[23] Overbury, *Wife* (1622), sig. C4v ('Ad Comitissam Rutlandiæ,' 21–24).

represents the genre in terms of a ridiculous love for the queen. This gesture need not involve disrespect to Elizabeth, any more than Beaumont's caricature of love poets applies to Sidney. Rather Beaumont was mocking popular views of the court: versifiers trying and failing to write in Sidney's style, and a lowly tailor 'hot in loue' with the queen.

As for the second of the two poetic genres that he ostensibly avoids—the poetry of praise, or epideictic—Beaumont's speaker facetiously reasons that, were he ever to praise a woman, he would choose one who, unlike Lady Rutland, deserves no praise, and so would appreciate his.

> Ile picke some woman out, as full of sinne
> As you are full of vertue, with a soule
> As blacke as yours is white, A face as foule
> As yours is beautifull,[24]

Thus Beaumont turned his poem into a praise poem even as he refused to write one. For every compliment that he offers Lady Rutland, Beaumont's speaker adds a corresponding detail to the ugly, sinful woman whom he contrasts to her. He enumerates the woman's 'loose skin,' her 'breath . . . horrible and vild,' her 'stinke,' and 'such a foot and such a nose,/As will not stand in any thing but prose.'[25] This strategy produces an anti-blazon that ranks Beaumont's poem with the period's most elaborate parodies of courtly love poetry, such as Donne's 'The Anagram' and 'The Comparison,' in which the speaker humorously distinguishes the addressee's 'Ranke sweaty' mistress from his own beautiful mistress.[26] As I discussed in the previous chapter, Donne's Flavia also contrasts sharply with a beautiful woman, if only one implied by the poem: the conventional mistress of courtly love poetry.

Yet Donne's comparisons of ugly and beautiful women tend to minimize the distinction between them, and ultimately flatter neither. Beaumont makes his praise of Lady Rutland comparatively unambiguous. His 'Ad Comitissam Rutlandiæ' praises an ideal woman—as does Overbury's poem 'A Wife.' In fact, Beaumont and Overbury reportedly composed these poems for the same ideal woman. According to William Drummond, Ben Jonson claimed to have read 'A Wife' to Lady Rutland

24 Overbury, *Wife* (1622), sig. C4v ('Ad Comitissam Rutlandiæ,' 28–31).
25 Overbury, *Wife* (1622), sigs C4v–C5r ('Ad Comitissam Rutlandiæ,' 37, 39, 44–46).
26 *Donne Variorum*, 2:51 ('The Comparison,' 7).

on behalf of Overbury, who 'was in love with her.'[27] When Henry Seile published Overbury's and Beaumont's poems together, he probably knew of Lady Rutland's relationship to each. Yet, regardless of what he knew about these verses, Seile put his customers in a position to recognize that both poems praise a woman by contrasting her to a decidedly less ideal counterpart: in the case of Beaumont's poem, to an ugly, unpraiseworthy mistress and, in that of Overbury's, to Frances Howard.

If the print-publishers of Overbury's poem indirectly evoked the countess of Somerset, the compilers of manuscript verse miscellanies ruthlessly exposed her. They did so by reproducing libels on her and her husband that no one would print. And they regularly juxtaposed these libels to each of the poems discussed in this chapter and others like them, including Beaumont's epideictic, and Donne's less complimentary, anti-courtly love poems. In the last section of this chapter, I argue that such juxtapositions amount to recontextualizations that are similar to, yet more radical than, Lisle's and Seile's. Before concluding with this argument, though, the next section considers how anti-courtly love poems and Somerset libels became simultaneously available to verse collectors. Their concurrent dissemination may have had something to do with the relationship between the men most closely associated with each genre, Donne and Somerset; but it may have also involved the family and friends of Somerset's enemy, the third earl of Essex.

DONNE, SOMERSET, AND ESSEX

Rather paradoxically, John Donne qualifies as both a quintessential coterie poet and the most popular author in seventeenth-century literary manuscripts.[28] Chronology, of course, explains part of this paradox. Initially, Donne restricted the audience for his poems to small groups of trusted readers. And later, in some cases decades after he had composed a poem, verse collectors disseminated them widely in manuscript. Donne's transformation from coterie to popular poet—or, more to

[27] Jonson, *Conversations*, 20.

[28] Arthur F. Marotti, *John Donne: Coterie Poet* (Madison: University of Wisconsin Press, 1986); Beal, *Index*, 1:1:243–568; *Donne Variorum*, 2:xlix.

the point, the circulation of his poetry beyond its original audience—may have begun to occur not only at about the same time as the Overbury affair did, but also for reasons connected to the scandal.

While Overbury was unknowingly ingesting poison in the Tower of London, Donne appealed to Carr, then viscount Rochester, for patronage and received the secretaryship that Overbury had just vacated under duress. Within weeks of the Somerset wedding, Donne celebrated it in an epithalamion ('Eclogue. 1613. December 26.'), and offered to write a defense of the bride's divorce from her first husband. Somerset evidently supported Donne 'for the next year or so.'[29] Near the end of that time, and just weeks before his ordination, Donne was unenthusiastically preparing to print a collection of his poems for Somerset. This plan required Donne to borrow an 'old book' of his own poems from his friend Sir Henry Goodyer, joking that it 'cost me more diligence, to seek them, then it did to make them.'[30] Donne has left no evidence of trying to print his poems before this attempt. Although he never did print them, Helen Gardner speculated that one of the most authoritative groups of Donne poetry manuscripts derived from a lost manuscript collection that Donne compiled at this time for Somerset.[31] This theory of transmission tempts one to imagine that, when Donne

[29] In his biography of Donne, R. C. Bald reproduced a letter that James, Lord Hay presented to Rochester on Donne's behalf, explaining: 'With Overbury removed, Rochester badly needed someone of similar ability on whom he could lean. Hence Donne's letter was even more successful than he had dared to hope. Shortly afterwards he was presented to Rochester by Hay, and he created so favourable an impression that Rochester not only felt sure of being able to make use of his talents but also urged him to put aside all thoughts of entering the Church. Subsequent letters make it clear that Rochester contributed generously to Donne's support for the next year or so.' Bald prints an excerpt from another letter in which Donne 'professed his ardour to write not merely an epithalamion but also a defense of the divorce' (*John Donne: A Life*, ed. Wesley Milgate (Oxford: Oxford University Press, 1970), 272–74). See also Annabel Patterson, *Reading Between the Lines* (Madison: University of Wisconsin Press, 1993), 195: 'We know, for instance, that Donne profited from the greatest scandal of James's reign, in which Frances Howard's divorce from the third earl of Essex and remarriage to the *other* and more famous Sir Robert Carr, now earl of Somerset, was made still more disreputable by the murder of someone who had resolutely opposed it. On September 14, 1613, Sir Thomas Overbury died in the Tower, poisoned, as it was later charged, by the countess through her accomplices. Donne, in the meantime, had not only sought out Somerset as a new patron, but had accepted the position as his secretary that Overbury's imprisonment had vacated.'

[30] Donne, *Letters*, 196–97.

[31] Gardner, *The Divine Poems*, lxiii–lxv. See Beal, *Index*, 1:1:245–46, 249–50.

began gathering his poems for Somerset, he made possible their remarkable scribal publication, even though he had intended the collection to be 'not for much publique view.'[32]

Yet, according to subsequent editors, 'no evidence exists that Donne ever successfully collected his poems.'[33] Ernest W. Sullivan II has come to this conclusion in his study of the Dalhousie manuscripts, two of several known copies of a group of poems that, he has hypothesized, the Essex family originally collected.[34] Regardless of who initially collected these texts, the first Dalhousie manuscript may record the earliest surviving literature to recontextualize Donne's poetry with the Overbury affair. The miscellany begins with two prose items on the Essex nullity case: a letter opposing the suit from one of the clerics whom King James had appointed to hear the trial, George Abbot, archbishop of Canterbury; and James' openly circulated rebuttal.[35] Following these texts on the Essex divorce, the main scribe copied the sequence of poems that has long interested Donne editors—and which includes, in addition to Donne's poems and Beaumont's 'Ad Comitissam Rutlandiæ,' verses by Sir John Davies, Sir John Harington, Sir John Roe, John Hoskyns, and Sir Henry Wotton, as well as some of the prose characters that appeared in print with Overbury's 'A Wife.'[36]

Sullivan's hypothesis that the Essex family originally compiled this group of poems gains considerable interest in the context of the Overbury affair. For it brings up the possibility that, while Somerset and even Donne himself were trying and possibly failing to get a hold of Donne's

32 Donne, *Letters*, 197.

33 Ernest W. Sullivan, II, ed., *The First and Second Dalhousie Manuscripts: Poems and Prose by John Donne and Others* (Columbia: University of Missouri Press, 1988), 10. Ted-Larry Pebworth concurs in 'John Donne, Coterie Poetry, and the Text as Performance,' *Studies in English Literature, 1500–1900*, 29/1 (Winter 1989), 69. In conversation, Prof. Sullivan has reiterated this point, and John Shawcross and Gary Stringer have agreed. I am grateful to each.

34 Sullivan, *The First and Second Dalhousie Manuscripts*, 4–7. Sullivan repeats the hypothesis in 'The Renaissance Manuscript Verse Miscellany: Private Party, Private Text,' in W. Speed Hill, ed., *New Ways of Looking at Old Texts: Papers of the Renaissance English Text Society, 1985–1991* (Binghamton NY: Medieval and Renaissance Texts and Studies, 1993), 289–97.

35 Texas Tech MS PR 1171 D 14 (Dalhousie I), fols 1r–2v; Sullivan, *The First and Second Dalhousie Manuscripts*, 15–17. See Bellany, *The Politics of Court Scandal*, 52–53.

36 'The most likely copyist or conduit from the court of James to the Dalhousie family would have been Sir John Ramsay, Viscount Haddington and Earl of Holderness (1580–1626)' (Sullivan, *The First and Second Dalhousie Manuscripts*, 5).

poems, Somerset's enemy Essex occupied the center of a social network that was circulating those same poems. In other words, this theory of transmission suggests that, when the spoils of the Overbury affair had been distributed, Somerset got the girl, but Essex got the poetry. Granted, a verse miscellany would hardly have provided adequate compensation for everything that Essex lost in his divorce. Nevertheless, such a book of verse would have represented one of Essex's greatest remaining assets: an impressive network of clients and friends, many of whom had served in his father's military campaigns. As Sullivan has suggested, several of these friends may have sent their own poetic compositions to the second earl, his sister (Penelope Devereux, Sidney's 'Stella'), or the third earl himself. By amending and disseminating the family poetry collection, the third earl would have been maintaining a circle of supporters who continued to show him respect even in his disgrace. When the earl and countess of Somerset fell from favor, they conspicuously lacked such loyal support.

Indeed, while the nullity case surely disgraced Essex, it did not provoke libelers to subject him to the sort of censure that they heaped on the Somersets in a number of poetic libels. If Essex acquired any of these libels on his ex-wife or her second husband, he did not keep or circulate them with the poetry collection that Sullivan has attributed to his family. For, even though some of the manuscripts derived from this collection include literature related to the Overbury affair, none of them includes a Somerset libel.[37] The compilers of other verse miscellanies, though, regularly gathered together Somerset libels and the poems that the Essex family seems to have collected. I suggest that, in doing so, these verse collectors established relationships between Donne's poems and literature on the Overbury affair that Essex did not promote, and that neither Donne nor Somerset would have appreciated. This argument requires assessing the politics of Donne's decision to dedicate his poems to Somerset and, so, considering his request for 'that old book' of Goodyer's in some detail.

37 Donne editors have labeled these the Group II manuscripts: Trinity College Dublin MS 877, fols 13r–161v (Dublin MS I); Houghton fMS Eng. 966.3 (a copy of Dublin MS I); British Library MS Lansdowne 740, fols 58r–136v; Texas Tech MSS PR 1171 D14 (Dalhousie MS I), fols 21r–62r; PR 1171 S4 (Dalhousie MS II), fols 5–34 (a copy of Dalhousie MS I); Trinity College, Cambridge MS R.3.12 (Puckering MS); British Library MS Add. 18647 (a copy of the Puckering MS); and National Library of Wales MS Dolau Cothi 6748.

Donne had apparently made the request once before he reminded Goodyer to send the book, and explained why he needed it, in his letter of 20 December 1614. Donne warned that Goodyer must keep the explanation secret from their mutual patron, Lucy Russell, countess of Bedford.[38]

One thing more I must tell you; but so softly, that I am loath to hear my self: and so softly, that if that good Lady were in the room, with you and this Letter, she might not hear. It is, that I am brought to a necessity of printing my Poems, and addressing them to my L. Chamberlain. This I mean to do forthwith; not for much publique view, but at mine own cost, a few Copies. I apprehend some incongruities in the resolution; and I know what I shall suffer from many interpretations: but I am at an end, of much considering that; and, if I were as startling in that kinde, as ever I was, yet in this particular, I am under an unescapable necessity, as I shall let you perceive, when I see you. By this occasion I am made a Rhapsoder of mine own rags, and that cost me more diligence, to seek them, then it did to make them. This made me aske to borrow that old book of you, which it will be too late to see, for that use, when I see you: for I must do this, as a valediction to the world, before I take Orders.[39]

Donne had good reason to keep his proposed Somerset collection secret from Lady Bedford. For, in the spring of 1614, she had made clear her opposition to Somerset by joining the effort—led in part by her kinsman, William Herbert, third earl of Pembroke (whom James had passed over when he appointed Somerset lord chamberlain)—to introduce to court James' next royal favorite, George Villiers (of whom, at the end of his letter, Donne tantalizingly promised to tell Goodyer more in person).[40] Despite the antagonism between Lady Bedford and Somerset, Donne apparently wanted to acknowledge his connection

[38] Donne does not refer to Lady Bedford by name in this letter but Bald, for one, identifies this 'good Lady' as she (*John Donne: A Life*, 295–96).

[39] Donne, *Letters*, 196–97.

[40] Donne, *Letters*, 198. See Beal, *Index*, 1:1:245–46. As Bellany explains, Somerset had been appointed lord chamberlain when his father-in-law left the office to become lord treasurer in the summer of that year; Pembroke had wanted the office for himself, and also disliked Carr's apparent anti-parliamentary, pro-Spanish leanings. Bellany lists among Pembroke's possible collaborators, George Abbot, archibishop of Canterbury; Henry Wriothesley, third earl of Southampton; Sir Ralph Winwood; Thomas Erskine, viscount Fenton; Thomas Howard, fourteenth earl of Arundel; and Sir Thomas Lake (*The Politics of Court Scandal*, 58, 66–67). See also Roger Lockyer, 'Villiers, George, first duke of Buckingham (1592–1628),' *ODNB*; Victor Stater, 'Herbert, William, third earl of Pembroke (1580–1630),' *ODNB*.

to the countess in his Somerset collection. He told Goodyer that he planned to include his verse letters to 'persons of rank,' presumably including the significant fraction of which he had addressed to Lady Bedford.

Donne's desire to register his associations with these two opponents at court brings up a similarity with another book of poems prepared for Somerset. As John Pitcher has suggested, Donne's politically balanced collection has a few things in common with one that Samuel Daniel began to compile for Somerset some eighteen months later.[41] Like Donne, Daniel had obligations to both Somerset and Lady Bedford. Also like Donne, he tried to manage these conflicting interests by including verses addressed to each of them in his presentation manuscript for Somerset. Furthermore, Somerset very well may have commissioned both Donne's and Daniel's books. Negotiating the simultaneous patronage of enemies at court, Donne and Daniel each seem to have been trying to depoliticize inevitably political books by acknowledging their connections to each of their patrons. Both poets seem to have given up trying: whereas Donne never printed and may not have even succeeded in collecting his poems, Daniel left his presentation manuscript incomplete.

If Donne was attempting to mitigate the political gesture of dedicating his poems to Somerset, most of those who collected them in verse miscellanies (beyond the Essex circle) demonstrated no such concern for political neutrality. For the poems that Somerset seems to have requested from Donne make quite a different political statement when juxtaposed to the libelous ones that Somerset unwittingly provoked. Instead of balancing Donne's poems with verses addressing a carefully selected range of court figures, verse collectors included them in miscellanies among libels that attack the most notorious courtiers. And of all the poetic genres that Donne would have represented in the collection that he planned for Somerset, miscellany compilers disproportionately favored his anti-courtly love poems, like 'The Comparison' and 'The Anagram.' By collecting Somerset libels and anti-courtly love poems together, verse collectors established an association

[41] John Pitcher, *Samuel Daniel: The Brotherton Manuscript: A Study in Authorship*, Leeds Texts and Monographs, new ser., 7 (The University of Leeds: School of English, 1981), 46, 65, 68–74.

between the sexualized and disgraced women who are the subjects of the two genres.

Of course Donne would not have made such a connection between Frances Howard and the negative representations of women in his most popular poems—at least not in a volume dedicated to her husband. And if the publishers Lisle and Seile suggested a relationship between Howard and the unworthy woman in Beaumont's anti-courtly love poem, they did so cautiously. Collectors of manuscript verse had no reason to adopt such caution. By consistently gathering together Donne's anti-courtly love poems and Somerset libels (along with Overbury's and especially Beaumont's poems), they made explicit and slanderous the relationships that Lisle and Seile implied. In doing so, verse collectors effectively turned Donne's writings against his own patron.

ANTI-COURTLY LOVE POEMS AND SOMERSET LIBELS IN MISCELLANIES

One of the libels on Frances Howard, which consists of pro and con verses on her character that are headed 'Petitio' and 'Responsio,' has a certain affinity with Beaumont's and Donne's comparisons of worthy and unworthy mistresses. More to the point, the hands responsible for the two known manuscript copies of this libel emphasized its similarity to such anti-courtly love poems. One transcriber added the libel to the verse collection of the Skipwith family of Cotes, Leicestershire, now at the British Library, which begins (in another hand) with Donne's elegies. The same hand responsible for the libel also transcribed Donne's satires and Beaumont's anti-courtly love poem, 'Ad Comitissam Rutlandiæ.'[42] Again, the Skipwiths most likely received their Donne poems from Sir Henry Goodyer, a relation by marriage. So, even if Goodyer failed to send 'that old book' of poems to Donne, he proved himself capable of disseminating those poems: copies of Donne's verses, written in Goodyer's own hand, appear among the papers of Sir Edward

[42] British Library MS Add. 25707, fols 31r–v ('A Letter to the Countesse/of Rutlande.//Madam: soe maye my verses pleasinge bee'), 46r ('Petitio//Looke, and lament behould a face of Earth'; 'Respontio.//It's strange to se a face soe highe in birth'). The hand responsible for these transcriptions is dominant in fols 29r–67r, which I collate as gatherings 6–11 in the appended manuscript description.

Conway, secretary of state.[43] The transcriber of the only other known copy of 'Petitio' and 'Responsio,' at Cambridge University Library, also copied a truncated version of Donne's 'The Anagram.'[44] In these two related miscellanies, compilers gathered together anti-courtly love poems that contrast good and bad women with a libel that puts Frances Howard in both positions.

Among Somerset libels, only 'Petitio' and 'Responsio' treat the countess so even-handedly: no other libel welcomes any debate regarding her character. So the other miscellanies that juxtapose Somerset libels to anti-courtly love poems assimilate her confidently to the latter's negative representations of women. Indeed, in another pair of closely related manuscript verse miscellanies, both in the British Library's Harley collection, Beaumont's 'Ad Comitissam Rutlandiæ' complements much harsher, and more popular Somerset libels, one of which uses initials to open with the phrase, *I see you are good Monsieur Carr*:[45]

I. C. V. R
good Mounsieur Car
about to fall

V. R. A. K
as most men say
and thats not all

V. O. Q. P
wth a nullitie
that shamelesse packe

S. X. Y. ff
whose wicked life
hath broke thy backe/[46]

Confronting Somerset with a prediction of his fall, the cryptic speaker tells him, 'V. R. A. K'—that is, *you are a kae* or jackdaw, proverbially

[43] British Library MS Add. 23229, fols 10r–14v ('Allophanes/Vnseasonable man, statue of Ice' '), 55r ('If yet I have not all thy l[o]ve'), 76r–77r ('Let mans Soule bee a Spheare And then in this').

[44] Cambridge University Library MS Add. 29, fols 18r–v (here headed 'Petitio' and 'Responsio'), 39r rev. ('Elegie. 10.//Marry & loue thy Flauia for shee').

[45] British Library MSS Harley 1221, fols 79v–80r ('Madam, so may my verses pleasinge bee'); Harley 6038, fols 222r–23v ('Madam, so may my verses pleasing bee').

[46] British Library MSS Harley 1221, fol. 91r; Harley 6038, fol. 28r ('I: C. V. R./good Monseiur Car'). Including these two, the poem is found in at least 27 manuscript copies, listed in the following appendix of verse texts.

known for its borrowed feathers, like the titles and estates that Somerset has borrowed from other men. 'And thats not all' that Somerset has taken from others. The speaker claims, 'V. O. Q. P. . . S. X. Y. ff': *you occupy Essex's wife.*

Another Somerset libel in this pair of Harley manuscripts represents Howard as a leaky sailing vessel, or 'pincke,' after her voyage from Essex to Rochester.

> ffrom Katherines docke was lanched a pincke
> w^{ch}: did leake but did not sincke
> Sometimes she lay by Essex shore
> expectinge rigging yeards and more
> but all disasters to preuent ~~wth~~
> wth winde in poope she sayled to Kent
> at Rochester she Anchor Cast
> w:^{ch} Canterbury did distaste
> but winchester wth Elyes helpe
> did hale a shore this Lyons whelpe
> she was weake sided and did reele
> tso som-were-sett to mend her keele
> to stopp her leake & sheath her
> and make her fitt for euery~~mend~~ [47]

In both of his miscellanies, the verse collector omitted the last word in each of the last two lines, which in another copy reads: 'And stopp her leake, and sheath her port/And make her fitt for any sporte.'[48] In the sequence of verses preserved in this collector's pair of anthologies, Frances Howard no longer resembles both the ugly and praiseworthy women whom Beaumont contrasted to one another. If, however, a reader of one of his manuscripts were to seek an example of the sort of reprehensible woman evoked in Beaumont's poem ('full of sinne' with a 'blacke' 'soule'), he or she would need to turn only a few pages to find one clearly presented in these Somerset libels.

Similarly, Frances Howard begins to resemble one of Donne's negative representations of a woman in the manuscript verse miscellany of

[47] British Library MSS Harley 1221, fol. 91v; Harley 6038, fol. 28v ('From Katherine docke was lanch'd a Pinke'). I list 23 copies of short versions of 'ffrom Katherines docke was lanched a pincke' in the following appendix of verse texts.

[48] British Library MS Egerton 2230, fol. 71r ('From Katherins dock there launcht a pinke').

one Edward Denny (not the earl of Norwich), now bound into the composite Haslewood-Kingsborough manuscript at the Huntington Library.[49] A few pages after a rare, long version of 'from Cathernes docke theer launch't A pritty Pinke,' the single hand responsible for virtually all of the text in this miscellany copied another lengthy libel on the countess of Somerset, beginning 'She that with Troupes of Bustuary Slaues.' Immediately following this Somerset libel, he transcribed a few of the fifty-two Donne poems that he collected, starting with 'The Curse.'[50] Needless to say, Denny or whoever compiled his miscellany paired two quite distinct poems when he juxtaposed 'She that with Troupes of Bustuary Slaues' and Donne's 'The Curse.' Yet he also accentuated each poem's acerbic tone, relentless pace, and crudeness. Referring to the medical examination that legally established her virginity during her divorce proceedings, the libel charges that Howard 'could wreake within the Armes of lust/yett then be search't and pass without mistrust':

> she that could cheate the Matrimoniall bed
> with A falce stampe Adulterate maydenhead
> and make the Husband thinke the Kisses Chast
> w:^{ch} weer stale Panders to his spouses wast
> she that consisted of all borrowed grace
> could painte her Hart as smothly as her face[51]

The libel represents Howard as supremely deceptive, especially to her trusting husband, who reportedly never suspected her adultery. In the

[49] Beal, *Index*, 1:1:253.

[50] Huntington MS HM 198, pt. 1, pp. 19–21 ('On the Countess of Sommersett,// from Cathernes docke theer launch't A pritty Pinke'), 33–34 ('verses made on the Cou: of Somersett://She that with Troupes of Bustuary Slaues'), 34–35 ('Duns Curse upon him that knew his m://whoesoeuer ghesses, thinkes, or dreames he knows'), 35–37 ('upon the loss of A Braclett://Not that in cullour it was like thy Haire'), 43–44 ('Come Madame come all rest my powers defye'). The only other known copy of the long version of 'from Cathernes docke theer launch't A pritty Pinke' is University of Texas at Austin MS HRC 79, pp. 97–101; transcribed in Norman K. Farmer, Jr., 'Poems from a Seventeenth-Century Manuscript with the hand of Robert Herrick,' *Texas Quarterly*, 16/4 (Winter 1973), 74–79; corrected in P. J. Croft, 'Errata in "Poems from a Seventeenth-Century Manuscript with the Hand of Robert Herrick. Edited, with Introduction and Facing Transcriptions, by Norman K. Farmer, Jr.,"' *Texas Quarterly*, 19/1 (Spring 1976), 165. A complete text of 'She that with Troupes of Bustuary Slaues' follows in an appendix.

[51] Huntington MS HM 198, pt. 1, p. 33.

next poem in Denny's miscellany, Donne's speaker puts a curse on another trusting man, whose mistress, according to the curse, will commit adultery with his enemies and will ruin him.[52] One need not exaggerate the similarities between these two very different poems in order to recognize their uncanny resonance when placed together.

In each of the miscellanies surveyed in this section, manuscript verse collectors chose to copy or bind anti-courtly love poems and Somerset libels together. Even collectors who distinguished the two groups of poems from one another did this. For instance, the London pharmacist Richard Glover (or whoever compiled the manuscript that he owned by 1638) began a miscellany now in the British Library's Egerton collection with poems by Donne (including 'The Curse'), Beaumont (including 'Ad Comitissam Rutlandiæ'), Bastard ('In Gætam'), and others. Later, after half a quire of blank pages, he added a substantial collection of Somerset and other libels.[53] This collector consciously separated the seemingly apolitical literature at the front of his miscellany from the libels at the back. Nevertheless, he chose to put both sets of poems in the same manuscript.

Another collector did more or less the same thing with anti-courtly love poems by others in a miscellany now in the Dyce collection at the Victoria and Albert Museum. He began this anthology with a copy, written partly in code, of Thomas Nashe's 'The choise of valentines,' and included later in the volume the quintessential anti-courtly love poems that Sir John Davies printed alongside Marlowe's translations of Ovid (as well as Davies' epigram 'In Librum').[54] He then concluded the

52 Huntington MS HM 198, pt. 1, pp. 34–35.

53 British Library MS Egerton 2230, fols 8v–9v ('Madam) soe may my verses pleasing bee'), 19v ('Geta, from woll and weauing first began'), 22r–v ('Curse//Who euer guesses, thinkes, or dreames he knowes'), 69r ('Tis painefull rowing gainst ye bigg swolne tide'; 'Ladye chang'd to venus doue'), 69v ('Were itt nott a brutish crueltye'; 'Braue worthy carter that wth thy bravado'), 70r ('The howse of the Howards'); 70v ('Heare lyeth he that once was poore'; 'A page, a knight, a viscount and an Erle'); 71r ('From Katherins dock there launcht a pinke'); 71v ('From Roberts coach to Robins carr'); 72r ('Poore Pilote thou hast lost thy Pinke'); 72v–73r (Richard Corbett's 'Ha^{d}st thou like other s^{rs}, and knights of worth').

54 Victoria and Albert MS Dyce 44, 25.F.39, fols 2r–4r, 57r ('I loue thee not for sacred chastity'), 57r–v ('Fayth wench I cannot courte thy piercing eyes'), 57v ('Sweet wench I loue thee yet I will not sue'), 80r ('Liber doth vaunt how chastly he hath liu'd'), 97r ('From Katharens docke was lanch'd a pinke'; 'I C V R good Mounsier Car'), 98v ('Poore pilot thow art like to loose thy pinke'; 'From Roberts coach to Robins carre').

manuscript with Somerset libels. Although, like several of his contemporaries, this collector preserved anti-courtly love poems and Somerset libels in the same miscellany, he too recognized distinctions between the two poetic genres.

These last two examples may suggest that collectors juxtaposed anti-courtly love poems and Somerset libels only when generic distinctions did not concern them; and that those collectors who arranged their miscellanies according to genre kept the two groups of poems separate. This hypothesis encounters trouble, however, in the pair of Folger and University of Nottingham miscellanies that the previous chapter introduced. Again, the compiler of these manuscripts showed a keener interest in genre than did virtually any of his fellow manuscript verse collectors. He organized each of his miscellanies with generic headings, and fit a wealth of libels on the Somersets under the appropriate rubric 'Satyres.'[55] Accordingly, in both of his miscellanies, he placed Donne's anti-courtly love poem 'The Anagram' in another section.[56] Yet in the 'Satyres' section of the Folger manuscript, he surprisingly included two of Donne's lyrics and highlighted their distinction from conventional love poetry. To 'The broken heart' he gave the heading 'Against Love' and he wrote over 'The triple fool': 'A Lover against himselfe.'[57]

These lyric poems of Donne's openly engage neither satire nor politics, yet the scribe who grouped them with political satires—and who demonstrated such unique attention to genre throughout his miscellanies—may not have simply misread the poems. Just as his

[55] Folger MS V.a.103, fols 66r–v ('A Satyre entituled the Witch; supposed to bee made/against the Lady Francis Countes of Somersett.//Shee with whom troopes of Bustuary slaves'), 68r ('On S Robart Carr Earle of Som[m]ersett.//When Carr in Court a Page at first began'; 'On the Lady Fran: Countesse of Som[m]ersett.//Lady kin to Venus dove'; 'On the same.//Plants ne're likely better prov'd'), 69v ('On the Lady Francis Countesse of Som[m]ersett.//At Katherins docke there launcht a Pinke').

University of Nottingham MS Portland PwV 37, pp. 135–36 ('A Satyre entituled the Witch; supposed to bee made/against the Lady Francis Countes of Somersett.//Shee with whom troopes of Bustuary slaves'), 142 ('On S Rob: Carr Earle of Sommersett.//When Carr in court a Page at first began'; 'On the Lady Francis Countesse of Sommersett.// Lady kin to Venus dove'; 'On the same.//Plants ne're likely better prov'd'; 'On the same.// At Katherins dock there launcht a Pinke').

[56] Folger MS V.a.103, fol. 54r–v ('D Dunne. The praise of an old Woman.//Marry and love thy Flavia, for shee'); University of Nottingham MS Portland PwV 37, pp. 112–13 ('D Dunne. The praise of an old Woman.//Marry and love thy Flavia, for Shee').

[57] Folger MS V.a.103, fols 68v ('Against Love.//Hee is starke madd who ever saies'), 69r ('A Lover against himselfe.//I am two Fooles, I know').

headings indicate, one can position both poems 'against' love poetry: 'The broken heart' opens calling anyone who claims to be in love 'starke madd,' and love makes 'The triple fool' what he is.[58] In other words, the compiler of this miscellany related these Donne poems to the same poet's anti-courtly love poetry. In giving them the individual and section headings that he did, this scribe made explicit what many miscellany compilers were doing in the early seventeenth century: associating poems that Donne wrote 'Against Love' with 'Satyres' on the Overbury affair.

I have already suggested one reason why Donne himself may not have approved of this association between his poetry and Somerset libels. When Donne began to collect his own verse for Somerset, he told Goodyer, 'I know what I shall suffer from many interpretations.'[59] Yet I doubt that he anticipated the interpretations that verse collectors would suggest in the context of the Overbury affair. Likewise, when Donne wrote in a verse letter to another friend, Rowland Woodward, that his muse 'to few, yet to too many'hath showne/How love-song weeds, and Satyrique thornes are growne,' he could not have known to how many verse collectors his poems would eventually be shown, nor that those poems would regularly accompany 'Satyrique thornes' on his future patron.[60] Collectors' recontextualization of Donne's poems in verse miscellanies may have surprised the poet and his friends for an additional reason, though. This possibility requires briefly returning to the late Elizabethan context that Beaumont evoked in 'Ad Comitissam Rutlandiæ,' in addition to considering religious politics.

The recontextualization of Donne's anti-courtly love poems with Somerset libels appears most radical in relation to the recent critical readings of the poems' original politics that I discussed in the previous chapter. Again, Donne scholars have argued that, particularly in poems that resist or parody the conventions of courtly love literature, the poet was mocking the late Elizabethan courtier best known for employing them at court, Sir Walter Ralegh, and may have even shown potentially dangerous irreverence for Elizabeth herself.[61] Well aware of Donne's

58 Folger MS V.a.103, fol. 68v.

59 Donne, *Letters*, 197.

60 *Complete Poetry of John Donne*, 197; ('To Mr. Rowland Woodward' ('Like one who'in her third widdowhood doth professe'), 4–5).

61 Young, '"O my America, my new-found-land"'; Hester, 'Donne's (Re)Annunciation of the Virgin(ia Colony) in *Elegy XIX*'; Guibbory, '"Oh, Let Me Not Serve So."'

Catholic background, these critics have thus suggested that he was showing irreverence to the culture of a protestant court. If Donne scholars have correctly discerned the original politics of his anti-courtly love poems, the collectors who anthologized them among Somerset libels brought about the most dramatic recontextualization considered in this chapter. Whereas Somerset libelers quoted late Elizabethan epigrams and the publisher Lawrence Lisle revived Overbury's early seventeenth-century poem during the scandal surrounding his death, manuscript verse collectors completely reversed the religious politics of anti-courtly love poetry. To be sure, they constructed other aspects of the genre's politics without changing them. For example, collectors continued to oppose the genre to the royal court, and to use it show a measure of disrespect to women at court. At the same time, however, they assimilated poems that arguably registered irreverent detachment from the court of a protestant monarch who persecuted Catholics to libels that attacked a woman from a powerful noble Catholic family—a family that, with its new connection to the royal favorite, had begun to look like a formidable crypto-Catholic faction that would promote pro-Spanish policy at court. After all, as a Catholic woman who married twice, the countess of Somerset cut a decidedly different figure from the protestant virgin queen. She had divorced the son of an honorable, militant, Elizabethan protestant in order to marry the royal favorite who, after the wedding, endorsed a marriage between Prince Charles and the Spanish Infanta.[62] As later libels on this Spanish match and James' next royal favorite George Villiers (who actually traveled with Charles to Spain) make clear, fears of a Catholic contingent at court came to dominate early Stuart manuscript verse miscellanies, and continued the radical recontextualization of anti-courtly love poetry.

[62] Bellany, *The Politics of Court Scandal*, 59, 62–65.

4

The Spanish Match and the History of Sexuality

The religious politics of the Essex divorce and Overbury murder must have outraged many observers of the early Stuart court. Of course, divorce and murder trials focusing on impotence and witchcraft would produce immediate sensation. Yet the religious identities of the players caused enduring, and grave, concern. Frances Howard's first marriage, to Robert Devereux, third earl of Essex, had reconciled her influential Catholic family to the heir of a legendary militant protestant who had consistently promoted war with Catholic Spain. Her divorce and prompt remarriage in 1613 signaled that Howard had refused her honorable English protestant husband and was poised to influence the low-born, Scottish royal favorite, who could in turn sway the king. When, after his wedding, Somerset began to promote a marriage between Prince Charles and Donna Maria Anna of Spain, and to discuss extending toleration to English Catholics, he confirmed the worst fears of many watching these events.[1] A pro-Spanish and so effectively pro-Catholic contingent at court was threatening to undermine both church and state.

Anyone who shared such a fear had cause for much greater alarm, then, in the spring of 1623, when word spread that James I had actually sent Prince Charles and George Villiers, then marquess of Buckingham, to Spain in order to negotiate a royal marriage with the Spanish Infanta. The resurgence of a noble Catholic family at court, and its alliance with the royal favorite, had provided more than enough reason to worry. If an English prince married a Spanish Catholic, and domestic Catholics gained toleration, the reformation would be lost in England.

[1] Bellany, *The Politics of Court Scandal*, 59–65, 70.

By regularly gathering together libels on the Overbury affair and the Spanish match, manuscript verse collectors suggested continuities between the two scandals. And by collecting these libels among other popular manuscript verses, including anti-courtly love poems, they surrounded these usually older, less topical texts with religious and political sentiments that had started to dominate miscellanies: nostalgia for the assuredly protestant Queen Elizabeth paired with disdain for, and fear of, Catholic women such as the countess of Somerset and the Spanish Infanta. Indeed, manuscript verse collectors joined in linking the two sentiments. Among the texts that they consistently anthologized, nostalgia for Elizabeth reached its greatest exaggeration in a set of Spanish match libels that represent her as a protestant saint. These verses consist of a petition from commoners to 'Saint Elizabeth'; a prayer that the commons ask her to mediate to God; and finally an answer-poem written in Saint Elizabeth's understanding yet demanding voice from heaven. The first section of this chapter argues that, with these Spanish match libels, manuscript verse collectors assimilated the genre of anti-courtly love poetry to a polemical neo-Elizabethanism directed against Catholic interests.

While such Spanish match libels continued to revere a legendary protestant queen and to oppose Catholic women, others introduced new elements to early Stuart manuscript culture. Virtually all of the political verses considered in this study thus far have reserved the brunt of their ridicule for women. Although Spanish match libels concern a Catholic woman, some of them turn their attention to a man and, rather without precedent in libels on early Stuart favorites, issues of *male* sexuality. George Villiers succeeded Robert Carr, earl of Somerset, as King James' royal favorite and eventually became the first duke of Buckingham. All of the similarities between Somerset and Buckingham make it surprising to find how differently libels represent the two favorites. James clearly favored both men in part because of their good looks. Each certainly enjoyed unrivalled access to and influence with the king. And each has led historians, with reason, to suspect an erotic or even sexual element to his relationship with James. Nevertheless, libelers did not focus on, or even mention, any such sexual relationship between Somerset and James; again, Somerset libels generally focus on the gender and sexuality of the countess, not the earl, of Somerset. Yet with Buckingham, the sexuality of the favorite—and, in turn, the king—became a central concern.

I suggest that this shift in the way libelers and verse collectors represented royal favorites marks a significant moment not only in the political and literary history of early seventeenth-century England, but also in the history of sexuality. For it shows the producers and consumers of political literature initiating a practice of worryingly scrutinizing same-sex relations at court that were hardly unprecedented. Erotic royal favoritism had emerged considerably earlier in the royal courts of Europe, England, and even James, yet early Stuart libelers did not mention it until the Spanish match. Their emboldened attitude toward court sexuality may have found its most eloquent and provocative articulation in a parody of Ben Jonson's Buckingham-sponsored court masque, *Gypsies Metamorphosed*, usually called 'The Five Senses.' As the second half of the chapter shows, 'The Five Senses' provided manuscript verse collectors with a fine example of literary appropriation that they in turn used to recontextualize anti-courtly love poetry. By surrounding examples of the genre with such Buckingham libels, collectors continued to oppose it to the court, yet redirected its parody of the courtly style of love to a court redefined by King James' love for Buckingham.

ELIZABETH I AND THE INFANTA IN SPANISH MATCH LIBELS

According to one verse collector, on '22 Iune of 1623' a copy of a poetic libel 'was founde in the hand of Queen Elizabeths tombe at West [minster].'[2] Less sure of the date, the hand responsible for another copy concurred that it had been 'put into the hand of Queene Elizabeths statue in Westminster by an vnknowne person.'[3] The author or authors of the libel addressed its first part 'To the blessed S:^{t} Eliza: of most famous memory' from 'her now most wretched and most Contemptible, the Com[m]ons of poore distressed England.' In a patently

[2] Folger MS V.a.275, p. 1.

[3] Bodleian MS Malone 23, p. 32. Except where noted, quotations from the commons' petitionary exchange are from this manuscript—whose pages were rebound in the wrong order after they were numbered.

nostalgic reconstruction of her reign, the collective speakers ask Saint Elizabeth to show them mercy in heaven, as she did on earth:

> O be not nowe lesse gratious then of old:
> When each distressed Vassall might be bold
> Into thyne open hand to putt his greife
> And thence receiue tymely and faire releife
> Be not lesse good, lesse gratious then before[4]

When Elizabeth reigned on earth, the speakers claim, her subjects could boldly put their complaints 'Into thyne open hand.' Now, though, they must resort to placing them in the hand of her tomb monument secretly. For, while they expect continuity between Elizabeth's earthly and heavenly courts, the speakers of the libel have recently become all too aware of what distinguishes their heavenly king from an earthly monarch (excepting Elizabeth, of course).

> In heauen the supplications of the poore
> Are heard assoone as suits of greatest kings....
>
> Where noe corruption, noe fraud, noe bribe
> Noe griping lawyer noe Avaritious scribe
> Noe fauorite, noe parasite, noe Mynion
> Cann leade, or alter the opinion
> Of that great Chancellour,[5]

The libel represents God's divine court as empty of all the characters and characteristics of an early modern court. Most pointedly, God has 'Noe fauorite.'

In the summer of 1623, anyone with the wherewithal to acquire this libel could have had no doubt as to which earthly king and royal favorite it invoked, and what recent developments provided evidence of their corruption. For in February of that year, King James had sent Prince Charles and Buckingham to Catholic Spain to secure the hand of the Spanish Infanta in marriage. For James, this match logically followed an agenda of pacifist ecumenism, as it offered to balance the 1613 marriage of his daughter Elizabeth to the Elector Palatine Frederick V, a Reformed Protestant. But few English protestants recognized any

[4] Bodleian MS Malone 23, p. 32.
[5] Bodleian MS Malone 23, pp. 32–33.

continuity between the two marriages; indeed, most must have feared that James was betraying both his daughter and the true church. A great many English protestants celebrated Princess Elizabeth's marriage to Frederick as 'a pan-European Protestant alliance against popery.'[6] Yet James had appeared to be breaking that alliance since 1620 or 1621, when he refused to intervene as Catholics ran Frederick and Elizabeth first out of Bohemia, and eventually off all their lands. James had allowed Catholics to defeat protestants and even his own family on the continent, and now seemed ready to welcome them into England.

In the context of the Spanish match, then, James could hardly have appreciated the libel's implicit comparison of him with a predecessor who had defeated the Spanish Armada.[7] Indeed, the speakers of the commons' petition to Saint Elizabeth tell her that their troubles began precisely when she died and James replaced her on the throne: 'When heauen was pleas'd honor'd soule to call the hence.... oh then begun our feares.'[8] Yet the glorious figure of Saint Elizabeth poses an additional contrast—with the Spanish Infanta. The emergence of this Catholic woman in manuscript miscellanies continued the process of recontextualizing anti-courtly love poetry. To be sure, the Infanta does not appear in the commons' petitions. Moreover, the Infanta never actually arrived in England (which made the return of Charles and Buckingham a cause for widespread jubilation).[9] The author or authors of the petitions may have considered it unwise to slander a woman who very well could marry the prince. Yet he, or they, also regarded the Spanish match as a literally unspeakable consequence of James' misdirected foreign policy. In any event, and despite its silence regarding her, this libel has everything to do with the Infanta. It dates, from internal evidence, to the marriage negotiations with Spain, and enumerates a number of Jacobean tribulations that culminated in the proposed match with the Infanta.[10]

[6] Diarmaid MacCulloch, *Reformation: Europe's House Divided 1490–1700* (London: Penguin, 2003), 490.

[7] 'James was simply condemned by the comparison.' McRae, *Literature, Satire and the Early Stuart State*, 96.

[8] Bodleian MS Malone 23, p. 33.

[9] Thomas Cogswell, *The Blessed Revolution: English Politics and the Coming of War, 1621–1624* (Cambridge: Cambridge University Press, 1989).

[10] Bellany and McRae, 'Early Stuart Libels,' Niv1. Internal dating seizes upon these lines: 'thrise seauen sonnes haue worne/Their Summer suits since wee begann to mourne', 'this one and twentie yeares.... Halfe fortie yeares and more are gone' (Bodleian MS Malone 23, pp. 36, 44).

The Spanish Infanta's national and religious difference from Queen Elizabeth provided more than enough reason to plead with heaven for mercy and deliverance. The libel hints at the religious difference between 'S:^{t} Eliza:' and the Infanta by reviving the long-standing relationship between Queen Elizabeth and the Virgin Mary. Over the course of Elizabeth's reign, her subjects increasingly applied Catholic Marian iconography to the monarch, as if to replace the Virgin Mary with the virgin queen in the English protestant imagination. Likewise, as Catharine Gray has noted in her discussion of this libel, the vocabulary of Marian devotion 'celebrates the very kind of competitive anti-Catholic assimilation of Catholic images into a cult of Protestant royalty that characterized Elizabeth's later self-representations.'[11] Indeed, the speakers of the libel promise to 'make the name of blest Eliza/Equall the Auies of that great Maria' and to build monuments that 'shall make proud Roome [Rome]/On pilgrimage to come, and att thy shrine/Offer their guifts as to A thing diuine.'[12] Insofar as such Marian representations of Elizabeth eclipsed the Virgin Mary, the libel engaged a long tradition. Yet, in the context of the Spanish match, this appropriation of Catholic imagery was also doing something new: it was hinting at the Spanish Infanta and so suggesting a stark contrast between an English protestant saint and a Spanish Catholic princess. With Charles and Buckingham negotiating a marriage in Spain, in other words, the libel's representation of Saint Elizabeth purposely outshone not only the Virgin Mary but also the Spanish Infanta. This libel, in other words, ironically appropriated Catholic iconography for openly anti-Catholic purposes.

In an appropriation of another feature of Catholicism, the speakers of the libel petition Saint Elizabeth as an intercessor or mediator—a traditional role for Catholic saints and especially the Virgin Mary which protestants generally eliminated from their religious practice. The speakers of the first part of the libel ask Saint Elizabeth to relay a

[11] Catharine Gray, 'Forward Writers/Critical Readers: Women and Counterpublic Spheres in Seventeenth-Century England' (PhD diss., State University of New York at Buffalo, 2001), 216–17. See also Gray, *Women Writers and Public Debate in 17th-Century Britain* (New York: Palgrave, 2007), 152. For an earlier, opposed, reading of the libel's Catholic imagery, see Ann Baynes Coiro, 'Milton and Class Identity: The Publication of *Areopagitica* and the 1645 *Poems*,' *Journal of Medieval and Renaissance Studies*, 22 (1992), 261–89.

[12] Bodleian MS Malone 23, pp. 33, 36.

prayer to God, to 'giue it to his hands that cann relieue vs.'[13] This prayer to God comes in the form of the libel's second, longer section, which presumably accompanied the first poem in the hand of Elizabeth's tomb monument: 'The most humble Petition of the/nowe most miserable the Com[m]ons of/long afflicted England.' Much of this prayer pleads with God to 'Awake thy mercie lett thy Iustice slumber' in response to the nation's collective sins.[14] The specifics of these sins emerge only toward the end of the poem.

> Was there A nation in the Vniuerse
> More daring, once more bold, more stout, more ferce
> And is there nowe vpon the earths broad face
> Any that cann be reckoned halfe soe base
> Is there A people soe much scorn'd dispised
> Soe laught soe trodd on soe vassaliz'd
> Wee that all Europe envy'd, wee euen wee
> Are slaues to those wee kept in slauerie

Unsurprisingly, given the context of the Catholic defeat of the Palatinate, the sins of the English turn out to be sins of omission: military omission.

> The bold and hardie Brittaines conquered are
> Without a drumb, a sword or sound of warr[15]

Repentant of their nation's failure to defend their protestant brothers on the continent, the speakers of the libel regard the Spanish match as defeat without a fight.

Most manuscript copies of the commons' petitions conclude with a third section: 'A Gratious answere from that/blessed Saint to her whilome/Subiects, with a diuine admo =/nition and a prophetiq con =/ clusion.' Before concluding with her prophecy, Saint Elizabeth confesses 'the truth of all' the commons' complaints and hopes for 'A period to your miseries.' But she also tells them that 'first your infinite iniquities/ Must haue an end.'[16] In another reference to the religious issues of the Spanish match, Saint Elizabeth represents the beginning of her reign in the terms of reformation propaganda. Directly addressing the English, she says:

13 Bodleian MS Malone 23, p. 33.
14 Bodleian MS Malone 23, p. 38.
15 Bodleian MS Malone 23, p. 13.
16 Bodleian MS Malone 23, p. 14.

> I found you like A humble scattered flocke
> Your very soules beating against the Rocke
> Of ignorance, and sup[er]stition[17]

The libel represents pre-reformation England as one of ignorance and superstition. The word 'ignorance' tellingly reappears in the prophecy at the end of the libel, among the tribulations that England may expect to suffer:

> The Gospell sunne shall loose his glorious light
> And ignorance as blacke as darkest night
> Shall spread her sable wings about this Isle
> And Babilons proud whore once more defile
> Albions white Cliffes,[18]

The light of the gospel will go out; ignorance will envelope the island; and the whore of Babylon—a standard signifier of the Catholic Church in reformation polemic—will 'once more defile' England. In the midst of the marriage negotiations with Catholic Spain, Saint Elizabeth, and through her the author or authors of this libel, were predicting that Catholicism would once again defile and darken the English church and state.

Again, the libels to and from the commons do not explicitly identify the Spanish Infanta. So this mention of the whore of Babylon does not necessarily refer to her. On the other hand, though, most English protestants would have recognized the Infanta as the individual poised to bring about the horrific developments described above. Even if they did not consider her the whore of Babylon, many would have recognized that the Infanta would bring the whore of Babylon along with her to England. Collectors of both the commons' petitionary exchange and other libels that do identify the Infanta surely made this connection. Another Spanish match libel, a song commonly found in the same sources as the petitions, features the Infanta at the very beginning, calling her in some copies 'the Spanish Lady' or in others 'the Golden Ladye,' referring to the dowry that she supposedly offered.[19]

17 Bodleian MS Malone 23, p. 16.

18 Bodleian MS Malone 23, pp. 46–47.

19 All quotations of 'All the newes thats stirringe now' are from Bodleian MS Malone 19, pp. 32–33. The 'Spanish lady' versions include Bodleian MS Rawl. D.1048, fol. 76r; Huntington MS HM 46323, fol. 9v–10v; and West Yorkshire Archive Service, Bradford MS 32D86/34, pp. 52–53. I list other copies of the libel in the following appendix of verse texts.

On the Spanish
match

All the newes thats stirringe now
Is of the Golden Ladye:
The Pope as yet will not agree
King Iames should bee her Dadye.

This opening facetiously casts the Spanish match as a custody battle over an infant. Although by no means scurrilous, this libel offers an irreverent representation of the Infanta—in a song that nevertheless considers the Spanish match a quite serious issue. Perhaps the author or authors of this song decided to feature the Infanta so prominently because it seemed to them 'doubtfull' that the marriage would take place:

And those false harted Englishmen,
Which wrought with him for Spaine,
Doe stand and scratch because the match
Doth doubtfull yet remaine.

Just as the commoners in the petitionary exchange presumed that loss of bravery had kept England from the Thirty Years' War, the speaker (or singer) of this libel considers the Englishmen who accompanied Charles to Spain and 'all that are Hispanioliz'd' to be 'false harted.'

But God preserve our Kinge & Prince,
A plague uppon their foes,
And all that are Hispanioliz'd
And would their Country loose.

The libel groups the 'foes' of the royal family here with 'all that are Hispanioliz'd,' all who for the sake of an alliance with Spain 'would their Country loose.' Lest there be any doubt as to the religious persuasion of such hispanophiles, the libel elsewhere specifies that Buckingham and other proponents of the match 'Us'd their best trickes with Catholiques/ To bring our Prince to Spain.' The song represents Catholics, hispanophiles, and a Spanish Catholic princess with that standard technique of poetic libelers: irreverence.

With such irreverent representations of the Infanta, paired with serious portrayals of the consequences of the match, manuscript verse collectors continued and intensified the process of recontextualizing anti-courtly love poetry. As with Frances Howard, collectors placed the Infanta where she became a target for the irreverence common to libels, anti-courtly love poems, and manuscript verse miscellanies in general. Yet, as a potential bride not to a royal favorite but to the prince, and as a representative of the country that many considered England's mortal enemy, the Infanta posed much more serious threats than had the countess of Somerset. Whereas the Howard family's opponents during the Overbury affair feared that English Catholics would use their influence with the royal favorite to promote a marriage alliance with Spain and toleration at home, the Infanta literally embodied, and made imminent, the possibility both of this alliance and of such toleration. The Infanta, in other words, represented the gravest English fears of a Catholic plot in 1623. In reaction to such a threatening figure, libelers greatly intensified early Stuart neo-Elizabethanism, especially by fashioning the commons' prayers to a paradoxically sainted Queen Elizabeth. For their considerable part, manuscript verse collectors circulated Spanish match libels and preserved them in miscellanies, where these verses on affairs of state modified the political associations of some of collectors' other favorite texts. As my second chapter has shown, even those collectors who most directly opposed Donne's anti-courtly love poetry to the Elizabethan court did not show or encourage any disrespect for Elizabeth. The next section returns to some of these collectors in order to show how, with the addition of libels that deify Elizabeth, they insisted on according unprecedented honor to the legendary protestant monarch. Furthermore, collectors subtly redirected the irreverence of anti-courtly love poetry toward the Spanish Infanta and the early Stuart court.

THE EFFECT OF SPANISH MATCH LIBELS IN MISCELLANIES

The Skipwith manuscript at the British Library offers an example of how Spanish match libels modified the political character of a miscellany. As mentioned in the previous chapter, this manuscript consists of several distinct sets of gatherings, beginning with five quires devoted to Donne's elegies and lyrics, and proceeding to six more that include Donne's satires, one of Beaumont's anti-courtly love poems, and the most restrained of the Somerset libels (the pro and con verses on Frances Howard headed 'Petitio' and 'Respontio'). To these gatherings, the Skipwiths added several others, one of which includes the commons' petitions to Saint Elizabeth and to Jehovah (without Elizabeth's response).[20] If the family members who produced and read the first eleven gatherings read into Donne's parodies of courtly love a response to the Elizabethan court, as did the collectors that I considered in Chapter 2, those who added the commons' petitionary exchange to the family poetry collection effectively removed the possibility of such a reading. Laughing at Elizabeth's court could have held little attraction and made little sense once she had become a saint. By adding the commons' petitions, the Skipwiths modified the political tenor of their family poetry collection.

Similarly, the scribe responsible for the two generically-headed miscellanies at the Folger and the University of Nottingham changed the political context of his core group of poems with the Spanish match libels that he added to just one of them.[21] He included no Spanish match libels in the Folger manuscript but added all three libels in the petitionary exchange to his fuller miscellany now at Nottingham, which also features a set of Donne's anti-courtly love poems. Among the poetic texts in the Nottingham manuscript's section of 'Panegyricks,' the scribe included three by Donne that model praise of a sort that hardly qualifies as conventional panegyric: the quintessential contreblazon on the ugly Flavia, 'The Anagram'; the ultimately moderate libertine poem 'In ye Praise of Change in a Lover,' usually entitled 'Change'; and the paradoxical encomium to a mature, if not aged, woman, 'The Autumnall.'[22] Even if Donne composed his 'Elogy of an Autumnall Face' as a sincere epideictic poem (which I consider most likely), these three poems together display Donne's characteristic antagonism to poetic convention, especially courtly love conventions. As I argued in Chapter 2, the

20 British Library MS Add. 25707, fols 76r ('To the famous S:^{r} of blessed memorye/Elizabeth, the Humble petic[i]on of her/now wretched, and Contemptible, the/Comons of England.//If S:^{ts} in heauen can either see or heare'), 77r–78r ('To the most heigh and myghty ye most pious and mercifull/the cheife Chancello^{r} of heauen, and onely Iudge of Earth/the most humble petic[i]on of the poore distressed Com[m]ons/of longe afflicted England.//If bleeding soules deiected hearts finde grace').

21 Folger MS V.a.103; University of Nottingham MS Portland PwV 37.

22 University of Nottingham MS Portland PwV 37, pp. 114–17.

respect that this collector showed to Ralegh and especially Elizabeth effectively prohibited his readers from opposing Donne's anti-courtly love poetry to Elizabeth's court.[23] When he added the full set of commons' petitions to one of the last sections of the Nottingham manuscript, headed 'Serious Poemes,' he strengthened this prohibition, but also redirected his volume's nostalgia for Elizabeth to the religious politics of the Spanish match crisis.[24] Especially since the collector deems them 'Serious Poemes' in this miscellany, the commons' prayers to Saint Elizabeth and Jehovah refer back to the epitaphs on Elizabeth that begin the anthology. In fact, the libels assimilate the epitaphs' proper respect for a recently deceased monarch to polemical invocations of that monarch composed two decades later. And they suggest that, if this verse collector associated Donne's negative representations of women with a public figure, she was not Elizabeth but the Spanish Catholic woman who drove the commons to petition Elizabeth as a saint.

In the hands of other manuscript verse collectors, the commons' petitions recontextualized not only Donne's but also Sir John Davies' and Francis Beaumont's anti-courtly love poetry. A manuscript apparently owned by Henry Lawson, now in the Bodleian's English Poetry collection, features several Donne poems, including 'The Anagram,' and, of the commons' petitionary exchange, only Elizabeth's response.[25] To this miscellany one of several hands added Davies' 'ffaire wench I cannot court,' one of the anti-courtly love poems that first appeared in print anonymously in Davies' and Marlowe's late Elizabethan *Epigrammes and Elegies*.[26] The compilers of this miscellany fittingly gathered together Donne's facetious praise of the antitype of the Petrarchan mistress with Davies' refusal of the arts of the courtly lover and brusque offer instead to '——the[e] soundly.' Yet they placed among these late Elizabethan anti-courtly love poems the prophecy to English commoners from a

[23] University of Nottingham MS Portland PwV 37, p. 1.

[24] University of Nottingham MS Portland PwV 37, pp. 243–52.

[25] Bodleian MS Eng. poet. e.14, fols 29v–30r ('D^r: Dun://Marry & Love thy Flavia; for she'), 49v–52r ('The fayned Answer of Q. Eliz: to her subiects/with a divine admonition & prophetick/Conclusion//Your bold Petitions Mortalls I have seene').

[26] Bodleian MS Eng. poet. e.14, fol. 75v. Davies and Marlowe, *Epigrammes and Elegies*, sig. D4r–v. See Fredson Bowers, 'The Early Editions of Marlowe's *Ovid's Elegies*,' *Studies in Bibliography*, 25 (1972), 150–73.

sainted Queen Elizabeth. In the company of such a libel, and in the context of the Spanish match, Donne's and Davies' rejections of the courtly love associated with Elizabeth's court could hardly indicate any disrespect for the protestant saint.

Similarly, Edward Denny, or whoever compiled the Huntington miscellany that he used repeatedly, added Francis Beaumont's anti-courtly love poem 'Ad Comitissam Rutlandiæ' to the collection of Donne poems and libels that includes one of the commons' petitions.[27] As discussed in the previous chapter, when Beaumont facetiously likened love poets to a ridiculous tailor in love with Queen Elizabeth, he suggested a certain tension between anti-courtly love poetry and the Elizabethan court. Yet the compiler of Denny's anthology placed examples of the genre by Beaumont and others in the company of a heavenly, rather than an earthly, Elizabeth, and so effectively erased any such tension. Indeed, he immersed Beaumont's and Donne's anti-courtly love poems in a manuscript environment populated by the figures who were animating the early Stuart political imagination. 'Ad Comitissam Rutlandiæ' follows not only Donne texts but also a series of verses on a spectrum of religious identities that, in the context of the Spanish match, had come to represent particularly antagonistic political commitments: 'A Protestant'; 'A Papist'; 'The true Puritan without disguise.'[28] Verses and prose characters on such religious figures abound in the miscellanies of this period, and their mockery of both puritans and Catholics as extremists provides important evidence that the Thirty Years' War and the Spanish match concerned more early modern verse collectors than could have possibly occupied the ideological fringes. In the heyday of early Stuart verse collecting, in other words, even collectors who, like the compiler of Denny's miscellany, positioned themselves as moderates, in between

27 Huntington MS HM 198, pt. 1, pp. 43–44 ('Come Madame come all rest my powers defye'), 62–63 ('To ower blessed S:^{t} Eliz: of famous memory ye Humble Petition of/her now most wretched & most Contemptable ye Comons of England://If Saints in Heauen can eyther see or heare'), 64 ('Elegy 6to//As the sweet sweat of Roses in A still'), 205–6 ('fletcher: to ye Countes of Rutland.//Maddam soe may my uerses pleasing bee').

28 Huntington MS HM 198, pt. 1, pp. 180–84 ('A Protestant//Soe will the Formalist be cald:'), 184 ('A Papist//A Romanist is such another thing'), 184–85 ('Religion//Religion the most sacred power on earth'), 185–89 ('The true Puritan without disguise//A Puritan is such A monstrous thing').

the extremes of Catholicism and puritanism, came to entertain the increasingly radical political views of poetic libels. In Denny's and others' anthologies, such radical politics recontextualized both Donne's and Beaumont's anti-courtly love poems.

In the miscellanies surveyed immediately above, I suggest that even verse collectors who included just one part of the commons' petitionary exchange in their miscellanies helped to immerse anti-courtly love poems in political and religious contexts quite unlike those in which these poets had written. Predictably, then, one of the greatest collectors of Spanish match libels did so as well. The professional scribe of the elaborate Rawlinson Poetry folio introduced in Chapter 2 went so far as to reapply the genre's irreverence to the Spanish Infanta. In his very neat folio, Spanish match libels surround anti-courtly love poetry. In originally loose gatherings that he then had bound together, this scribe transcribed all three texts in the exchange between the commons and Saint Elizabeth; some of Donne's quintessential anti-courtly love poems (including 'The Anagram' and 'To his Mistress going to bed,' in separate quires); and the other Spanish match libel that I have discussed ('All the cheife talk is now/Of the golden Lady,' here with a heading that indicates that it was sung 'TO THE/tune of Vir=/ginia').[29] When he arranged the loose gatherings for binding, the compiler placed five additional Spanish match libels just a few folios after Donne's 'To his Mistress going to bed' and 'The Bracelet.'[30] Like 'All the cheife talk is now,' these other match libels openly criticize the Spanish Infanta. One of the libels, which

[29] Bodleian MS Rawl. poet. 160, fols 16r–v ('TO T[H]E BLESSED ELIZA/OF FAMOVS MEMORIE/The humble petic[i]on of the/wretched & most contemptible/ the poore com[m]ons of England//If Saints in heaven can either see or heare'), 16v–18v ('TO T[H]E MOST/high and mightiest the/most iust and yet most/mercifull the greatest/Chancellor of heaven and/the cheife Iudg of ye earth.//If bleeding hearts deiected soules find grace'), 18v–20v ('A GRATIOVS/Answeare fro[m] the blessed S.^{t}/to her whilome subiects w.th a/devine admonition and a/propheticall conclusion://Your bould petition mortalls I haue seene'), 104r–v ('Marry and loue thy fflauia for she'), 171r–v ('AN ELIGIE//Come madam come, all rest my powers defy'), 171v–72v ('VPON/A gold cheyne lent/and loste.//Not that in colo^{r} it was like thy haire'), 177v–78r ('TO THE/tune of Vir=/=ginia.//All the cheife talk is now').

[30] Bodleian MS Rawl. poet. 160, fols 176v–77r ('WHOOPE/doe me noe harme/ good man//Our eagle is flowne to a place yet vnknown'), 177v–78r ('TO THE/tune of Vir=/=ginia.//All the cheife talk is now'), 178v–79v ('A SONG//Heaven bless king Iames our Ioy'), 179v–80v ('A SONG//The Scottishmen be beggars yet'), 180v–81v ('VPON/Prince Charles his/arrivall from/Spaine Oct[ober]/5:th 1623.//The fift of August and the fift'), 181v–82r ('A SONG//In Sussex late since Eighty Eight').

begins 'The Scottishmen be beggars yet,' refuses to give the Infanta an honorific title, and somewhat flippantly calls her 'ye Spanish girle.'[31] Likewise, a song 'VPON/Prince Charles his/arrivall from Spaine Oct-[ober]/5:th 1623' reports rather irreverently that the prince 'went into Spayne to fetch a thing.'[32] Up to this line of verse, the libelous representations of the Infanta that I have cited have remained cautiously irreverent: not very respectful but by no means scurrilous. Yet in early modern English, and especially in the poems that the compilers of manuscript verse miscellanies preferred, the word 'thing' commonly referred to genitalia. Now, if this miscellany referred so crassly to the Infanta only once, one might conclude that this instance of the word 'thing' connotes nothing sexual. A nearby poem makes a similar reference, however. A song, set to the tune of numerous bawdy songs, 'WHOOPE/doe me noe harme/good man,' begins by reporting that 'Our eagle is flowne to a place yet vnknown/To meet with the Phœnix of Spaine,' and concludes with an overtly sexualized portrayal of this meeting: 'o^{r} Northpole shalbe put in ye hole/of the Southerne inferior beare.'[33]

These obscene references to the Spanish Infanta's 'thing' and 'hole' constitute the most sexually explicit representations of the princess in Spanish match libels and, indeed, in manuscript verse miscellanies. Moreover, these word choices complement similar references in the anti-courtly love poems that the scribe of this Rawlinson Poetry manuscript transcribed. Consider Donne's obscene description of Flavia in this collector's copy of 'The Anagram,' 'Whome Dildoes bedstaues & the veluet glasse/would be as loth to touch as Ioseph was.'[34] Also, just a few leaves before the songs in the Rawlinson Poetry manuscript, Donne's 'To his Mistress going to bed' famously features not only the disrobing of the speaker's mistress but also, at the very center of the poem, the speaker's erection, or 'flesh vpright.'[35] To be sure, Spanish match libels and Donne's elegies differ in many important respects. The

31 Bodleian MS Rawl. poet. 160, fols 179v.

32 Bodleian MS Rawl. poet. 160, fols 180v.

33 Bodleian MS Rawl. poet. 160, fols 176v–77r. Tom Cogswell mentions that the poet responsible for these lines 'could scarcely contain his delight with the thought that "our north pole shall bee put in the hole/Of the Southerne Inferior beare."' *The Blessed Revolution*, 46.

34 Bodleian MS Rawl. poet. 160, fol. 104v.

35 Bodleian MS Rawl. poet. 160, fol. 171r.

libels satirize identifiable individuals; plus, people could sing them. Donne's elegies, on the other hand, do not lend themselves to singing. Furthermore, if 'The Anagram' and 'To his Mistress going to bed' originally satirized anyone, they did so with such subtlety that their early Stuart collectors and readers could not have recognized their original targets. Yet neither this scribe nor his readers needed to overlook such distinctions in order to notice that their common focus on genitalia and their presence in the same miscellany form a relationship between anti-courtly love poems and Spanish match libels.

The libels that focus on the Spanish Infanta, and the miscellanies that feature these verses among anti-courtly love poems, conclude one major strain of this book's argument. Much of this book has focused on representations of women, specifically noble and royal women. I have argued that manuscript verse collectors associated the parodies of late Elizabethan court poetry with attacks on women who threatened to influence early Stuart courts, especially the countess of Somerset and the Spanish Infanta. If anti-courtly love poets originally hinted at any disrespect for Elizabeth, manuscript verse collectors were then maintaining some consistency in the genre's class politics and gender politics. In other words, they were rather consistently opposing the genre to powerful women at court, or poised to join the court. Yet, in terms of religion, verse collectors would have been dramatically altering the politics of anti-courtly love poetry. They grouped poems that registered subtle criticism of the court of a protestant queen with slander on women of quite different religious associations: the Catholic wife of a royal favorite and a prince's Catholic fiancée. The collectors of the Spanish match libels considered in this section made the religious distinction between these women quite clear. They also completed a major phase in the recontextualization of anti-courtly love poetry by aligning poems that responded playfully to the court of a protestant queen to attacks on powerful Catholic women.

Yet Spanish match libels also contributed to a new phase in the political recontextualization of anti-courtly love poetry. The authors of these libels worried not only about the Infanta. They criticized a range of court figures, including the royal favorite and even, on occasion, the king. In turning their attention from a Spanish Catholic woman to the English king and his favorite, libelers did something unprecedented in the popular verse dedicated to early Stuart court scandal. They kept focusing on sexuality but, rather than remaining primarily concerned with women's sexuality, also began to consider issues of *male* and *royal* sexuality. As the next section demonstrates, libelers' and collectors' new interest in same-sex relations at court would have consequences not only for the reception of anti-courtly love poetry but also for political history and even, arguably, the history of sexuality.

'THE FIVE SENSES' IN THE HISTORY OF SEXUALITY

While the Spanish Infanta necessarily played a prominent role in Spanish match libels, an ultimately more contentious character emerged in even some of the poems and manuscripts discussed above: George Villiers, first duke of Buckingham, who would eventually serve as royal favorite to both James I and Charles I. As mentioned in the previous chapter, a determinedly protestant or 'patriot' court faction led by William Herbert, third earl of Pembroke, and George Abbot, archbishop of Canterbury, had orchestrated the young Villiers' replacement of Robert Carr, earl of Somerset, as royal favorite. Again, both radical and moderate protestants had opposed Somerset, in part, because of his alliance with a powerful Catholic family and his support for a Spanish match. Therefore, Buckingham must have bitterly disappointed those who had put him in power when he came to endorse the same Spanish match, going so far as to accompany Charles to Spain.

Thus Buckingham came to demonstrate greater similarity to his predecessor than his initial supporters had hoped. Of course, the court faction that masterminded Buckingham's ascendance must have planned for him to operate like Somerset in several respects. Its members chose him for his good looks, his fine dancing, and his general ability to replace Somerset in the king's affections. So, to any of them aware of the emotionally intense and possibly sexual relationship between Somerset and James, Buckingham's similar relationship with the king could not have come as much surprise. For one, Pembroke certainly understood the eroticism that had developed between monarch and favorite. He and his younger brother had numbered among the king's first English favorites. Furthermore, he had watched in frustration as Somerset superseded him in the king's affections. When James appointed Somerset lord chamberlain instead of Pembroke, Pembroke retaliated by successfully promoting the young Villiers at court, going so far as to loan him the clothes that a new favorite would need in order to turn the king's attention from Somerset.[36] Pembroke and, if only through him, his collaborators in this venture surely understood the role that Villiers would play with the king.

Despite the many similarities between Somerset and Buckingham, the authors and collectors of early Stuart libels made a major distinction between James' two great favorites. After ignoring the sexually charged relationship between Somerset and James in virtually all of the scurrilous poems on the Overbury affair, they began to criticize the sexuality of Buckingham and, rather more cautiously and dangerously, the king. Moreover, they had found unremarkable the subject of Buckingham's sexuality for the first several years of his exceptional rise, until the royal favorite endorsed the revived Spanish match negotiations. Perhaps the Spanish match simply coincided with revelations or rumors that Buckingham had developed a more openly erotic or sexual rapport with James than had his predecessors. Yet, to the strident anti-Catholics who had promoted Buckingham such as Pembroke and Abbot, his endorsement of the Spanish match would have come as a greater shock than his adoption or even his intensification of the erotics of Jacobean royal favoritism. Similarly, the unknown author of one of the first and most eloquent poetic libels to sexualize Buckingham seems to have been responding not so much to disclosures of the royal favorite's sexuality as to news of his religious politics.[37] To be sure, the libel usually headed 'The Five Senses' criticizes Buckingham's sexuality at length. And this chapter ultimately proposes that the poem has played a more significant role in the history of sexuality than scholars have recognized. Yet it also proposes that 'The Five Senses' can make its greatest contribution to the history of sexuality in the local context of early Stuart libels, and in the manuscript environments that it shares with a certain anti-courtly love poem.

[36] Paul Hammond, *Figuring Sex between Men from Shakespeare to Rochester* (Oxford: Clarendon, 2002), 128–29, 136–37; Roger Lockyer, 'Villiers, George, first duke of Buckingham (1592–1628),' *ODNB*; Stater, 'Herbert,' *ODNB*.

[37] While acknowledging that Folger MS V.a.345, p. 59 ascribes it to one 'Iames Iohnson,' Andrew McRae has revived William Drummond's candidacy for the authorship of the poem, relying on an ascription to the famous poet in Bodleian MS Eng. poet. c.50, fol. 25r–v, and admitting that 'critical opinion is generally against' the attribution to Drummond. Bellany and McRae, 'Early Stuart Libels,' L8; *Literature, satire and the early Stuart state*, 75–82.

In the archive of libels on early Stuart royal favorites, 'The Five Senses' emerges as one of the very first to allege that a royal favorite had a sexual relationship with another man, and one of the few to suggest that the king did as well. Thus, in its generic and material contexts, this poem shows how, and ultimately why, early Stuart libelers began to censure a mode of sexuality that they had previously treated as unremarkable. As Chapter 3 has proposed, these poets had no problem attacking court sexuality or royal favoritism. But they did not remark upon James' allegedly sexual relationships with either of his two great favorites until 'The Five Senses.' When its author finally brought up the issue of same-sex relations at court, he offered a simultaneously reactionary and subversive response. His attack on the royal favorite helped to initiate an unprecedented subgenre of early Stuart libels, which would have a major effect on Buckingham's career and ultimately even on the political history of early modern England. Furthermore, this libeler's willingness to consider the king's natural body as a desiring and, so, potentially sinful one would help to begin the ultimately revolutionary process of demystifying early Stuart kingship.

'The Five Senses' issues a parodic, line-by-line, answer to a song from Ben Jonson's 1621 court masque, *The Gypsies Metamorphosed*. Buckingham sponsored and performed in Jonson's masque and, on 3 August 1621, presented it to the king at Burley-on-the-Hill, Buckingham's country house. James enjoyed the drama so much that he ordered two more performances: two days later at the earl of Rutland's house, Belvoir, and probably the next month at Windsor Castle. To the final performance at Windsor, Jonson added the song (among other things), which consists of a long blessing on the king's senses and a prayer that those senses be preserved from a series of minor discomforts. For example, Jonson's first stanza, on the sense of sight, begins:

ffrom a *Gypsie* in the morninge
  Or a paire of squint-eies torninge,
ffrom the *Goblin* and the spectre,
  Or a drunckard, though wth nectar,
ffrom a woman true to no man,
  And is vglie, beside com[m]on. . . .
Blesse the soueraigne, and his *seeinge*.[38]

[38] *Ben Jonson*, 7:610–11 (*The Gypsies Metamorphosed*, 1329–32, 1338).

Repeating this stanzaic and syntactic formula, Jonson proceeded to 'Blesse' each of the king's senses 'from' the mildest of offences. He hoped for protection of the king's hearing 'From a fidle out of tune.' He blessed his '*Smelling*' 'From a Ladie that doth breathe/Worse aboue then vnderneathe'; and his '*Tasting*' 'From bad venison, and worse wine.'[39] In regards to the king's final sense, Jonson wrote:

From a needle or a thorne
I' the bed at euen or morne,
Or from any Gout[es] least grutching,
Blesse the soueraigne, and his *Touching*./[40]

Having wished James a life free of even the 'least' discomfort, Jonson concluded the song with a blessing of longevity and a witty recognition of the king's two bodies.

Bless him, ô blesse him, heau'n, and lend him long
To be the sacred burthen of all song,
The Act[es] and yeares of all o^{r} *Kings* to outgoe,
And, while hee'is mortal, wee not thinck him so./[41]

The medieval political theory that the early Stuarts adopted held that the body politic effectively purified the king's mortal or natural body. In a truncated, terse reiteration of this theory, Jonson joked that they simply amounted to ignoring the king's mortality, but he nevertheless promised that James' subjects would gladly do exactly that. The libel that parodied Jonson's song would engage these same theories, but with a subversive result.

Manuscript verse collectors excerpted Jonson's song from the dramatic text and disseminated it on its own in no fewer than the 17 copies extant today. Many of the copies of Jonson's song accompany transcriptions of the libel that mocks it. Yet verse collectors evidently preferred the libel to Jonson's original. They made 'The Five Senses' one of the most popular early Stuart libels, leaving at least 41 copies.[42] In short, the libeler replaced Jonson's catalogue of mildly offensive stimuli with a

[39] *Ben Jonson*, 7:610–11 (*The Gypsies Metamorphosed*, 1345, 1363, 1355–56, 1371, 1367).

[40] *Ben Jonson*, 7:610–11 (*The Gypsies Metamorphosed*, 1378–81).

[41] *Ben Jonson*, 7:610–11 (*The Gypsies Metamorphosed*, 1386–89).

[42] Lists of known manuscript copies of both 'The Five Senses' and Jonson's original song appear in the following appendix of verse texts. See James Knowles, '"Songs of baser alloy": Jonson's *Gypsies Metamorphosed* and the Circulation of Manuscript Libels,' *Huntington Library Quarterly*, 69/1 (2006), 153–76.

complex of serious threats to the king and kingdom. He thus turned Jonson's facetious wish that James be kept from a gypsy and a woman with bad breath into a fervent prayer that the king be kept from someone who 'may p[ro]ue the Ruine of the land.'

> from such a face whose excellence
> may captiuate my Soue^r^ignes sence
> and make him Phæbus like his throne
> resigne to some young Phaeton
> whose skillesse and vnsteady hand
> may p[ro]ue the Ruine of the land[43]

As the rest of the libel makes clear, the excellent 'face' in the first line belongs to the royal favorite, Buckingham. So too does Buckingham emerge as the 'young Phaeton' who threatens to usurp the throne of Phœbus/James. The author of this libel was not only parodying Jonson but also caricaturing his patron, Buckingham.

The first stanza continues to explain that Phaeton, or Buckingham, 'may p[ro]ue the Ruine of the land' if Jove, or God, does not strike him down:

> vnles great Iove downe fro[m] the skie
> beholding Earths calamitye
> strike wth a hand that cannot erre
> that proud vsurping charioter
> and cure (though Phæbus) grieue) our woe
> fro[m] such a face as can doe soe
> where soe e're that haue a being
> blesse my Soue^r^igne & his seing.

This passage contrasts Jove's infallible hand with the young favorite's 'skillesse and vnsteady hand.' Although its contrast between an infallbile god, or God, and a corrupt man hardly qualifies as unorthodox, this passage rather provocatively leaves the king's hand out of the equation. As Andrew McRae has discussed, 'The Five Senses' subverted the theory of the king's two bodies, which Jonson light-heartedly invoked at the end of his song.[44] The libel, by contrast to both the political theory and Jonson's song, implies both that James' indulgences may harm the body

[43] Unless otherwise noted, quotations of 'The Five Senses' are taken from University of Edinburgh MS H.-P. Coll. 401, fols 51r–v.

[44] McRae, *Literature, Satire and the Early Stuart State*, 80.

politic, and that James' hand can indeed err. In an ostensibly loyal and quite serious prayer for James, the author of this libel began to fracture the early Stuart theory of kingship, which would crumble over the next few decades.

The second stanza of the libel proceeds to the sense of hearing. In Jonson's original masque song, he wished that James would never hear the sounds of 'a foole' or 'Heapes of phrases, and no stile.'[45] The playwright may have been flattering himself in this line, and transparently hoping that James would never allow a lesser poet than Jonson himself to entertain the court. The libeler too must have had Jonson's court entertainments in mind when he wrote:

from Iests p[ro]phane and flattering tounges
fro[m] bawdy tales and beastly songs
fro[m] after supp[er] suites that feare
a Parliament or Consells Eare
from Spanish treaties that may wound
the Contries peace or Gospells sound

The libeler regarded at least some Jacobean court poets as 'flattering tounges' and at least some court entertainments as 'Iests p[ro]phane,' 'bawdy tales and beastly songs.' If William Drummond did compose this libel, then he may have been criticizing his friend Jonson here. On the other hand, if Drummond both wrote the poem and expected Jonson to see the libel, he may have been trusting one of the most prolific authors of Jacobean court entertainments to appreciate his harsh criticism of them! Regardless of who wrote libel, though, he or she clearly regarded court entertainments as not only morally but also politically harmful, since they could lead directly to 'suites' (perhaps edible sweets and musical suites but certainly also court suits) that cannot be heard by the ear of Parliament—or, worse, to 'Spanish treaties' that would endanger both church and state.

This reference to 'Spanish treaties' would seem to corroborate the date of 1623 given the libel in three manuscripts, and to place the poem firmly in the context of the Spanish match.[46] The author of 'The Five

[45] *Ben Jonson*, 7:610–11 (*The Gypsies Metamorphosed*, 1339, 1344).

[46] Regarding the poem's date, McRae cites three manuscripts that date the poem to 1623: Bodleian MS Rawl. poet. 26, fol. 72r; British Library MS Stowe 962, fol. 144v; and Folger MS V.a.345, p. 59. *Literature, satire and the early Stuart state*, 75, 76 n.107.

Senses' clearly considered such 'Spanish treaties' a serious threat to both church and state: again, they would 'wound/the Contries peace or Gospells sound.' Following this mention of the Gospel, the stanza on hearing represents the Spanish match as a disaster of Biblical proportions.

> fro[m] Iobs false freind that would entice
> my Soueraigne fro[m] heauens Paradice
> from Prophets such as Ahabs were
> that flattering would entice his eare
> his frowne more then his makers fearing
> blesse my So^{r}igne & his hearing

The 'flattering tounges' in the beginning of this stanza apparently belong to court poets like Jonson, authors of tales and songs. Once the libel links such entertainments to a political agenda, though, courtly flatterers acquire much more serious associations. The poem likens them to Job's 'false freind,' and to Ahab's false prophets.[47] Like these misguided and misguiding Biblical figures, James' flatterers 'would entice' him 'fro[m] heauens Paradice.'

Lest readers overlook the religious significance of James' turning from 'Paradice,' the third stanza on 'Tasting' catalogues a series of specific references to Catholicism:

> fro[m] the candide poysoned Baites
> of Iesuits & their deceipts
> Italian sallets, romish druggs
> the milke of Babells proud-whores duggs
> fro[m] wine that can destroy the Braine
> & fro[m] the dangerous figgs of Spaine-
> At all Banquets at all feasting
> blesse my So^{r}igne & his tasting.

The threats to the king's sense of taste proceed from Catholic centers: from Italy, Rome, Babylon, or—worst of all—Spain. Recognizing that the reference to Spain 'perhaps alludes to the Spanish match,' McRae has noted that the fig was 'considered an aphrodisiac, and a word sometimes used euphemistically for the vagina' (80). The moral seriousness of 'The Five Senses' may suggest that its author would not have

[47] Job, 1 Kings 18.

intended an obscene reference to the Spanish Infanta with this reference. On the other hand, however, in a manuscript such as this Rawlinson Poetry miscellany, full of the 'bawdy' songs on the Spanish match discussed above, readers surely could have detected or imposed this possible meaning.

Even if this line on the 'figgs of Spaine' does refer to the Spanish match, the libel focuses not on the relationship between the Infanta and Charles, but on the king's relationship with Buckingham, and Buckingham's influence on the king's senses. In the fourth stanza on his sense of touch, the speaker prays that the king be kept:

> fro[m] such a smooth and Beardles Chinne
> as may p[ro]uoake or tempt to sinne
> fro[m] such a hand whose moist Palme may
> my Sou^{r}igne lead out of the way
> fro[m] things polluted & vncleane
> fro[m] all that bestiall & obscene
> fro[m] what may set his soule a reeling
> blesse my Sou^{r}aigne & his feeling

The excellent face with which the poem begins thus comes to feature 'a smooth and Beardles Chinne.' Likewise, the 'skillesse and vnsteady hand' that, in the first stanza, threatened to misguide the ship of state reappears here with a 'moist Palme' that could mislead 'my Sou^{r}igne'—mislead him into 'things polluted & vncleane . . . bestiall & obscene' that 'may set his soule a reeling.'

In the stanza on the fifth sense, 'Smellinge,' the focus on this tempting young man widens to take in the poem's most complete representation of Buckingham:

> next I craue
> thou wilt be pleasd (great god) to saue
> my Sou^{r}aigne fro[m] a Ganimede
> whose whorish breath hath power to leade
> his excellence wch way he list
> o let such lips be neuer kist
> fro[m] a breath in stinke excelling
> blesse my Sou^{r}aigne & his smelling

Since Buckingham began his career at court as a cupbearer to James, contemporaries regularly called him Ganymede, who was cupbearer to

Zeus. More generally, though, Ganymede 'became a popular euphemism for a "catamite": the passive partner in homosexual coupling.'[48] Lest his readers suspect that the Ganymede in this poem served merely as James' cupbearer, the poet pointed out the young man's 'whoreish breath' and 'lipps' that would kiss. Assuming the worst of the royal favorite, and worrying over the king's sexuality and spirituality, the speaker was pleading with God to 'save' James from Buckingham, to 'lett such lipps be never kist.'

'The Five Senses' deserves attention for a number of reasons. Its author produced in this poem a daring piece of literary appropriation that matches or exceeds the literary quality of Ben Jonson's masque song. The libel simultaneously mocks Jonson's original and turns Jonson's relative frivolity into utter seriousness regarding church and state. Furthermore, the poem helped to realize the potential of emergent modes of dissent in early modern England, which would not prove idle. Within six years of this libel's composition, John Felton would assassinate Buckingham. As the next chapter explains, poets and verse collectors encouraged, foretold, celebrated, and justified the murder in a great many libels and manuscripts, which surely made the duke the most libeled figure in early Stuart England. In fact, one could partly credit or blame the cultures of libeling and verse collecting for Buckingham's assassination and, more specifically, for establishing the forums in which the authors and collectors of libels made his murder thinkable and commendable. The verse collectors who cultivated these cultures prized and preserved 'The Five Senses.'

The dissent fostered by this libel did not stop at censure of Buckingham. As a prayer of blessing on the king's desiring and fallible body, 'The Five Senses' demonstrated an ostensibly loyalist means of effectively undermining the early Stuart theory of kingship. The libel's apparent loyalty may have worked quite effectively on its highest profile reader. In the year that it was written, 1623, Buckingham learned of two poetic

[48] McRae, *Literature, satire and the early Stuart state*, 79–80. Cites James M. Saslow, *Ganymede in the Renaissance: Homosexuality in Art and Society* (New Haven: Yale University Press, 1986); Roger Lockyer, *Buckingham: The Life and Political Career of George Villiers, First Duke of Buckingham 1592–1628* (New York: Longman, 1981); Frederick W. Fairholt, ed., *Poems and Songs Relating to George Villiers, Duke of Buckingham; and his Assassination by John Felton* (London: Percy Society, 1850), 49. See also Gregory W. Bredbeck, *Sodomy and Interpretation: Marlowe to Milton* (Ithaca: Cornell University Press, 1991), 3–30.

libels on his character (one that had been 'sett up at Court' and another 'that went abroad') and offered rewards (one for the sizeable sum of £1000) 'to know the author.'[49] Yet James apparently acquired a copy of 'The Five Senses' and decided that he actually liked the poem: he reportedly 'made light' of the libel and excused its anonymous author by saying, 'this fellow wished good things for him.'[50] Nevertheless, 'The Five Senses' remained dangerous literature, even for its collectors. After Buckingham's assassination, Alexander Gil, an outspoken critic of the royal favorite and John Milton's friend, ran into serious trouble with the authorities, who seem to have recorded that he had a copy of 'The Five Senses' in his possession.[51]

Beyond the political history of early Stuart England, 'The Five Senses' may have also played a role in the history of sexuality. Michel Foucault never completed his proposed Renaissance volume of *The History of Sexuality*.[52] Numerous histories of early modern sexuality have filled the gap that he left—including, to name just a few, influential contributions by Alan Bray, Jonathan Goldberg, Jeffrey Masten, Bruce Smith, and Valerie Traub.[53] James' royal favorites have not gone unnoticed in such studies; nor has the poem that, I suggest, marks the shift of libelers' attention to the sexuality of Jacobean royal favoritism.[54] Indeed, Bray

[49] James Knowles, 'To "scourge the arse/Jove's marrow so had wasted": Scurrility and the Subversion of Sodomy,' in Dermot Cavanagh and Tim Kirk, eds., *Subversion and Scurrility: Popular Discourse in Europe from 1500 to the Present* (Aldershot: Ashgate, 2000), 80. Quotes Sir Simonds D'Ewes, *The Diary of Sir Simonds D'Ewes, 1622–1624*, ed. Elisabeth Bourcier (Paris: Didier, 1974), 112–13.

[50] Bellany, *Politics of Court Scandal*, 258. British Library MS Add. 28640, fol. 105v.

[51] McRae, *Literature, Satire and the Early Stuart State*, 76 n.107. National Archives MS SP 16/111/51.

[52] Michel Foucault, *The History of Sexuality*, trans. Robert Hurley, 3 vols. (New York: Random House, 1978–86; rpt. 1988–90).

[53] Alan Bray, *Homosexuality in Renaissance England* (London: Gay Men's Press, 1982; rpt. New York: Columbia University Press, 1995); ___, *The Friend* (Chicago: University of Chicago Press, 2003); Jonathan Goldberg, *Sodometries: Renaissance Texts, Modern Sexualities* (Stanford: Stanford University Press, 1992); ___, ed. *Queering the Renaissance* (Durham: Duke University Press, 1994); Jeffrey Masten, *Textual Intercourse: Collaboration, Authorship, and Sexualities in Renaissance Drama* (Cambridge: Cambridge University Press, 1997); Bruce R. Smith, *Homosexual Desire in Shakespeare's England: a Cultural Poetics* (Chicago: University of Chicago Press, 1991); Valerie Traub, *The Renaissance of Lesbianism in Early Modern England* (Cambridge: Cambridge University Press, 2002).

[54] In a section devoted to 'James I and his Favourites,' Paul Hammond discusses, and transcribes in full, 'The Five Senses' (*Figuring Sex*, 128–50, esp. 141–43).

quoted 'The Five Senses' twice in his ground-breaking *Homosexuality in Renaissance England*: on one occasion, to show that his subjects considered even the king susceptible to the debauchery that led to sexual and other related vices; and, on another occasion, to debunk the nineteenth-century myth that the English Renaissance had tolerated homosexuality.[55] In each instance, Bray treated 'The Five Senses' as representative of dominant attitudes regarding sexuality.[56] Yet, considered in the context of previous libels on early Stuart favorites, 'The Five Senses' hardly appears a common depiction of same-sex desire or royal favorites. On the contrary, among contemporary libels and in manuscript verse miscellanies, it emerges as a quite unprecedented poem that helped to initiate a policy among early Stuart libelers and verse collectors of scrutinizing a mode of court sexuality that they had previously treated as unremarkable.

This observation fits with what historians and critics of early modern sexuality have suggested, in general, about male–male friendships in early modern England—specifically that contemporaries considered same-sex erotic relationships unexceptional, unless they became implicated in social disorder.[57] Recast in these terms, the lack of attention, in early years, to James' emotionally intense and possibly sexual relationships with his favorites suggests that even contemporary libelers and verse collectors considered these relationships orderly. Accordingly, when libelers decided to remark upon issues of male court sexuality, and collectors in turn prized their unprecedented poetic representations of a royal favorite, they implied that James' erotic relationship with Buckingham had become disorderly—not merely that it had gotten out of hand, but that it had begun to threaten social order.[58] Suddenly, the king's relationships were no longer his business alone; they became the

[55] Bray, *Homosexuality*, 16, 60–61.

[56] Curtis Perry also cites 'The Five Senses' as representative of a long-standing discourse on corrupt royal favoritism, which involves but is not limited to sexuality. *Literature and Favoritism in Early Modern England*, 96.

[57] Bray contributed the most thoughtful and elaborate investigation of early modern friendship in *The Friend*. For an extended consideration of Bray's work, see Jody Greene, ed., 'The Work of Friendship: In Memoriam Alan Bray,' special issue of *GLQ: A Journal of Gay and Lesbian Studies*, 10/3 (2004), 319–541.

[58] Mario DiGangi uses the terms 'orderly' and 'disorderly' in his introductory discussion of homoeroticism in early modern drama. *The Homoerotics of Early Modern Drama* (Cambridge: Cambridge University Press, 1997), 1–23.

business of his discontented subjects as well. More to the point of 'The Five Senses,' James suddenly needed to master more than his kingdom; he had to demonstrate mastery of himself as well, of his desires and his senses. Foucault's *The History of Sexuality* began a genealogy of just such self-mastery, including within its expansive concept of sexuality a range of self-disciplines.[59] Given Foucault's interest in the dispersal and decentralization of power in this project and in general at the end of his life, it is fitting that subjects attempted to impose this standard of sexual self-control on the monarch, rather than the other way around.

Collected together, as the compilers of numerous manuscript verse miscellanies arranged them, poetic libels on early Stuart royal favorites demonstrate that libelers began to censure same-sex relations at court not when James initiated his first erotically charged relationship with a royal favorite, Somerset; not when that favorite's career ended in disgrace; and not even when James began a second affectionate relationship with another favorite, Buckingham. In fact, after more than a decade of evidence and rumors of sexual relations between monarch and favorite, such issues became a subject for open discussion in libels and miscellanies only when Buckingham had apparently betrayed protestant interests by demonstrating his support for the Spanish match. That is, libelers first censured same-sex relationships at the Jacobean court when they became implicated in a much more troubling *hetero*sexual union: one between the Prince of Wales and Spanish Infanta. The problem with this union, of course, was not the gender or sexuality of its participants, but their religious commitments. A Spanish match would compromise or even end the English reformation, not least by returning England to a policy of tolerating domestic Catholics.

FANTASIES OF THE ROYAL BEDCHAMBER

In manuscript verse miscellanies, verse collectors surrounded less topical literature with 'The Five Senses' and other libels on the Spanish match and Buckingham. As a result, the clusters of information and opinion in the libels redrew the frames of reference for the less overtly political texts. To return to the central example of this study, verse collectors

[59] Foucault, *The History of Sexuality.*

circulated anti-courtly love poems concurrently with Spanish match and Buckingham libels. And they regularly related parodies of courtly love to libels' slanderous critiques of love at court. In other words, collectors assimilated mockeries of late Elizabethan courtiers' love poetry to rebukes of provocative relations between Charles and the Infanta, and between James and Buckingham. Ironically, this process of recontextualization may have actually recalled certain verse collectors' constructions of one anti-courtly love poem's late Elizabethan politics. Specifically, 'The Five Senses' returned its readers' attention to the royal bedchamber that the collectors featured in Chapter 2 evoked in their settings of Donne's 'To his Mistress going to bed.' These collectors suggested that when, after several decades of ignoring it, libelers eventually turned their attention to the royal bedchamber, their imaginative representations of a sexual relationship between monarch and favorite arguably had a precedent in this popular anti-courtly love poem.

As I discussed in Chapter 2, critics who have historicized the original politics of Donne's elegies have focused in particular on 'To his Mistress going to bed.' They have pointed out that the poem mockingly dramatizes the sexual implications of the Elizabethan discourse of colonialism, especially where that discourse involved the late Elizabethan royal favorite, Sir Walter Ralegh. Some scholars, then, have read Donne's poem as an irreverent response to Ralegh's western design. Like Ralegh, Donne's mock-colonialist speaker petitions his mistress, as if she were a monarch, for a license to explore a colony that he has already identified with her. Once the woman grants the license, though, her lover not only explores but also conquers her; once a queen regnant, she becomes colonized. By 'inverting the central conceit' of the discourse of early English colonialism in this way, Donne facetiously 'literalized (or eroticized)' its sexual implications in a fictional bedroom scene.[60] In a reading such as this, the poem becomes an irreverent fiction of a privy chamber conversation that enacted the sexual implications of the early discourse of English colonialism.

Other than 'The Five Senses' and 'To his Mistress going to bed,' very few fantasies of royal bedchambers appear in early modern manuscript verse miscellanies. Yet, again, verse collectors fabricated another one

[60] Young, '"O my America, my new-found-land,"' 41. Hester, 'Donne's (Re)Annunciation,' 56.

starring Ralegh and Elizabeth after their deaths. One of the collectors of the conflation of love lyrics by Thomas Carew and Sir Robert Ayton headed it with the words: 'Sr Walter Ralegh to ye Queen.'[61] Interestingly, this copyist imagined the relationship between the royal favorite and his sovereign in a manuscript that already contained a copy of 'Nay pish, nay pew, infaith but will you? fye.'[62] He thus associated with both Ralegh and Elizabeth a style of love that this anti-courtly love poem opposed elsewhere in the miscellany.

More interestingly, the other verse collector who erroneously represented this lyric as from 'SIR/Walter Ralegh to/Queene Eliza=/=beth' also included 'The Five Senses' in the Rawlinson Poetry miscellany discussed above, in addition to the other poems that this chapter has already considered: the full set of commons' petitions with Saint Elizabeth's reply; the substantial group of Spanish match ballads; and, shortly before these songs, Donne's 'To his Mistress going to bed.'[63] Such an array of poems required their collector, and any close readers of his very legible anthology, to imagine erotic relationships between Ralegh and Queen Elizabeth; the Spanish Infanta and Prince Charles; and Buckingham and King James. The scribe thus placed Donne's bedroom scene in a miscellany laced with specific references to imaginary royal bedrooms. Lest Queen Elizabeth's role in his representation of love and sex at court do her any dishonor, this scribe idealized her by including the commons' petitionary exchange with Saint Elizabeth. Rather than show the same respect to early Stuart monarchs, he immersed Donne's poem, and virtually all of the other texts that he collected, in a political and literary culture dominated by fears over the erotic relationship between James and Buckingham.

Only these two manuscript verse collectors claimed that Ralegh wrote these love lyrics specifically for Elizabeth I. Several others, however, helped to establish the relationship between Donne's fantasy of the

[61] British Library Add. 22602, fols 30v–31r ('Sr Walter Ralegh to ye Queen.//Our Passions are most like to Floods and streames').

[62] British Library Add. 22602, fol. 19v ('A Gentlewoman, while a Gentleman/ Courted her.//Nay pish, nay pew, infaith but will you? fye').

[63] Either when he arranged the gatherings for binding or when he copied the libel, the compiler of Bodleian MS Rawl. poet. 160 placed 'The Five Sences' immediately before the commons' petitionary exchange (fols 14v–15r). In a similar fashion, he positioned his large group of Spanish match ballads following Donne's 'To his Mistress going to bed' (fols 171r–v, 176v–82r). I return to this miscellany in the next chapter.

Elizabethan bedchamber and the prayer for its Jacobean counterpart, 'The Five Senses.' Although relatively few people may have recognized the similarity between these two poems in the seventeenth century, several of their collectors and copyists did collect them together. 'To his Mistress going to bed' and 'The Five Senses' show up in twelve of the same manuscripts. This means that 'To his Mistress going to bed' accompanies nearly one third of the 37 known seventeenth-century manuscript copies of 'The Five Senses.'[64] I propose that the verse collectors responsible for these twelve manuscripts effectively established a relationship between the two poems. Yet this argument depends less on the total number of manuscripts that feature both poems than on the individual miscellanies that do. So the remainder of this section briefly surveys a few more of these manuscripts, and demonstrates in some detail how verse collectors associated Buckingham libels with anti-courtly love poems and, especially, 'The Five Senses' with 'To his Mistress going to bed.'

For example, the main compiler of the Rosenbach miscellany introduced in Chapter 2 placed his copy of the Ayton–Carew conflation,

[64] Bodleian MSS Eng. poet. c.50, fols 25r–v ('Seeinge./from such a face whose excellence'), 42v ('Come madam Come all rest my powers defie'); Rawl. poet. 117, fols 23v–24v ('The sences/From such a face whose excellence'), 222v–21r rev. ('Come M^{ris} come all rest my powers defye'); Rawl. poet. 160, fols 14v–15v ('T[H]E FIVE SENCES/SEEING//From such a face whose excellence'), 171r–v ('AN ELIGIE//Come madam come, all rest my powers defy'); British Library MS Stowe 962, fols 82v–83r ('An Elegie•or/vndressinge of ons/mistresse.//Come madame, come, all rest my powers defie'), 144v–46r ('The fiue Sences. 1623.//Seeinge./ffrom such a face whose excellence'); Folger MS V.a.345, pp. 59–61 ('Of ye fiue senses by Iames Iohnson 1623/Seeing. 1/from such a face whose excellence'), 80–81 ('Dr Dunne to his m^{rs} goign to bed//Come Maddam, come, al rest my powers defy'); Houghton MS Eng. 686, fols 35v–36v ('Come Madam come, all rest my powers defye'), 59r–60v ('ffrom such a face whose excellence'); Huntington MS HM 198, pt. 1, pp. 30–32 ('The fiue Sences/Seing//From such A face whose excellence'), 43–44 ('Come Madame come all rest my powers defye'); Leicestershire Record Office MS DG7/Lit.2, fols 281r ('Come Madam come all rest my powers defy'), 333v–34r ('Seeing.//From such a face whose excellence'); Morgan MS MA 1057, pp. 4–5 (last six lines of 'goinge to Bedd' beginning, 'defie,/Thers no pennance due to innocence'), 80–81 ('Seeinge//From such a face whose excellence'); Rosenbach MS 239/27, pp. 47–48 ('Vpon on goeinge to bed to his mistresse.//Come madam come, all rest my powers defye'), pp. 58^{b}–60 ('On the fiue senses./1 Seeinge.//ffrom such a face whose excellence'); St. John's, Cambridge MS S.32, pp. 31r–32r ('The Senses/Seeinge.//ffrom such a face whose excellence'), 37v–38r ('To his M^{rs} as shee was comeing to bed.//Come Madame, come, all rest my powers defie'); Westminster Abbey MS 41, fols 14v–15r ('Come, Madam come, all rest my powers defy'), 21r–22r ('5 Senses./i Seeing.//from such a face whose excellence').

headed 'Sr Walter Rawleigh to his M^{ris},' among not only anti-courtly love poems by Donne but also a range of Buckingham libels.[65] In addition, just a few pages following his juxtaposition of the styles of love associated with Ralegh and Donne, this verse collector produced perhaps the most elaborate extant setting of 'The Five Senses.' He began this remarkable sequence of libels with verses on Buckingham's military failure, along with a critical anagram on the duke and a Somerset libel.[66] Next he placed his copy of the libel 'On the fiue senses,' followed by both Jonson's original, headed 'Another to K: Iames,' and a rare poem superscribed, 'The Letany.'[67] 'The Letany' adopts the catalogue format of the two preceding poems, abandoning their focus on the senses and replacing their refrain about King James with the liturgical Latin phrase, 'Libera nos domine' (Save us, Lord).

ffrom Mahomett & Paganisme
ffrom heriticks, from sects, & schisme
ffrom highway rascalls & cuttpurses
ffrom citty bawds & old dry nurses
ffrom glister pipes, & d^{rs} whistles
ffrom begginge schollars stale Epistles
ffrom turnestile bootes & longlane beauers
ffrom agues & from drunken feauers
Libera nos domine.

Although it says virtually nothing about the king or royal favorite, 'The Letany' makes a perfect companion piece to 'The Five Senses' and Jonson's song. Like them, it devotes nearly every line to prepositional

65 Rosenbach MS 239/27, pp. 47–48 ('Vpon on goeinge to bed to his mistresse.//Come madam come, all rest my powers defye'), 49–50 ('Loues voyage into the Netherlands.//The haire a forrest is of ambushes'), 50 ('Sr Walter Rawleigh to his M^{ris}.//Passions are likened to floods & streames'), 50–51 ('Wronge not deare empresse of my heart').

66 Rosenbach MS 239/27, pp. 54^{b}–57^{b} ('On the Duke//And art return'd againe with all thy faults'), 57^{b} ('The Dukes ffarewell.//And wilt thou goe great Duke & leaue vs heare'; 'Anagram[m]a://Georgius Villerus. Regis, vulgi elusor').

67 Rosenbach MS 239/27, pp. 58^{b}–60 ('On the fiue senses.//1 Seeinge.//ffrom such a face whose excellence'), 60–62 ('Another to K: Iames.//from a gipsy in the morninge'), 62–64 ('The Letany://from Mahomett & Paganisme'). 'The Letany' also appears in Bodleian MS Ashmole 36, 37, fol. 46v, and in each edition of the printed miscellany *Merry Drollery*: W.N., et al., *Merry Drollery . . . The First Part* (London: J.W. for P.H., 1661; Wing M1860), 164–66; _____, *Merry Drollery, Complete* (London: Simon Miller, 1670; Wing M1861), 174–76; _____, *Merry Drollery Compleat* (London: William Miller, 1691; Wing M1862), 174–76.

phrases beginning with the same word. Moreover, 'The Letany' shares certain concerns with each of the preceding poems: it petitions the Lord to save its collective speakers from both serious threats to the church and state, rather like those catalogued in 'The Five Senses,' and minor ones to the individual, somewhat like those that Jonson hoped would never bother the king. Indeed, 'The Letany' oscillates between national and personal enemies or problems. Beginning on an even grander scale than 'The Five Senses,' it first evokes 'Mahomett & Paganisme'; then tightens its focus in the next line to Christian enemies of the true faith; and by the third line has zoomed in on quite small-scale threats to one's property, health, or comfort. Much of 'The Letany' maintains this attention to relatively minor troubles: 'itches'; 'the watch at 12 a clock'; 'a wife thats leane & meager.' Yet every so often the poem widens its focus to glance at larger issues. It asks the Lord, for instance, to deliver its speakers 'From a bastard thats the clargies'; 'From the spanish inquisition'; 'From a gripinge Spanish Cullion'; 'ffrom a pastor too too zealous.' Like many of the poems on religious difference in contemporary manuscript verse miscellanies, these scattered lines position the poem's speakers in the moderate religious space between Spanish Catholics and zealous English protestants. Yet these lines also distance their speakers from hypocrites in the Anglican establishment (or from their illegitimate children). By placing 'The Letany' right after 'The Five Senses' and Jonson's masque song, the main compiler of the Rosenbach miscellany exhibited their close intertextual relationship. He also, therefore, demonstrated his own attention to the order of the poems in his anthology. In light of his thoughtful arrangement of these three texts, his juxtaposition of Ralegh's courtly and Donne's anti-courtly love poems, introduced in Chapter 2, looks more perceptive than it might otherwise. So too does his decision to place Ralegh's and Donne's opposing representations of desire next to this sequence of Buckingham libels. Evidently conscious of his editorial role, the main compiler of this Rosenbach miscellany represented both Ralegh and Buckingham as lovers at court, and affiliated Donne's apparent rejection of Ralegh's style of love with libelers' attacks on Buckingham's relationship with King James. As my next chapter will show, this manuscript verse collector dramatically concluded his account of early modern royal favorites and their detractors with libels on the duke's assassination.

Of the other manuscripts that contain both 'The Five Senses' and 'To his Mistress going to bed,' two Oxford miscellanies deserve particular attention. George Morley, who had attended Christ Church when it was becoming the nation's most prolific center for collecting verse and compiling miscellanies, owned and may have partially compiled one of these anthologies, now held at Westminster Abbey. Within the span of ten leaves, Morley's octavo features Donne's 'The Anagram' and 'To his Mistress going to bed,' 'All the newes that is stirring now,' and 'The Five Senses.'[68] Readers of these few pages proceed quite quickly from Donne's parodies of late Elizabethan courtly love poetry to censures of the early Stuart court—and from Donne's playful dramatization of the sexualized rhetoric of an Elizabethan courtier to the prayerful criticism of a sexualized Jacobean royal favorite in 'The Five Senses.'

Later, Morley's anthology features not only Jonson's original song from *The Gypsies Metamorphosed* but also another Jonson lyric paired with a parodic answer-poem.[69] Several early modern verse collectors extracted the last stanza of the fourth poem in Jonson's 'A Celebration of Charis in Ten Lyrick Peeces' from the longer sequence and transcribed it on its own. Nearly half of these collectors made sure to accompany Jonson's verse with its unauthorized companion piece.[70] Jonson's original stanza begins with the question, 'haue y^{u} seene the white lilly grow/Before rude hands haue toucht it.' After a series of related questions—about the addressee's experience with snow, swans, and honey—the stanza culminates in a complex simile: 'o so white, ô so soft ô so sweet/so sweet so sweet is shee.' In Morley's manuscript and others, Jonson's stanza immediately precedes another which facetiously begins, 'Haue you seen a blackheaded maggot.' This answer-poem simply replaces the traditionally white, soft, and sweet ingredients of Jonson's verse with their opposites, ultimately exchanging Jonson's beautiful Charis for a woman described in the exclamation: 'O so black, o so rough o so sour is shee.' Although it lacks the complexity and difficulty of Donne's Ovidian elegies, this crude little mock-poem performs a similar function by isolating a standard feature of certain anti-courtly

68 Westminster Abbey MS 41, fols 14r–15r, 18r–v, 21r–22r.

69 Westminster Abbey MS 41, fols 27v–28v, 88v–89r.

70 Jonson's stanza appears with the answer-poem in five manuscripts, and on its own in six others. See the following appendix of verse texts for lists of these manuscripts. *Complete Poetry of Ben Jonson*, 121–31, 125.

love poems, such as 'The Anagram': a parodic refusal of the conventions and the beautiful mistress of courtly love poetry. The two parodies of Jonson in Morley's miscellany reserve most of their criticism for two of verse collectors' favorite targets for ridicule: courtly love and royal favorites. By placing these answer-poems to Jonson among other anti-courtly love poems and additional Buckingham libels, the compilers of Morley's manuscript contributed to the political recontextualization that verse collectors were bringing about in the early seventeenth century. They were assimilating anti-courtly love poetry to criticisms of the Jacobean court.

In another Oxford octavo, now at Harvard University's Houghton Library, two men associated with New College and, later, with the Inns of Court immersed Donne's anti-courtly love poems in a manuscript environment predominated by Spanish match and early Buckingham libels. The first ten numbered leaves of this small manuscript book feature a series of five consecutive Spanish match libels.[71] The next poem in the manuscript shows to what extent the Spanish match had recontextualized earlier poetry. As I mentioned in the introduction, verse collectors reapplied Sir Henry Wotton's poem on James I's daughter and icon of the international protestant cause, Elizabeth, Queen of Bohemia, to other royal women. Like the other collectors who read the Spanish Infanta into Wotton's poem, the compilers of this Houghton miscellany redirected it 'To the Spanish Lady.'[72] They may have made this radical appropriation by mistake. Yet, even as a mistake, it utterly transformed the religious politics of Wotton's poem.

In addition to this appropriated verse in praise of the Infanta, the Houghton miscellany contains an unusually high number of texts celebrating the match, one of them quite rare.[73] Yet it also includes

[71] Houghton MS Eng. 686, fols 2r–4v ('On the Spanish match.//The day was turnd to starr light & was runne'), 5r–6r ('On the Spanish match./Dr Corbet to the Duke of Buckinghame//I've read of Ilands floating & removed'), 6v–7r ('Reply to the former// ffalse on his deanery, false, nay more Ile lay'), 7v–8r ('On the Spanish Match.//All the newes that's stirring now/Is of the Golden Lady'), 8r–9v ('On the Princes going to Spayne.//ffrom England happy & vnequall state//John Harvey'). This poem is also attributed to 'Iohn Harvy' in Bodleian MS Malone 19, pp. 35–37, where it begins 'One the Princes goeinge/To Spayne.//ffrom Englands happy & vnequall state.'

[72] Houghton MS Eng. 686, fols 9v–10r ('To the Spanish Lady//Yee meaner beauties of the night').

[73] John Harvey's poem is found in only the two copies listed above. 'The day was turnd to starr light & was runne' also appears in Beinecke MS Osborn b62, pp. 63–69; Bodleian MSS Ashmole 47, fols 25v–29r; Malone 19, pp. 21–26; British Library MSS

the more popular libels that oppose the marriage, such as 'All the newes that's stirring now,' an incomplete copy of the second commons' petition, and 'The Five Senses.'[74] Their interest in the full range of libels on the Spanish match shows that the compilers of this Houghton manuscript attended closely to the religious politics of the mid-1620s, yet makes their own views on the match difficult to discern. Into this politically conscious manuscript environment they transcribed other popular lyrics circulating around Oxford in the 1630s. In between their incomplete copy of the second commons' petition and 'The Five Senses,' they copied a set of exemplary anti-courtly love poems: the anonymous 'Nay pish, nay phew, in faith & will you? ffye'; Donne's 'To his Mistress going to bed'; and his Ovidian 'Natures Lay Ideot, I taught thee to love.'[75] While their reapplication of Wotton's poem on the queen of Bohemia to the Spanish Infanta constitutes a dramatic act of appropriation, these collectors' addition of Donne's anti-courtly love poems to a miscellany so involved with the Spanish match assimilated them to a new political context.

When libelers turned against Buckingham, the figure of the sexualized royal favorite reemerged in manuscript verse miscellanies. A late Elizabethan version of this character was already lurking in any of these anthologies that included Donne's enormously popular 'To his Mistress going to bed,' particularly in the manuscripts introduced in Chapter 2. Yet few collectors and readers of Donne's love elegy could have discerned the late Elizabethan royal favorite, Ralegh, in the midst of epitaphs on Elizabeth I and libels on Jacobean court scandals. Over the second half of Buckingham's career, however, libelers and verse collectors made sure that their readers focused on this early Stuart favorite. The collectors who gathered together Buckingham libels and

Add. 47111, fol. 18r; Egerton 923, fols 40v–43v; Sloane 542, fols 21r–23r; Brotherton MS Lt q 11, no. 41; Folger MS V.a.162, fols 46r–48v; Houghton MS Eng. 686, fols 2r–4v; National Library of Wales MS NLW 12443A, pt. 2, pp. 248–59; New York Public Library MS Arents S288, pp. 118–23; Corpus Christi, Oxford MSS 309, fols 80r–v; 328, fol. 70v–72v; Rosenbach 239/27, pp. 1–6. I thank Julian Reid for checking the Corpus manuscripts for me.

[74] Houghton MS Eng. 686, fols 29r–30v, 59v–60v.

[75] Houghton MS Eng. 686, fols 35r ('Nay pish, nay phew, in faith & will you? ffye'), 35v–36v ('Come Madam come, all rest my powers defye'), 37r–v ('vppon a woman who the Author taught/to love & Complement.//Natures Lay Ideot, I taught thee to love').

anti-courtly love poems, in other words, chronicled decades of politically sensitive reactions to early modern English courts. And, whether or not they realized that they were doing so, those who put 'The Five Senses' and 'To his Mistress going to bed' in the same miscellanies suggested a relationship between an especially provocative pair of such reactions, each of which offers fantasies of sexual relations between a monarch and a royal favorite.

AFTER THE MATCH

When Prince Charles and Buckingham abandoned the Spanish match negotiations and returned to England without the Infanta, the country erupted in jubilant celebration.[76] And as the prince and favorite reversed their foreign policy and pressed for war with Spain in the following months, collaborating with a 'patriot' coalition at court and in Parliament, Buckingham briefly became a hero of the protestant cause. Although libelers had attacked Buckingham while he promoted the match, they changed their minds about the duke once he turned on Spain. One libel of late 1623, beginning 'The Prince is now come out of Spayne,' explained how the tables had turned, both for Catholics and for Buckingham's reputation among libelers:

> But when the Prince to England came,
> And brought not home the Spanish Dame,
> The Papists hung their eares....
>
> I love the Prince, and every name
> That honours noble Buckingham[77]

Libels written the following year acknowledged how the failure of the match strained relations between Buckingham and the Spanish ambassadors, to the delight of the poems' anonymous authors:

> Theres naught can asswage Spaines Ambassadors rage
> But the great Duke of Buckingham's head,

[76] Cogswell, *The Blessed Revolution*, 6–76.

[77] Bodleian MS Rawl. poet. 26, fol. 22r–v ('Of the Prince's returne/from Spayne. 1623.//The Prince is now come out of Spayne'); Bellany and McRae, 'Early Stuart Libels,' Nv17.

For the barbarous Don knowes whilst it is on
'Twill bee to their terror and dread.[78]

Another 1624 libel directly addressed James in defending Buckingham against the ambassadors (and conflated them with Moors): 'let not that head satisfy the thirst/Of Morish pride.' This libel went so far as to rank Buckingham 'the very first/of all thy fauourites' that 'E're vndertooke/His Countryes Cause and thus did overlooke/Spanish Deceiueings. ffor he hath done more/Then twenty of thy fauourites before.'[79] Once perhaps the most hated royal favorite of early modern England, Buckingham had become the darling of militant protestants.

Yet, as Bellany has shown, 'Buckingham's career as a charismatic exemplar of Protestant military virtue was short lived.'[80] The war with Spain turned out to be a disaster; and, as Lord Admiral and Warden of the Cinque Ports, Buckingham received much of the blame. Even before his worst military defeat, at the Ile de Ré in 1627, libelers recuperated the negative representations of the duke that they had developed in the years leading up to the Spanish match negotiations. One well-distributed poem, written on the occasion of the duke's departure for Ré, catalogued several of the commonplaces on the favorite.

And wilt thou goe, great Duke, and leave us heere
Lamenting thee and eke thy Pupill deare
Great Charles? Alas! who shall his Scepter sway,
And Kingdome rule now thou art gone away?
Are there noe Whores in Court to stay thee? Must
Thy hate to France and Spaine exceed thy Lust?
Hast thou no Neece to marry? Cannot an Inne
Or bawdy house afford thee any kinne
To cuckold Lords withall? Hast not a Foe
To poison heere at home? And wilt thou goe
And thinke the Kingdome plagu'ed sufficiently?
Most gracelesse Duke, wee thanke thy charitie,

[78] British Library MS Sloane 826, fols 159r–160v, as transcribed in Bellany and McRae, 'Early Stuart Libels,' Oi1. Bellany notes that, in early 1624, the Spanish ambassadors Don Carlos Coloma and Marquis Juan Hurtado de Mendoza Inijosa made several attempts to turn James against his favorite, going so far as to charge Buckingham with planning 'to usurp the Stuart line by marrying his daughter to the son of the Elector Palatine' ('Early Stuart Libels,' O).

[79] Bodleian MS Eng. poet. c.50, fol. 21r; Bellany and McRae, 'Early Stuart Libels,' Oi2.

[80] Bellany, '"Raylinge Rymes,"' 301.

> Wishing the Fleet such speed, as thou but lost,
> Though wee bee conquer'd, wee have quitted cost.[81]

Now the royal favorite of King Charles I, Buckingham yet again provoked representations as an overreacher, a sexual profligate, and a poisoner, since James I's physician had charged the duke with poisoning James.

A popular libel written in response to the debacle at Ré held Buckingham solely responsible, and reiterated the poisoning charge (among others). 'And art return'd againe with all thy Faults' poses a series of taunting questions to the duke: did he retreat because of a 'queasie stomach (gorg'd with sweet-meates),' or 'for want of Wenches,' or because he feared losing his power to other courtiers or a parliament at home? The poem then depicts Buckingham as 'vext' by all of these questions in battle, which worked on his guilty soul just as the favorite's poison had worked on James:

> All these, noe question, with a restlesse motion
> Vext thy bespotted soule, as that black Potion
> Tortur'd the noble Scott, whose Manes tell
> Thy swolne Ambition made his carkasse swell.

After associating Buckingham with religious extremism (both radical Brownism and ceremonialist Arminianism), the libel proceeds to demonstrate how far the favorite had strayed from the protestant religious mean, by reminding readers of his Catholic mother: 'Could not thy Mothers Masses, nor her Crosses,/Nor Sorceries prevent these fatall losses?' The poem concludes by charging Buckingham with 'Trechery, Neglect, and Cowardise' and by calling for him to stay at court, to leave warfare to proper soldiers, and to put an end to his overreaching: 'be govern'd by the state'; 'For if but one yeare more thou lordst it thus,/ Thou draw'st confusion on thy self and us.'[82] This 1627 couplet sounds ominous, even threatening, as if the speaker would not tolerate 'one yeare more' of Buckingham's power. Over the next year, such threats would become increasingly common and pointed in libels. And in 1628, one of these libels fell into the hands of a decidedly active reader and collector.

[81] British Library MS Sloane 826, fol. 161r, as transcribed in Bellany and McRae, 'Early Stuart Libels,' Oii5.

[82] British Library MS Sloane 826, fols 161v–64r, as transcribed in Bellany and McRae, 'Early Stuart Libels,' Oii12.

5

Verse Collectors and Buckingham's Assassination

When the unemployed and disgruntled lieutenant John Felton reached over the shoulder of a colonel bowing to greet Buckingham, and stuck a knife in the duke's chest, he brought to a certain culmination the long, libelous discourse on early modern English favorites.[1] At the same time, he renewed and transformed the discourse. Although Felton acted alone, and found motivation in his personal grievances against the duke (who twice passed him over for promotion, twice declined to hire him, and indefinitely postponed issuing his back pay), the disaffected soldier learned *by collecting and reading libels* that others shared his complaints. Nursing physical and psychological wounds from Buckingham's failed invasion of the Ile de Ré, and renting quarters in John Donne's London parish of St. Dunstan-in-the-West, Felton found himself in the heart of the city's vibrant trade in political manuscripts. At the shop of the scribe George Willoughby, whom Felton hired to draw up his petitions for back pay, he discovered that Willoughby devoted much of his labor to copying political tracts. Felton then frequented Willoughby's shop both to pursue his business interests and to collect libels, many of which allowed him to connect his individual discontents with those of a great many others.

At Willoughby's shop, Felton learned about the Windmill Tavern in Shoe Lane, a hot spot for political texts and talk, and about Lawrence Naylor, a bakery delivery boy who distributed poetic libels in addition to bread. Shortly before he headed south to confront Buckingham at Portsmouth, Felton received from Naylor one of several short verses

[1] Thomas Cogswell, 'John Felton, Popular Political Culture, and the Assassination of the Duke of Buckingham,' *The Historical Journal*, 49/2 (2006), 357–85; Alastair Bellany, 'Felton, John (*d.* 1628),' *ODNB*.

circulating in 1628 that baldly promised that someone would soon kill the duke. In Felton's hands, these two little lines must have called out to their reader and demanded a response. According to a copy among Willoughby's papers, scribbled by one of his clients, the verse read:

> lett Charles & george doe what they can
> yet george shall dye like Doctor Lambe[2]

Less than two months before Felton killed Buckingham, the duke's astrologer Dr. John Lambe attended a play at the Fortune Theatre, after which a growing crowd followed him through the streets. Even though Lambe quickly hired a bodyguard of sailors, the crowd started throwing rocks. Lambe ironically took shelter first in the Windmill, where the astrologer must have stood out among more than a few of his patron's unpaid soldiers and enemies. But the bartender made him leave. The doctor then sneaked into a house, where the crowd found him, forced him to the street, and stoned and clubbed him. Hardly recoiling from the grisly murder, neighborhood libelers were threatening more of the same. In this and other libels, they assured readers that someone would give Buckingham the same treatment that Lambe received. Felton's subjective response to this libel must have effectively matched the announcement that he made as he emerged from the kitchen at the Greyhound Inn and into the chaos surrounding the duke's body: 'I am the man.'

For some time in the summer of 1628, Felton had tried and failed to get Willoughby to loan him a copy of the House of Commons' 'Remonstrance,' which represented Parliament's final, and unsuccessful, attempt to curtail the duke's abuse of power. After he stridently refused Felton, Willoughby allowed his employee Richard Harwood to borrow a copy, which Harwood promptly took (where else?) to the Windmill to read with Felton. There, Felton finally laid eyes on perhaps the most official verification of his countrymen's discontents with Buckingham, as well as the record of their failure to restrain him diplomatically. Harwood loaned the 'Remonstrance' to Felton in exchange for his promise to return it, which Felton never did. In fact, he had the 'Remonstrance' on his person when he killed Buckingham. With this

[2] National Archives MS SP 16/114/32; Bellany and McRae, 'Early Stuart Libels,' Pi1; Cogswell, 'John Felton, Popular Political Culture,' 378.

political document in his pocket, and with what he must have regarded as the support of countless libelers and countrymen at his back, Felton acted on the criticisms and threats that had been mounting in manuscript libels for years, and especially in recent months. Although the government tried hard to find accomplices, Felton assumed full responsibility for the assassination, doing no more to spread the blame than explaining, '[t]hat which drawed mee to this horrid sinfull fact, was some foule reports.' As Tom Cogswell has suggested, 'these "foule reports," which were ubiquitous, effectively represented Felton's accomplices.'[3] Felton conspired with no one, in other words, except libels. Without these political texts, he surely would have lacked the support, the justification, and the grand religious and political rationale to kill Buckingham. He turned into a killer, to put it another way, by reading.

When he resolved to kill the duke, this reader of libels turned into an author of two that must have quickly become highly sought among collectors. In addition to keeping the copy of the 'Remonstrance' in his pocket, Felton had sewn into his hatband two manuscripts defending his actions, and challenging those who would presume to judge him. According to a copy that reached a collector as far north as Chester, Felton had written:

> Let noe man discommende mee ffor doinge itt, but rather discommende
> them selues; ffor iff god had not taken awaye our hartes, ffor
> our ssins, he had not liued thus lounge vnpunished./
> Iohn ffelton./

> That man in my opinion is cowardlye base, deserues nether
> the name off a gentleman, nor a souldyer, that is vnwillinge
> to ssacriffice his lyffe, ffor the honnor of god, the kinge, and
> the goode off his Cuntrye./
> Iohn ffelton./[4]

Do not judge my actions, he explained to contemporaries; judge your inaction, your cowardice, your reticence to sacrifice your life for God, king, and country. Felton's pen may have been less mighty than his sword. Yet the pens of libelers encouraged Felton's mightiest, or at least his most consequential, act with a blade. And, in addition to giving

[3] John Felton, *The Prayer and Confession of Mr. Felton* ([London]: n.p., 1628; STC 10762), 3; Cogswell, 'John Felton, Popular Political Culture,' 384–85.

[4] Cheshire Archives MS ZCR 63/2/19, fol. 69r.

manuscript collectors the two self-defenses above, Felton gave libelers the inspiration to take up their pens again. They responded with dozens of poems celebrating the assassination and many more defending and praising Felton himself. Thus after collecting, reading, and even writing a few libels, Felton became a subject of a great body of poems glorifying him and reveling in Buckingham's death. Felton, in other words, encouraged a rather unprecedented set of libels, marked by celebration and dedicated to a godly hero of the people.

In verse collectors' manuscript miscellanies, these triumphant libels on Felton and the deceased Buckingham put earlier literature in a starkly new context. They made clear that the threats on the duke's life composed earlier in the year had been anything but idle. They claimed as justification for the murder criticisms of Buckingham's sexuality, religion, and politics written earlier in the decade. They drew on the rhetoric deployed against previous royal favorites, most obviously including the duke's immediate predecessor, Somerset. Yet this rhetoric emerged long before Somerset and even James. Of all the earlier royal favorites whom verse collectors might have evoked in their anthologies, they most often chose Sir Walter Ralegh. As Chapter 2 suggested, Ralegh's detractors had criticized some of the same characteristics that libelers would later identify in Somerset and Buckingham: relatively humble origins; unseemly ambition; the accumulation of abundant honors, titles, and estates; suspicious religion; and allegedly erotic intimacy with the monarch. Yet, in the years since Ralegh had last exhibited intimacy with a monarch, manuscript collectors had helped to rehabilitate his reputation, in no small part by promoting the fallen courtier as a critic of Somerset. While some collectors attributed popular Somerset libels to Ralegh, others circulated his letter asking Carr not to accept Ralegh's forfeited lands at Sherborne as a gift from James in 1608–9.[5] In contrast to his early Stuart successors, Ralegh thus came to

[5] Bodleian MS Eng. poet. e.14, fol. 49r ('S^{r}. Walter Raleigh to ye Ld Carr//I.C.V.R. good mounser Carr'); West Yorkshire Archive Service, Leeds MS WYL156/237, fol. 56v ('Of Fauorites//Dazled with the height of place//Sr Water: Raleigh'). For Ralegh's letter to Carr, which also appears in other manuscripts, see British Library MS Harley 6038, fols 31r–32r; Cambridge University Library MS Ee.5.23, p. 418; Huntington MS EL 6232. Bellany discusses the letter in *The Politics of Court Scandal*, 171. See also Senate House MS 313, fol. 15r ('Sir Walter Rawleye sent a bible/to Earle Somersett being in the tower/ he desiring to haue a Bible with a/leafe turned downe at the xxiijth/Chapter of Ecclesiasticus verse xiijth/¶ Remember thy father and/mother &c and soe to the end/of the Chapter'). I thank Richard Temple for checking this manuscript.

represent the relatively glorious Elizabethan past, even for those verse collectors who positioned him at the start of the problem with royal favorites that Felton ultimately solved. In their miscellanies, poems on these three courtiers in particular delineate a brief history of increasingly corrupt, and increasingly sexual, royal favoritism that culminated in Buckingham and concluded (if only for a time) thanks to Felton. By including assassination libels among other verses on these men, collectors imparted a sense of foreboding, if not inevitability, to earlier literature on favorites. That is, they effectively subsumed the earlier political poems in a suggestive teleology, as if to say that someone had to put an end to England's succession of progressively wicked royal favorites.

This final chapter begins with miscellanies whose compilers suggested just such a progression of favorites, from Ralegh to Buckingham. Especially by gathering supposed Ralegh lyrics among assassination libels, these anthologists proposed a certain beginning and a decidedly revolutionary end to the recent history of erotic royal favoritism. In addition, they exhibited a corresponding development in poets' methods of censuring favorites. For, of course, they showed that favorites had grown worse by demonstrating, more directly, how they provoked increasingly intense opposition from poets. For instance, only in the latest attacks on Buckingham did libelers demand or celebrate the duke's murder. The authors of earlier libels on the duke fixated not on his death but on his sexuality. And the opponents of Somerset had focused not directly on the earl's sexual misconduct, but on that of his wife. The diction and tone of Ralegh libelers came to pale in comparison to those deployed against Somerset and especially Buckingham. When verse collectors gathered together libels on favorites from Ralegh to Buckingham in their miscellanies, they displayed how both favorites and libelers had become bolder and stronger over the last four or five decades. And when they included assassination libels in such collections of political verse, they exhibited how the history of libeling early modern English favorites culminated in Felton's revolutionary act, and poets' praise of it.

Yet collectors of late Buckingham libels generally preferred Donne's parodies of Ralegh's courtly love to libelers' more overt criticisms of the late Elizabethan courtier. In the first few miscellanies discussed below, they collected Donne's anti-courtly love poems among both love lyrics attributed to Ralegh and late Buckingham libels. These particular collectors not only displayed the tension between Ralegh's courtly and Donne's anti-courtly love. They also positioned Donne's sexually explicit elegies as early, tame attempts to mock a royal favorite. In the hands of these collectors, Donne's anti-courtly love poems assumed a place in the history of opposing great courtiers, in which his relatively subtle mockery of Ralegh comes to look rather polite. By placing Donne's poems in this context, these anthologists suggested that, just as Ralegh helped to initiate the style of courtiership that Buckingham would later exploit, Donne preceded early Stuart libelers in deploying manuscript verse against royal favorites.

Most collectors of late Buckingham libels and anti-courtly love poems, however, copied no Ralegh texts in their miscellanies. In part by omitting such late Elizabethan references from the manuscript contexts that they supplied for anti-courtly love poetry, these more numerous anthologists effectively completed the process of recontextualization that this book has analyzed. Needless to say, they immersed the genre in a literary and political culture that had changed dramatically from the late Elizabethan environment of its emergence. More to the point, such collectors helped to remove anti-courtly love poetry from the place that certain collectors had assigned it in the rather tame, early days of mocking royal favorites. Those who excluded Ralegh from their anthologies of anti-courtly love poems and libels on early Stuart favorites may have made it difficult for their readers to chart the ideological distance between these two genres. Without Ralegh, such miscellanies of erotic and political verse appear to be quite miscellaneous, and parodies of late Elizabethan courtly love begin to look simply, if inexplicably, compatible with some of the most revolutionary literature of the early seventeenth century.

Not even in the rest of Charles I's troubled reign, in the years leading up to the civil wars, would libelers circulate more revolutionary verses than those that encouraged and praised Buckingham's assassination. As a result, Buckingham's assassination continued to define recent English history for verse collectors throughout the 1630s and well into the 1640s. Given their disdain for the Catholic Spanish Infanta, one might expect libelers to have later attacked Charles I's French Catholic bride, Henrietta Maria. Yet few libels even mention her, and none slander her.[6] And, given their censures of early Stuart royal favorites, one may look for libels on Charles I's chief councillor of 1639–40, Thomas Wentworth, earl of Strafford. Yet, apart from one passing, derogatory reference, libelers considered Strafford only in ambivalent epitaphs, which weigh his positive attributes against negative ones.[7] When Felton killed Buckingham, and libelers turned from censuring the duke to praising his assassin, they effectively concluded the most revolutionary body of poems on affairs of state to emerge from early seventeenth-century England. And when verse collectors in turn gathered the last of these libels among anti-courtly love poems, they completed the first of several major recontextualizations that anti-courtly love poetry would undergo at the hands of anthologists, editors, and readers. In doing so, these collectors demonstrated that, like other literary agents, they exercised considerable influence in both literary and political matters.

[6] Queen Henrietta Maria appears briefly in a few libels that are largely concerned with others. In a verse letter ostensibly written from prison before Buckingham's voyage to Ré, beginning 'In reading these my Lord youll see I've got,' the speaker briefly registers that he and his fellow prisoners discuss, among other political issues, the queen's Catholicism: 'The Queene should nowe be crown'd shee was converted' (Bodleian MS Malone 23, pp. 58–61; Folger MS V.a.276, pt. 2, fol. 33v; Bellany and McRae, 'Early Stuart Libels,' Oii4, l. 51). Another libel on Ré, a mock song, concludes with a possibly flippant, but by no means scurrilous, blessing on the queen: 'God blesse the Church and Parliament,/Our Queene God blesse, and Wee' (British Library MS Sloane 826, fols 167r–71r; Bellany and McRae, 'Early Stuart Libels,' Oii7, ll. 108–9). 'The progresse' begins, 'See what a love there is betweene/The K: & his endeared Queene' and proceeds to slander members of the queen's household (Folger MS V.b.110, pp. 88–90; Bodleian MS Ashmole 36, 37, fol. 264r; Bellany and McRae, 'Early Stuart Libels,' R5). Likewise, 'A health to my Lady Duchess' offers ironic toasts to a series of courtiers with links to the queen, without openly criticizing her (British Library MS Harley 6383, fols 49r–50r; Bellany and McRae, 'Early Stuart Libels,' R6). Bellany and McRae note the 'anachronistic air' of these last two libels, suggesting that they may have been composed quite late.

[7] A 1640 libel identifies Sir Thomas Wentworth, earl of Strafford and Lord-Deputy of Ireland, as 'blacke Tom Tyrant of Ireland' (British Library MS Harley 6947, fol. 210r–v; National Library of Scotland MS Advocates' 19.3.8, fol. 33r; Trinity College Dublin MS 806, fol. 535r; 'Early Stuart Libels,' R8, l. 2). The ambiguous epitaphs on Strafford, most likely composed in the following year, each registered both the popular love and the hate that he inspired: 'Epitaph on the Earle of Strafford.//Here lies wise and valiant dust' (British Library MSS Add. 22602, fol. 36r; Add. 37719, fol. 193v; Bodleian MSS Eng. poet. c.50, fol. 122r; Eng. poet. e.97, p. 193; University of Wales, Bangor MS 422, p. 108); 'An Epitaph upon the Earle/of Strafford.//Here lyes wisdome, Courage, witt' (British Library MS Egerton 2725, fol. 78r); 'An Eligie on ye Earle of Strafford//Great Strafford, worthy of that name, though all' (Bodleian MS Ashmole 36, 37, fol. 33v; Beinecke MS Osborn b200, p. 279; British Library MS Egerton 2725, fol. 78r–v).

ROYAL FAVORITES FROM RALEGH TO BUCKINGHAM

This study of the collectors of anti-courtly love poems got under way, in Chapter 2, with those who also attributed love lyrics to Ralegh. This final chapter begins by returning to the miscellanies of two of those compilers, for they also included late Buckingham libels in their anthologies. By so doing, they placed anti-courtly love poetry in a brief history of erotic royal favoritism that stretches from Ralegh's courtly love poetry to Buckingham's assassination—approximately parallel to the history of favoritism that I have sketched in this book. One of these collectors figured largely in the previous chapter, on account of the Spanish match libels that he transcribed, with a fair hand, into his attractive folio now in the Bodleian's Rawlinson Poetry collection. After his booklets of poems were bound together with blank gatherings, he copied into a recto near the back of the volume two libels that ostensibly address Buckingham in harsh tones before and after his 1627 expedition to the Ile de Ré, respectively. In the middle of the page, he separated these two texts with one of the chronograms praying for the duke's death in 1628.[8] Elsewhere, he had included funeral elegies on two Englishmen who died at Ré.[9] Thus the scribe lamented the loss of individuals who perished in the invasion, and placed the blame for their deaths squarely on Buckingham. Whereas he mourned the deaths of the duke's soldiers, this collector registered Buckingham's own death only hopefully, in the chronogram, or indirectly, in one of the most popular epitaphs on Felton, which begins 'Here vninter'd suspends (though not to save/surviving freinds th'expences of a grave).'[10] This excellent poem offers a meditation on the body of Felton hanging in

[8] Bodleian MS Rawl. poet. 160, fol. 198r ('ON/The Duke of/Bucks.//And wilt thou goe, great duke, & leave vs here'; 'GEorgIVs DVX $_{B}$VC$_{K}$I$_{NGA}$MI$_{\AE}$/1628//Thy numeros name with this year doth agree'; 'Art thou return'd great Duke w.th all thy faults').

[9] Bodleian MS Rawl. poet. 160, fols 22r–23r ('AN ELEGIE/vpon the death of Sr Iohn/Burgh slaine in the/Isle of Ree w.th a mus=/=ket shott A.^{o}/1627//Oh wound vs not with this sad tale forbeare'), 53v–54r ('AN/Elegie vpon y^{e} death/of Sr Charles Rich/Slaine at y^{e}/Isle of/Ree.//How faine would we forget this fatall war').

[10] Bodleian MS Rawl. poet. 160, fol. 53r ('VPON FELTON/That kild y^{e} Duke of/Bucks & was hang'd/in Chaines.//Here vninter'd suspends (though not to save').

chains at Portsmouth, on Charles I's orders, after the lieutenant's execution. It proposes that, despite the king's attempt to disgrace him publicly, the heavens and earth recognize and affirm Felton's glory: the stars adorn his tomb of air; the skies rain down embalming tears; and the birds '[c]ontend to reach his body to his soule.' In this verse collector's piecemeal account of 1627–28, the departed soldiers who fought at Ré receive due honor; only their commander deserved to die.

The scribe responsible for this miscellany sharpened its contrast between the deaths of valiant protestants and Buckingham with the inclusion of an elaborate, and quite rare, 1626 funeral elegy, complete with a prefatory address to the reader. When he arranged his booklets of poems for binding, he decided to begin his folio with this elegy on 'y^{t} most execrable murther of Thomas Scott/Preacher.' According to the rest of the scribe's heading, Scott 'was kild by an English soldier in a Church=/=Porch at Vtrecht, as he was entring to deuine seruice.'[11] The soldier, John Lambert, stabbed Scott in the stomach with a rapier.[12] Scott thus died rather like Buckingham would. Despite the similarities between them, the compiler of this miscellany represented the murders of Scott and Buckingham in pointedly opposite fashion. Throughout his accounts of notable deaths, the deceased almost always receive the attention and praise. Killers deserved, at best, passing references—that is, until the collector reached Buckingham and Felton. For these two influential men, he reversed his policy: the poems that he collected praise the assassin and censure the victim. The compiler of this miscellany joined a large number of early modern poets and verse collectors in reserving unusually harsh treatment for Buckingham, and in defending Felton. Yet, by opposing Buckingham's assassination to that of Thomas Scott, this collector arguably pronounced uncommon support for the militant, protestant ideology that spurred Felton on.

Perhaps more than any other writer, Scott had expressed in controversial prose the radical sentiments evident in so many of the verse libels of the 1620s. Published widely first in print and then in manuscript, his 1619 *Vox populi or Newes from Spayne* offered a fictional, yet beguiling,

[11] Bodleian MS Rawl. poet. 160, fols 5r ('A distracted Elegie vpon y^{t} most execrable murther of Thomas Scott/Preacher whoe was kild by an English soldier in a Church=/= Porch at Vtrecht, as he was entring to deuine seruice//Keep thy teares reader & y^{t} softer sorrow'), 5r–10r ('Not more lamented for soe hard a fate').

[12] Sean Kelsey, 'Scott, Thomas (*d.* 1626),' *ODNB.*

account of a report that the Spanish ambassador, Gondomar, delivered in Madrid after his first embassy to England. Among his machinations to subdue England to Rome and Spain, Scott's Gondomar boasts of orchestrating the downfall and, he hopes, the execution of 'that admirable Engine *Raleigh*,' whose western design threatened Spain's colonial empire.[13] *Vox populi* caused an uproar and an official search for the identity of the author, who had escaped to the continent. Back in England, the authorities arrested the former soldier and newswriter Thomas Gainsford as a suspect, confiscating his manuscript work 'Vox spiritus, or, Sir Walter Ralegh's ghost.'[14] In later works, Scott adopted Gainsford's ghost trope. He resurrected another royal favorite of Elizabeth's in his 1624 pamphlet *Robert Earle of Essex his Ghost*.[15] And in one of his last tracts, he invoked Ralegh in order to report on yet another 'secret Consultation, newly holden in the Court of Spaine.'[16] In *Sir Walter Rawleighs Ghost, or Englands Forewarner*, Gondomar meets 'the Ghost of Sir *Walter Rauleigh K*night, a Noble famous English-man and a renowned Souldier.'[17] Before the dazzling apparition, Gondomar confesses that, among his extensive sins, he 'did both plot, pursue, effect and consumate' Ralegh's demise; that he 'made thine end my beginning, thy fall the fulnesse of my perfection, and thy destruction the last worke or master peece of all my wisedome and pollicie.'[18] In the throes of the Spanish match crisis, Scott dramatically opposed Ralegh's protestant virtue to the deception of the Spanish ambassador. In large part because of Scott, Ralegh had passed on to a politically useful afterlife.

As an impressive collector of political literature including the elegy on Scott, the compiler of the Rawlinson Poetry miscellany most likely recalled the polemicist's resurrection of Ralegh's reputation when he copied the composite love poem purportedly by 'SIR/Walter Ralegh to / Queene Eliza=/=beth.'[19] Regardless of whether he knew about Scott's prose on Ralegh, though, this verse collector was enlisting the departed

13 *Vox Popvli. Or Newes from Spayne* ([London?]: n.p., 1620; STC 22098.5), sig. C1r.

14 S. A. Baron, 'Gainsford, Thomas (*bap.* 1566, *d.* 1624),' *ODNB*.

15 *Robert Earle of Essex His Ghost* (Printed in Paradise [London: J. Beale?], 1624; STC 22084).

16 *Sir Walter Rawleighs Ghost, or Englands Forewarner* (Vtricht: Iohn Schellem, 1626; STC 22085), sig. A1r.

17 *Sir Walter Rawleighs Ghost*, sig. B2v.

18 *Sir Walter Rawleighs Ghost*, sigs B4v, C3v–C4r.

19 Bodleian MS Rawl. poet. 160, fol. 117r.

Elizabethan courtier in an outstanding presentation of political sentiments that Scott had shared. While this collector did not invoke Ralegh as a ghost in his miscellany, he did represent Elizabeth as a protestant saint in his copies of the commons' petitionary exchange. He thus recast Ralegh's lyric intimacy with the queen as holy and, moreover, zealously protestant, given Saint Elizabeth's objections to the forces that threatened the church and state in her absence. More importantly, though, this anonymous collector produced a miscellany with an unusually consistent political outlook. By doing so, he effectively appropriated the composite lyric that he ascribed to Ralegh, along with virtually all of the other texts that he transcribed, including his anti-courtly love poems.

Having now engaged this Rawlinson Poetry miscellany in a series of early Stuart contexts, one can draw a few conclusions about its compiler's political views, or those of its intended audience. In addition to his extensive collection of verses opposing the Spanish match and Buckingham, and defending militant English protestants, he collected a number of other texts that suggest a commitment to the protestant cause at home and abroad: an anagram on 'THE GVNNE POWDER/CONSPIRRACIE'; a series of five verses praising the defender of the faith, Gustavus Adolphus, King of Sweden; three poems on English protestants' best connection to their embattled brethren on the continent, Elizabeth, Queen of Bohemia; a letter to the pope from Lucifer; and an epitaph on Dr. Theodore Price, the ceremonialist Anglican clergyman who allegedly 'dyde a roman/Catholicke' and therefore, in the words of the poem, a 'false Iem.'[20] Moreover, the texts that this verse collector left out of his miscellany say as much about his politics as do

[20] Bodleian MS Rawl. poet. 160, fols 34r–v ('THE GVNNE POWDER/CONSPIRRACIE/Anagrammatized/NOWE GOD CAN PRE=/=SERVE T[H]E PRINCE//Now now I see though earth, & hell, conspire'), 38r–v ('AN/Encomiastick Epicedium/in memory of the/illustrious & eu[er]/renowned late/k: of Sweth=/=land//There needs noe trumpet but his name'), 38v ('VPON/The glorious King/of Sweden://Seeke not sad reader, here to find//Tho: Roe. Eques Auratus'; 'Another//Gustauus, in the bed of honor dyde'), 39r ('AN:/Elegie consecrated to y^{e}/pious memory of y^{e}/most renowned/king of Swe=/=den://Oh for a laureat, a Sydneyan quire!//M:^{r} W:^{m} Hodgson'), 39v–41r ('AN/Elegie vpon the Victorious/King of Sweden//Like a cold fatall sweat, y^{t} vshers death//Hen: King'), 84r–v ('TO/The queene of/Bohemia.//Bright soule of whome, if any countrey$_{(known}$'), 84v ('AN OTHER//Shine on maiestick soule, abide//G: H:'), 109r–v ('ON my Princesse & M.^{rs}/the Lady Elisabeth elected/Queene of Bohemia.//Yow violets

the texts that he transcribed. Many of his contemporaries collected the sort of decidedly protestant, anti-Catholic texts that he did. Yet most verse collectors moderated the political sentiments in such literature, for instance by including anti-puritan verses in their anthologies as well. None of the texts that the compiler of this Rawlinson Poetry manuscript copied in his miscellany distances him from puritans. This anonymous verse collector qualifies then as an unusually radical collector of libels and especially of anti-courtly love poems.

As I suggested in Chapter 2, the compiler of the Rawlinson Poetry miscellany effectively positioned Ralegh, in his guise as the courtier poet responsible for the Carew–Ayton conflation, as the target of Donne's parody in 'To his Mistress going to bed.' Furthermore, having offered Ralegh as the earliest in his miscellany's series of eroticized royal favorites, which ends with the murdered Buckingham, this verse collector assigned Donne's anti-courtly love poetry a role in the history of writers opposing favorites. He established a remarkable relationship between the representations of love and the political sentiments in his miscellany. For his choice in libels expresses a much more consistent political outlook than most miscellanies offer, so much so that this collector's personal politics effectively envelope all of the texts that he transcribed. The compiler of the Rawlinson Poetry miscellany did what perhaps no other collector of the genre accomplished in manuscript: he assimilated anti-courtly love poetry to radical protestant politics.

Contrast the militant protestant ideology of the Rawlinson Poetry manuscript to the political balance exhibited in the Rosenbach miscellany that Chapter 2 also introduced. The copyist who began this Rosenbach manuscript started with visually impressive settings of two Spanish match libels: one a mythological epithalamium composed on the assumption that the marriage would occur, and the other a poetically ambitious record of the jubilant celebrations that followed the

y^{t} doe first appeare//S:^{r} Hen: Wotton'), 159v–61v ('A COPIE OF A/Letter sent vnto the/Pope/To the most pious vertuos and religious/Primate of all Christendome, Vrban y^{e}/Eighth of that name and my Vice=/=gerent here vpon earth: I Lucifer god/of the world, Lord of Gehenna, Kinge/of Tartara, prince of Abyssus, and sole/comander of the infernall feinds send/Greeting//Most reverent and Deare sonne whose holines'), 163r ('AN/Epitaph on Dr Price/subdeane of Westm[inster]/who dyde a roman/Catholicke//This stone hides him who for the stone'). On Price, see J. F. Merritt, 'Price, Theodore (*c.*1570–1631),' *ODNB*.

failure of the match.[21] When a second compiler took over the task of transcription, he resumed with an enormously popular verse addressed to Felton in prison, which encourages the assassin to 'Enjoy thy bondage make thy prison knowe/Thou has a liberty thou can'st not owe.'[22] This pro-Felton libel lends fatal seriousness to the negative representations of Buckingham that the second compiler transcribed in the following pages: a composite text of three libels that registers the duke's excessive power, and the libels that taunt Buckingham before and after Ré.[23] Elsewhere, this verse collector copied the epitaph on Felton hanging in chains among both negative and positive representations of Buckingham.[24] Felton remains a hero in this Rosenbach manuscript, yet his victim occasions some disagreement. If the compilers of this miscellany recorded more criticism of Buckingham than praise, they were only providing a representative sample of libels on the duke. While they acknowledged the extreme unpopularity of both the Spanish match and Buckingham, they also countenanced, and indeed facilitated, debate on the controversial political events and players of the 1620s. Whereas the compiler of the Rawlinson Poetry manuscript above used his miscellany to define a consistent position on early Stuart politics, the collectors of the libels in the Rosenbach manuscript surveyed a variety of such positions, effectively moderating discussion on recent developments in English history. Indeed, these collectors appreciated a measure of polyphony that the individual authors in their miscellany could not have achieved on their own.

[21] Rosenbach MS 239/27, pp. 1–6 ('Verses vpon the Princes returne from/Spaine.// The day was turn'd to starlight, & was runne'), 6–10 ('Another on the same.//Oh for an Ovid or a Homer now'). 'Oh for an Ovid or a Homer now' also appears at Beinecke MS Osborn b356, pp. 149–56; Brotherton MS Lt q 44, fols 31v–33v.

[22] Rosenbach MS 239/27, pp. 45–46 ('To his confined freind M^{r} ffelton.//Enjoy thy bondage make thy prison knowe').

[23] Rosenbach MS 239/27, pp. 46 ('Verses one the state//Our states a game att cardes, the counsell deale'), 46–47 ('Iustice of late hath lost her witts'), 47 ('A thing gott by candle light'), 54^{b}–57^{b} ('On the Duke//And art return'd againe with all thy faults'), 57^{b} ('The Dukes ffarewell.//And wilt thou goe great Duke & leaue vs heare'). See Bellany and McRae, 'Early Stuart Libels,' Oiii10, Oi13, Oiii15, Oii5, Oii12.

[24] Rosenbach MS 239/27, pp. 318 ('On the Dukes death.//Some say the Duke was vertuous gracious, good') 318–19 ('The Dukes Ghoast//I that my Country did betray'), 319 ('Another on the Duke//Loe in this marble I entombed am'; 'On Felton suspended.// Heere unterr'd suspends (though not to saue'), 384–86 ('On the Duke of Buck[ingham]s: death//when Poetts vse to write, men vse to saye'). See Bellany and McRae, 'Early Stuart Libels,' Pii5, Pii15, Pi34, Piii15.

The expansive view of particularly the second, and dominant, compiler of the Rosenbach miscellany may have enabled him to recognize the roles that courtly and anti-courtly love poetry had played in recent English history. It certainly made him a less ideologically invested collector of Ralegh texts than the compiler of the Rawlinson Poetry manuscript, especially of the Carew–Ayton conflation that he too attributed to the once-great courtier. As I discussed in Chapter 2, the main compiler of the Rosenbach manuscript recognized the relationship between Ralegh's courtly and Donne's anti-courtly love poetry. For, in addition to ascribing Carew's and Ayton's composite representation of suffering love to Ralegh, he juxtaposed it to Donne's 'Loues Progresse' and 'To his Mistress going to bed.'[25] He thus credited Ralegh with a fitting, albeit misleading, example of courtly love, and visually opposed it to Donne's most sexually explicit elegies. In doing so, he offered a particularly compelling reconstruction of the politics of anti-courtly love poetry. Although he also collected a few laudatory epitaphs for Elizabeth and Ralegh, he left out of his anthology the texts (on Thomas Scott and Saint Elizabeth) that lend the Elizabethan favorite such glory in the Rawlinson Poetry miscellany.[26] Even though Ralegh poses as the author of Carew's and Ayton's courtly love lyrics in both miscellanies, the legendary courtier plays a less ideologically overdetermined role in the Rosenbach manuscript.

Nevertheless, the compiler of the Rosenbach miscellany also offered Ralegh as the earliest in his series of sexualized royal favorites, leading up to the deceased Buckingham. He placed his cluster of Ralegh and Donne poems within one of his sequences of libels on early Stuart favorites from Somerset to Buckingham.[27] Within the first several pages that he filled after taking over the task of transcription, this anonymous collector exhibited several key texts in the history of royal favoritism, and in the culture of mocking royal favorites in verse. In his miscellany, one can see a development in the erotics of favoritism from

[25] Rosenbach MS 239/27, pp. 47–52.

[26] Rosenbach MS 239/27, pp. 324 ('In mortem Elizab: Reginæ//Weepe greatest Ile, and for thy mistresse losse'), 325 ('Another.//The queene was brought by water to white Hall'; 'Another•//Spaines rodd. Romes ruine, Neitherlands releife'), 357–58 ('On Sr Walter Rawleighs death//Great heart who taught thee soe to dye').

[27] Rosenbach MS 239/27, p. 57 ('On the Lord Carr.//When Carr att first in court a page beganne').

Ralegh's courtly love to Buckingham's seductions in 'the fiue senses.'[28] One can also recognize a corresponding progression in the rhetoric of these favorites' enemies. This progression culminates, again, in libelers' celebrations of Buckingham's murder; and it also includes less virulent representations of Buckingham, as well as Somerset. I suggest that this particular verse collector's series of poetic responses to royal favorites also includes the anti-courtly love poems that he acquired. By juxtaposing Donne's sexually explicit elegies to the composite love lyric that he attributed to Ralegh, the compiler of this Rosenbach miscellany arguably positioned anti-courtly love poems as early, comparatively sedate examples of a poet mocking a royal favorite. In other words, this verse collector effectively placed Donne's anti-courtly love poems at the beginning of his account of poetic opposition to royal favorites.

Similarly, this collector surrounded anti-courtly love poems by other authors with additional verses on favorites ranging from Ralegh to Buckingham. He followed the anonymous, salacious monologue 'Nay pish, nay pheu, nay faith but will you, fy' with Buckingham libels; and he placed Davies' quintessential anti-courtly love poems among Ralegh poems, a Somerset libel, and another verse on Buckingham.[29] In other words, he kept Ralegh close to Somerset and Buckingham, and anti-courtly love poems near verses on these royal favorites. While I argue that he thus positioned anti-courtly love poems in the history of libeling royal favorites, I consider it undebatable that this verse collector thoroughly recontextualized anti-courtly love poetry with early Stuart libels, including the last verses on Buckingham. The verse collectors surveyed in the rest of this chapter did the same, even though they diminished or eliminated Ralegh's role in their miscellanies. While they thus did little or nothing to reconstruct the original context of anti-courtly love

[28] Rosenbach MS 239/27, pp. 58^{b}–60.

[29] Rosenbach MS 239/27, pp. 157 ('A maides denyall.//Nay pish, nay pheu, nay faith but will you, fy'), 167 ('Verses on the Duke, if read backward/in a contrary sense.//Mens bona non vagasors, virtus no[n] gratia Regis'), 167 ('GeorgIVs DVX bVCkInghaMIæ 1628'), 175–77 ('Goe soul the bodies guest//S.^{r} W: R:'), 182 ('The rusticke gallants wooinge.//ffaire wench I cannot court thy spritelike eyes'), 182 ('The lowest shrubbs haue topps, ye ant her gall'), 187 ('On the shortnesse of mans life.//W^{t} is our life? a play of passion'), 194 ('To the Duke of Buckingham.//The kinge loues you, you him, both loue ye same'), 194 ('On a Lady.//There was att Court a Lady of late'), 206 ('On a downright suitor//Faith wench I loue thee, but I cannot sue').

poetry, they did plenty to recontextualize the genre with the latest and most radical libels on early modern English royal favorites.

In Henry Lawson's miscellany, for instance, Ralegh appears without suggesting much about the late Elizabethan politics of the anti-courtly love poems in the anthology. Buckingham and Felton, on the other hand, play such large roles in this manuscript that they necessarily affect the politics of the genre. Ralegh's name shows up just once, attributing a popular Somerset libel to him.[30] The primary compiler of the miscellany may have also had Ralegh in mind when he transcribed a series of three poems: Ayton's 'Wrong not deare emprese of my hart,' with neither an attribution nor Carew's prefatory lines, and two epigrams on tobacco, which Ralegh famously promoted.[31] The copyist did not name Ralegh in connection to these verses, though. Moreover, he does not seem to have regarded them as related to the manuscript's few examples of anti-courtly love poetry, which appear elsewhere in the volume.[32] The multiple compilers of this verse miscellany did, however, immerse their courtly and anti-courtly love poems, along with virtually all of the other texts that they collected, in a political culture profoundly shaped by the Buckingham assassination.[33] Apparently unconcerned about the original politics of anti-courtly love poetry, the verse collectors who collaborated on Henry Lawson's miscellany nevertheless demonstrated their ability to alter those politics by putting the genre in the context of Buckingham's death. As the next section of the chapter makes clear, they were joining a number of other verse collectors in completing a major effort of recontextualization.

30 Bodleian MS Eng. poet. e.14, fol. 49r ('S^{r}. Walter Raleigh to ye Ld Carr//I.C.V.R: good mounser Carr').

31 Bodleian MS Eng. poet. e.14, fol. 19r ('A Song/38//Wrong not deare emprese of my hart'; 'On Tobacco/39//Our gallants of tobacco well esteeme'; 'On the praise of the same/40//Nature Idea Phisicks rare perfection').

32 Bodleian MS Eng. poet. e.14, fols 29v–30r ('D^{r}: Dun://Marry & Love thy Flavia; for she'), 75v ('A wooer/211//ffaire wench I cannot court thy sprightly eyes').

33 Bodleian MS Eng. poet. e.14, fol. 12v ('Here vnenterred suspends though to saue'; 'Immortall man of glory, whose stout hand'; 'Iohn Felton: NO FELLON'), 13r ('On the D. of Buck// I that my cuntry did betray'; 'Rex and Grex alike doth sound'), 14v ('verses written to M.^{r} ffelton by Mr T.//Enioy thy bondage make thy prison knowe'), 15r ('The Duks epitaph//If idle travilers ~~be~~^{aske} aske who lys here'), 15r–v 'In the praise of the Duke//Yet were bidentalls sacred, and the place'), 15v ('His Epitaph//Reader stand still loe here I am'), 19r ('On ye D: of B//Some say the D: was gratious virtious good'), 19r–v ('A diologue between Caron and ye D: of B://C At porchmouth D: I can noe longer stay').

THE END OF A COLLECTIVE EFFORT OF RECONTEXTUALIZATION

The previous two chapters have considered Edward Denny's manuscript verse miscellany, now at the Huntington, focusing especially on its remarkable sequence of Donne poems and libels on the duke of Buckingham and the countess of Somerset.[34] This brief series of verses features two of libelers' most elaborate attempts to sexualize and shame these court figures: 'The fiue Sences' and 'She that with Troupes of Bustuary Slaues.' Immediately following these libels, Denny or whoever compiled his anthology transcribed two Donne poems that also mix sex and shame, 'The Curse' and 'The Bracelet.' In each of these poems, Donne both sexualizes a woman and issues a curse. Again, the speaker of the former poem curses any man who attempts to discover the identity of his mistress with an unattractive, unfaithful mistress of his own, who will (according to the curse) publicly shame him. For its part, 'The Bracelet' concludes with a curse on the person who finds the lost bracelet of the speaker's mistress. Like Donne's sexually explicit lines in these poems, his curses resonate with the libels in Denny's miscellany; 'The Bracelet' even mentions libels by name. Donne's speaker hopes that whoever finds the bracelet will also stumble upon 'libels, or some Interdicted thing/w^{ch}: neglegently left thy ruine bring.'[35] In other words, he hopes that the finder of the bracelet will become a careless verse collector, causing his own 'ruine' by 'neglegently' leaving libels where others, perhaps the authorities, can find them. When Donne originally made this reference to libels, he could not have foreseen how the word's meaning would change as Buckingham provoked unprecedentedly radical examples of the genre over the course of his career.

[34] Huntington MS HM 198, pt. 1, pp. 30–32 ('The fiue Sences/Seing//From such A face whose excellence'), 32–33 ('If shaddoues be A pictures excellence'), 33–34 ('verses made on the Cou: of Somersett://She that with Troupes of Bustuary Slaues'), 34–35 ('Duns Curse upon him that knew his m:^{rs}//whoesoeuer ghesses, thinkes, or dreames he knowes'), 35–37 ('upon the loss of A Braclett://Not that in cullour it was like thy Haire'), 43–44 ('Come Madame come all rest my powers defye'), 44–46 ('And art return'd againe with all thy faults').

[35] Huntington MS HM 198, pt. 1, p. 37. I thank Peter Beal for transcribing these lines for me. See also *Donne Variorum*, 2:7, 40 ('The Bracelet,' 101–2).

Likewise, he could not have expected careful verse collectors like Denny to keep the libels that they found among Donne's own poems, where their sexual content and ranting tones ironically complement one another. Nevertheless, in Denny's miscellany, Donne's mention of libels comes to point suggestively to the manuscript's verses on Buckingham. As its compiler updated the anthology's collection of poems on the duke, the significance of Donne's word choice continued to change.

A few pages after these two Donne poems, and immediately following 'To his Mistress going to bed,' the scribe copied the libel taunting Buckingham after Ré (beginning 'And art return'd againe with all thy faults'). In this mocking verse, the tone of Donne's curses finds a particularly strong complement. In fact, the miscellany's transition from Donne's erotic monologue to the Ré libel offers an interesting counterpoint to the structure of 'The Bracelet' a few pages before. Like 'To his Mistress going to bed,' 'The Bracelet' addresses the speaker's mistress, positively representing her beauty even while playfully refusing to treat her according to the conventions of courtly love. The speaker of this elegy, however, eventually redirects his address, first to the twelve gold coins that he sadly will have to have melted down in order to replace his mistress' bracelet, and then to the bracelet's finder. In cursing him, Donne's persona does not merely invoke libels; he also anticipates the railing tone and pace of so many of these political verses, including the Ré libel nearby in Denny's miscellany. In this particular anthology, the structure of 'The Bracelet' curiously mirrors the relationship between Donne's anti-courtly love poem and the Ré libel a few pages later. As 'The Bracelet' tranforms from an unidealizing love poem into a harsh curse, Denny's consecutive copies of another Donne elegy and a Buckingham libel together turn attention from a beautiful mistress to a despised man.

In the unique manuscript context of Denny's miscellany, one could go so far as to see in 'The Bracelet' a microcosm of the anthology's cumulative representation of Buckingham. As Donne's elegy turns from a subject of desire to the subject of the speaker's curse, Denny's collection of Buckingham libels follows the duke's transformation from the attractive tempter in 'The fiue Sences' to the subject of derogatory assassination libels. Toward the end of the volume, its compiler added a fine group of poems on the duke's murder. Within a span of seven pages, he transcribed the verse encouraging Felton in prison; the ironically self-incriminating response to the 'Remonstrance' written in the duke's voice; a possibly unique poem on the tears of Buckingham's widow; the laudatory epitaph 'on felton' beginning, 'Immortall man of glory'; and the critical epitaph addressing the duke, 'And art thou who whilom thoughts[t] thy state/to be exempted from the power of fate.'[36] By adding this cluster of assassination libels to Denny's miscellany, its compiler completed a predominantly (but not entirely) negative representation of the deceased Buckingham that updates the preceding pages' depictions of the duke.[37] For instance, in the assassination libel written in his voice, Buckingham effectively accepts the blame for the failure of the Ré expedition assigned him in Denny's copy of 'And art return'd againe with all thy faults.' 'Immortall man of glory' spends more lines attacking Buckingham than praising Felton and confirms the oversexed depiction of the duke in 'The fiue Sences' toward the front of the miscellany. This group of assassination libels modifies the significance of the earlier Buckingham libels in Denny's miscellany, and completes the anthology's negative representation of the duke.

As assassination libels altered the picture of Buckingham in this miscellany, so too did they change the political context of Denny's extensive collection of Donne's poems. For, if the tone of Donne's curses had already complemented the voices of Buckingham's earliest detractors, that tone began to sound particularly consequential when libelers continued to deploy it against the duke even after his death. Furthermore, if Donne's sexualized figures sat comfortably next to representations of Buckingham's sexuality, the politics of such sexual verse changed when libelers celebrated the duke's murder as just punishment for his myriad sins. Assassination libels thus came to dominate both the manuscript environment and the social context of Denny's copies of anti-courtly love poems, not only those by Donne but also others by Beaumont and Carew (in particular, the former's poem for the countess

36 Huntington MS HM 198, pt. 1, pp. 152 ('To ffelton in Prison//Enioy thy bondage make thy prison know'), 156 ('on the Duke of Buckinghams Tombe://Theis are the solem obsequyes'), 157–58 ('The Coppy of A Rodomantatho sent by the Duke to the house of Comons 28: In: 1628:/by the lord Grimes: his graces seruant://Auaunt y^{u} giddy headed Multitude'), 158–59 ('on felton://Imortall man of glory whose braue hand'), 159 ('And art thou who whilom thoughts thy state').

37 In addition to the verse on the tears of Buckingham's widow, Denny's miscellany includes another laudatory poem on the duke's death: 'Geo: D: Buckinghame://Twas fatall unto the that in thy race' (Huntington MS HM 198, pt. 1, p. 96).

of Rutland and Carew's popular 'The Rapture').[38] Denny, and any readers of his quite legible manuscript, may have recognized the anachronism of the new relationships established between these poems in this miscellany. Yet even if they could not disentangle the miscellany's older, politically subtle poems from its newer, overtly seditious ones, readers encountered in this anthology the phenomenon of recontextualization that this book has analyzed. They saw sexualized representations of fictional women mingle with those of identifiable men, and rejections of courtly love poetry related to censures of the early Stuart court. More to the point, by including some of the latest Buckingham libels in the book, the compiler of Denny's miscellany helped to complete this process of recontextualization.

Buckingham's murder likewise defines the political character of an outstanding manuscript verse miscellany purportedly owned by Sir John Reresby, and now held at West Yorkshire Archive Service, Leeds, in Sheepscar. In this anthology too, the assassination anachronistically dominates the context of the anti-courtly love poetry in the folio. Together, the numerous compilers of Reresby's anthology placed a few excellent examples of the genre near the front of the book: 'Nay pish, nay pue, nay faith and will you? fy'; Beaumont's exemplary anti-courtly love poem for the countess of Rutland; 'As I aloane lay slumbringe in my bedd'; and Carew's gentle engagement of anti-courtly love, 'The Rapture.' Elsewhere one of these collectors transcribed Donne's ever-popular 'To his Mistress going to bed.'[39] The compilers of Reresby's anthology also assembled two substantial groups of ideologically diverse assassination libels. In a section of the miscellany devoted to epitaphs (including one each on Ralegh and Elizabeth I), a series of four leaves exhibits the full range of libelers' posthumous representations of Buckingham and Felton. On these folios, a possibly unique lament for the duke precedes a mock-dialogue between him and Charon before they cross the River Styx. Thereafter, John Eliot's sympathetic poems in

[38] Huntington MS HM 198, pt. 1, pp. 117 ('A rapture://I will enioye the now my Celia come'), 193–94 ('The hayre A forrest is of Ambushes'), 205–6 ('fletcher: to ye Countes of Rutland.//Maddam soe may my uerses pleasing bee').

[39] West Yorkshire Archive Service, Leeds MS WYL156/237, fols 6r ('A maides deniall//Nay pish, nay pue, nay faith and will you? fy'), 9r–v ('Madame so may my uerses pleasing bee'), 18r–v ('A Maydes dreame//As I aloane lay slumbringe in my bedd'), 19r–21r ('Caries Rapture.//I will enioy thee, now (my Cælia) come'), 59v–60v ('A louer to his m^rs^//Come Madam come, all rest my powers defy').

Buckingham's voice surround a critical answer to just the sort of apology that Eliot offers, plus a defense of Felton. The sequence then concludes with two laudatory Felton epitaphs.[40] Later in the volume, its compilers copied other Buckingham libels within several leaves of one another. They transcribed a poem on the duke's son and an admission of guilt written in Buckingham's voice a few leaves before Owen Felltham's defense of the duke and Zouch Townley's popular libel encouraging Felton in prison.[41]

Almost as if to interrupt his apology for Buckingham, someone inserted an extra gathering right in the middle of Felltham's poem. In addition to several libels related to James I's reign, this insert features Richard Corbett's funeral elegy on Donne and an anonymous pair of verses that demonstrate several features of the anti-courtly love poetics that Donne had perfected. In the first of these two poems, headed 'A Letter to his M^{rs},' a male speaker denies his beloved the stock Petrarchan compliments: 'Lett others sweare their mistrisses bee fayre/Like Starrs their eyes like threds of gould their hayre.' In 'Her Answer,' a female voice directs her lover's attention from her 'face' to 'some other place,' concluding with the suggestive promise, 'In tyme thou maist inioye the Parke, the Deare, and all.'[42] The female speaker here adopts the metaphor of Venus in one of the most famous and scintillating passages from Shakespeare's Ovidian epyllion, in which the goddess tells Adonis:

40 West Yorkshire Archive Service, Leeds MS WYL156/237, fols 30v ('On Sr Walter Raleighes death//Great hart, who taught the so to dye'), 31r–v ('An Epitaph on the Duke of Buckingham//Long let this word hang on thy lipps' Hee's dead'), 31v–32r ('Caron At Porchmouth (Duke) I can no longer staye'), 32r–v ('Yet war Bydentales sacred, and the place'), 32v–33r ('Mr Cooe hauing writt some verses which hee/intituled, An Apologie for the Duke,/this answer was sent him . . . // So earst did the Plutonian Cart-wheele creake'), 33r ('Som say the Duke was gratious ~~good~~ vertuous good'), 33r ('An Epitaph on the Duke/of Buckingham//Reade, stand still and looke. Loe heere I am'), 33v ('Verses directed to Felton the/Murderer of the Duke//Immortall man of glory, whose braue hand'), 34r ('Feltons Epitaph//~~Heren~~^{Herein} interd,^{suspends} (though not to saue'), 35v ('Vppon the dead body of Queene Elizabeth/brought from Richmond to White Hall// The Queene is come from Richmond to White Hall').

41 West Yorkshire Archive Service, Leeds MS WYL156/237, fols 79r ('On A sonne of the Duk of Buckingham//Made of course and churlish clay'), 80v ('On the Duke of Buckinghame//I (that my countrey did betray'), 82v–83r ('On the Duke of Buckinggame//Sooner may I a fixed Statue bee'), 83v ('An other To Felton//Enioy thy bondage; make thy prison knowe').

42 West Yorkshire Archive Service, Leeds MS WYL156/237, fols 82^{i}v–82^{k}r ('A Letter to his M^{rs}//Lett others sweare theire mistrisses bee fayre'), 82^{k}r–v ('Her Answer//S^{r} you say some prayse ther M^{rs} for her face').

Ile be a parke, and thou shalt be my deare:
Feed where thou wilt, on mountaine, or in dale;
Graze on my lips, and if those hils be drie,
Stray lower, where the pleasant fountaines lie.[43]

In addition, the poetic exchange in Reresby's miscellany rehearses several gestures of shorter anti-courtly love poems, and hearkens to the examples of the genre elsewhere in this manuscript. In an unusual instance of the relationship that verse collectors established between anti-courtly love poetry and Buckingham libels, once the female speaker completes her offer to her lover at the end of the inserted gathering, Felltham abruptly resumes defending the duke, and an anonymous libeler praises Felton.

In a miscellany associated with Oxford, an anonymous manuscript verse collector arranged another page spread that politicizes anti-courtly love poetry with Buckingham libels. Possibly with the collaboration of a partner, he gathered together verses from Christ Church, anti-courtly love poems, and ideologically diverse Buckingham libels. Like the compilers of Reresby's manuscript, he also demonstrated a tendency to group related verses together. For instance, he juxtaposed two Donne elegies; and either he or his partner gathered together a few other anti-courtly love poems elsewhere in the quarto, now in the Bodleian's English Poetry collection.[44] Furthermore, within just a few pages, the main compiler of this manuscript transcribed three positive or ambivalent Buckingham libels: John Eliot's poems composed in Buckingham's confident voice from the grave and the laudatory epitaph attributed in another manuscript to one Dr. Lewis.[45] The predominant compiler of this miscellany moderated the account of Buckingham in these verses with two others that represent the duke somewhat less positively: the

43 William Shakespeare, *Venus and Adonis* (London: Richard Field, 1594; STC 22355), sig. Ci^{v}.

44 Bodleian MS Eng. poet. e.97, pp. 101–2 ('Docter Donne to his M.^{ris}//Till I haue peace with thee warre other men,'), 103–4 ('Docter Donnes speech to his m.^{ris}/going to bedd.//Come Madam, Come, all rest my powers defie;'), 184 ('A Maidens Dreame.//As I lay slumbring in my naked bed'), 185 ('A maides Deniall.//Nay pish, away I pray, nay will you, fie'), 187–89 ('Loues Rapture.//I will Enioy thee now my Cælia! Come,').

45 Bodleian MS Eng, poet. e.97, pp. 57–58 ('On the death of the Duke.//Yet were Bidentalls Sacred, & the place'), 58 ('His Epitaphe.//Reader stand still. Looke here I am'), 60 ('On the Duke of Buckingham.//Hee that can ~~read~~^{spell} a Sigh, or read a teare'). For the attribution to 'Dr Lewis,' see Bodleian MS Rawl. poet. 26, fols 37v–38r.

poem that he and others attributed to Zouch Townley, 'To ffelton in the Tower,' and, just below Townley's relieved approval of the murder, an early libel 'To the Duke' beginning, 'The king loues you, you him.'[46] Placed immediately below Townley's encouraging poem to Felton, this second libel would initially seem to offer some explanation for the assassination, as it hints at sodomy and flippantly attributes the singular royal favor that Buckingham enjoyed to mere 'Luck.' Yet the main collector complicated the political significance of the libel by uniquely ascribing it to 'Richard Corbett,' who had composed and distributed laudatory poems to his patron, Buckingham. Indeed, among twelve accepted Corbett poems, this miscellany features a respectful verse written expressly 'To the Duke of Buckingham' from 'Doctor Corbett.'[47] This miscellany thus registers Corbett's respect for his patron and, in so doing, suggests a unique interpretation of 'The king loues, you, you him.' In Corbett's voice, the libel loses much of its political bite. The subscription to the duke's patronage client effectively curtails each of the libel's politically sensitive gestures, as if to say that the poem could hardly defame Buckingham if his client had written it.

On the page facing this unique interchange of Buckingham libels, the main compiler of this Oxford miscellany placed one of the anti-courtly love poems that he collected. Right after his Townley and Corbett attributions, he copied Sir John Davies' 'ffaire wench, I cannot court your spritlike Eyes' in a quite consistent script.[48] Indeed, he introduced something of a visual rhyme to this page spread with his dramatic inscriptions of the letter *Z* in both 'Zouch Tounly' and Davies' punchline: 'Zounds I can loue thee soundly.' Similarly, in the first words of verse on these facing pages, the majuscule character *ff* in Townley's 'ffarewell' finds a visual parallel in Davies' invocation of his 'ffaire wench.' Thus, on one page of this collector's miscellany, Townley bids good riddance to a court controlled by Buckingham, and Corbett is made to lighten up an acknowledgement of the excessive love between

[46] Bodleian MS Eng. poet. e.97, pp. 91–92 ('To ffelton in the Tower.//Enioy thy bondage, make thy prison know//Zouch Tounly'), 92 ('To the Duke.//The king loues you, you him//Richard Corbett').

[47] Bodleian MS Eng. poet. e.97, p. 154 ('To the Duke of Buckingham.//When I can pay my parents or my King//Docter Corbett.').

[48] Bodleian MS Eng. poet. e.97, p. 93 ('The Rustick-Gallant's wooing.//ffaire wench, I cannot court your spritlike Eyes').

the king and favorite. Then, on the next page, Davies explicitly rejects a style of love associated with the court. By the point that he does so in this Oxford miscellany, Townley has already criticized the 'Court' that the 'fauorite' ruled, and Corbett has purportedly acknowledged the 'loue' that the duke shared with the king.[49] Thus when Davies' speaker refuses to 'court' his mistress in this anthology, the manuscript context redefines his defiant gesture with libelers' various reactions to the 'loue' that defined the late Jacobean court.

By arranging these poems together, the main compiler of this Oxford miscellany highlighted their common, yet distinct, attention to the sort of love found at court. Yet, as English courts had changed over the past several decades, the style of love associated with them had changed as well. Indeed, Buckingham had altered the connotations of the English words *court* and *love* since Davies had chosen them for his poem. Late Buckingham libels, in other words, affected not only the political order in England, but also the English language and, with it, the cultural coordinates upon which the intelligibility of texts depends. Effectively dominating verse collectors' accounts of recent English history throughout the 1630s, these libels shifted the frame of reference for the earlier poems that collectors also kept in their miscellanies. When old poets mocked the sort of love associated with royal favorites in these anthologies, and in this political culture, they no longer retained control of the meanings of their own poems. Verse collectors had effectively taken control of them. In their hands, the love that characterized the court had become a far more contentious and openly political subject than it had been for Davies or anyone else who had mocked courtly love in Elizabeth's day. And in their miscellanies, parodies of courtly love acquired an affinity for other poets' bold representations of the love between royal favorite and king.

A FUTURE ROYALIST TURNS DONNE INTO A SUPPORTER OF FELTON

In the late 1630s, the future royalist captain Nicholas Burghe compiled the perfect miscellany with which to conclude this study. In

[49] Bodleian MS Eng. poet. e.97, pp. 91–92.

his composite manuscript, now among those that Elias Ashmole bequeathed to the Bodleian, Burghe collected a fine sample of nearly all of the sorts of poems considered in this book, from epitaphs on Elizabeth I to an ideologically diverse range of Buckingham libels; from popular to rare anti-courtly love poems. From the very first page of his anthology, Burghe gave John Donne a peculiarly exalted role in his account of recent English literary history. On that page, he incorrectly credited Donne with verses possibly by the poet's friend Sir Henry Wotton. On the next page, he misattributed one of Sir Francis Bacon's poems to Donne, apparently before a collaborator corrected his mistake.[50] Thus, although he demonstrated a greater interest in authorship than many of his fellow verse collectors, Burghe tended to get his Donne attributions wrong. Of the twelve or thirteen texts that he assigned to the poet, Burghe's contemporaries seconded only six, and Donne's editors have accepted only five.[51] The relative inaccuracy of Burghe's attributions, however, hardly makes them inconsequential. Indeed,

[50] Bodleian MS Ashmole 38, pp. 1 ('Doctor Donn's valadiction/to the ~~warld~~ worlde//Farewell yea guilded follies, pleasing troubles'), 2 ('On mans Mortalite by ~~Doctor Dunn/~~ *Sr Fran: Bacon*//The worlds A buble and thy lyfe of man'). In this note, I have italicized the text in the second hand. I consider this hand that of a collaborator because Burghe continued working on the manuscript even after the second hand added text. Burghe completed one of the collaborator's partial transcriptions: '*And art thou back returnd wth all thy faults,*' pp. 133–35), and added short texts under other texts in the second hand: '*from Kathirn'gs dock was launch'd A pinck*'; 'Vppon S^{t} paule pynderes begin[in]ge to repayre s^{t} Paules Church//St Paule sainct Paule hath brauely ^{Glorius} decte w^{t}hin' (p. 135); 'On the Countes of Sommersett//From Katherins Docke was launcht a Pincke'; '*If thou beleiu'st I loue thee, thou art lost*'; 'Wee are A game att Cardes; the Counsell deale' (p. 136). The second hand distinguishes itself from Burghe's with its secretary *c* and, occasionally, *C*; epsilon *E* and, occasionally, *e*; uncrossed *A*; ampersand; and generally thick, dull appearance.

[51] Burghe copied his five accepted Donne poems in Bodleian MS Ashmole 38, pp. 14 ('To Christ://Wilt thou forgiue those sinns whear I begune//finis D Donn'), 40 ('A Satire against the Court/wrighten by Doctor Dunn, In/Queene Elizabeths Raigne//Well I may now receyue and dye; my sinn'), 49 ('A Comination wrigten by/D. Donn//Who euer guesses, dreames or thinkes hee knowes'), 63 ('Come Maddame, come; all rest my powers defye//D Donn'), 202 ('An Epitaphe wrighten by Doctor Donne ~~of~~/on the death of Marqesse Hambleton//Wheather that soule that now Coems vpp to you').

Burghe also attributed to Donne six lines of dialogue in verse, the first two in a woman's voice and the last four in that of a man. Bodleian MS Ashmole 38, p. 152 ('S^{r} say not that you love vnless you doe//D: Donn'). Other verse collectors attributed the man's part to Donne: Folger MS V.a.170, p. 49 ('A Lady to Dr Donne.//Say not you love, vnlesse you doe:'; 'His answer, to the Lady.//Madam I love: and love to doe:'); Huntington MS HM 116, p. 12 ('A Gentlewoman to Doctour Dun//Say not you loue, vnlesse you doe'; 'Dr Dun to his Wife giuing him ye Lye//You say I Lie, I say you lie').

partially because he proved such a poor witness of authorship, Burghe offers an especially good example of verse collectors' unique literary agency, as distinct from that of authors.

Among other verses, Burghe put Donne's name on Elizabethan satire and anti-courtly love poetry, and—surprisingly—even the popular epitaph on Felton's body hanging in chains at Portsmouth. Both recognizing and exaggerating Donne's literary reputation, Burghe claimed that the same poet who mocked Elizabethan courtiers came out of literary retirement to applaud the demise of the last great early Stuart favorite. He gave his copy of 'Here vnInter,'d, Suspends, though not to saue' the poem's only surviving early modern attribution of authorship with the dubious yet intriguing heading: 'Io: Feltons Epitaph made/By D: Donn.' Specifying the *doctor* Donne throughout his miscellany, and including one of Donne's religious poems, Burghe put into the mouth of the esteemed divine the libel's ironic subversion of the state's ritual to shame Felton. The verse collector thus lent the ecclesiastical weight of the dean of St. Paul's to the libel's contention that 'heauen; and A thousand fayre,/And glorious Diomond starrs' serve as the assassin's incorruptible tomb, and that 'pittiing foule' will deliver Felton's body to his 'soule.'[52] Before Burghe's error, Donne's only connection to Felton had likely been that of the ceremonialist vicar of St. Dunstan-in-the-West to one of the parish's disaffected, puritanical soldiers. Burghe offered an alternative history, however, in which Donne reached across the ideological divide in the Church of England in order to condone his parishoner's violent act.

Burghe invoked Donne not only as a doctor of divinity but also as a specifically Elizabethan satirist. Of Donne's five satires, Burghe copied only the fourth, in which the speaker encounters a caricature of a courtier, and provided the accurate heading: 'A Satire against the Court/wrighten by Doctor Dunn, In/Queene Elizabeths Raigne.'[53]

Yet no other early modern verse collectors agreed with Burghe's other Donne attributions. In addition to the misattributions discussed above, he placed Ben Jonson's translation from Petronius Arbiter in the middle of his page of 'Doctor Donn verses' (although he did not put Donne's name directly above or under this poem) and subscribed William Basse's epitaph on Shakespeare 'Dr Doone.' Bodleian MS Ashmole 38, p. 62 ('Doinge A filthye pleasure is, ~~some say~~ and short'), 203 ('on Mr Shak=speare// Renowned Spencer, lye a thought more neere').

[52] Bodleian MS Ashmole 38, p. 20.

[53] Bodleian MS Ashmole 38, pp. 40–43 ('Well I may now receyue and dye; my sinn// D; D;').

Burghe's Donne thus defamed courtiers from Elizabeth's day to Buckingham's murder. Moreover, Burghe placed the Felton epitaph in an account of early modern English satire that includes not only Donne but also another Elizabethan satirist, John Marston, who like Donne also became an early Stuart cleric. The collector attributed to Marston two copies (one crossed out) of a 1628 chronogram hoping for Buckingham's death:

> GeorgIVs VIlleres DVX BVCkIngaMIæ
> 1628
>
> Thy Numerous Name wth this yeare doth agree
> but twentye nyne god graunte thou neuer see
>
> made some few monthes before
> he was murthered by } Iohn Marston:[54]

By 1628, Marston had long ago retired from the London stage in favor of the country parish, arguably making his authorship of a timely Buckingham libel even less likely than Donne's.[55] Nevertheless, in Burghe's account, Marston contributes just the sort of threatening libel that encouraged Felton to act, both on the page before and a few pages after Donne honors the assassin with a laudatory epitaph. Even these misattributions, however, indicate Burghe's rather perceptive understanding of the development of satire between the reigns of Elizabeth I and Charles I. Simply by applying the names of Elizabethan satirists to assassination libels, Burghe tersely summarized the evolution of Renaissance satire into early modern libel. In his counter-factual literary history, Burghe made more or less the same mistake that subsequent literary historians have made, by overestimating the role of canonical authors to the exclusion of other literary agents. Rather than authors like Marston and Donne, it was verse collectors such as Burghe himself who were recognizing and negotiating the relationship between satire and libel.

Other verses that Burghe misattributed to Donne ironically demonstrate his awareness of Donne's reputation as an anti-courtly love poet.

54 Bodleian Ashmole 38, p. 25. The crossed-out copy appears on page 19 ('~~GEORGIVS DVX BVCkInghaMIæ:/1628//Thy Numorous name wth this year doth a gree,/but terntye nyne, god graunt thou neuer see/made some few monthes before hee was/killd by Iohn Marston~~'). See Albert H. Tricomi, 'John Marston's Manuscripts,' *Huntington Library Quarterly*, 43 (1979–1980), 87–102.

55 James Knowles, 'Marston, John (bap. 1576, d. 1634),' *ODNB*.

His only organized series of purported Donne texts presently fills one page spread. The verso begins with the heading 'Doctor Donn verses'; proceeds to three poems, none of them actually Donne's; and concludes with a subscription to 'D. Donn.' The facing page correctly ascribes to 'D Donn' the ubiquitous 'To his Mistress going to bed.'[56] Juxtaposed to this quintessential anti-courtly love poem, the three texts that Burghe mistook for Donne compositions exhibit a common, non-idealizing regard for women. The first begins with a gentle rendition of a familiar anti-courtly love gesture: 'I knowe as well as you, she is not faire/nor hath she sparkling eyes.' The speaker proceeds to deny his mistress both beauty and virtue in a contreblazon, yet finally retreats to affirm that, even though for no good reason, he loves her. By slight contrast, the last poem on the page demands a 'faire' mistress, 'yet not Extremly soe.' While less attractive and less overtly sexualized than the addressee of 'To his Mistress going to bed,' the women in these poems complement Donne's mistress in the love elegy on the next page. Burghe arranged these poems thoughtfully, and even put some thought into his misattributions—or else he reproduced someone else's intelligent arrangement. Regardless, when he copied poems that refuse to idealize women, he knew to invoke the name of the master of anti-courtly love poetry.

Burghe's acknowledgement of Donne's status as the preeminent anti-courtly love poet makes his misattribution of the Felton epitaph particularly interesting. For it shows how, more dramatically than virtually any of his contemporaries, Burghe placed Donne and his anti-courtly love poetry in the context of Buckingham's murder, going so far as to miscast the poet in the role of the assassin's supporter. Again, Burghe joined a significant number of his fellow verse collectors in recontextualizing anti-courtly love poetry with early Stuart court scandals. Indeed, he followed their example when he added anti-courtly love poems by other authors to his manuscript, without putting those authors' names on libels. But Burghe reserved a special place for Donne in his

[56] Bodleian MS Ashmole 38, pp. 62 ('Doctor Donn verses//I knowe as well as you, she is not faire'; 'Doinge A filthye pleasure is, ~~some say~~ and short'; 'When I doe loue, my Mistres must be faire//D. Donn.'), 63 ('Come Maddame, come; all rest my powers defye'). Again, Ben Jonson translated 'Doinge A filthye pleasure' from Petronius Arbiter (*Complete Poetry of Ben Jonson*, 269). Although a stub remains in between these two pages, the rest of the leaf must have been removed before Burghe added page numbers to the manuscript.

miscellany. He imagined the well-known poet lending the respectability of his religious and satirical verse to a textual monument for Felton. And he used Donne's name to connect anti-courtly love poetry to Buckingham libels.

This chapter began with a radical verse collector whose manuscript verse miscellany defines a consistent political and religious position. As a future captain in the royalist army, Nicholas Burghe may represent the ideological opposite of that collector. Yet Burghe acquired too diverse a range of early Stuart libels to have agreed personally with all of them. Moreover, he probably completed his miscellany before he could have possibly identified with the royalist cause. He inscribed the date 1638 in his book a few years before parliament threatened the monarchy enough for royalism to emerge as a coherent political cause.[57] In the years following the completion of his anthology, Burghe's personal politics may have developed rather like those of James Smith, whom Burghe probably indicated with the initials that he inscribed under a summer 1628 Buckingham libel: 'I. S.'[58] Written in the duke's voice, this libel ostensibly responds to the parliament's 'Remonstrance' against Buckingham, yet ironically concedes and augments the parliament's charges. Later that year, James Smith wrote another libel (which Burghe did not collect) disputing the justice of Felton's execution, and concluding with a laudatory epitaph for the assassin.[59] Yet Smith made his most significant literary contributions in mid-century coteries and printed miscellanies that espoused royalist politics. Apparently for Smith, and reasonably enough, having libeled Buckingham in 1628 did not require him to oppose Charles I in the middle of the century. Similarly for Burghe, collecting a range of libels both attacking and defending the duke in the 1630s did not preclude him from fighting on the side of royalists in the following decade. As future royalists who wrote or collected Buckingham libels, Smith and Burghe demonstrate the royal

[57] Bodleian MS Ashmole 38, p. 165. Robert Wilcher charts the emergence of constitutional royalism in impressive detail in *The Writing of Royalism, 1628–1660* (Cambridge: Cambridge University Press, 2001). On the date of the manuscript, see *The Poems of John Cleveland*, eds. Brian Morris and Eleanor Withington (Oxford: Clarendon, 1967), lii–liii.

[58] Bodleian MS Ashmole 38, pp. 44–45 ('~~On~~ The Duke of Bucking[ham] Roddomontados//Auante you Giddie Headed Multitude//I. S•').

[59] 'You auntient Lawes of Right; Can you, for shame,' Bellany and McRae, 'Early Stuart Libels,' Pii12.

favorite's extreme unpopularity even among those who would defend the monarchy when threatened. That is, they exhibited the difference between attacking a royal favorite and deposing a king, or the difference between the political contexts of the 1620s and the 1640s.

The distinction that Smith and Burghe must have eventually drawn between murdering the royal favorite and executing the king also delimits the bounds of the present study. Whereas this book has analyzed the verse collectors who assimilated anti-courtly love poetry to early Stuart court scandals, the following epilogue briefly surveys a few of the verse collectors who redeployed the genre in the quite distinct political environment of the 1650s. Despite his eventual military commitments, not to mention his imaginative revision of recent literary history, Burghe left the royalist appropriation of anti-courtly love poetry to these later verse collectors. Instead, he joined a great many other verse collectors in relating the genre to the political texts and contexts that mattered to them in the 1620s and '30s: the libels on the early Stuart court scandals that culminated in Buckingham's assassination.

Epilogue: Redeploying Anti-Courtly Love Poetry Against the Protectorate

As verse collectors began to print certain anti-courtly love poems in the middle of the seventeenth century, they continued assimilating them to new contexts. Yet, working in a different medium and political moment from the collectors featured in the preceding chapters, the editors and publishers of mid-century verse miscellanies initiated a distinct phase in the recontextualization of anti-courtly love poetry. Whereas most of their predecessors had placed the genre in the contexts of early Stuart court scandals, mid-century anthologists redeployed anti-courtly love poetry against a novel protectorate government determined to advance moral reform.

Back in 1632, when John Marriott registered his plans to print the first edition of Donne's poems, the Stationer's Company 'excepted' five of the love elegies on the grounds that Marriott lacked the 'lawfull authority' to publish them. These effectively censored texts included some of Donne's most popular and precise demonstrations of anti-courtly love poetry: 'To his Mistress going to bed,' 'Loues Progresse,' and 'Loves War.' Although Marriott added the other 'excepted' elegies to his second edition of Donne's *Poems* (without leaving behind evidence of his 'lawfull authority' to do so), he never printed the censored anti-courtly love poems. Indeed, these three elegies did not appear in a single-author volume of Donne's verse until Henry Herringman published the seventh edition of *Poems* in 1669.[1] The compilers and

[1] Arber, *Registers of the Company of Stationers*, 4:*249 (* here indicates duplicate page number); *Donne Variorum*, 2:lxxvi–lxxxii, 144, 147, 165, 175, 304, 311; John Donne, *Poems* (London: by M.F. for Iohn Marriott, 1633; STC 7045); ___, *Poems* (London: T.N. for Henry Herringman, 1669; Wing D1871), 66–68, 94–99.

publishers of multi-author poetry books had printed these salacious Donne verses several years earlier, however, in a few of the anthologies of the mid-1650s. In the first printed miscellany to feature any of Donne's banned elegies, Robert Chamberlain's 1654 *The Harmony of the Muses*, the editor included full or partial copies of all three poems in addition to other Donne verses and the classic anti-courtly love poems 'Nay pish, nay pew, nay faith, and will you, fie,' and Beaumont's poem to the countess of Rutland. Chamberlain thus introduced some of the period's most provocative texts to the medium of print, and to the political context of the protectorate, in an anthology of anti-courtly love poetry and other verse that nevertheless bears some resemblance to the manuscript verse miscellanies analyzed in the preceding chapters.

Indeed, in his facsimile edition of *The Harmony of the Muses*, Ernest W. Sullivan II points out the textual relationship between this printed book and Nicholas Burghe's verse miscellany, the last manuscript considered in the previous chapter. Burghe's anthology features fourteen of the poems that Chamberlain published, with three pairs of verses in the same order.[2] Chamberlain began his printed miscellany with one of these pairs of texts: an unattributed copy of a poem that Burghe incorrectly ascribed to Donne, 'When I do love, my Mistris must be fair,' and 'Come Maddam come, all stay my powers deny,' which Chamberlain correctly headed, '*An Elegie made by J.D.*'[3] Chamberlain and Burghe must have drawn on related manuscript sources, if only distantly related. To be sure, though, Chamberlain's sources had more in common with Burghe's miscellany than with the single-author collection of Donne's poems that Marriott had presented to the Stationer's Company. In fact, the manuscripts that Mariott and Chamberlain must have used to edit their respective printed books could represent the two major groups of extant Donne poetry manuscripts: the few dozen single-author collections that Marriott and subsequent Donne editors

[2] '"On the Choice of a Mistris" and "An Elegie made by J. D.", "On a Fly that flew into Celia's Eye" and "On the Snow falling on his Mistris breast", and "The Question of a Lady that was newly wedded" and "Dr. Dun's Answer to a Lady."' Sullivan adds that Corpus Christi, Oxford MS 328 contains 27 of Chamberlain's poems in a similar order, including poems that appear in no other known manuscript. *The Harmony of the Muses by Robert Chamberlain, 1654*, ed. Ernest W. Sullivan, II (Aldershot, Hants: Scholar, 1990), xii.

[3] Robert Chamberlain, *The Harmony of the Muses* (London: T.W. for William Gilbertson, 1654; Wing C105), 1–3.

have preferred, and the much more numerous miscellanies whose compilers made Donne's anti-courtly love poems more popular than most of his other works. Whereas for decades the printed books that drew on the single-author manuscripts excluded some of Donne's most representative anti-courtly love poems, those reminiscent of miscellanies highlighted these sexually explicit verses.

Chamberlain marketed his miscellany as reminiscent of more than the heyday of manuscript verse collecting. On his title page, he promised poems by nine named authors, first among them 'Dr. *Joh. Donn,*' 'And others of the most refined Wits of those TIMES.' In his preface 'TO THE READERS,' Chamberlain praised 'those TIMES' with a sly reference to the form of government that characterized them, at least from his perspective in the 1650s:

Poetry *in their dayes flourished, and they flourished with it, and gave a Crown unto that which hath crowned them with Honor, and perpetuall* Fame. . . . *There were never in one Age so many contemporary Patterns of* Invention, *or ever* Witt *that wrought higher or cleerer.*[4]

In his study of seventeenth-century printed miscellanies, Adam Smyth has demonstrated how such 'appeals to, and celebrations of, a past—never clearly defined, but generally located in *near* history—had the obvious function of distancing texts from the contemporary and thus implicitly, sometimes explicitly, offering criticism of Interregnum government.'[5] Indeed, shortly after Oliver Cromwell assumed the title *Lord Protector* instead of *King*, Chamberlain's repetitive choice of the words '*Crown*' and '*crowned*' registered nostalgia specifically for the monarch.

Embracing royalism in this way, Chamberlain effectively appropriated the fine collection of anti-courtly love poetry that he printed in his miscellany. He did so in part by listing Donne and Beaumont on the title page among royalists such as John Cleveland and Sir Kenelm Digby. Yet he also suggested affinities, on the title page and beyond, between anti-courtly love poems and the works of the Caroline courtier Thomas Carew, several of which Donne had indeed influenced. Carew served as gentlemen extraordinary of the privy chamber and as sewer in

4 *The Harmony of the Muses*, sig. A3r.

5 Adam Smyth, *'Profit and Delight': Printed Miscellanies in England, 1640–1682* (Detroit: Wayne State University Press, 2004), 169.

ordinary to the king. Yet he died before hostilities between the crown and parliament made royalism a viable political alternative.[6] Carew thus provided something of a link, however loose, between the anti-courtly love poets and the royalists in *The Harmony of the Muses*, or between the deceased authors who had parodied the literature of Elizabeth I's court and those living who had defended the court of Charles I and the institution of monarchy. Yet, even as Carew served to associate Donne and other rather early poets with the Caroline court and ultimately with royalism, Chamberlain was appropriating Carew as much as Donne, claiming both poets for a political cause that emerged after their deaths.

In the opening pages of his miscellany, Chamberlain juxtaposed a few of Donne's and Carew's representations of attractive mistresses and sexual desire, including 'To his Mistress going to bed.'[7] A few pages on, he placed one of Carew's most popular and sexually explicit poems, 'The Rapture,' here beginning, 'I will enjoy thee now, my *Cœlia*, come' and headed, '*Loves Elizium*.'[8] Chamberlain also arranged an extended, and intriguing, series of Donne and Carew poems near the middle of the volume. In this sequence, Carew's persuasion poem '*To his coy Mistris*' pleads with a young woman to love now while she still has her beauty, for 'if your beauty once decay,/You'l never know a second *May*.'[9] Chamberlain perceptively placed Donne's 'The Autumnall' next, which resumes the reader's tour through the seasons of a woman's beauty, here beginning, 'No Spring or Summer beauty hath such grace/As I have seen in an Autumnall Face.'[10] Again, Donne's poem overturns the conventional association of youth and beauty in order to pay a compliment to a

[6] 'Quite simply there were no cavaliers in the 1630s—if the term is intended to delineate a coherent political group. And as description of a style, gallant and swaggering, it was by no means confined to the court. Indeed many of those known as "cavalier poets"—Carew and Suckling for example—died before the first blood had been spilled in the English civil war.' Kevin Sharpe, *Criticism and Compliment: The Politics of Literature in the England of Charles I* (Cambridge: Cambridge University Press, 1987), 27; see also 109, 111.

[7] *The Harmony of the Muses*, 2–3 ('*An Elegie made by J.D.*//Come Maddam come, all stay my powers deny,'), 3–4 ('*The Rapture, by* J.D.//Is she not wondrous fair? but yet I see'), 4 ('*The Extreames, by* T.C.//Ile gaze no more on her bewitching face'), 6–7 ('*To his Mistris.*//Here let me War, in these Armes let me lie').

[8] *The Harmony of the Muses*, 18–23.

[9] *The Harmony of the Muses*, 44–47.

[10] *The Harmony of the Muses*, 47–49.

woman in the autumn of life. Yet his praise of a woman who deviates from the stereotype of female beauty likely reminded Chamberlain or his readers of the derogatory descriptions of women in anti-courtly love poems like Donne's 'The Anagram' or Beaumont's 'Ad Comitissam Rutlandiæ,' the second of which Chamberlain included elsewhere in *The Harmony of the Muses.* Even if 'The Autumnall' did not put Chamberlain or his readers in mind of anti-courtly love poetry, though, the following text confronted them with the genre. The common heading that Chamberlain reproduced in his printed book, '*A Maids Denyall*,' invokes a younger woman as the speaker of the anonymous monologue here beginning, 'Nay pish, nay pew, nay faith, and will you, fie.'[11] Yet, unlike the women in the immediately preceding texts, the female in this anti-courtly love poem is not silently considering the appeals of a poetic speaker; she is talking through her unsuccessful, and eventually half-hearted, resistance of a man who is forcing himself on her. Spoken in a woman's voice rather than a man's, this poem does not end until well after the sexual encounter has finished. The poem thus not only provides a stark contrast to Carew's nearby persuasion poems; it also suggests a rude, narrative conclusion to them, a simultaneously titillating and sobering counterpart to any number of the love lyrics in the miscellany.

By gathering together verses by Donne and Carew, and by juxtaposing anti-courtly love poems with more polite love lyrics, Chamberlain was doing something that many manuscript verse collectors, including Burghe, had done before him: he was demonstrating collectors' ability to recontextualize literature. Yet he was also doing a few things that no verse collector had done before him. He was printing some of these poems for the first time. He was placing them in the quite unprecedented context of the fledgling protectorate. He was claiming them for the royalist cause in his preface. And he was thus beginning a distinctly new stage in the history of the politics of anti-courtly love poetry.

To be sure, other royalists had collected anti-courtly love poems in manuscript, and so had helped to develop the canon of texts and the model of the miscellany that Chamberlain and others would transfer to the medium of print. The transformation of the early Stuart manuscript verse miscellany into the royalist anthology took place nowhere more

11 *The Harmony of the Muses*, 49–50.

intensely than in Oxford. Many of the verse collectors active at Christ Church in the 1630s, England's most prolific center for collecting verse and compiling miscellanies at the time, must have become royalists when Charles I moved his headquarters to the college in 1642, as the threat to the crown, and the opportunity to defend it, became clear. After all, the verse collectors of Christ Church had contributed greatly to a college culture that was perfectly disposed to welcome the exiled king. As political events unfolded, and as those at Christ Church rearticulated their allegiance to Charles accordingly, the verse collectors among them assimilated their favorite poems and their miscellanies to their developing contexts and commitments.

Chamberlain surely did the same. In appreciation for his services as a clerk, the solicitor-general to Queen Henrietta Maria sent Chamberlain to Exeter College, Oxford in 1637, where he most likely acquired many of the poems that he would print in *The Harmony of the Muses*.[12] Like many others, Chamberlain sided with the king when hostilities arose, and later hoped for the restoration of the monarchy. Yet, unlike most Oxford verse collectors, Chamberlain kept neither his verse miscellany nor his political inclinations private. He published both in print. In transferring his miscellany from one medium to another, he effectively redeployed the poems therein for the purposes of an oppositional political party. Employing a device foreign to manuscript verse collectors—the preface—he enveloped his entire collection within a politically motivated nostalgia. With his preface, Chamberlain anachronistically represented Donne's and others' anti-courtly love poetry as opposed to a puritan regime.

The Harmony of the Muses contributed to a model which other opponents of Cromwell's government soon adopted. Smyth's survey of printed miscellanies documents a surge in the production of these books at the start of the protectorate. The publishers of two very popular miscellanies had competed only with one another when they reprinted their 1640 anthologies in the early '40s, mid-40s, and early '50s. They encountered increasing competition, however, as Cromwell consolidated power: from *The Harmony of the Muses* in 1654; from three new anthologies in 1655; and from four new titles, plus a reprint, in 1656.[13]

[12] Peter Ball served as Henrietta Maria's solicitor-general.

[13] Smyth, *'Profit and Delight,'* 178–79.

The compilers of these printed miscellanies generally shared Chamberlain's nostalgia, his taste in bawdy literature, and his ill will toward the protectorate. Several also shared his royalism; but not all of them did. Rather, royalists such as Chamberlain made the printed verse miscellany such an effective means of opposing the protectorate that even a nonroyalist could adopt the model in order to register the discontent that much of the nation developed with Cromwell's government. For instance, the verse collector responsible for the last two printed miscellanies that this book considers redeployed anti-courtly love poetry against the protectorate without conceding the genre to royalists.

John Milton's nephew, John Phillips, almost certainly contributed to the two miscellanies that Nathaniel Brook (or Brooke or Brooks) published in 1656 in reaction to recent developments in the protectorate. And the government responded. Late in the previous year, Cromwell had established a team of regional major-generals to ensure local security and to advance 'a reformation of manners.'[14] The major-generals sought out royalists, thieves, and those indulging in a range of licentious activities. In other words, they criminalized, along with threats to the government and personal property, immoral or ungodly behavior. According to historians, the major-generals seem not to have considered the regulation of printing central to their mission.[15] Yet, at the same time that he was organizing the major-generals, Cromwell issued an order against 'Unlicensed and Scandalous Books and Pamphlets.'[16] Moreover, Cromwell's council recognized the scandalous nature, and likely the politics, of at least one of Phillips and Brook's miscellanies.

Phillips had pronounced his support for the republic and even for Cromwell in recent publications, one of them published by Brook. Having begun his education and writing career under his uncle's direction, Phillips printed a Latin apology for Milton's 1651 *Defensio pro*

[14] John Morrill, 'Cromwell, Oliver (1599–1658),' *ODNB*.

[15] Christopher Durston, *Cromwell's Major Generals: Godly Government During the English Revolution* (Manchester: Manchester University Press, 2001); Peter Gaunt, *Oliver Cromwell* (Oxford: Blackwell, 1996), 189–92.

[16] *Orders of His Highness The Lord Protector... against Printing Unlicensed and Scandalous Books and Pamphlets* (London: Henry Hills and John Field, Printers to His Highness, 1655; Wing C7151). Shawcross dates the order to 28 August 1655 and its execution to 9 October. *The Arms of the Family: The Significance of John Milton's Relatives and Associates* (Lexington: University Press of Kentucky, 2004), 123.

populo Anglicano, the 'first defense' of the nascent English republic that Milton wrote as Cromwell's secretary for foreign tongues.[17] In 1654 he wrote a satire against religious hypocrites, which Nathaniel Brook published in the following year to quite receptive audiences.[18] Probably in January 1656, Brook then published Phillips' translation of Las Casas' unfavorable account of Spanish colonialism, *The Tears of the Indians*, which Milton's nephew dedicated to Cromwell, celebrating the lord protector as a righteous opponent of Spanish Catholics.[19]

Yet this endorsement of the lord protector did not extend to his recent moral reforms, at least as they concerned literature. At approximately the same time that they produced the Las Casas translation, Phillips and Brook printed the first of their two miscellanies, *Wit and Drollery*, which signaled their opposition to the 'reformation of manners.'[20] In his epistle to the 'Courteous Reader' of this miscellany, Phillips promised to provide the poems '*of Sir* J.M. *of* Ja. S. *of Sir* W.D. *of* J.D. *and other miraculous Muses of the Times*.'[21] The first two initials likely refer to the royalists Sir John Mennes and James Smith who, as Timothy Raylor has shown, had recently become 'the benchmarks by which such collections were judged,' thanks to their association with the successful 1655

[17] John Phillips, *Responsio ad apologiam anonymi* (Londini: Typis Du-gardianis, 1652; Wing P2098); John Milton, *Joannis Miltoni Angli defensio pro populo Anglicano* (Londini: Typis Du Gardianis, 1651; Wing M2168).

[18] He ran two issues of the first edition and a second edition in the same year; the poem went through seven more editions in the next 55 years. John Phillips, *A Satyr against Hypocrites* (London: for N.B., 1655; Wing P2101); Shawcross, *The Arms of the Family*, 119.

[19] Bartolomé de las Casas, *The Tears of the Indians*, trans. John Phillips (London: J.C. for Nath. Brook, 1656; Wing C799).

[20] John Phillips, ed., *Wit and Drollery* (London: for Nath: Brook, 1656; Wing W3131). The legendary book collector George Thomason evidently purchased his copies of *Wit and Drollery* and *The Tears of the Indians* within days of one another in January 1656. Apparently modifying the title page's new style publication year with the date of purchase in old style, Thomason inscribed in his copy of *The Tears of the Indians* the date 9 January 1655/6 (Huntington, Rare Books, 9769), and in *Wit and Drollery*, 18 January 1655/6 (British Library, Printed Books, E.1617.(1.)).

The pseudonymous epistle 'To the Reader' of *Sportive Wit* mentions that 'a Book intituled *Wit and Drollery*' 'formerly came forth.' As I discuss below, on 19 April, Brook testified that his printers produced this miscellany 'about two months since.' John Phillips, ed., *Sportive Wit* (London: for Nath: Brook, 1656; Wing P2113), sig. A3r; John Thurloe, *A Collection of the State Papers of John Thurloe, Esq.*, vol. 4 (London: Printed for the executor of F. Gyles, 1742), 717.

[21] *Wit and Drollery*, sig. A3r–v.

miscellany, *Musarum Deliciae*.[22] Indeed, Smith likely composed the first three poems in *Wit and Drollery*. Mennes may have written nothing therein, however, and the royalist Sir William Davenant and the long-deceased John Donne (the only apparent 'J.D.' in the volume) had each written just one of the anthology's poems. Nevertheless, the miscellany's Donne selection, 'Loves Progresse,' resonated with the bawdy literature that royalist anthologists had recently associated with opposition to the protectorate.[23] This anti-courtly love poem complemented, in particular, an exchange of verses in the Donnean voice of an inconstant lover, '*A Song by Sir* John Suckling,' which begins, 'Out upon it, I have lov'd, three whole dayes together.'[24] Like his fellow courtier Carew, Suckling died before he could have become a royalist. Yet the late-1630s verses that Phillips and Brook attributed to him could not help but sound royalist in the mid-1650s. In particular, the speaker of an answer-poem who expressly identifies himself as 'Suckling' must have seemed openly royalist when he boldly pronounced: 'I am *John* for the King.'[25] Although Suckling wrote this poem in response to a satire regarding Charles I's late-1630s conflict with the Scots, and not his 1640s fight with parliament, its reproduction in *Wit and Drollery* anachronistically turned Suckling's service to the monarch into royalist support for the restoration of the monarchy.

This answer-poem also helped to associate the bawdy verse exchange that Phillips and Brook elsewhere attributed to Suckling with Donne's anti-courtly love poem, 'Loues Progresse,' at the end of the book. Adopting the model of the royalist printed miscellany that Chamberlain, Mennes, and Smith had recently made famous, Phillips and Brook employed these anti-courtly love poems by Suckling and Donne to satisfy the miscellany genre's requirement of sexually explicit verse.

[22] Timothy Raylor, *Cavaliers, Clubs, and Literary Culture: Sir John Mennes, James Smith, and the Order of the Fancy* (Newark: University of Delaware Press, 1994), 206.

[23] *Wit and Drollery*, 157–60.

[24] *Wit and Drollery*, 40. On p. 41, '*The Answer by the same Author*' begins, 'Say, but did you love so long? in sooth I needs must blame ye.' In his online database of printed miscellanies, Adam Smyth attributes the answer-poem to Sir Toby Matthews. 'An Index of Poetry in Printed Miscellanies, 1640–1682,' http://www.adamsmyth.clara.net/ accessed 19 August 2007.

[25] *Wit and Drollery*, 46. The satire '*Upon Sir* John Suckling' begins, 'I'le tell thee *Jack* thou'st given the King' (44–5). '*Sir* John Suckling*'s Answer*' responds, 'I'le tell thee foole who e're thou be' (46–7).

About a month after publishing their first miscellany, they printed three sections of additional verse and released them under a single title page: *Sportive Wit*. This time, they included among the requisite bawdy texts the ever-popular 'Nay pish! nay phew! nay faith and will you?'[26]

Two months later, on 19 April 1656, one of the deputies appointed by the commissioners for the regulation of printing discovered what Brook had been selling at his shop at the Angel in Cornhill. That same afternoon, the deputy had the publisher in front of Sir John Barkstead, lieutenant of the Tower of London, major-general of Westminster and Midddlesex, and deputy to the official yet aged major-general of London. Presented with '3 books bound in black calves leather, intitled, *Sportive witt*,' Brook named the buyer of the present copy as well as the printers of the 950 that he had received and the 700 that he had sold. But when the questions turned to authors, Brook grew evasive. Asked for the author of the book, he explained, 'they are only the collection of sundry papers, which he procured of several persons, and added together for that purpose.' Asked for the authors of the poems then, Brook again evaded the question, naming only one source and reasserting his responsibility for compiling the miscellany: 'The rest he had from several other musicians and other persons, and put them together as aforesaid.' Finally, asked for the author of the epistles, he named Phillips. A few days later, on 25 April, the council of state determined that 'the book contains much scandalous, lascivious, scurrilous and profane matter'; charged 'the Lord Mayor of London and the other Commissioners for the regulation of printing' to seize all copies and have them burned publicly; and fined Brook, the printers, and Phillips.[27]

Within days, the council issued a similar order for another printed miscellany produced by other hands. And in the 1682 edition of Phillips and Brook's first anthology, *Wit and Drollery*, the prefatory epistle claims that it suffered the same fate.

> This sort of Wit hath formerly suffered Martyrdom; for *Cromwell*, who was more for Policy than Wit, not only laid the first Reviver of these Recreations in the Tower, but also committed the innocent Sheets to the mercy of the Executioners fire; as being some of them too kind, as he thought, to the Royal Partie.[28]

[26] *Sportive Wit*, 41–42.

[27] Thurloe, *State Papers*, 4:717–18.

[28] *Wit and Drollery* (London: Obadiah Blagrave, 1682; Wing W3133), iii.

The 1682 publisher of *Wit and Drollery* may have confused it with *Sportive Wit* in this statement. Nevertheless, both the compilers and the investigators of such miscellanies recognized that, in the context of the protectorate, these books registered opposition to the government. Even if, as he claimed before the council, Brook compiled *Sportive Wit* himself, Phillips surely realized that his prefatory epistles promoted literature that the government would not like.

Yet this little act of opposition to the protectorate's moral reforms hardly makes Phillips, recent defender of the republic and proponent of Cromwell, a royalist. Milton scholars have pointed to the two verse miscellanies that he produced with Brook as evidence of Phillips' estrangement from his uncle, and of his wavering from Milton's political ideals. Yet John Shawcross has recently marshaled a great deal of evidence to call into question both Phillips' supposed rift with Milton and his alleged political instability.[29] Indeed, unless Phillips underwent an incredible political conversion between the January 1656 production of *The Tears of the Indians* and that of *Wit and Drollery* in the very same month, he contributed to Brook's printed miscellanies not out of royalism but out of a much more precise opposition to the government's recent activity, perhaps especially its promotion of the 'reformation of manners' or regulation of printing. Royalists, in other words, had so exploited the oppositional potential of both the printed verse miscellany and anti-courtly love poetry that even a nonroyalist could use them to voice his discontents loudly enough for the government to hear.

By the time that mid-century anthologists printed anti-courtly love poems in their oppositional miscellanies, these bawdy verses had undergone a remarkable series of recontextualizations, from their original Elizabethan context to those of the scandals surrounding James VI and I's great royal favorites to the protectorate. Although the continuing popularity and persistent relevance of these poems attests to the eloquence of their authors, these poets remained relatively passive throughout the transmission and reception history of the genre. Not authors but verse collectors did the work of incrementally assimilating anti-courtly love poetry to ever-new historical contexts.

[29] Shawcross, *The Arms of the Family*, 95–133.

APPENDIX 1:
Selected Verse Texts

This appendix supplies full texts of the least accessible poems discussed in the preceding pages. I have chosen texts from manuscripts that pertain to this book, and not necessarily the earliest or most authoritative versions of poems available. I have also listed additional manuscript copies of the poems, without recording variant readings from those sources. The transcripts retain original spelling and punctuation, as far as possible. Yet I have expanded a number of abbreviations in square brackets.

1 Anti-Courtly Love Poems

Anonymous, 'Naye, phewe nay pishe?'

Lasciua est nobis pagina vita proba est.

Naye, phewe nay pishe? nay faythe and will ye, fye.
A gentlman deale thus? in truthe ille crye.
Gods bodye, what means this? naye fye for shame
Nay, Nay, come, come, nay faythe yow are to blame.
Harcke sombodye comes, leaue of I praye
Ile pinche, ille spurne, Ile scratche, nay good awaye
In faythe you stryue in vayne, you shall not speede.
You ~~hurt~~ marr my ruffs, you hurte my back, my nose will bleed
Looke, looke the doore is open some bodye sees,
What will they saye? nay fye you hurt my knees
Your buttons scratche, o god ~~?~~ what coyle is heere?
You make me sweate, in faythe here is goodly geare
Nay faythe let me intreat leue if you lyste
Yow marr the bedd, you teare my smock, but had I wist,
So muche before I woulde haue kepte you oute.
It is a very proper thinge indeed you goo aboute.
I did not thinke you woulde haue vsed me this.
But nowe I see to late I tooke my marke amysse
A lytle thinge woulde mak vs two not to be freends.
You vse me well, I hope yow will make me amends.
Houlde still Ile wype your face: you sweat amayne
You have got a goodlye thinge wth all this payne.
O god how ~~whott~~ I am come will you drincke

Ife^{we} goe sweatinge downe what will they thinke
Remmember I praye howe you haue vsde me nowe
Doubte not ere longe I will be quite with you.
Ife any one but you shoulde vse me so
Woulde I put vp this wronge? in faythe sir no
Nay goe not yet: staye supper here with me
Come goe to cardes I hope we shall agree.
Finis

Source: Bodleian MS Rawl. poet. 85, fol. 4r.
Other texts: Beinecke MSS Osborn b62, pp. 96–97; Osborn b200, pp. 430–31; Bodleian MSS Ashmole 38, p. 150; Ashmole 47, fol. 54r–v; Don. d.58, fol. 44^{b}v (p. 90); Eng. poet. e.97, p. 185; Eng. poet. f.27, pp. 149–50; Malone 19, pp. 75–76; Rawl. poet. 199, pp. 10–11; Rawl. poet. 214, fol. 73v rev.; British Library MSS Add. 22582, fols 43v–44r; Add. 22602, fol. 19v; Add. 22603, fol. 64r–v; Add. 30982, fol. 53r; Egerton 923, fol. 65r–v; Egerton 2421, fol. 21r; Harley 6057, fol. 48r–v; Sloane 542, fol. 36v; Sloane 1792, fol. 125r–v; Corpus Christi, Oxford MS 328, fol. 87r; Folger MSS V.a.97, pp. 52–53; V.a.124, fols 48v–49r; V.a.262, pp. 74–75; V.a.319, fol. [51r–v]; V.a.322, p. 43; V.a.339, fol. 188v; V.a.345, pp. 7–8; Houghton MS Eng. 686, fol. 35r; National Library of Wales MS NLW 5390D, pp. 532–31 rev.; New York Public Library MS Arents S288, p. 34; Rosenbach MSS 239/18, p. 42; 239/27, p. 157; 1083/15, p. 3; Trinity College Dublin MS 877, pt. 2, fols 232v–33r; University of Newcastle MS Bell/White 25, fol. 23v; University of Wales, Bangor MS 422, p. 50; West Yorkshire Archives Service, Leeds MS WYL156/237, fol. 6r.

Sir John Davies, Sonnet-Epigrams

I loue thee not for sacred chastity
Whoe loues for that nor for thy spritely wit
I loue thee not for thy sweet modestie
wch makes thee in perfections throne to sit
I loue thee not for thy inchaunting ey
Thy beauties ravishing rare perfection
I loue thee not for thy vnchast luxurie
Nor for thy bodies fayre proportion
I loue thee not for that my soule doth danse
And leape wth pleasure when those lips of thyne
Giue musicall & gracefull vtterance
To some (by thee made happie) poets line
I loue thee not for voyce both sweet or small
But wilt thow know wherefore fayre Sweet for all.

Source: Victoria and Albert MS Dyce 44, 25.F.39, fol. 57r.
Other text: Trinity College Dublin MS 652, fol. 358r.

Fayth wench I cannot courte thy piercing eyes
W^th^ the base vial plac'd between my thighes
I cannot lispe nor to some fidle singe
Nor run vpon a hyghe streacht minikin
I cannot whyne in puling elegies
Intombing Cupid wth sad obsequies
I am not fashioned for these amorouse tymes
To courte thy beautie wth lasciviouse rimes
I cannot dally caper danse or singe
Oyling my Saint wth supple sonetting
I cannot crosse my armes & sigh ay mee
Ay me forlorne egregiouse fopperie. [*folio break*]
I cannot busse thy cheeks play wth thy hayre
Swearing by loue thow art most debonayre
Not I in fayth but shall I tell thee roundlye
Harke in thyne eare Zounds I can ( ) thee soundly

Source: Victoria and Albert MS Dyce 44, 25.F.39, fol. 57r–v.
Other texts: Beinecke MSS Osborn b200, p. 128; b205, fol. 28r; Bodleian MSS Eng. poet. e.14, fol. 75v; Eng. poet. e.97, p. 93; Eng. poet. f.27, p. 171; Malone 21, fol. 51v; Rawl. poet. 199, pp. 9–10; British Library MSS Add. 30982, fol. 73v; Harley 6931, fol. 31v; Folger MSS V.a.245, fol. 56r; V.a.345, p. 34; Kinzers, Pennsylvania, The Family Album, Edwin Wolf II MS, p. 50; Rosenbach MSS 239/27, p. 182; 240/7, p. 17; 243/4, p. 1; 1083/16, pp. 47–48; 1083/17, fols 98v–99r; St. John's, Cambridge MS S.32, fols 3v–4r; Trinity College Dublin MS 652, fol. 358v; University of Newcastle MS Bell/White 25, fol. 25v; West Yorkshire Archive Service, Bradford MS 32D86/17, fol. 14v.

Sweet wench I loue thee yet I will not sue
Or shew my loue as muskie Courtiers doe
I'le not carouse a health to honoure thee
In this same bezling drunken curtesie
And when all's quaf't eate vp my bouzing glasse
In glorie that I am thy servile asse
Nor will I weare a rotten Burbon locke
As some sworne pesant to a fæmall smocke
Well featured lasse thow knowest I loue thee deare
Yet for thy sake I will not bore myne eare
To hang thy durtie silken shoe=tyes there
Nor for thy loue will I once gnash a bricke
Or some pied coloures in my bonet sticke
But by the chaps of hel to doe thee good
Ile freely spend my thrice decocted bloud.

Source: Victoria and Albert MS Dyce 44, 25.F.39, fol. 57v.
Other texts: Bodleian MSS Douce f.5, fol. 19r–v; Rawl. poet. 199, p. 9; Folger MS V. a.345, p. 29; Rosenbach MSS 239/27, p. 206; 243/4, p. 1; 1083/17, fol. 99r; Trinity College Dublin MS 652, fol. 358v.

Francis Beaumont, 'Ad Comitissam Rutlandiæ'

A Letter to the Countesse
of Rutlande./

Madam: soe maye my verses pleasinge bee,
soe maye you laugh at them, and not at mee,
As somethinge to you I would gladly saye,
but how to doe it cannot finde the waye:
I would avoyde the comon troden wayes
to Ladies vs'd, wch bee, or loue, or prayse:
As for the first that little witt I haue,
Is not yett gone soe neere vnto the graue
but that I can by that dym[m]e fadinge light
perceaue of what, and vnto whome I write:
Lett such as in a hoplesse, wittlesse rage
can sigh a quire, and reade it to a page:
Such as can make tenn Son[n]ets ere they rest,
When each is but a greate blott at the best.
Such as can backes of bookes, and windowes fill,
Wth their too furious diamond, and ^{their} quill;
Such as are well resolu'd, to end their dayes
Wth a loude laughter blowne beyond the seas:
Who are soe mortefied; that they can lyve
Contem'd by all the Worlde, and yett forgive /
Write Loue to you, I would not willingely
bee pointed at in eu[er]y Companie,
As was the little taylor, that till death
was hott in Loue wth, Queene Elyzabeth:
And for the last: in all my idle dayes
I neuer yet did lyvinge woman prayse
In verse, or proes, and when I doe begyn,
Ile pick some woman out, as full of synne
as you are full of vertue, wth a soule
as black, as yours is white; a face as foule
as yours is bewtifull; for it shalbee
out of the rules of Phisiognomye
soe farr, that I doe feare I must displace
the arte a litle, to lett in her face:
It shall at least foure faces bee belowe
the Devells, and her parched corps shall showe
in her lose skin as yf a spright shee were
kept in a bagg by some greate Coniurer:
Her breath shalbee as horrible, and vilde
as every worde you speake is sweete, and milde: [*folio break*]

It shall bee such a one as cannot bee
couer'd, wth anie arte, or pollicie:
But lett her take all pouders, fumes, and drincke
she shall make noe thinge, but a dearer stincke:
Shee shall haue such a foote, and such a nose
that will not stand in anie thinge but proes:
If I bestowe, my prayses vpon such
tis charetie; and I shall merrit much:
My prayse will come to her like a full boule
bestowed at most neede, on a thirstie soule:
Where yf I singe your prayses in my ryme
I lose my Inke, my paper, and my tyme
Add noethinge to your ouer flowinge store,
and tell you naught, but what you knew before:
Nor doe the ^{worthy} minded; wch I sweare
Madam I think you are, indure to heare
their owne perfections into question brought
but stop their eares at them, for yf I thought
You tooke a pride to haue your vertues knowne
Pardon mee Madam; I should thincke them none./
To what a length is this strange letter growne
In seekinge of a subiect; yett findes none:
But yf your braue thoughts, wch I must respect
aboue your glorious titles, doe accept
these few ill scattered lynes, I shall ere longe
Dresse vp your vertues new, in a new songe
Yet farr from all base prayse, and flatterie
although I knowe what ere my verses bee
they will like the most seruile flatterie shew
Yf I write trewth, and make my subiect you./

F B./

Source: British Library MS Add. 25707, fols 31r–v.
Other texts: Bodleian MSS Don. b.9, fols 56v–57v; Eng. poet. c.53, fol. 13r–v; Rawl. poet. 31, fols 37v–39^{a}r; British Library MSS Add. 25303, fols 102v–3v; Egerton 2230, fols 8v–9v; Harley 1221, fols 79v–80r; Harley 3910, fols 15v–16v; Harley 4064, fols 268r–69r; Harley 6038, fols 24r–25r; Lansdowne 740, fol. 120r–v; Sloane 1446, fols 73v–74r; Derbyshire Record Office MS D258/34/26/1, fols 40v–41v; Houghton MSS Eng. 966.3, fols 43v–44r; Eng. 966.7, fol. 63v; Huntington MSS HM 198, pt. 1, pp. 205–6; HM 198, pt. 2, fol. 114r–v; Leicestershire Record Office MS DG9/2796, pp. 24–28; Morgan MS MA 1057, pp. 105–6; Texas Tech MSS PR 1171 D14 (Dalhousie I), fols 52v–53r; PR 1171 S4 (Dalhousie II), fols 26r–27r; Trinity College Dublin MS 877, fols 44r–45r; University of Edinburgh MS Laing.III.493, fols 98r–99r; University of Kansas MS 4A:1, pp. 56–57; West Yorkshire Archive Service, Leeds MS WYL156/237, fol. 9r–v.

Ben Jonson, from 'Ten Lyrick Pieces for Charis'

haue y^{u} seene the white lilly grow
Before rude hands haue toucht it
haue y^{u} markt the fall of the snow
Before the earth hath smutcht it
Haue y^{u} felt the woole of Beuer
  or Swanns Downe euer
  haue y^{u} smelt of the bud 'o' the beyre
    or ye nard o in the fier
  or haue y^{u} tasted the bagg 'of the bee
  o so white ô so soft ô so sweet
    so sweet so sweet is shee.

Source: Westminster Abbey MS 41, fol. 88v.
Other texts: Bodleian MSS Don. d.58, fol. 26v; Rawl. poet. 199, p. 74; British Library MSS Add. 19268, fol. 14r; Sloane 1792, fol. 92r; Stowe 962, fol. 179v; British Library, Printed Books, C.39.a.37, fols 9v–10r; Folger MS V.a.170, pp. 30–31; Huntington MS HM 46323, fol. 3r; Trinity College Dublin MS 412, fol. 31v; University of Nottingham MS Portland PwV 37, p. 64.

Anonymous, parody of Jonson

Haue you seen a blackheaded maggot
crawling on a dead dog
or an old witch with a faggott
swayling of a hedghogg
Haue you smelt Cousbobby toasted
  or a sheepskin roasted
Have you smelt to' the babe in the whittle
  Or the leaper in the spittle
Or have tasted the Sabin tree
  O so black, o so rough o so sour is shee

Source: Westminster Abbey MS 41, fol. 89r.
Other texts: British Library MSS Add. 19268, fol. 14r; Sloane 1792, fol. 92r; Stowe 962, fol. 179v; Folger MS V.a.170, p. 30.

2 Somerset Libels

Anonymous, 'The Witch'

A Satyre entituled the Witch; supposed to bee made
against the Lady Francis Countes of Somersett.

Shee with whom troopes of Bustuary slaves,
Like Legion sojournd still amongst the Graves;

And there laid plots wch made the silver Moone
To fall in labour many times too soone:
Canidia now drawes on.

Shee that in every vice did so excell
That shee could read new principells to Hell;
And shew the Fiends recorded in her lookes
Such deedes as were not in theire blackest bookes:
Canidia now drawes on.

Shee that by spells could make a frozen stone
Melt and dissolve wth soft affection;
And in an instant stricke the Factours dead
That should pay duties to the Marriage bed:
Canidia now drawes on.

Shee that consisted all of borrowed grace
Could paint her heart as smoothly as her face;
And when her breath gave wings to silken words,
Poisons in thought concieve and murthering swords:
Canidia now drawes on.

Shee that could reake wthin thee sheets of lust,
And there bee searcht, yett passe wthout mistrust;
Shee that could surfle up the wayes of sinne
And make streight ~~gates~~ Posternes, where wide gates had bein:
Canidia now drawes on.

Shee that could cheat the matrimoniall bed,
Wth a false=stampt adulterat maidenhead;
And make the Husband thinke those kisses chast
W^{ch} were stale Panderes to his Spouses wast:
Canidia now drawes on. [*page break*]

Whose breast was that Aceldama of bloud,
Whose vertue still became the Cankers food;
Whose closett might a Golgotha bee stil'd,
Or else a Charnell where dead bones are pil'd:
Canidia now drawes on.

Whose waxen pictures made by Incantation,
Whose Philters, Potions for love's propagation;
Count Circe but a novice in that trade
And scorne all druggs, that Colchos ever made:
Canidia now drawes on.

Oh lett noe bells bee ever heard to ring,
Lett not a chime the nightly houres sing;

Lett not the Lyrique Larke salute the day,
Nor Philomele tune the sad darkes away:
Canidia still drawes on.

Lett croaking Ravens, and death-boding Owles,
Lett groneing Mandrakes, and the gastly howles,
Of men unburied bee, the fatall knell,
To ring Canidia downe from Earth to Hell:
Canidia still drawes on.

Lett wolves and Tygers howle, let Serpents cry,
Lett Basiliskes bedew their poysoning eye;
Lett Pluto's dogg streatch high his barking ~~throate~~, note,
And chant her dirges with his triple throate:
Canidia still drawes on.

Under his burthen lett great Atlas quake,
Lett the fix't Earth's unmoved Center shake;
And y[e] faier heavens wrap't as itt were with wonder,
That divills dy speaks out their loudest thunder:
Canidia still drawes on.

No longer shall y[e] pretty Marygolds,
Ly sepulcherd at night in their owne folds;
The Rose should flourish and through out ye yeare
No leafe nor plant once blasted would appeare
Were once Canidia gone.

[*sideways, in the gutter:*]

*The starrs would seeme as glorious as ye moone,
And shee like Phæb[u]s in his brightest noone;
Mists clouds, and Vapours all would passe away
And ye whole yeare bee as Halcyons day!
Oh were Canidia gone.

Source: Folger MS V.a.103, fol. 66r–v.
Other texts: Bodleian MS Malone 23, pp. 8–10; British Library MSS Harley 3910, fols 26r–27r; Sloane 1792, fols 2v–4r; Huntington MS HM 198, pt. 1, pp. 33–34; Senate House MS 313, fol. 16v–17r; University of Nottingham MS Portland PwV 37, pp. 135–136.

Anonymous, 'A Page, a knight, a vicount and an earle' (early version)

A libell made on y[e] earle of
Sommerset
A page, a knight, a vicount and an earle

all foure were married to an english gerle
the like was neuer seene betweene foure
A wife, a witch, a countesse and a whore

Source: University of Wales, Bangor MS 422, p. 59.
Other texts: Bodleian MSS Ashmole 38, p. 116; Rawl. D.1048, fol. 64r.

Anonymous, 'A page, a knight, a vicount and an earle' (late version)

A page, a squire a viscount and an Earle
were marryed all vnto a lustfull girle
A match well made for she was likewise fow^{er}
A wife, a witch, a murdresse, & a whore;

Source: Bodleian MS Rawl. poet. 160, fol. 163r.
Other texts: Bodleian MSS Don. c.54, fol. 23r; Malone 19, p. 38; Malone 23, p. 7; Tanner 465, fol. 96v; British Library MSS Add. 44963, fol. 40r; Egerton 2230, fol. 70v; Sloane 1489, fol. 9v; Cheshire Archives MS ZCR 63/2/19, fol. 11r; Chetham's MS Mun. A.4.16, p. 37; Folger MSS V.a.162, fol. 62v; V.a.262, p. 139; Houghton MS Eng. 686, fol. 10r; Leicestershire Record Office MS DG7/Lit.2, fol. 261v; Senate House MS 313, fol. 17v (two copies); University of Edinburgh MS H.-P. Coll. 401, fol. 43^{b}r; University of Texas, Austin MS HRC 79, p. 85; West Yorkshire Archive Service, Bradford MS 32D86/34, p. 81.

Thomas Bastard, 'In Getam'

Geta, from woll and weauing first began
Swelling, and swilling to a gentleman
When he was a gentleman, and brauely dight
He left nott swelling till he was a knight
Att last, forgetting what hee was att first
Hee swell'd to bee a lord, and then he burst:/

Source: British Library MS Egerton 2230, fol. 19v.
Other text (six-line version): St. John's, Cambridge MS U.26, p. 144.
Other texts (eight-line version): Bodleian MS Don. d.58, fol. 34v; British Library MS Harley 1836, fol. 16r; New York Public Library MS Arents S288, p. 102.

Anonymous, 'When Carr in Court a Page at first began'

On Sr Robart Carr Earle of Som[m]ersett.

When Carr in Court a Page at first began
Hee swell'd and swell'd into a Gentleman,
And when a Gentleman, and bravely dight;
He swell'd and swell'd till Hee became a Knight:

At last forgetting what Hee was at first,
Hee swelld into an Earle, and then Hee burst.

Source: Folger MS V.a.103, fol. 68r.
Other texts: Beinecke MS Osborn b62, pp. 42–43; Bodleian MS Malone 19, p. 151; Folger MS V.a.162, fol. 63v; Houghton MS Eng. 686, fol. 13v; Rosenbach MS 239/27, p. 57^{b}; University of Nottingham MS Portland PwV 37, p. 142.

Anonymous, 'I. C. V. R.'

I. C. V. R
good Mounsieur Car
about to fall

V. R. A. K
as most men say
and thats not all
V. O. Q. P
wth a nullitie
that shamelesse packe

S. X. Y. ff
whose wicked life
hath broke thy backe/

Source: British Library MSS Harley 1221, fol. 91r.
Other texts: Bodleian MSS Don. c.54, fol. 22v; Douce f.5, fol. 34v; Eng. poet. e.14, fol. 49r; Firth d.7, fol. 152r; Rawl. D.1048, fol. 64v; Rawl. poet. 160, fol. 162v; Sancroft 53, pp. 48, 58 (second copy crossed out); British Library MSS Add. 15227, fol. 42v; Add. 15476, fol. 1r; Add. 30982, fol. 22r; Harley 4955, fol. 81r; Harley 6038, fol. 28r; Harley 7316, fol. 4v; Sloane 1489, fol. 9v; British Library, Printed books, C.39.a.37, fol. 12v; Cambridge University Library MS Add. 4138, fol. 47r; Cheshire Archives MS ZCR 63/2/19, fol. 13r; Chetham's MS Mun. A 4.16, p. 37; Duke of Rutland, Belvoir Castle MS, *Letters and Papers*, Verses, Vol. XXV, fol. 53r; Folger MS V.a.162, fol. 35r; Rosenbach MSS 1083/15, p. 140; 1083/16, p. 172; Somerset Record Office MS DD/SF C/2635, Box 1; University of Edinburgh MS H.-P. Coll. 401, fol. 43^{b}r; Victoria and Albert MS Dyce 44, 25.F.39, fol. 97r.

Anonymous, 'ffrom Katherines docke was lanched a pincke' (early version)

ffrom Katherines docke was lanched a pincke
w^{ch}: did leake but did not sincke
Sometimes she lay by Essex shore
expectinge rigging yeards and more
but all disasters to preuent ~~wth~~
wth winde in poope she sayled to Kent

at Rochester she Anchor Cast
w:^{ch} Canterbury did distaste
but winchester wth Elyes helpe
did hale a shore this Lyons whelpe
she was weake sided and did reele
~~t~~so som-were-sett to mend her keele
to stopp her leake & sheath her
and make her fitt for euery^{mend} (struck through: ~~mend~~)

Source: British Library MSS Harley 1221, fol. 91v.
Other texts: Bodleian MSS Ashmole 38, pp. 135, 136 (two copies); Don. c.54, fol. 23r; Firth d.7, fol. 151r; Malone 19, p. 94; Rawl. D.1048, fol. 64v; Rawl. poet. 26, fol. 18r–v; Rawl. poet. 84, fol. 68r–67v rev.; Rawl. poet. 160, fol. 163r; British Library MSS Add. 34218, fol. 165r; Add. 61944, fol. 77v; Egerton 2230, fol. 71r; Harley 6038, fol. 28v; Harley 6057, fol. 13v; Harley 7316, fol. 4r–v; Sloane 2023, fols 60v–61r; Chetham's MS Mun. A 4.15, fol. 68v; Folger MS V.a.103, fol. 69v; Senate House MS 313, fol. 16r; University of Nottingham MS Portland PwV 37, p. 142; University of Texas, Austin MS HRC 79, p. 83; Victoria and Albert MS Dyce 44, 25.F.39, fol. 97r.

Anonymous, 'from Cathernes docke theer launch't A pritty Pinke' (late version)

On the Countess of Sommersett,
from Cathernes docke theer launch't A pritty Pinke
leake she did often, butt did neuer sinke,
in falling downe to Essex pleasant shore
long she exspected rigging, and yards store [*page break*]
but out of hope theer to obteine content
with wind in Poope, away she flyes for Kent
and faine she would att Rochester cast Anchor
but hideous dangers, and chill feares much blank her
beside to Cross good Canterburyes house
and london too, did cross the Ocean lawes
yet winchester auerd she might, and Ely
by scriptum est would proue itt, did not he ly
well wheer she would bee, they tow tugd her thether
Maugre the sea, the Tide, the winde, the wether,
them Som=are=sett to Caulke, and fresh her beake
make yare her gear new yard her, stop her leake
and brauly furnisht now with all munition
to sea she goes upon an expedition
her Canuas spreading, when she was inclind too
up she would fetch, whome ere she had A mind too

clap him A boord, take the best things he had
and in exchang gaue him some oreworne bad
Manny A Gallant Top, foreyard, and Mast
her rude incounters layde in helpless wast
and now her beake comaunds what ere she please
without controule euen ouer all the seas,
in triumph thus she reueld, till debate
arose betweene his m^{r}: and his mate
the Pinke was tender sided and unsteady
att euery Gust to turne her Keele up ready
the mate deserning that, did sore distast her
his thoughts, her faults, discouers to the M^{r}:
forwarning him such tempest weer A bruing
as not to leaue her brought apparant ruine
the m^{r}: wholly on his Pinke enamour'd
into his head ~~head~~ could haue no councell hamerd
still he would keepe her, like her, loue her best
but doth in hart his honnest Mate detest
consults with his belou'd, A fitt time watches
when by A tricke they clapt him under hatches
wheer fed with Art composed Tart he lay
tell att A port hole he was made away
thus Ouer=bury=ed head and eares in water
was't not great pitty she should act this slaughter
this Treacherous practise Neptune winnowed out
and uowed Iust uengance all the seas aboute
the grudging winds with Angry murmer swell
and sad disasters in blacke stormes fortell
no rest, no refuge the proude Pinke wuld haue
tust, tumbled, rumbled on the boystrous waue
her ends, her frends preuailes not, nor her prayers
up she was cast att the black fryers stayres
wher in requitall of his former Iadeing
ransack't and rifled, mard & bard from trading
on Ground she sitts, and tho as yett she splitts not
crackt and halfe rackt, for sea againe shees fitt not [*page break*]
nay though her owners safly of should wind her
no man A liue would euer uenture in her
but her deare m^{r}: close unto A mountaine
was driuen A shore nigh Ignoramus fountaine
from whence the stormes increasing, fury strooke him
downe to A Moore wher now you may goe looke him

Source: Huntington MS HM 198, pt. 1, pp. 19–21.
Other text: University of Texas, Austin MS HRC 79, pp. 97–101.

3 Spanish Match Libels

Anonymous, Commons' petitionary exchange

TO T[H]E BLESSED ELIZA
OF FAMOVS MEMORIE

The humble petic[i]on of the
wretched & most contemptible
the poore com[m]ons of England

If Saints in heaven can either see or heare
Or helpe poore mortalls; oh then lend thyne eare
Looke downe (bles'd Saint) oh heare oh heare vs now
whose humble hearts lowe as o^{r} knees doe bowe
Looke on o^{r} sufferings thinke but on o^{r} wrongs
that hardly can be tould by mortall tongues
Oh be not now lesse gratious then of ould
when each distressed vassaile might be bould
Into thy open hand to put his greife
And timely thence for to receiue releife
Be not lesse good lesse gratious then before
In heaven the supplicac[i]ons of the poore
Are heard as soone as suits of greatest kings
If o^{r} petic[i]on then (bles'd S.^{t}) want wings
To mount them to the Iudge of Iudges throne
Oh helpe them (mighty Sou[er]aigne) with thyne owne
Carry o^{r} iust complaints (since iust they are)
And make a tender of them at the barre
where noe corrupc[i]on, fraud, noe freind noe bribe
noe wrangling lawyer noe vsurping Scribe
noe favorite noe parasite noe minion
can either lead or alter the opinion
Of that great chancellor there, oh laye them (downe
And merit praise on earth, in heaven renowne
Soe intricate is this our wretched storye
Where to begin (Defendor of all glorye
Heaven knowes we doe not know, nay wch is worst
Thyne once bles'd Subiects, haue soe oft bin curst
ffor offering vp petic[i]ons of this kind
Soe as we tremble when we call to mind
Thy wonted goodnes, y.^{t} oh y.^{t} doth cheere vs
That only giues vs hope y.^{t} thou wilt heare vs
When heaven was pleas'd (great S.^{t}) to take ye hence
And soe make wretched for some vile offence

This sinfull land oh then began o[r] feares
And had we then this kingdome drown'd in teares
And in those floods convay'd o[r] soules to heaven
to waite on thyne we had not now bin driven
To crye and call the from thy fellow Saints
to heare and pitty theis o[r] iust complaints [*folio break*]
Oh pardon thou but such o[r] grosse comission
And deigne to pardon this o[r] poore petition
And we will make the name of bles'd Eliza
Equall the Avies of the great Maria.
Noe snuffling rascall through his horn=pipe nose
Shall tell thy story in his ill tun'd prose
Or shewe thy Statute to each penny groome
the monuments wee'le raise, shall make proud Roome
on pilgrimage to come, and at thy shrine
Offer their guifts as to a thing devine
And on thy altar fram'd of richest stones
weele dayly tender teares, & sighes & grones
Eternity shall sleepe and long tongu'd fame
fforget to speake ere we forget thy name
Read (blessed S.[r]) oh read it & beleeue vs
and giue it to his hands y[t] can releiue vs.

TO T[H]E MOST
high and mightiest the
most iust and yet most
mercifull the greatest
Chancellor of heaven and
the cheife Iudg of y[e] earth.

If bleeding hearts deiected soules find grace
thou all disposer turne not back thy face
from vs thy suppliants; thrice 7 sonns haue worn
their som[m]er suits since we began to mourne
Egipts Tenne plagues we haue endur'd twice told
since bles'd Eliza was with S.[ts] inrold
Thy messengers of wrath their vyalls powre
Dayly vpon our heads nay every howre
Plagues beget plauges, & fearefull vengeance gro[wes]
As if there were noe end set to o[r] woes
Haue o[r] great sin[n]s rais'd vp soe great a cloud
twixt heaven and vs as cryes though nere soe loud
Can get noe entrance to thy mercye seate
Are o[r] iniquities (good god) soe great?
Soe infinite as neither groanes nor teares
Can get a passage? Remember but y[e] yeares

Of o^{r} affliction, then forget we crave
o^{r} sins, bury them in the deepest grave
Of darke oblivion, Hyde them in the syde
of our Redeemer, oh let them be tyde
in chaynes that they may never rise againe
Let vs noe longer sue or begg in vayne. [*folio break*]
Let this o^{r} Supplication, this complaint
tendred by o^{r} late Soveraigne now thy Saint
At last find grace, was't not we humbly pray
Enough that first thou tooks't y^{t} Queene away
was not y^{t} Doue that lambe of innocence
Sufficient sacrifize for our offence?
Oh noe! our sins outliu'd her & our crimes
Did threaten to outliue the last of times
Thou didst remooue her that she might not se
the sad begining of our misirie
Then like a showre of hailestone fell ye darts
of angry Death how many thowsand hearts
were wounded in one yeare? how many bled
and wish'd to dye when all they lou'd was dead
Mothers left childles, children quite bereft
of carefull parents; nay there was not left
A paire of freinds to comfort one an other
whoe wanted not a sister whoe a brother?
where was the husband where the wife could$_{say}$
we shall not be devour'd this night this daye?
Death soe his powre and large comission shewd
That men on earth as corne on ground wert strew'd
The sad remembrance of it still remaynes
Then the strict hand of vengeance bound in chains
The fruitfull feilds till, birds, beasts, hearbs plants trees
Did famish, faint, drop, dye, wither and freeze
And nothing issued from the barren earth
But y^{t} leane monster meagre palefac'd Death
Next invndations rose, such as before
Since Noahs flood ne're touch'd ye Brittish shore
where men and beasts alike ingrau'd their bones
Vnder moist waues instead of marble stones
How often hath the sunne w.thdrawne his light
And turned daye into the shape of night
Had Egipt greater darknes then had we
when cleirest eyes at Midday scarce could see
Vnwholsome mists; strange foggs rumors of wars
Evill pretending cometts, blazing starrs

Prodigious births & most vn=naturall seasons
spurring Philosophers beyond their reasons
ffrighting the poore, the drowsy rich exhorting
from of their downy beds where they lye snorting
Heaven seemed in combustion y^{e} skye in armes
The spheares beat drum[m]s, y^{e} orbes bid sound alarmes
The ayre did often bloody colou^{r}s spread
And all to rouze vs from o^{r} downy bedd
Of base securitye, yet nought could fright vs
Till heaven had robd vs, of w^{t} did most delight vs
Henry o^{r} Ioye, Henry whose every limbe
threatned to conquer Death, & Death not him [*folio break*]
Henry our pride even Henery the bles'd
In whome great Brittaine set vp all her rest
Resolving loosing him to playe noe more
but liue for ever wretched ever poore
whoe had not in that one an ample share
what subiect, had not rather lost his heire?
What tender mother did not wish y^{t}' dart
Had glanc'd from him & hit her darlings heart
All that were vertuous all y^{t} then were good
turn'd their eyes Rivers into Seas of blood
Th' Egiptian waters bitter were, but knowe
this touch'd the very soule, they did not soe
O pardon heaven all plagues y^{t} went before
Had lost themselues in this, and were noe more
to be remembred, this oh this alone
might well haue made vs weepe o^{r} selues to stone
The spaune of Pharoah could their bloods be priz'd
All the first borne y^{t} soe were sacrifiz'd
All that base fury compar'd to this o^{r} Henery
Deserues noe mention, noe thought noe memorye
Lusting Sodome (such hath thy mercy bin
Although we did abound in crying sinne)
could not take fire vntill they were remoou'd
that thou in mercy like in goodnes lou'd
Anne thy anoynted, she must leaue this Cittye
before it was destroy'd, such was thy pittye
Such was thy goodnes, oh is there yet tenne
is there (good God) a number yet of men
whose innocence may slacke thy kindling ire
and saue thy Sodom Brittaine from the fire
Of thy iust anger? Is there yet a soule
whose vertue power hath but to controule
thy heau'd vp hand of Iustice, if there be

for his, or her sake rouse thy clemencye
Awake thy mercy let thy Iustice slumber
and saue the greater by the lesser number
ffor his or her sake we doe humbly praye
respite of time giue vs a longer daye
And then enabled by thy grace and favor
weele purchase pardon by o^{r} good behavior.
Plagues famine, darknes, and Invndations
we haue indur'd, feare of Innovations
with expectation of the worst can followe
dayly torments vs, and we howrely swallowe
Our very spittle with feare and horror
we nightly sleepe in feare awake in terror
Nor are we all this while from vermine free
the Caterpillers hang on every tree
Lowsy Proiectors Monopoly=mongers
A crew of vpstart Rascalls, whose greedy hungers [*folio break*]
Can ne're be satisfi'd, A sort of slaues
More miserable far then whores or graues
A crew of vpstart parasites that rise
And doe more mischeife then th' Egiptian flies
Theis in our gardens theis in our howses swarme
One drinks a manno^{r}, another eats a farme
This with a Lordship warmes his lusting whore
That by the sale of iustice doth procure
A tenem.^{t} or Twoe, which being gott
by violence he drowneth in the pott
they enter, citties corporations
worke not yet liue by ocupations
They haue noe trade and yet noe trade is free
from paying them a taxe, a fine, a fee,
They eate the corne and fruite of eu[er]y feild

And we haue skip=iack courtiers I dare saye
that doe devower more in one poore daye
Then they in Pharoahs age could ere haue done
They bounded were, prey'd but fro[m] sunne to sunne
but theis for three apprentiships haue eate
the fruits of all o^{r} labors, all our sweate.
Have we not froggs? oh yes, in every ditch
Devouring poore, impoverishing the rich
busie Intelligencers base informers
like toads and froggs lye croaking in all corners
Promooting rascalls whose venemous tongus
Haue done thy suppliants infinite great wrongs
Where they desire to enter, there's noe defence

noe auntient title noe inheritance
Can serue for plea, they wretch & strech ye lawe
keepe magistrates and officers in awe
they plucke the ballance from faire Iustice fist
And make her Iniustice, they'le doe w^{t} they list
there is noe equitye noe lawe noe right
All causes goe by favor or by might
Oh God! of misery w^{t} can more be said
Iustice is bought and sold become a trade
Honor confer'd on base vnworthy groomes
And clownes for coyne are pearch'd in highest roomes
Iob he had many stabbs but none so bad
As we this one and twenty yeares haue had
Egipt had botches, murrens, sores y^{t} smarted
but yet they lasted not they soone departed,
Halfe fforty yeares in this sadd wildernesse
we now haue travel'd is there noe redresse;
Bowman, and Iowler, Ringwood & his mate
compar'd to vs are in a better state. [*folio break*]
They can be heard 'tis they can be rewarded
when we are slighted curst & vnregarded
Is there (oh heaven) a people falne a degree
belowe the condic[i]on of a dogg but wee?
Was there a nation in the vniverse
more daring once more stout, more bold, more^{feirce}
And is there now vpon the worlds broad face
Any that can be recconed halfe soe base?
Is there a people soe much scorn'd despiz'd
soe laugh'd at trodden & soe vassailiz'd?
Where is our auntient nobilitye become
Alas they are supprest and in their roome
Like proud vsurping Lucifers there sitts
a Crew of vpstart fawning parasites
Where is the Gentry? All oppres'd disgrac'd
And errant knights aboue them now are plac'd
ffidlers and fooles w.th Dancers and Rymers
Are now in England the greatest clymers
We had a Parliam.^{t} a cure for soares
A Magna Charta; Alls cast out of dores
The bould and hardy Brittains conquered are
without a drumme a sword, a sound of warre
If without cause (Iust heaven) we doe complain
Then send o^{r} supplicac[i]ons back againe
Much more we could say, much more we could speak
but with the thought of this o^{r} hearts even break

As humbly then as we began we crave
A gratious answeare; oh be pleas'd to saue
the remnant of thy people turne thy face
and let vs once more tast thy saving grace
  fforsake vs not for ever Lord; but giue
  More life to those y[t] now desire to liue
ffinis

Source: Bodleian MS Rawl. poet. 160, fols 16r–18v.
Other texts: Beinecke MS Osborn b197, pp. 96–97, 86–91; Bodleian MSS Ashmole 36, 37, fols 303r–4v; Eng. poet. c.50, fols 8r–10v; Eng. poet. f.10, fols 107r–11r; Malone 19, pp. 15–19 (second poem); Malone 23, pp. 32–36, 11–12, 37–44, 13–14; Rawl. D.398, fols 222r–26r; Top. Cheshire c.7, fols 3r–5v; British Library MSS Add. 5832, fol. 202r–v (first poem); Add. 25707, fols 76r, 77r–78r; Add. 34217, fols 39v–40v; Sloane 363, fols 11r–14v; Sloane 1479, fols 6v–8v (second poem); Brotherton MSS Lt 28, fols 2r–5v; Lt q 44, fols 2r–5v; Folger MS V.a.275, pp. 1–7; Houghton MS Eng. 686, fols 29r–30v (partial copy of second poem); Huntington MS HM 198, pt. 1, pp. 62–63 (first poem); St. John's, Cambridge MSS K.56, no. 59; K.56, no. 60; University of Edinburgh MS H.-P. Coll. 401, fols 45r–47v; University of Nottingham MS Portland PwV 37, pp. 243–48; University of Texas, Austin MS HRC 79, pp. 330–37; West Yorkshire Archive Service, Bradford MS 32D86/34, pp. 93–94, 96–100.

A GRATIOVS
Answeare fro[m] the blessed S.[t]
to her whilome subiects w.[th] a
devine admonition and a
propheticall conclusion:

Your bould petition mortalls I haue seene
and found it full of passion full of spleene
Prayers that enter heaven & gayne a hearing [*folio break*]
Are wing'd with charitye, there's noe appearing
with supplicac[i]ons fraught with ire and gall
I doe confesse (poore soules) the truth of all
and wish a period to yo[r] miseries
But first yo[r] infant young iniquities
must haue an end alas yow must begin
to loue faire virtue as yow haue done sin
Yow must redeeme the time that's lost and know
As heaven hath ever bin to vengeance slowe
Soe by degrees is grace and virtue wonne
Eyes that are sore by gazing at the sonne
Increase their greife, if yow wold mercy gaine
from vniust acc[i]ons yow must first abstayne
How dares a wicked servant once require
from his iust master either grace or hire?
Yow must put of your shooes, w.[th] w.[ch] yow trode
the waye to sinne: ere yow dischourse w.[th] god

Give me encouragem.^{t} of com[m]endation
of your amendm.^{t} then your supplication
I will deliver; I left yow rich 'tis true
but prow'd withall, yow fear'd none, all fear'd yo.^{w}
yow were soe farre from feare y^{t} yow deny'de
to paye him feare that gave yo.^{w} cause of pride
Yow must be humbled, heaven e're punish'd yet
All kind of Cankers with an opposite
He that will surfet, e're he gaine his health
must strictly fast, had yow sate still in wealth
yow never would haue bow'd yor stubborn knee
either to God or S.^{t} to heaven or mee
I will not greive yor trobled soules too much
yet guilty, yor ingratitudes i'le touch
And that yow may the better know yor errors
I will vnto yor memories call some favors
by yow forgoth, vnthankfully forgotten
long time before the hearse I wore was rotten
It is noe ostentation to relate
Curt'sies done to such as are ingrate
I found yow like a hurrying scatter'd flock
yor very soules beating against the rocke
of blinded ignorance and superstition
Iust in the high way vnto foule perdition
I playd the Pilot and the sheppard too
And got noe lambe noe fleice more then my due
I ne're exacted from the comon store
we all alike were rich, we all were poore
for mine and thine, & thine & mine are things
not to be knowne twixt subiects & their kings
Princes should sun=like fro[m] the ayre exhall, [*folio break*]
The wealth they raise; & then in showres let fall
in every place as they see cause a share
And not consume them in the wanton ayre
then full Exchequers should lik conduits be
open to all to rich and poore like free
And subiects shold like feilds be full of springs
that nat'rally still fall towards their kings
The comonwealth shold be in motions
Seas fall to brookes, & brooks shold fall to Ocians
such loyall acts, loyall comunitye
keepes kings and subiects, still in vnitye
I cannot say I greive, this place as free
from passion is as from iniquitie
But yet I muse since Scotland w.th yo.^{w} ioyn'd

Englands Exchequer is noe better coyn'd
Sure there's falce play, I feare y^{e} younge^{r} brother
is growne too wise, too crafty for the other
It is an ill made marriage where y^{e} bride
spends faster then the husband can provide
I did meynteyne (far be vayne glory hence)
A well=rig'd navy still for your defence
A royall fleete y^{t} like a brazen wall
circled this land, the armies were not small
the garrisons and forts I did vphold
kept yow in peace, like sheepe w.thin a fould
What well deserving soldier went away
without reward? much lesse without his pay?
To neighbo.^{r} states in amity we lent
money and men; what servants ever went
without his hire? w^{t} pension was deny'de
from my first howre vntill the howre I dy'de?
I breife I sildome borrowed oft did lend
yet left enough to giue enough to spend
How comes it then since neither fleete nor fort
Army nor garrison nor howse nor court
wages nor debts, nor ought repayr'd nought paid
purchas'd nor built, nought, lent^{nor} yet defray'd
And is there nought remaynes nought to be found
All is not perfect sure all is not sound
I noe lesse muse to see the woods cut downe
The auntient lands revenewes of the crowne
Disported oft to favorite and freind
that should hereditarily descend
ffrom king to king even as the Diadem
ye land o'th' crowne is the crownes cheifest Iem
Customes fines, Subsedies and accedents
and nought substantiall but ye annuall rents
[*obscured*] deservers sure y^{t} service doe [*folio break*]
That must not be made knowne to heaven or yo.^{w}
Princes are gods on earth and subiects eyes
vpon their acc[i]ons must not stand as spyes
It is a dangerous and vngodly thing
to prye into the chamber of the king
That Arke of state is sanctifi'de and must
be only touch'd of such are put in trust:
But answeare yow expect of yor petition
then know (poore soules) i'ts given me in comission
ffrom heavens great king to tell yo.^{w} all y.^{ts} past
to what's to come is but a sparke or blast

Yo^r sorrowes yet alas like weomens flowers
Doe goe and come but there must follow showers
E're England be deliver'd, that will make
Yo^r entrailes bleed yor very soules to quake
The daye will come when stowtest men shall mourn
And children wish they neu[er] had bin borne
The sword shall take w^t famine hath o're slip'd
And fire consume w^t famine hath not nip'd
The Gospells sunne shall lesse her glorios light
And ignorance as black as darkest night
shall spread her sable wings about this Isle
And Babilons proud whore shall then defile
Albions white cliffes, the Isra'litts must duble
the bricks they make yet be allow'd noe stubble
An Egiptian with an hebrew shall contend
and t'hebrew want a Moses to his freind
there is a sin incurable lyes hid
And such an one doth modestye forbidd
Any Sex to name, till y^t be brought to light
And Achan punish'd yo.^w shalbe put to flight
before the men of Ai; yow shall not stand
nor shall ought prosper that yo.^w take in hand
The Levite from his wife shalbe divorc'd
and from the truth to goe shalbe enforc'd
Vriah shalbe murthered for his wife
And Naball sleepe in danger of his life
Yow lusted for a king (heavens king releiue yo.^w)
And grant yow pardon as I doe forgiue yo.^w
Yow tooke a surfett at my happy reigne
And payd my well deserving wth disdaine
But oh! yow cas't me not away twas not I
yo.^w slighted it was the lord of hoasts most high
And therefore yow shall cry & call in vayne
bootles yo.^w shall lament, bootles complaine
ffrom forth the Northerne p[ar]ts is come at last
The Lyon rows'd from Den, y^t shall laye wast,
yor townes and Citties whoe stand vp alas
to stopp the gapp where such hie wrath shold pase
He shall by pollicye and craft doe more [*folio break*]
Then all the world by force could doe before
Yet know his end, his last conclusion
shall misery be and eke confusion.

But harke heavens Organs summon me away
my comission's ended and I dare not staye
the blessed Quiresters of heaven I heare

tuning their voyces to their Sou[er]aignes eare
ffarewell poore soules goe pray repent & fast
the Deafe and vniust Iudge is wonne at last
by importunitie; much more will hee
that is inclin'd and prone to clemencye
I shall attend yo[r] prayers every howre
And to the vtmost will extend my powre
with him that can and may releiue yo[r] owne
Greiue for whats past with resolution
T'amend yo[r] liues referre the execution
Vnto t'howers of th'alteration.
ffinis

Source: Bodleian MS Rawl. poet. 160, fols 18v–20v.
Other texts: Beinecke MS Osborn b197, pp. 92–96; Bodleian MSS Eng. poet. c.50, fols 10v–12r; Eng. poet. e.14, fols 49v–52r; Eng. poet. f.10, fols 111r–13v; Malone 23, pp. 14–16, 45–48; Rawl. D.398, fols 226r–28v; Top. Cheshire c.7, fol. 6r–7v; British Library MS Sloane 363, fol. 15r–17r; Brotherton MSS Lt 28, fols 6r–8r; Lt q 44, fols 6r–8r; Cheshire Archives MS ZCR 63/2/19, fols 33r–34v; Folger MS V.a.275, pp. 8–9; St. John's, Cambridge MSS K.56, no. 61; K.56, no. 62; U.26, pp. 6–11; University of Edinburgh MS H.-P. Coll. 401, fols 48r–50r; University of Nottingham MS Portland PwV 37, pp. 249–52; University of Texas, Austin MS HRC 79, pp. 338–42; West Yorkshire Archive Service, Bradford MS 32D86/34, pp. 94–96.

Anonymous, 'All the cheife talk is now'

TO THE
tune of Vir=
=ginia.

All the cheife talk is now
of the golden Lady
The Pope will not allow
king Iames shalbe her Daddy
Charles could get noe victualls
sufficient for his traine
His horses and his trumpetters
are all come back againe
With a hey downe downe
with a hey downe downe
With a hey downe downe derry
If this be soe
thres many more
Besides vs wilbe merry.

2

Gundamore whose breech is sore
he rides besides the saddle
H'as long bin hatching eggs
which now may prove all addle
And those halfe hearted English
that with him wrought for Spaine
Begin to scratch because y[e] match
doth doubtfull still remayne
With a hey downe &c

3

But shall I tell yow w.[t] I thinke
I doubt tis but a rumor
The foxes they know how to winke
to sound the peoples humor
ffor questionles all doubts were scand
before y[t] Charles went thither
And now a navy is at hand
to saile the lord knowes whither
with a hey downe &c

4

Earle Rutland is o[r] Admirall
and Windsor hees y[e] Rere [*folio break*]
Lord Morley cannot doe withall
except his wench were there
God send them all a merry gale
and send then free on shore
And grant all papists loue y[e] prince
as Morley loues his whore
with a hey downe &c

5

The Navy is well furnished
with papists wondros store
And Captaines many & Admiralls
that never fought before
Lets pray then that o[r] mariners
to their tacklings stout may stand
And fling the papists overbard

to floate vnto the land
with a hey downe &c

6

Duke Buckingham & Cottington
with the Endimion swaine
Vse their best tricks with Cotholicks
to bring o^{r} prince to Spaine
But now hees there we need not feare
the Lady must not marry
God send our Charles safe home againe
and let her worship tarry
with a hey downe &c

7

Now God preserve o^{r} king and prince
and a plauge vpon his foes
And all that are Hispagnioliz'd
or wold their Country loose
And grant y^{t} those whoe matches make
before the parties woe
May goe sell matches vp and downe
as now poore frenchfolkes doe
with a hey downe downe
with a hey downe downe
With a hey down down ~~down~~ derry
if this be soe
theres many moe
besides vs wilbe merrye. ffinis

Source: Bodleian MS Rawl. poet. 160, fols 177v–78r.
Other texts: Beinecke MSS Osborn b197, pp. 222–23; Osborn b356, pp. [292–94]; Bodleian MSS Don. b.8, p. 117; Malone 19, pp. 32–33; Rawl. D.1048, fol. 76r; Rawl. poet. 26, fol. 24v; British Library MSS Add. 5832, fols 200v–1r; Add. 29492, fols 30v–31v; Add. 61683, fol. 73r; Harley 907, fol. 75v; Sloane 1792, fols 52v–53v; Cambridge University Library MS Gg. 4. 13*, p. 48; Cheshire Record Office MS ZCR 63/2/19, fols 32v–33r; Folger MS V.a.162, fol. 73r–v; Houghton MS Eng. 686, fols 7v–8r; Huntington MS HM 46323, fols 9v–10v; Rosenbach MS 1083/16, pp. 250–51; St. John's, Cambridge MS K.56, no. 72; University of Texas, Austin MS HRC 79, pp. 343, 345–46 (two copies); West Yorkshire Archive Service, Bradford MS 32D86/34, pp. 52–53; Westminster Abbey MS 41, fol. 18r–v.

4 'The Five Senses' and Related Texts

Anonymous (possibly William Drummond), 'The Five Senses'

On the fiue senses.

1 Seeinge.

ffrom such a face whose excellence
may captiuate my soueraignes sence
And make him Phæbus like, his throne
Resigne to some yonge Phaeton,
Whose skilllesse & vnsteady hand
May proue the ruine of our land
Except greate Ioue doth from the sky
Beholdinge earthes calamitie
Strike with his hand, that cannot erre
The proude vsurpinge charrioter,
And turne (though Phæbus greiues) our woe
From such a face which can doe soe
Wheresoere itt hath a beinge
Blesse my soueraigne and his seeinge

2 Hearinge.

From jests prophane & flatteringe tongues
ffrom bawdy tales & beastly songes
ffrom after supper suites that feare
A Parliam^t house or counsells eare
From Spanish treatie that may wound
Our countryes peace or Gospells sound
From Iobs false freinds, that would entice
My soueraigne from heauens paradise
From prophetts such as Ahabs were
That flatteringe would abuse his eare
His frowne more then there makers fearinge
Blesse my soueraigne & his hearinge

3 Tastinge.

[*page break*]

ffrom all fruite that is forbidden
Such for which old Eue was chidden
ffrom bread of labours sweate & toyle
ffrom the poore widdowes meale & oyle
ffrom blood of innocents oft wrangled
ffrom there estates, & for that strangled

From the candide poison'd baites
From Iesuites & there deceites
Italian sallads, Romish druggs
The milke of babells proud horn'd duggs
From wine that can destroy the braine
And from the dangerous figgs of spaine
Att all banquetts & all feastinge
Blesse my soueraigne and his tastinge.

4 ffeelinge

ffrom pricke of Conscience such a stinge
That slayes the soule, heauen blesse my kinge
From such a bribe as may withdrawe
His thoughts from equity & lawe
ffrom such a smoath & beardlesse chinne
As may prouoke or tempt to sinne
ffrom such a one whose moyst hand may
My soueraigne leade out of the way
ffrom thinges polluted & vncleane
ffrom that's beastly & obscene
ffrom that may sett his soule one reelinge
Blesse my soueraigne & his feelinge

5 smellinge

Where myrre and frankinsense is throwne
And altars built to gods vnknowne
O lett my soueraigne neuer smell
Such damn'd perfumes are fitt for hell
Lett noe such fume his nosthrills staine
ffrom smells that poison can the braine [*page break*]
Heauens still preserue him; next I craue
Thou wilt be pleas'de greate god to saue
My soueraigne from a Ganamede
Whose whorish breath hath power to lead
His highnesse which way itt lists,
Lett such lipps be neuer kist
ffrom a breath soe farre excellinge
Blesse my soueraigne & his smellinge.

Seeinge.

And now just god I humbly pray
That thou wilt take that filme away
That keepes my soueraignes eyes from veiwinge
Those thinges that will be our vndoeinge.

hearinge

Then lett him heare o god the sounds
As well of men, as of his houndes.

tastinge

Giue him tast & timely feelinge too
Of what his subjects vndergoe

ffeelinge and smellinge.

Giue him a feelinge of there woes
And then noe doubt his royall nose
Will quicklie smell ye raskall forth
Whose blacke deeds haue ecclipsd his worth
They found & scourg'd for there offences
Heauen blesse my soueraigne & his senses.

Source: Rosenbach MS 239/27, pp. 58^{b}–60.
Other texts: Beinecke MSS Osborn b54, p. 877; Osborn b356, pp. 67–68; Bodleian MSS Eng. Poet. c.50, fol. 25r–v; Eng. poet. e.37, pp. 72–74; Malone 23, pp. 28–31; Rawl. poet. 26, fols 72r–73r; Rawl. poet. 117, fols 23v–24v; Rawl. poet. 160, fols 14v–15v; Tanner 465, fol. 97r; British Library MSS Add. 23229, fols 99r–100r; Add. 25303, fols 133r–34r; Add. 28640, fol. 105r; Egerton 923, fols 30r–31r; Harley 367, fol. 153r–v; Stowe 962, fols 144v–46r; Brotherton MS Lt q 44, fols 1r–2r; Chetham's MS Mun. A 3.47, fols 1r–2r; Downing, Cambridge MS Bowtell 'Wickstede's Thesaurus,' pt. 2, fols 106v–7v; Durham Cathedral MS Hunter 27, fols 94v–95r; Folger MSS V.a.275, p. 175; V.a.276, pt. 2, fols 40v–42r; V.a.339, fol. 263r; V.a.345, pp. 59–61; X.d.235; Hatfield House MS 206/100r–v; Houghton MS Eng. 686, fols 59v–60v; Huntington MS HM 198, pt. 1, pp. 30–32; Leicestershire Record Office MS DG7/Lit.2, pp. 333v–34v; Morgan MS MA 1057, pp. 80–81; Mount Stuart, Bute MS 104; National Library of Scotland MS Advocates' 19.3.8, fols 47r–48v; National Library of Wales MS NLW 12443A, pt. 2, pp. 125–30; Rosenbach MS 1083/16, pp. 84–87; St. John's, Cambridge MS S.32, fols 31r–32r; Somerset Record Office MS DD/SF C/2635, Box 1; University of Edinburgh MS H.-P. Coll. 401, fol. 51r–v; University of Nottingham MS Portland PwV 37, pp. 198–200; University of Texas, Austin MS HRC 79, pp. 325–37; West Yorkshire Archive Service, Bradford 32D86/34, pp. 65–66; Westminster Abbey MS 41, fols 21r–22r.

Ben Jonson, from *The Gypsies Metamorphosed*

Another to K: Iames.

ffrom a gipsy in the morninge
ffrom a paire of squint eyes turninge
ffrom the goblins & the specter
ffrom a drunkard though with nectar
From a woman true to noe man [*page break*]
Which is vgly, besides com[m]on.

ffrom a rampant smock that itches
To be puttinge one the breeches
Wheresoere they haue there beinge
Blesse our soueraigne and his seinge.

ffrom vnproper serious toyes
ffrom a Lawyer 3 parts noise
ffrom impertinence like a drum[m]e
That beates his dinner & his roome
From a tongue without a file
All of phrase & yett noe stile
From the candlesticks of Lothbury
And loue pure wiues att Banbury
Only eare and time outwearinge
Blesse &c:

ffrom gapinge oisters, & fride fish
ffrom a sowsbaby in a dish
From any portion of a swine
From bad venison & worse wine
ffrom lynge whatsoeuer cooke itt boyle
Though itt be sauc'd with mustard oyle
ffrom the durt & the knowledge
Of the students of Beere colledges
ffrom these & what may keepe men fastinge
Blesse. &c.

ffrom a trauellinge tinkers sheete
ffrom a paire of Carriers feete
ffrom a Lady that doth breath
Worse aboue then beneath
From Tobacco & the tipe
Of the Diuells glisterpipe
ffrom a stinke all stinkes excellinge
ffrom a fishmonger & his dwellinge
Blesse &c. [*page break*]

ffrom birdlime, tarr & from all pitch
ffrom a doxy & her itch
ffrom the bristles of a hogge
From the ringworme of a dogge
ffrom the courtship of a briar
ffrom S[t] Anthonies old fire
ffrom a needle, pinne, or thorne
In his bedd att euen or morne
ffrom the gow't or the least grutchinge
Blesse &c.

Blesse him still in all pretences
In his sport or in his senses
ffrom a boy to crosse his way
ffrom a foole or a fowle day
O blesse him heauen & send him longe
To be the subject of each songe
The acts & yeares of all our kinges t' outgoe
Though he is mortall weele not thinke him soe.
Finis ~

Source: Rosenbach MS 239/27, pp. 60–62.
Other texts: Bodleian MSS Ashmole 47, fols 90r–91r; Eng. poet. f.16, fol. 9r–v; British Library MSS Add. 30982, fols 155r–54v rev.; Sloane 1792, fols 64r–65r; Folger MSS V. a.125, pt. 1, fols 21v–22r; V.a.170, pp. 67–68; V.a.245, fol. 62r–v; Huntington MS HM 46323, fol. 15r–v; Morgan MS MA 1057, pp. 82–83; St. John's, Cambridge MS S.32, fols 27v–28v; University of Aberdeen MS 29, pp. 80–82; University of Nottingham MSS Cl LM 43; Portland PwV 37, pp. 197–98; West Yorkshire Archive Service, Bradford MS 32D86/34, pp. 67–68; Westminster Abbey MS 41, fols 27v–28v.

Anonymous, 'The Letany'

The Letany:
ffrom Mahomett & Paganisme
ffrom heriticks, from sects, & schisme
ffrom highway rascalls & cuttpurses
ffrom citty bawds & old dry nurses
ffrom glister pipes, & d[rs] whistles
ffrom begginge schollars stale Epistles
ffrom turnestile bootes & longlane beauers
ffrom agues & from drunken feauers
Libera nos domine.
From all seuerall kind of itches
From pickadills & cloakebagg britches
ffrom Carbonado'de suites of sarges [*page break*]
From a bastard thats the clargies
ffrom thredd points and caps of cruell
ffrom the danger of a duell
ffrom a tally full of noches
ffrom 2 priuy seales of botches.
Libera nos domine.
From a whore thats neuer pleasant
But in lusty wine & pheasant
ffrom the watch att 12 a clock
ffrom Besse Broughtons button'd smock
ffrom hackney coaches & from panders
That doe boast themselues com[m]anders

ffrom a taylors tedious bill
ffrom pilgrimage vp Holborne hill
Libera nos domine.

From damages & restitutions
From all cursed executions
From all new found way of sinninge
From the scurfe and sable linnen
From ye pox & the Phisitian
From the spanish inquisition
From a wife thats Leane & meager
From both lice & winters Leaguer
Libera nos domine.

From a gripinge Spanish Cullion
ffrom the gow't & the strangullion
ffrom a mountebanke his potion
ffrom his searinge & his lotion
ffrom the buttock of Priscilla
That dietts with salsa = perilla
ffrom a pastor too too zealous
ffrom the tubb of old Cornelius
Libera nos domine. [*page break*]

ffrom bawdy courts & ciuill Doctors
ffrom drunken sum[m]ers & there proctors
ffrom occasion for to reuell
With a Lawyer to the diuell
ffrom sergeants yeomen & there maces
ffrom false freinds with double faces
ffrom an enemy more mighty
Then vsquebaugh or aqua vitæ.
Libera nos domine.

Source: Rosenbach MS 239/27, pp. 62–64.
Other text: Bodleian MS Ashmole 36, 37, fol. 46v.

5 Buckingham Assassination Libels

Zouch Townley, 'Enjoy thy bondage make thy prison knowe'

To his confined freind M^r ffelton.

Enjoy thy bondage make thy prison knowe
Thou hast a liberty thou canst not owe
To these base punishments; kept entire since
Nothinge but guilt shackells the Conscience
I dare not tempt thy valiant blood to whay

Infeeblinge itt with pitty, nor dare pray
Thine act may mercy find, least thy great story
Loose somethinge of itts miracle & glory
I wish thy meritt freindly crueltie
Stout vengeance best becomes thy memory
For I would haue posterity to heare
He that can brauely doe, can brauely beare
Tortures seeme great vnto a cowards eye
Tis noe great thinge to suffer, lesse to dye
Should all the cloudes fall out & in y[r] strife
Lightninge & thunder sent to take my life
I would applaud the wisdome of my fate
Which knewe to valew me att such a rate
As att my fall to trouble all the skye
Emptyinge vpon me Ioues whole armory.
Serue in your sharpest mischeifes vse your rack
Enlarge each joynt & make each sinew crack
Thy soule before was streightned (thanke thy doome)
To shewe her vertue she had larger roome
Yett sure if euery artery were broke
Thou wouldst find strength for such another stroke
And now I leaue thee vnto death & fame
Which liues to shake ambition att thy name [*page break*]
And if itt were not shame ye Court by itt
Should hourely sweare before the fauourite.
Farewell, for thy braue sake we shall not send
Henceforth com[m]anders enemies to defend
Nor will itt euer our just Monarch please
To keepe an Admirall to loose the seas.
Farewell, vndaunted stand & joy to bee
Of publike sorrowe ye Epitome
Lett the Dukes name solace & crowne thy thrall
All wee in him did suffer thou for all
And I dare boldly write as thou darst dye
Stout ffelton Englands ransome here doth lye.
If idle trauellors aske who lyes here
The Dukes tombe may this inscription beare
Paint Cales & Ree make French & Spanish laugh
Mixe Englands shame & theres his Epitaph.

Source: Rosenbach MS 239/27, pp. 45–46.
Other texts: Beinecke MS Osborn b62, pp. 36–38; Osborn b200, pp. 120–21; Osborn b356, pp. 138–39; Bodleian MSS Don. b.8, pp. 212, 368 (two copies of last 4 lines); Eng. poet. c.50, fol. 26r (last 4 lines); Eng. poet. e.14, fols 14v–15r; Eng. poet. e.97,

pp. 91–92; Malone 21, fol. 4r–v; Malone 23, pp. 205–7; Rawl. poet. 26, fol. 34r; Rawl. poet. 142, fol. 42v; Rawl. poet. 153, fol. 10r (last 4 lines); Rawl. poet. 199, pp. 62–63; British Library MSS Add. 29492, fols 42v–46r; Add. 30982, fol. 86r; Add. 33998, fols 42v–43v; Add. 44963, fol. 40r (last 4 lines); Add. 47111, fol. 4v (lines 11–20); Egerton 2026, fols 12r (last 4 lines), 65r; Harley 6383, fol. 28v; Harley 6931, fol. 48r–v; Harley 7319, fol. 2r; Sloane 826, fols 192v–93v; Sloane 1199, fol. 74v; Sloane 1792, fols 114v–15r; Sloane 4178, fol. 63r; Corpus Christi, Oxford MS 328, fol. 51r–v; Folger MSS V. a.97, pp. 21–22; V.a.125, pt. 2, fol. 11v–r rev.; V.b.43, fols 33v–34r; Houghton MS Eng. 1278, item 11; Huntington HM 198, pt. 1, p. 152; Leicestershire Record Office MS DG7/Lit.2, fol. 353r–v; London Metropolitan Archives MS ACC/1360/528, fols 13r–v (77v–r rev.); Rosenbach MSS 239/27, pp. 45–46; 240/2, fol. 93r; St. John's, Cambridge MS S.32, fol. 29r–v; Trinity College Dublin MS 877, fols 168v, 169r–v; Victoria & Albert MS F48.G.2/1, item 3; West Yorkshire Archive Service, Leeds MS WYL156/237, fol. 83v.

Anonymous, epitaph for John Felton

Io: Feltons Epitaph made
By D: Donn/

Here vnInter,'d, Suspends, though not to saue
Surviuing freends, the expences of a graue;
Feltons dead Earth; w^{c}h to the world shall bee;
his owne Monument; his Elegie;
As large as Fame; but whether; bad; or good:
I dare not say; by hym, twas wright In blood,
for w^{c}h; his bodye, Is Intombd, In Ayre:
Archt ouer w^{c}h heauen; and A thousand fayre,
And glorious Diomond starrs; A Sepulcher,
That tyme, shall neuer Ruinatte; and whear,
The Impartiall worme, is nott bribed to sparr,
Princes, Corruptt In Marble; shall not share
his flesh; w^{c}h yf the Charritable skyes•
Imbalme wth Teares; doing Those obsequies,
Belonge to men; shall liue; tell pittiing foule,
Contend, to reach his bodye to his soule

Source: Bodleian MS Ashmole 38, p. 20.
Other texts: Beinecke MSS Osborn b62, p. 19; Osborn b197, p. 27; Osborn b200, pp. 130–31; Osborn Poetry Box VI, fol. 27v; Bodleian MSS Ashmole 47, fol. 48r; Eng. poet. c.53, fol. 9r; Eng. poet. e.14, fol. 12v; Eng. poet. f.27, p. 17; Malone 21, fols 4v–5r; Malone 23, p. 210; Rawl. poet. 84, fol. 114v–r rev.; Rawl. poet. 147, p. 40; Rawl. poet. 160, fol. 53r; Rawl. poet. 199, pp. 56–57; Tanner 465, fol. 71v; British Library MSS Add. 15226, fol. 28r; Add. 47111, fol. 4v; Egerton 923, fols 26v–27r; Egerton 1160, fol. 241v;

Harley 3511, fol. 241v; Harley 6057, fol. 6v; Sloane 826, fol. 197v; Corpus Christi, Oxford MS 328, fols 11v, 62r–v; Folger MSS V.a.97, p. 8; V.a.125, pt. 2, fol. 12r rev.; V.a.319, fol. 1r; V.a.322, p. 27; V.b.43, fol. 34r; Leicestershire Record Office MSS DG9/2796, pp. 10–11; DG7/Lit.2, fol. 354v; National Library of Wales MS NLW 12443A, pt. 2, pp. 100–1; Rosenbach MSS 239/27, p. 319; 240/7, p. 82; St. John's, Cambridge MS S.32, fols 28v–29r; West Yorkshire Archive Service, Leeds MS WYL156/237, fol. 34r.

APPENDIX 2:
Manuscript Descriptions

Since this book places such emphasis on early modern verse collectors, I have had to verify that they, as opposed to modern book dealers or librarians, compiled the miscellanies and juxtaposed the texts that pertain to this study. The following manuscript descriptions exhibit the bibliographic evidence that they did so. The descriptions focus, therefore, on those parts of miscellanies that anthologists put together in the early seventeenth century, to the relative exclusion of the texts, gatherings, and bindings that others added to some of them in subsequent decades and centuries. For instance, in the case of the Huntington Library's Haslewood-Kingsborough manuscript, I describe only its first part, which constitutes a unified miscellany in a single, seventeenth-century hand; and, for the present purposes, I ignore the second miscellany and the other documents that were bound with this anthology in the nineteenth century. Yet in the case of another composite manuscript in a modern binding, the British Library's Skipwith manuscript, I account for every gathering in the volume, given the likelihood that members of the Skipwith family first bound them together in the seventeenth century. In other words, the following descriptions focus rather exclusively on the early modern features of manuscripts in order to demonstrate the work of early modern verse collectors.

Each description begins with a manuscript's location and shelfmark and, in some cases, an informal title. If the identity of an early modern compiler or owner survives, this information appears next in the description. The collation of the manuscript follows. The collation offers a hypothetical account of a manuscript's construction and, in some cases, its partial destruction. It begins with the manuscript's format: 8° for octavo; 4° for quarto; and the rare, yet consistent, 2° for folio. It proceeds to list each of the manuscript's gatherings or quires in Arabic numerals of regular font size, and then, in superscript, the number of leaves that each gathering originally contained. If a gathering has lost any leaves, these are recorded in parentheses with a minus sign. Thus the collation for an octavo in eights (Houghton MS Eng. 686) begins as follows:

$8°$: $1–3^{8}$ 4^{six} $5–13^{8}$ $14^{8}(-14.2)$ $15^{8}(-15.6)$ $16–18^{8}$ $19^{8}(-19.3)$ 20^{8}

Immediately following the format (8°), the characters '$1–3^{8}$' indicate that each of the first three gatherings originally had eight leaves, and that all of these leaves remain. When the evidence does not permit a reasonably certain hypothesis regarding the original construction of a gathering, I spell out the number of remaining leaves, as in '4^{six}.' The sign '$14^8(-14.2)$' indicates that the second leaf of the fourteenth gathering is missing.

Much of the evidence for a collation comes from watermarks. So the description proceeds to a chart that locates each watermark and, if applicable, countermark in the manuscript. The watermark chart for the Houghton octavo begins in this fashion:

1	2 a	3 A	4	5	6	7	8

Each cell of the chart corresponds to a leaf in the manuscript, or a leaf that the manuscript once contained. And each row represents a quire. The outermost cells in the row represent one conjugate pair of leaves, as do the second and seventh cells, the third and sixth, and the innermost two boxes in the row. The numbers in the cells refer to the Houghton manuscript's modern folio numbers. The lower-case *a* stands for the lower portion of the first watermark in the manuscript, and indicates that the second leaf displays this portion of the watermark. Accordingly, upper-case *A* refers to the upper part of the watermark, which appears on the third leaf. In other gatherings, brackets indicate missing leaves. Empty brackets point out that a missing leaf did not feature a watermark, and was extracted before the manuscript was foliated. If a missing leaf did contain a watermark, the symbol for that mark appears in brackets: [a]. (Elsewhere parentheses indicate leaves that are extant but unnumbered.) In octavo gatherings made of a single sheet of paper, like those in this Houghton manuscript, watermarks regularly appear on the second and third leaves of a quire, or on its first and fourth leaves. The recurrence of watermarks on these particular leaves throughout the Houghton manuscript supports the collation.

Next I describe the watermarks in the manuscript, with reference to the standard authorities on the paper one finds in early seventeenth-century manuscript verse miscellanies.[1] In some cases, the appearance of a single watermark throughout suggests a manuscript's bibliographic unity. Sometimes the uniform gatherings displayed in the collation and watermark chart argue for a manuscript's physical coherence. But even some manuscripts made of multiple paper stocks and irregular gatherings demonstrate unity. Especially for complicated manuscripts such as these, the description proceeds from the codicological

[1] Charles Briquet, *Les Filigranes* (Leipzig: K. W. Hiersemann, 1923); Edward Heawood, *Watermarks, Mainly of the 17th and 18th Centuries* (Hilversum, Holland: Paper Publications Society, 1950); Daniel W. Mosser and Ernest W. Sullivan, II, *The Thomas L. Gravell Watermark Archive* http://wiz2.cath.vt.edu:8200/ accessed 27 August 2007.

evidence introduced above to paleographical features, numbering and, if appropriate, distinguishing a manuscript's early modern hands. When possible, the description also considers design features, especially ruling.

The description concludes with transcriptions of the headings and first lines of selected texts, most of them early Stuart libels and anti-courtly love poems. This final section thus demonstrates a manuscript's relevance to the present book. Following the collation and watermark chart, the list of selected contents show where in the codex verse collectors placed examples of these two poetic genres and, therefore, precisely how they related them to one another. Furthermore, after the section on hands, this last section points out which verse collectors put these poems in the same miscellany.

Beinecke MS Osborn b62

Collation

8°: $1^8(-1.1,2)$ $2^8(-2.6)$ $3–5^8$ $6^8(-6.4)$ 7^8 $8^8(-8.3)$ 9^8 10^8

Watermark chart

Like most octavos in eights, this manuscript has quires each made of a single sheet of paper. Such gatherings usually show bits of a watermark on four leaves: either the second, third, sixth, and seventh; or the first, fourth, fifth, and eighth.

[ ]	[a]	1 a	3	5	7 a	9 a	11
13 a	15	17	19 a	21 a	[ ]	23	25 a
27	29 a	31 a	33	35	37 a	39 a	41
43	45 a	47 a	49	51	53 a	55 a	57
59 a	61	63	65 a	67 a	69	71	73 a
75 a	77	79	[a]	81 a	83	85	87 a
89	91 a	93 a	95	97	99 a	101 a	103
105 a	107	[ ]	109 a	111 a	113	115	117 a
119	121 a	123 a	125	127	129 a	131 a	133
135	137 a	139 a	141	143	145 a	147 a	149

Paper

This manuscript contains only one paper stock. Its watermark (*A* in the chart above) features the initials 'MV' on a single-handled pot with a crescent on top (on a flower with four petals, on the central of five circles, on top of five ovals spread in a fan). Similar initials appear in Heawood 3595 and 3638, but in two rows and in pots with more elaborate bases and fans. Pots with the initials 'MV' also appear in Gravell POT.051.1 and POT.256.1, but these lack crescents. The crescent, flower, fan, and base resemble those in Heawood 3608.

Hand

A single, amateur hand transcribed the great majority of the manuscript, including all of the texts listed below. Additional hands have added text to the back of the book, from p. 107 forward. Yet the main chunk of text on p. 107 leaves open the possibility that the primary hand changed scripts or styles here and so may be responsible for some or even most of the text following as well.

Selected contents

'Sr Thomas Ouerberryes Epitaph / on himselfe // The span of my dayes measur'd here I rest' (p. 1); 'One Felton that kild the duke // Here vnterd suspends (though not to saue' (p. 19); 'On felton in prison that kild the Duke / by Zouch Townly o Ch: Ch: // Enjoy thy bondage, make thy prison knowe' (pp. 36–38); 'on the faith of a woman // Catch me a stare that's falle[n] fro[m] the skye' (p. 38); 'On felton hangd in chaines // wants he a graue who[m] heauen couers? was hee?' (p. 39); 'on the Corps of Queene Elizabeth / beinge brought by water from Greene= / widge to white hall // The queene was brought fro[m] greenewidge to whitehal' (p. 42); 'On Sr Robert Carr / earle of Sommerset // When Carre in Court a page began' (pp. 42–43); 'Epithalamiu[m] // The day was turnd to starr-light & was runn' (pp. 63–69); 'The glosse // This Poeme is noe sybill nor noe Prophet' (p. 69); 'On a masq acted before prince / Charles in Spaine // y^{e} Prince of Wales wth all his stately traine' (pp. 73–75); 'on Queene Elizabeth // weepe great Iland for thy M^{ris} death' (p. 77); 'A maidens Dreame // As I lay slumbring in my naked bed' (pp. 79–80); 'A Gen$^{\text{woma[n]}}$ to a ge$^{\text{ma[n]}}$ busy wth her // Nay pish, nay phewe, nay faith but will y^{u}, fye' (pp. 96–97); 'Dr Dun • to his M^{ris} // Come Madame come, all rest my powers defye' (pp. 97–98); 'A Dreeme // Methought one night I went vnto my deere' (p. 103).

BEINECKE MS OSBORN B200

Compilers

Anonymous verse collectors with connections to Christ Church, Oxford. The predominant compiler could have started transcription no earlier than 1634, and could have transcribed pages 150 forward no earlier than 1636.

Collation

4°: (+1) $1–3^8$ $4^8(-4.5–8)$ $5^8(-5.1–5)$ $6–9^8$ $10^8(-10.3,4)$ $11–13^8$ $14^8(-14.8)$ $15–17^8$ $18^8(-18.2)$ $19–21^8$ $22^8(-22.8)$ $23–36^8(+1)$

Watermark chart

Most of the gatherings in this quarto were made of two full sheets folded independently and then fit one within the other. All of its gatherings could have been made in this fashion. But several must have been (specifically 1–4, 8–11, 16, 18–20, 22–28, 30, 32, 36), for the innermost and outermost leaves of these gatherings feature either too many or too few watermarks to have been made of a single sheet. Conjugate pairs in this quarto must feature either no watermark or top and bottom portions of the same mold.

---

i							
ii	iii A2	1 A1	3	5	7 a1	9 a2	11
13	15 A2	17 A1	19	21	23 a1	25 a2	27
29	31 a1	33 a2	35	37	39 A2	41 A1	43
45 a2	47	49	51 a1	44 A1	[56]	[58]	[60 A2]
[62]	[64 a1]	[66]	[68 w]	[70 w]	72	74 A1	76
78 A1	80	82 a2	84	86	88 A2	90	92 a1
94 a2	96	98 a2	100	102	104 A2	106	108 A2
110 a2	112	114	116 A2	118 a2	120	122	124 A2
126 a2	128	130	132 a1	134 A1	137	3139	131 A2
3143 a2	3145	[ ]	[a1]	147 A1	149	151	153 A2
155 a2	157	159	161 a1	163 A1	165	167	169 A2
171 a2	173	175 a2	177	179	181 A2	183	185 A2
187	189 A2	191	193 A2	195 a2	197	201 a2	203
205 a2	207	209 A1	211	213	215 a1	217	[A2]
219 A2	221	223 A1	225	227	229 a1	231	233 a2
235 A1	237	239	241 A2	243 a2	245	247	249 a1
251 A1	253	255 A1	257	259	261 a1	263	265 a1
267	[269 A2]	271 a2	273	275	277 A2	279 a2	281

283 A1	285	287	289 a1	291 A1	293	295	297 a1
299	301 A2	303 A1	305	307	309 a1	311 a2	313
315 a2	317	319 a2	321	323	325 A2	327	329 A2
331 a2	333	335	337 a1	339 A1	341	343	[A2]
345 A1	347	349	351 a1	353 A1	355	357	359 a1
361	363 A2	365 a2	367	369	3571 A2	373 a2	375
377	379 a1	381 a2	383	385	387 A2	389 A1	391
393 A1	395	397	399 A2	401 a2	403	405	407 a1
409 A1	411	413	415 A2	417 a2	419	421	423 a1
425	427 a1	429 A2	431	433	435 a2	437 A1	(439)
(441)	(443) a1	(445)	(447) A2	(449) a2	(451)	(453) A1	(455)
(457)	(459) A2	(461) A1	(463)	(465)	(467) a1	(469) a2	(471)
(473) A1	(475)	(477) a2	(479)	(451)	(453) A2	(455)	(457) a1
(459) a2	(461)	(463)	(465) A2	(467) a2	(469)	(471)	(473) A2
(475)	(477) A2	(479)	(481) A2	(483) a2	(485)	(487) a2	(489)
(491)	(493) A2	(495)	(497) a1	(499) A1	(501)	(503) a2	(505)
(507) A1	(509)	(511) A1	(513)	(515)	(519) a1	(521)	(523) a1
(525) A1	(527)	(529)	(531) A2	(533) a2	(535)	(537)	(539) a1
(541)							

Paper

This manuscript is made of one paper stock, whose pair of watermarks displays a single-handled pot with the initials 'PBR,' with the 'P' above 'BR.' Each pot is topped by a crescent on a flower with four petals (which is on the middle of five circles, each of which is on one of five ovals spread in a narrow fan). One of the pair has a mangled crescent on a symmetrical flower, and a narrow band at the bottom of the base. The flower on the other mark has a lopsided bottom leaf, and a wide band at the bottom of the base. In the watermark table, *A1* and *a1* stand for the upper and lower portions of the mark with the malformed crescent, respectively; and *A2* and *a2* indicate the pair with the asymmetrical flower. *W* stands for an unknowable watermark. The pots with the tops that most closely resemble these are Heawood 3608 and 3633. Some of the same initials appear in the probably unrelated pots in Heawood 3625, 3575, 3576, 3562, 3563, and Briquet 12806, 12794, 12786, 12793, 12704.

Ruling

Two red rules appear throughout: one down the left edge, another across the header, intersecting at the upper left corner. The consistent ruling strongly suggests that the manuscript was ruled before transcription began. Does it also suggest that the manuscript was made and sold as a blank book?

Hands

'[V]arious,' says the Beinecke finding aid accurately. Yet the primary hand is responsible for the great majority of the transcription through p. 165. Pages 168–201 are clearly in a distinct, more uniformly italic script, and thus may be in a second hand. The first script or hand resumes, though, on p. 202 and carries on until p. 267. A third hand seems to have been responsible for pp. 268–89. Hand 1 reappears on pp. 290–92, 341–79, 407–13, and 427–36. At least one additional hand shows up on pp. 295–301. Pages 380–81 and 383 may be the work of a new hand, two new hands, or one of the hands appearing earlier, perhaps hand 2.

I suspect that Hand 1 first transcribed the majority of the texts in this manuscript, separating them by genre, rather like the compiler of British Library MS Egerton 2230 did; and that, later, additional hands filled in some of the leaves that the first hand left blank. All headings and first lines transcribed below are in the primary hand.

Selected contents

'Prince Charles his enterteinment / In Spayne: 1618: // The Prince of Wales, wth all his stately trayne' (pp. 1–3); 'A Womans faythe• / Catch me A Starre y^{ts} falling fro[m] ye Skie' (p. 3); 'on ye retourne of Buckingham fro[m] ffrance. // And art retournd agayne wth all thy faults' (pp. 50–53; pagination skips 52); 'Chronogram[m]a in eunde[m] Villars. // Georgius Dux Buckinghamiæ' (p. 53; dots appear beneath underlined letters); 'In eundem• // A thing was got by candle light' (p. 53); 'A Dialogue betweene Charon, & G: Villars, / Duke of Buckingham• // Ch: At Portsmouth (Duke) I will noe longer stay' (p. 54); 'I, y^{t} my Countrey did betray' (p. 54); 'In eundem• // Rex & Grex ye same thing sound' (p. 55); 'In laude[m] eiusdem. // Yet were Bidentalls sacred, & y^{e} place' (p. 55); 'Womans Inconstancy• // Goe & catch a falling Starre' (p. 92); 'To ffelton in y^{e} Tower for killing Villars / Duke of Buckinghame. // Enioy thy bondage, make thy Prison know' (pp. 120–21); 'A rustick Gallant's wooing. // ffayre wench, I cannot court thy Sp'rit=like ~~li/kes~~^{eyes}' (p. 128); 'On ffeltham hanging / in Chaynes. // Heere vninter'd suspends (though not to save' (pp. 130–31); 'To his M^{rs} as she was goeing to bed. // Come (Madam) come, all rest my powers defy' (pp. 208–9); 'On Madam ffowler desyring to have / A Sonnet written on her. // Good Mada[m] ffowler doe not trouble me' (p. 218); 'On Sir Robert Car's wife. // There was at Court A Lady of late' (p. 409); 'On A Lady sitting stradling. // A gallant Lady sitting in A muse' (p. 430); 'A Maydes denyall• // Nay pish, nay phu, infayth: but will you? ffy' (pp. 430–31); 'An excellent remedy for ye greene sicknes. // A | Mayden fayre of ye greene sicknes late' (p. 431); 'On A Clowne. // A rustick Swayne was cleaving of A block' (p. 431).

BODLEIAN MS ASHMOLE 38, PP. 1–223, 240

Collation

2°: 1^{10}(−1.1) 2^{10} 3^{10}(−3.1,4) 4^{10}(−4.5) 5^{8} 6^{6} 7^{6} 8^{8} 9^{10}(−9.7) 10^{8}(−10.8) 11^{10}(−11.1,6–8) 12–13^{8} 14^{8}(−14.7,8) 15^{6}(−15.1–3) 16^{nine}(+1)

Watermark chart

In a folio, of course, one leaf of a conjugate pair has a watermark, and its mate has none. Page 200 has probably been cut from another location in the volume and inserted in its present location with its ruling upside down. The brackets with question marks represent stubs of leaves that are now missing and may or may not have once featured a watermark. Damage makes the watermarks on pp. 45–51, and especially the one on p. 47, difficult to distinguish.

[a]	1	3 a2	5 a2	7 a2	9	11	13	15 a2	17
19 a1	21 a1	23	25	27 a2	29	31 a	33 a2?	35	37
[a]	39	41	[ ]	43	45 a1	47 a	49 a1	51 a2	53
55 a2	57	59 a2	61 a2	[a]	63	65	67	69 a2	71
	73	75	77 a2	79 a2	81	83	85 a2	87 a2	
		89 a2	91	93 a1	95	97 a1	98^{b}		
		98^{d}	98^{f} a2	100 a2	102	104	106 a1		
	108	110	112	114	116 a2	118 a2	120 a2	122 a2	
124 a1	126	128 a1	130	132 a2	134	[w]	136	138 a1	140
	142	144 a2	146 a1	148 a1	150	152	154	[w]	
[ ]	156 a1	158	160 a1	162 a2	[ ]	[ ]	[A]	164	166 a1
	168	170 a2	172 a2	174 a2	175	176	178	180 a2	
	182 a1	184 a1	186 a1	188	190 a2	192	194	196	
	198 a2	240	202 a1	204 a1	206	208	[w]	[ ]	
		[ ]	[ ]	[ ]	210 a1	212 a1	214 a2		
[?]	216	218 a2	[?]	[?]	[?]	[?]	220	222 a1	
[200 a2]									

Textual evidence for the collation

The text on p. 199 continues on p. 240, and that on p. 241 resumes on p. 202.

Paper

Although the insertion of several originally loose papers (now foliated as 224–39, 241–43, despite the fact the rest of the manuscript is paginated) has turned this manuscript into a composite volume, the original folio contains just one watermark throughout: a coat of arms with a quartered shield and a crown on top. In each mold of this mark, the upper left hand quartering displays three bobbles: two circles in a row made of two wires and the third bobble on its own. In one of the molds, the individual bobble is beneath the other two (*A1*); in the other mold, it is above them (*A2*; see pp. 124 and 200 for particularly legible examples). Each of the other quarterings contains a four-footed animal. At the bottom of the coat are a few intitials. In *a1*, only two letters appear, 'IL,' as the space for the initials is pinched on the right side. In *a2*, three show up: 'ILL' or possibly '166.' Compare Heawood 576–77.

Ruling

Simple rules in pencil marking the left and top margins (and occasionally the right margin and columns) remain on pp. 6–45, 47–50, 52–139, 141–48, 152–64, 167–208. The rules on 149–50 are in ink.

Hands

The verse miscellany that constitutes the bulk of this manuscript is in the hand of Nicholas Burgh or Burghe, signed and exemplified on pp. 165–66 (where he solemnly and charmingly swears to have personally collected the tree leaves whose 'true portrayture' he has drawn below 'in s^t^ Iohns wood by marribone parke pale on the 3^d^ of Iune 1638 In the presence of m^r^ Roger Dalton'). Burghe is also responsible for the prose beginning at the back of the volume (pp. 223–208 rev.). His mixed hand varied in size and care, and he often wrote too casually to have been working for anyone other than himself and perhaps friends or family. His predominant script features a horizontal stroke through *O*; unusually deliberate forms of *v* and *w*, beginning and ending with horizontal strokes; a small, circular ampersand with a loop proceeding counter-clockwise from the top of the character to the lower right; secretary forms of terminal *s*; and both secretary and italic *e*. While Burghe's mixed hand occasionally did without hardly any secretary letterforms, he reserved for special emphasis a pure italic script more akin to monumental engraving than to print.

Early pagination

Burghe added the manuscript's earliest page numbers after the removal of several leaves, assigning to current pp. 1–97 the numerals 1–55, 57–70, 72–73, 74–98 (skipping numbers 56 and 71 without missing a page, and missing the page between 73 and 74). After missing three extant leaves, his pagination resumes with the still current numbers 99–106. A second pagination in his hand begins on the verso immediately following his drawings of tree leaves, assigning numbers 1–31 to present pp. 167–95; someone cut out page numbers 10–11 along with several lines of text.

Selected contents

'Doctor Donn's valadiction / to the ~~warld~~ worlde // Farewell yea guilded follies, pleasing troubles' (p. 1); 'On mans Mortalite by ~~Doctor Dunn~~ / Sr Fran: Bacon // The worlds A buble and thy lyfe of man' (p. 2; the attribution to Bacon probably in a second hand); 'To Christ: // Wilt thou forgiue those sinns whear I begune // D Donn'; 'Heape, on the Duke of Buckingham // I that my Cuntry did betraye'; 'Another by the same man In / the Dukes Comendation // Honor, worth, greatnes or what parts so eare' (p. 14); '~~GEORGIVS DVX BVCkingha-MIæ: / 1628 // Thy Numorous name wth this year doth a gree // Iohn Marston~~' (p. 19); 'On the Murder of the Duke of Buck: / 1628 // Soner I may some fixet statue bee'; 'Io: Feltons Epitaph made / By D: Donn // Here vnInter,'d Suspends, though not to saue' (p. 20); 'GeorgIVs Villeres DVX BVCkIngaMIæ / 1628 // Thy Numerous Name w^{c}h this yeare doth agree // Iohn Marston' (p. 25); 'An Epitaphe on the Thrice Excellent / Princes Queen Elizabeth // Kings, Queens. mens, Iudgements Eyes' (p. 36); 'on Crux, on word of the / Duke of Buckin[ghams] motto // Rex and grex are of a sound' (p. 44); '~~On~~ The Duke of Bucking[hams] Roddomontados // Auante you Giddie Headed Multitude' (pp. 44–45); 'A Comination wrigten by / D. Donn // Who euer guesses, dreames or thinkes hee knowes' (p. 49); 'He that would my mri^{s} knowe' (pp. 49–50); 'Doctor Donn verses // I knowe as well as you, she is not faire'; 'Doinge A filthye pleasure is, ~~some say~~ and short'; 'When I ^{doe} loue, my Mistres must be faire // D. Donn' (p. 62); 'Come Maddame, come; all rest my powers defye' (p. 63); 'Mr Caryes Rapture // I will Inioye the now; my Cælia; Come' (pp. 68–71); 'A Maydens Deame // As I lay slumbring once w^{c}hin my Bedd' (p. 85); 'vppon S. R. C. and the Ladye F.H: // A page a knight a Vicount, and an Earle' (p. 116);

'And art thou back return'd wth all thy faults' (pp. 133–35; first 40 lines in second hand); 'from kathirn'gs dock was launch'd A pinck' (p. 135; second hand); 'On the Countes of sommersett // From Katherins Docke was launcht a Pincke' (p. 136); 'Res este Sacra miser noli mea tangere tata / sacrilogæ bustis abstinuere Manus; // Yet weare bydentalls sacred, and the place'; 'The Epitaph // Reader stand still and gaze; loe here I am' (p. 142); 'A mayds Denyall // Nay pish, nay ^{pue}~~fye~~; nay fayth, and will you fye' (p. 150); 'When on man Guides the shipp'; 'S^{r} say not that you loue vnles you doe' (p. 152); 'A fayre Ladye washing hur selfe in a Riuer // A Nimphe, when as the summer beames made hott the Cooler Ayre' (p. 153); 'On Queene Elizabeth Queene of / England // Kings, Queens, mens ~~eyes~~, Iudgments eyes' (p. 167); 'On Queene Elizabeth // Eliza: that great Maiden Queen lies here // Char, Best' (p. 172); 'On Queen Elizabeth // she was, she is, what Can there more be said' (p. 189); 'When Charles, hath got ye Spanish Gearle' (p. 229).

Bodleian MS Ashmole 47

Collation

8°: 1^8(−1.1,2) 2–23^8 24^8(−24.8)

Watermark chart

In an octavo, conjugate pairs usually display either portions of the same half of the watermark, or no watermark evidence at all.

[ ]	[A]	a	1	2	3 a	4 A	5
6	7 A	8 a	9	10	11 a	12 A	13
14 a	15	16	17 A	18 A	19	20	21 a
22 a	23	24	25 A	26 A	27	28	29 a
30 a	31	32	33 A	34 A	35	36	37 a
38 a	39	40	41 A	42 A	43	44	45 a
46	47 A	48 a	49	50	51 a	52 A	53
54 a	55	56	57 A	58 A	59	60	61 a
62 A	63	64	65 a	66 a	67	68	69 A
70 a	71	72	73 A	74 A	75	76	77 a
78 A	79	80	81 a	82 a	83	84	85 A
86 a	87	88	89 A	90 A	91	92	93 a
94	95 A	96 a	97	98	99 a	100 A	101
102	103 A	104 a	105	106	107 a	108 A	109
110	111 A	112 a	112^{c}	113	114 a	115 A	116

117 a	118	119	120 A	121 A	122	123	124 a
124 A	126	127	128 a	129 a	130	131	132 A
133	134 A	135 a	136	137	138a	139 A	140
141	142 A	143 a	144	145	146 a	147 A	148
149 a	150	151	152 A	153 A	154	155	156 a
157	158 A	159 a	160	161	162 a	163 A	164
165	166 A	(167) a	(168)	(169)	(170) a	(171) A	(172)
(173) a	(174)	(175)	(176) A	(177) A	(178)	(179)	(180) a
(181) a	(182)	(183)	(184) A	(185) A	(186)	(187)	[a]

Paper

The only watermark in the manuscript shows a coat of arms with a clover on top. On the bottom, beneath an equilateral cross, a cartouche features a series of letters beginning with 'M,' concluding with 'NVRIN,' and so possibly spelling 'MENVRIN,' as in Heawood 660.

Ruling

The texts in the main hand are set off by simple rules, in ink, for the left and top margins.

Hand

One hand is responsible for most of the miscellany (fols 8v–130r), presumably the dull, mixed hand of Elias Ashmole.

Selected contents

'On y^{e} spannish Match T: M: // The day was turn'd to starre light and was $_{runne}$' (fols 25v–29r); 'On y^{e} Duke of Buckinghams death // Some say our Duke was vertuous, gratious good' (fol. 31r); 'Dr Dunn to a gentlewoman // you say I Lye; I say you lie iudge whether'; 'on women // Catch mee a starre y^{ts} falling from y^{e} skye' (fol. 36r); 'on ffelton y^{t} Kild y^{e} Duke of Buckingham // Here vnwinterd suspends though not to $_{save}$' (fol. 48r); 'on a Ladye // A Ladye once y^{t} newly was besped' (fol. 52r–v); 'on a mayd // A meer mayd fflesh above and fish belowe'; 'A lover to his M^{rs} // Ile tell you how y^{e} rose did first grow red' (fol. 52v); 'To y^{e} duke of Buckingham // The King loves you you him' (fol. 53r); 'on a Ladye // A Vertuous Ladye sitting in a muse' (fol. 53v); 'A mayds denyall // Nay pish, nay pew, nay ffayth, and will you, fye' (fol. 54r–v); 'A gentlewoman to a gentle man // say not you Love vnlesse you doe'; 'His replye // Madam I Love and love to doe' (fol. 54v); 'A mayds embleme // Downe in a garden my sweete Rose did sport her' (fols 54v–55r).

Bodleian MS Eng. Poet. e. 14

Earliest known owner

'Henry Lawson' (or possibly Lamson or Lanison) (fol. 101v rev.)

Collation

8°: 1^8(−1.1,2) 2^8(−2.4,5,7) 3–5^8 6^8(−6.8) 7^8(−7.1,2,7,8) 8^8 9^8(−9.3–7) 10^8 11^8(−11.1,3,6,8) 12^8(−12.6) 13^8(−13.4,5,8) 14^8(−14.1,8) 15^8(−15.1,8) 16^{six}

Watermark chart

This octavo in eights features a very unusual distribution of watermarks. In most quires, including the first, large parts of the watermark appear on just two leaves (invariably the sixth and seventh leaves of the gathering). Yet in a few other quires, such as the second, small portions of the watermark show up on four leaves (always the outermost and innermost ones of these gatherings). In a quire like the third, the first and last leaves display fragments of the lower half of the watermark; the fourth and fifth feature bits of the mark's upper half; and the other leaves have no watermark at all. In a gathering like the first, though, so much of the watermark appears on the sixth and seventh leaves that virtually no part of it can be seen on the leaves conjugate to them.

[ ]	[ ]	2	3	4	5 A	6 a	7
8 a	9	10	[A]	[A]	11	[ ]	12 a
13 a	14	15	16 A	17 A	18	19	20 a
21	22	23	24	25	26 A	27 a	28
29	30	31	32	33	34 A	35 a	36
37 a	38	39	40 A	41 A	42	43	[a]
[ ]	[ ]	44	45	46	47 a	[A]	[ ]
48 a	49	50	51 A	52 A	53	54	55 a
56	57	[ ]	[ ]	[ ]	[A]	58 a	59
60	61	62	63	64	65 A	66 a	67
[a]	68	[ ]	69 A	70 A	[ ]	71	[a]
72	73	74	75	76	[A]	77 a	78
79	80	81	[ ]	[ ]	82 A	83 a	[ ]

[ ]	84	85	86	87	88 A	89 a	[ ]
[ ]	90	91	92	93	94 A	95 a	[ ]
	96	97 a	98	99	100 A	101	

Paper

Despite its irregular distribution throughout the volume, only one watermark appears in this manuscript: an elaborate crest with a clover on top and, on the bottom, an equilateral cross above a cartouche enclosing a series of letters, possibly 'VIGER' or 'WGER.' The watermark is faint and often obscured by the octavo format; the initials are most legible on fols 6 and 58. Compare Heawood 660.

Hands

Several hands produced the text in this manuscript in a number of stages, with the second and last hands doing most of the work. The earliest transcriptions in the manuscript must be the epitaphs that appear upside-down at the back of the volume (according to the orientation imposed by the modern foliation). The first few of these texts are in a mixed but primarily secretary hand, which adopts an increasing number of italic letterforms over the course of just a few pages. One can see the italicization of this hand (A) develop gradually in the epitaph on Sir John Spencer at the top of fol. 95r rev. The first word of the poem ('Here') features full-fledged secretary characters. But the second word ('lies') includes an epsilon *e*, which later recurs; the third word ('S^{r}') slips in an italic *r*, which appears repeatedly hereafter; and the third line introduces an italic *H*, which this hand employs exclusively from this point on.

The rapid development of this initial hand leaves open the possibility that it is also responsible for the next script in the manuscript. Yet I suspect that this second script is the work of a separate hand (B), based on the following features: the tight loop and horizontal stroke that begins *H* and, especially, the unusual bend in *l*, giving it a vague resemblance to a secretary *h*. Hand B probably filled in the blank space that hand A left on the bottom of his last leaf (fol. 93v rev.); transcribed three more poems beginning on the next recto (now fols 92v–90r rev.); turned the volume over; and started anew from the other side, leaving plenty of blank leaves. Hand B is a very consistent, slanted italic with both epsilon and italic forms of *e* throughout. The first two hands are fair enough to leave open the possibility of professional involvement or training, up to this point in the manuscript's production.

By contrast, the next few scripts added to the manuscript are too casual to have been professional. Before the next major hand took over transcription, probably four others added a few texts each. One of them added poems to the inside cover of the initial, back sequence of poems (fol. 101r rev.) in a casual italic (C). A distinct, scratchy italic hand (D) filled in just the few leaves following hand B's work in the back portion of the miscellany (fols 89v–88r rev.). Another hand (E) contributed texts following hand B's work on both ends of the manuscript. (In the back end, he filled fols 87v–84v, 84r, 83v rev. From the other end, he wrote on fols 9r, 10r–11r, 11v–14r, 57r, 58v.) Hand E wrote in an upright, variable, and often sloppy italic with all three common forms of *e* and secretary characters for several capitals. Yet another sloppy italic (this one with a secretary *e*) filled in just fol. 40v (hand F). And a very light hand, which bears a resemblance to hand B but lacks its epsilon *e* and has a distinct ampersand and capital *I*, added verses to fols 71r–v (hand G).

Thereafter, an occasionally nice, but more often excessively close, secretary hand (H) filled in most of the rest of the miscellany and numbered all of the poems. Texts in this hand appear specifically on fol. 93r rev.; the bottoms of fols 91r, 90r, 84v–83v rev.; all of fols 83r–76v rev. (the conclusion of the back sequence); the bottoms of fols 9r, 10r, 11r, 14r; all of fols 14v–24v; the bottoms of 25v, 26v, 29r, 30r, 32r, 33r, 34r, 35v, 37v, 38v, 42r; the bottom of 43r through fol. 49r; the bottom of 52r through the verso; the bottoms of 57r, 60r, 61r, 64r, 64v, 66v, 68r, 69v, 70r, 70v, 71r; and 72r–76r, the end of the longer sequence. Hand H's poem numbers for the back sequence proceed 1–2, 8–172, indicating at least one missing leaf in between fols 100 and 101 rev., and skipping crossed-out poems on fols 88v, 88r, 86r, 78r rev. His numbers for the front sequence proceed 1–109, 117–142, 149–166, 170–173, 177–189, 197–217, skipping cancelled text on fol. 19r, and indicating missing leaves between fols 47 and 48, 57 and 58, 67 and 68, 68 and 69, and 71 and 72. The other missing leaves noted in the collation and chart must have been extracted before hand H numbered the poems.

The 'Henry Lawson' who inscribed the back cover also practiced his secretary hand with the fragmentary name, 'Sr Hen... wotton / wotton' on fol. 68v. Perhaps the difficulty that he had with his secretary *w* suggests that this Lawson was a relatively late, modern owner.

Selected contents

'Here vnenterred suspends though to saue'; 'Immortall man of glory, whose stout hand'; 'Iohn Felton: NO FELLON' (fol. 12v); 'On the D. of Buck // I that my cuntry did betray'; 'Rex and Grex alike doth sound' (fol. 13r); 'verses written to M.^{r} ffelton by Mr T. // Enioy thy bondage make thy prison knowe' (fol. 14v); 'The Duks epitaph // If idle travilers $^{\#\#}$# aske who lys here' (fol. 15r); 'In the praise of the Duke // Yet were bidentals sacred; and the place' (fol. 15r–v); 'His Epitaph // Reader stand still loe here I am' (fol. 15v); 'On y^{e} D: of B // Some say the~~y~~ D: was gratious virtious good' (fol. 19r); 'A diologue between Caron and y^{e} D: of B: // C At porchmouth D: I can noe longer staye' (fol. 19r–v); 'A song // Madam becoverd why stand you bare' (fols 19v–20r); 'A song // Downe in a garden sitts my dearest deare' (fol. 24v); 'D^{r}: Dun: // Marry & Love thy Flavia; for she' (fols 29v–30r); 'D: Dun: // Till I have Peace with thee warre other Men' (fols 33v–34r); 'S^{r}. Walter Raleigh to ye Ld Carr // I.C.V.R: good mounser Carr' (fol. 49r); 'The fayned Answer of Q. Eliz: to her subiects / with a divine admonition & prophetick / Conclusion // Your bold Petitions Mortalls I have seene' (fols 49v–52r); 'A Comparison of two Mistresses // As ye sweete sweate of Roses in a Still' (fols 60v–61r); 'On a Gentlewoman seene naked // As I alone' (fols 65r–66v); 'A neglected Lover angry wth ye female / sexe. W. T. // Hard-harted-foolish Mayds, whose high swolne Pride' (fol. 69v); 'In the praise of a gentlewoman // Her haire but thin in all they are but three' (fol. 73r); 'In the praise of his M^{tris} // My mistrise hath a precious eye / But that alas it looks awry' (fol. 73r–v); 'A wooer // ffaire wench I cannot court thy sprightly eyes' (fol. 75v); 'On Iohn ffelton // Wants hee a graue whom heauens doe couer? was hee' (fol. 76v rev.).

Bodleian MS Eng. Poet. e. 97

Collation

4°: 1^8(−1.1–3) 2^{12} 3^8(−3.1) 4^{12} 5^8(−5.4) 6–10^8 11^8(−11.1) 12^8(−12.3) 13–14^8 15^8(−15.1) 16^8 17^8(−17.4) 18–21^8 22^8(−22.2,6,7)

Watermark chart

Each of the quires in this quarto was constructed by folding two or three sheets together. Its conjugate pairs feature either opposite ends of a watermark or no watermark at all.

		[a]	[ ]	[a]	1^a	2^a	3 A	5	7 A		
9	11	13	15 B	17 B	19 B	21 b	23 b	25 b	27	29	31
		[b]	33 b	35	37	39	41	43 B	45 B		
47 b	49 b	51 b	53	55	57	59	61	63	65 B	67 B	69 B
		71 b	73 b	75	[ ]	77	79	81 B	83 B		

85	87 b	89	91 B	93 b	95	97 B	99
101	103	105 B	107 B	109 b	111 b	113	115
117	119 B	121	123 B	125 b	127	129 b	131
133 b	135 b	137	139	141	143	145 B	147 B
149 b	151 b	153	155	157	159	161 B	163 B
[ ]	165	167 B	169 B	171 b	173 b	175	177
179	181	[B]	183 B	185 b	187 b	189	191
193 b	195 b	197	199	201	203	205 B	207 B
209	211	213 B	215 B	217 b	219 b	221	223
[ ]	225	227 B	229 B	231 b	233 b	235	237
239 b	241	243 B	245	247	249 b	251	253 B
255 b	257 b	259	[ ]	261	263	265 B	267 B
269	271 b	273	275 B	277 b	279	281 B	283
285 b	287 b	289	291	293	295	297 B	299 B
301 b	303 b	305	307	309	311	313 B	315 B
317 b	319	321 B	323	325	327 b	329	331 B
333 b	[b]	335	337	339	[ ]	[B]	341 B

Paper

The watermark partially visible in only two leaves of the first gathering (A) features two posts or pillars separated by a bunch of grapes on one end. The visible ends of these pillars are even and symmetrical, each composed of a small bobble connected to an oblong and then a shorter, curved shape. The grapes are in rows of 1, 2, 3, 4, 3, and 2. Compare the upper portions of Heawood 3492–93.

The watermark throughout the rest of the book (B) displays a single-handled pot with a crescent on top (on a four-leaf clover, on a crown) and bold (double-wire) initials 'IC' (unless the two wires used for the first letter were meant to form a 'U'). Heawood shows similar top elements in 3607, 3632.

Ruling

Before transcription, simple ruling was added in pencil along the left and top margins of pp. 3–197.

Hands

Although the verse miscellany that predominates this manuscript book (covering pp. 1–196) features a range of writing styles, these scripts display several common characteristics and, more importantly, they alternate. So the visually varied text of the miscellany is the product either of a single scribe showcasing his range, or of a few hands who have developed related writing styles and necessarily collaborated on this book.

For instance, if more than one scribe produced the text of the miscellany, the one who wrote in the elaborate secretary exemplified at the bottom of p. 94 must have worked on this page after the writer of the larger, more italic text immediately above. The copyist responsible for this large italic script also filled in the bottom of p. 67, after the writer of yet another style had finished a poem in his close secretary hand on the top of that page. And, on p. 60, the scribe who wrote in this close secretary filled in the blank space left by the same ornate secretary hand visible on p. 94. If these texts are the work of more than one hand, no one of them could have started working on the manuscript after the other had finished. They must have worked together.

Yet, compare the following letterforms in the two scripts on p. 94: the two-stroke *O*, the wide secretary *H*, the *w* distinguished by a closed initial minim (that is, the first down and upstrokes completely overlap), the epsilon ampersand, the uncrossed *A*. On pp. 66–67, consider the recurrence of that secretary *H*, the distinctive *w*, the epsilon ampersand, the uncrossed *A*; compare *r*, *g*, *b*. On p. 60, one finds in both writing styles the same secretary *H*, identical forms of *G*, the same *w*, similar characters for *E*, *h*, and *c*. Given these paleographical relationships, I consider it plausible that one scribe did most of the writing in this miscellany.

Selected contents

'Kinge Iames his verses on the blazing starr. // Yee men of Brittaine wherefore gaze yee soe'; 'On the same Starr. // A Starre of late appeard in Virgo's traine' (p. 11); 'Rex, Grex, Dux & Crux. // Rex and Grex haue both one sound' (p. 31); 'On the death of the Duke. // Yet were Bidentalls Sacred, & the place' (pp. 57–58); 'His Epitaphe. // Reader stand still. Looke here I am // Doctor Iuxon (some say) / Nondum Constat' (p. 58); 'On the Duke of Buckingham. // Hee that can ~~read~~^{spell} a Sigh, or read a teare' (p. 60); 'To ffelton in the Tower. // Enioy thy bondage, make thy prison know // Zouch Tounly' (pp. 91–92); 'To the Duke. // The king loues you, you him // Richard Corbett' (p. 92); 'The Rustick-Gallant's wooing. // ffaire wench, I cannot court your spritlike Eyes' (p. 93); 'Docter Donne to his M.^{ris} // Till I haue peace with thee warre other men' (pp. 101–2); 'Docter Donnes speech to his m.^{ris} / going to bedd. // Come Madam, Come, all rest my powers defie' (pp. 103–4); 'On a Shew p^{r}sented before Prince Charles / in the Spanish Courte. // The Prince of Wales withall his royall traine' (pp. 167–68); 'Sir H: Wottons Invitac[i]on of his m:^{rs} to goe fish. // Come live with mee & bee my Love' (p. 183); 'A Maidens Dreame. // As I lay slumbring in my naked bed' (p. 184); 'A maides Deniall. // Nay pish, away I pray, nay will you, fie' (p. 185);

'Loues Rapture. // I will Enjoy thee now my Cælia! Come // Tho: Cary' (pp. 187–89).

Bodleian MS Malone 19

Collation

4°: $1^8(-1.8)$ $2–5^4$ $6^4(-6.2,3)$ $7–10^4$ $11^4(-11.1)$ $12–13^4$ $14–16^8$ $17^8(-17.7,8)$

Watermark chart

In quartos like this one, conjugate pairs usually feature either opposite halves of a watermark or no watermark at all. While most of the gatherings in this manuscript could have been made by folding one or two sheets twice, the ninth quire must have been made with two half-sheets.

[A]	1 a	3	5	7	9	11 A	13 a
		15 B	17	19	21 b		
		23 b	25	27	29 B		
		31 b	33	35	37 B		
		39 B	41	43	45 b		
		47	[w]	[w]	49		
		51 B	53	55	57 b		
		59	61 b	63 B	65		
		67 a	69 a	71 A	72 A		
		75 a	77	79	81 A		
		[a]	83	85	87 A		
		89 A	91	93	95 a		
		97	99 A	101 a	103		
105	107	109 a	111 A	113 a	115 A	117	119
121	123 a	125	127 A	129 a	131	133 A	135
137 a	139 a	141	143	145	147	149 A	151 A
153	155 a	157	159 A	161 a	163	[A]	[ ]

Paper

The watermark that appears in the first quire and the last several quires (*A*) depicts a pair of pillars or posts with grapes on top, partially obscured in the gutter. Compare Heawood 3499. The second watermark, in the second through the eighth gatherings (*B*), shows a single-handled pot with a crescent on top (on three circles and the central oblong element of a crown) and, in the bowl, the letters: 'I / OO.'

Ruling

Rules in ink mark all four margins on pp. 1–121, 125–54 (although only the left and bottom rules appear on 139).

Hands

Although several hands have added texts to this manuscript, a single, fair secretary hand transcribed the original miscellany (on pp. 15–118, 125–54), using italic for headings and subscriptions, and ultimately mixing it into his book script. Poems in this hand regularly conclude with two vertical lines.

Pagination

In the manuscript's earliest pagination, the primary hand assigned page numbers 1–154 to current pp. 15–162. The absence of his original page numbers 35–38 and 73–76, combined with the watermark evidence, indicates that the leaves identified above were lost in between the original and the current paginations.

Selected contents

'To the most high & mightye, the most pious, & / mercifull, the cheife Chancellor of heaue[n] / and onely Iudge of earth: The most / humble petition of the poore / distressed Com[m]ons of long / afflicted England. // Thou all=disposer, turne not backe thy face' (pp. 15–19); 'Dum gener infaustis tentat temerarius armis // While thy sonnes rash vnluckye armes attempt' (p. 20); 'On the Spanish Match. // The day was turn'd to starre light & was runne' (pp. 21–27); 'On the Spanish match. / Dr Corbett to the Duke of / Buckingham. // I'ue read of Ilandes floating, & remou'd' (pp. 27–30); 'The Replye to the / former. // ffalse one his deanarye, false nay more, Ile say' (pp. 30–32); 'On the Spanish / Match. // All the newes that's stirringe now' (pp. 32–33); 'One the Princes goeinge / To Spayne. // ffrom Englands happy & vnequall state // Iohn Haruy' (pp. 35–37); 'To the Spanish Lady. // Ye meaner beautyes of the night' (pp. 37–38); 'To Buckinghame. // The Kinge loues you, you him'; 'One the Earle of ~~Essex~~ Sum[m]erset. // A Page, a Knight, a Viscount, & an Earle' (p. 38); 'Anagram. // ffrances Howard' (p. 53); 'On my L. Carre his Wife. // Theare was at Court a Ladye of late' (p. 74); 'A vertuous Ladye sitting in a Muse'

(p. 75); 'Nay phew, nay pish, in faith, & wil you? ffye' (pp. 75–76); 'ffrom Katherine docke was lanchd a pinke' (p. 94).

Bodleian MS Malone 21

Collation

8°: 1^8(−1.1,2) 2–12^8 13^8(−13.2,4,5) 14–15^8 16^8(−16.8)

Watermark chart

The proportions of the watermark (*A*) and countermark (*C*) account for their unusual distribution in this octavo. Since the countermark is much wider than it is tall, it appears on conjugate leaves. In some gatherings, such as the first, so much of the countermark appears on one conjugate pair (pp. 1 and 2) that it shows up on no other leaf. In the second quire, however, the upper portion of the countermark (*C*) is visible on one conjugate pair (pp. 7 and 12), while the lower portion (*c*) appears on another conjugate pair (pp. 8 and 11). The taller, slimmer watermark, however, invariably appears not on conjugate leaves but on leaves that were cut after folding.

[ ]	[ ]	i	1 C	2 C	3 A	4 a	5
6	7 C	8 c	9	10 A	11 c	12 C	13 a
14	15	16	17 C	18 C	19 A	20 a	21
22	23	24	25 C	26 C	27 A	28 a	29
30	31	32	33 C	34 C	35 A	36 a	37
38	39	40 c	41	42 A	43c	44	45 a
46	47	48	49 C	50 C	51 A	52 a	53
54	55	56	57 C	58 C	59 A	60 a	61
62	63	64 c	65	66 A	67 c	68	69 a
70	71	72	73 C	74 C	75 A	76 a	77
78	79	80	81 C	82 C	83 A	84 a	85
86	87	88	89 C	90 C	91 A	92 a	93
94 c	[ ]	96	[ ]	[ ]	99 a	100 A	101 c
102	103 C	104	105	106 a	107	108 C	109 A
110	111 C	112	113	114 a	115	116 C	117 A
118	119 C	120	121	122 a	123	124 C	[A]

Paper

The bottom of the watermark features a coat of arms over an equilateral cross and, beneath this, a rectangle enclosing the letter *C*, a heart, and the letter *B*. The letters are bold (that is, made of double wires) and the small heart is raised, as if superscript. The countermark consists of a cartouche with bold letters, 'NLHERITIER' or 'MHEBITIER.'

Hands

One casual hand filled in fols i^{v}–26r, 43v–58r, 62r–94r. On fol. 1v, he made an 'Index 1æ p[ar]tis,' and on fols 43v–44v an 'Index 2^{dæ} partis.' A slanted, close italic added texts to fols 26v–38r.

Selected contents

'To his confin'd ffreind / M^{r} ffelton // Enjoy thy bondage, make thy prison know' (fol. 4r–v); 'On M^{r} ffelton hanging / in chaines // Here uninter'd suspends (though not to save' (fols 4v–5r); 'A rusticke Gallants woeing // ffaire wench I cannot court thy spirit-like eyes' (fol. 51v); 'On ye Duke of Buckingham / returneing from the Isle of Ree // And art returnd againe wth all thy faults' (fols 56v–58r); 'On a deformed Gentlewoman / y^{t} sunge exquisitely // I chanc'd sweet Lesbia's voice to heare' (fols 64v–66r).

Bodleian MS Rawl. Poet. 160

This description is completely indebted to the much more thorough investigation that B. C. Barker-Benfield of the Bodleian Library carried out on the manuscript during its repair in 1986–87. His technical notes and collation chart, along with Beta-radiographs of watermarks and a reversed print of fol. 225r, are available upon request in Duke Humfrey's Library.

Collation

2°: 1^{8}(−1.1,2) 2–4^{10} 5^{8} 6^{8}(−6.1) 7^{10} 8^{6} 9–12^{8} 13^{10}(−13.8,9) 14^{10}(−14.2,7) 15^{8}(−15.6) 16–19^{8} 20^{12}(−20.9–11, +20.11) 21^{12} (−21.11,12) 22–25^{8} 26^{8}(−26.8) 27^{8}(−27.5) 28^{8}(−28.1,2,8) 29^{8}(−29.4,5)

Watermark chart

Of course in a folio, only one of the leaves in a conjugate pair features a watermark. (See overleaf for chart.)

Paper

Barker-Benfield has distinguished six watermark patterns in a total of 16 different states. Each version of watermark *A* features two posts or pillars flanking a cartouche with initials, which supports a bunch of grapes. The initials read, 'WM,' 'MM,' or (if the beta-radiograph is backwards) 'MN.' *A1* has a distorted center foot. *A2* has an additional bobble beneath that foot, in what looks like a series of three circles at the bottom of the design. And *A3* shows those three bobbles leaning to the left (or, in any event, to the side of the illegible letter in the cartouche). As Barker-Benfield suggests, *A2* and *A3* 'may represent the same mould at different stages of degradation' (3).

Watermark *B* also displays posts under a bunch of grapes, but with different characters in the cartouche: 'G\ARD' in *B1* and *B2*; and 'GALD' in *B3–B6*. A narrow right pillar, slimming near the cartouche, distinguishes *B2* from *B1*. The left column of *B3* has a wavy outer edge; that of *B4* becomes narrow at the cartouche. Also, whereas a chain-line runs almost down the middle of the grapes in *B3*, the right edge of the grapes in *B4* just touches a chain-line. Several elements in *B5* lean to the left: the tops of both posts; the base of the right one; the grapes, so much so that they just touch the pillar on one side and a chain-line on the other. The left column in *B6* gets quite narrow by the cartouche and has a chain-line running just to the right of the center of the grapes. Barker-Benfield compares Heawood 3503 and, for the cartouche-word, 3506, 3508, 3511, 3531.

Watermark *C* displays a cartouche with the year '1629' above the initials 'I' and 'G,' between another pair of posts, and beneath another bunch of grapes. In one of two molds (*C1*), the year is legible, but the penultimate bobble below is broken, causing the last circle to stray to the left. In the other mold (*C2*), the bobbles are clear, but the '2' in the year is difficult to make out. Barker-Benfield identifies the same initials with another year in Heawood 3498, and just the letters in 3528–9.

Appearing only once, watermark *D* shows another set of posts with grapes, this one with the initials 'RDP' in the cartouche.

Watermark *E* presents a fleur de lis in a shield with a crown on top and, below, the bold (double-wire) initials, 'IF / M.' In one mold (*E1*), the central ornament in the crown slants to the left. In the other mold in the pair (*E2*), the right petal on the fleur de lis has drooped.

		ii [w]	[ ]	iii	1	2 a3	3 a1	4 a1	5		
	6 a1	7 b3	8 b3	9	10 b4	11	12 b4	13	14	15	
	16	17 e1	18 e1	19	20 d	21	22 e2	23	24	25 e2	
	26 b4	27 b4	28 b4	29 b4	30 b4	31	32	33	34	35	
		36	37	38 c1	39	40 c1	41	42 c1	43 c2		
		[ ]	44 c1	45 c2	46 c1	47	48	49	50 c2		
	51	52 b6	53 b5	54 c2	55	56 c1	57	58	59	60 b6	
			61 c1	62	63 c2	64	65 c1	66			
		67	68 c1	69 c1	70 c2	71	72	73	74 c1		
		75 a1	76	77	78 a1	79	80 a2	81 a1	82		
		83 a2	84	85 a1	86 a1	87	88	89 a2	90		
		91 a1	92	93 a1	94	95 a3	96	97 a1	98		
	99 c1	100 b4	101	102 b4	103	104 b4	105	[w]	[ ]	106	
	107	[ ]	108	109 b5	110 b6	111	[ ]	112 b6	113 b6	114 a3	
		115	116	117	118	119 c2	[w]	120 c2	121 c2		
		122	123	124	125	126 a3	127 a3	128 a3	129 a3		
		130 a2	131	132	133 a1	134	135 a1	136 a2	137		
		138 a1	139	140	141	142 a1	143 a3	144 a3	145		
		146	147	148	149 a3	150	151 a1	152 a1	153 a1		
154 a2	155	156	157 b3	158	159	160 b4	161 b4	[ ]	[c]	[w] +b4	163
164	165	166	167	168 b3	169	170 b4	171	172 b4	173 b3	[w]	[w]
		174	175 f1	176	177	178 f2	179 f1	180	181 a2		
		182	183	184	185 a1	186	187 c2	188 c1	189 c2		
		190	191 a2	192	193	194 a1	195 a1	196	197 a2		
		198	199	200 a2	201	202 a2	203	204 a1	205 a1		
		206	207	208 a2	209	210 a1	211	212 a1	[w]		
		213 b1	214 b1	215	216 b1	[ ]	217 b2	218	219		
		[?]	[w]	220 b1	221	222 b2	223	224	[?]		
		225 b2	226	227	[?]	[?]	228 b1	229b1	230		

The final watermark in the manuscript (*F*), features a coat of arms with a quartered shield, a crown on top, and a monogram at the bottom, possibly 'HRL' or 'HBL.' In one mold (*F1*), the central ornament in the crown is relatively deformed and leaning to the left. In the other mold (*F2*), the monogram slants down to the left and up to the right. Contrast Heawood 602–3.

Ruling

Barker-Benfield used the marginal rules to demonstrate that, despite this manuscript's wide range of watermarks, its scribe constructed it 'in a single campaign' (8). He concluded that, using a mixed lot of paper stocks, the scribe first constructed eighteen separate gatherings, and added rules and text to them. He then had them professionally bound with eight blank quires interspersed among them, and three more at the end of the book. The scribe then resumed transcription, adding rules and texts to the blank leaves in the bound folio (11). The rules made in the original gatherings before binding proceed quite far into the gutters and occasionally leave wet offsets on facing pages, but never on those of another gathering. Post-binding rules, on the other hand, end well before the gutters and leave frequent wet offsets even between gatherings. The original gatherings are 2–11, 13–15, 20–23, and 26. The rules range in color from brilliant red to faded brown or purple over the course of the manuscript. The same colored ink appears in the designs and elaborate letterforms that adorn certain headings (fols 1r–v, 3r–125r, 154r–201r, 206r–v).

Hand

All of the early modern texts are in the hand of 'a single scribe of good standard,' in Barker-Benfield's judgement (10). The scribe used an upright, slightly rounded secretary script for most text, and italic for headings and special emphasis. The quality of his hand and the brilliance of the ruling makes this the most beautiful, and certainly professional, book that I have analyzed for these manuscript descriptions.

Binding

Barker-Benfield dates the binding of polished brown calf to the seventeenth century. He notes that its covers are 'decorated with gilt centerpieces and with three fillet-lines (two blind around a central gilt) around the edges' and that the spine retains evidence of 'decorative bands in gilt' (2).

Selected contents

'A distracted Elegie vpon y^{t} most execrable murther of Thomas Scott / Preacher whoe was kild by an English soldier in a Church= / =Porch at Vtrecht, as he was entring to deuine seruice // Keep thy teares reader & y^{t} softer sorrow' (fol. 5r); 'Not more lamented for soe hard a fate' (fols 5r–10r); 'T[H]E FIVE SENCES / SEEING // From such a face whose excellence' (fols 14v–15v); 'TO T[H]E BLESSED ELIZA / OF FAMOVS MEMORIE / The humble petic[i]on of the / wretched & most contemptible / the poore com[m]ons of England // If Saints in heaven can either see or heare' (fols 16r–v); 'TO T[H]E MOST / high and mightiest the / most iust and yet most / mercifull the greatest / Chancellor of heaven and / the cheife Iudg of ye earth. // If bleeding hearts deiected soules find grace' (fols 16v–18v); 'A GRATIOVS / Answeare fro[m] the blessed S.^{t} / to her whilome subiects w.th a / devine admonition and a / propheticall conclusion: // Your bould petition mortalls I haue seene' (fols 18v–20v); 'AN ELEGIE / vpon the death of Sr Iohn / Burgh slaine in the / Isle of Ree w.th a mus= / =ket shott A.° / 1627 // Oh wound vs not with this sad tale forbeare' (fols 22r–23r); 'VPON FELTON / That kild y^{e} Duke of / Bucks & was hang'd / in Chaines. // Here vninter'd suspends (though not to save' (fol. 53r); 'AN / Elegie vpon y^{e} death / of Sr Charles Rich / Slaine at y^{e} / Isle of / Ree. // How faine would we forget this fatall war' (fols 53v–54r); 'AN OT[H]ER // Noe spring nor somer beawty hath such grace' (fols 103v–4r); 'Marry and loue thy fflauia for she' (fol. 104r–v); 'TO HIS M^{rs} // Dearest thie tresses are not threds of gold' (fol. 115r); 'SIR / Walter Ralegh to / Queene Eliza= / =beth: // Our passions are most like to floods & strea^{mes}' (fol. 117r); 'FROM / Count: Somerset daughter / to Katherine Countesse / of Suffolke: // From Katherines dock was launch'd a pink'; 'A page, a squire a viscount and an Earle' (fol. 163r); 'AN ELIGIE // Come madam come, all rest my powers defy' (fol. 171r–v); 'VPON / A gold cheyne lent / and loste. // Not that in colo^{r} it was like thy haire' (fol. 171v–72v); 'WHOOPE / doe me noe harme / good man // Our eagle is flowne to a place yet vnknown' (fols 176v–77r); 'TO THE / tune of Vir= / =ginia. // All the cheife talk is now' (fols 177v–78r); 'A SONG // Heaven bless king Iames our Ioy' (fols 178v–79v); 'A SONG // The Scottishmen be beggars yet' (fols 179v–80v); 'VPON / Prince Charles his / arrivall from / Spaine Oct [ober] / 5:th 1623. // The fift of August and the fift' (fols 180v–81v); 'A SONG // In Sussex late since Eighty Eight' (fols 181v–82r); 'ON / The Duke of / Bucks. // And wilt thou goe, great duke, & leave vs here'; 'GEorgIVs DVX $_{B}$VC$_{K}$I$_{NGA}$MI$_{\AE}$ / 1628 // Thy numeros name with this year doth agree'; 'Art thou return'd great Duke w.th all thy faults' (fol. 198r).

British Library MS Add. 25707 (Skipwith MS)

Compilers

The Skipwith family of Cotes, Leicetershire.

Collation

2°: 1^{10} 2^{4} $3–4^{6}$ 5^{2} 6^{4} 7^{6} 8^{two} 9^{4} 10^{8} 11^{4} 12^{12} 13^{16} 14^{8} 15^{12} 16^{8}(−16.7–8) 17^{8}(−17.1) 18^{4}(−18.2) 19^{14}(−19.11, 12, or 13) 20^{8} 21^{two} 22^{four} 23^{40}(−23.1)

Watermark chart

In a folio, only one leaf of a conjugate pair features a watermark. The chart lacks the huge final gathering, which would be represented by an exceedingly long row. (See overleaf.) This quire shows watermarks on fols 150–52, 155–56, 158–59, 162–64, 166, 168, 172–73, 176, 179–80, 184–85 (that is, 23.4–6, 9–10, 12–13, 16–18, 20, 22, 26–27, 30, 33–34, 38–39).

Paper

Most of the manuscript (specifically gatherings 1–7, 9–16, 18–20, and 22) features a pair of pot watermarks with the letters 'P O,' resembling Heawood 3583. The two molds are easily distinguishable, as one has a lopsided base and wide handle (*B2*), and the other a level base and narrow handle (*B1*). Other watermarks are found on fol. 4, throughout gathering 17 (a distinct pot watermark in a quire devoted to Juvenal), and in the huge last quire. The main pot watermark supports the case for this composite manuscript's bibliographic unity.

Hands

At least a dozen hands are distinguishable in the Skipwith MS. Of particular interest is the italic hand that predominates gatherings six through eleven (fols 29r–67r), and is responsible for the first few texts highlighted in the contents below. The commons' petitionary exchange, however, appears in a distinct, mixed hand. After the entire composite MS was collected together and its incomplete set of page numbers added, an italic hand filled in virtually all of the margins with verse, much of it either love poetry or poetry associated with the poets already represented in the MS. The case for the volume's unity ultimately depends on the date of this final hand. The script shares several features common to mid-seventeenth-century hands. Yet, if it dates from a later period, so too might the binding that brought these quires together.

			1	2	3	4 a	5 b1	6	7	8 b2	9 b2	10 b2			
						11	12	13 b1	14 b1						
					15	16 b1	17 b2	18	19	20 b1					
					21	22	23 b2	24	25 b1	26 b1					
							27	28 b2							
						29	30 b1	31	32 b1						
					33	34	35	36 b2	37 b2	38 b2					
							39	40							
						41 b1	42	43 b1	44						
				45 b1	46 b1	47 b2	48 b2	49	50	51	52				
						53 b1	54 b2	55	56						
		57 b2	58	59	60	61 b2	62 b1	63	64	65 b1	66 b2	67 b2	68		
69 b2	70	71 b2	72	73 b1	74	75 b1	76	77 b1	78	79 b2	80	81 b1	82	83 b1	84
				85 b1	86	87	88	89 b2	90 b2	91 b1	92				
		93 b1	94 b1	95 b1	96	97 b1	98	99 b2	100	101 b2	102	103	104		
				105	106	107 b1	108 b1	109	110	[w]	[w]				
				[ ]	111	112 c	113 c	114	115	116 c	117 c				
						118 b2	118[b] [w]	119	120						
	121 b2	122	123	124	125 b2	126 b2	127 b2	128	129	130	131 b1	132 b2	[?]	133	
				134 b2	135	136	137	138 b2	139 b1	140 b1	141				
							142	143							
						144 b2	145 b2	146 b2	147 b2						

Selected contents

'A Letter to the Countesse / of Rutlande. // Madam: soe maye my verses pleasinge bee' (fols 31r–v); 'Petitio // Looke, and lament behould a face of Earth'; 'Respontio. // It's strange to se a face soe highe in birth' (fol. 46r); 'To the famous S:[t] of blessed memorye / Elizabeth, the Humble petic[i]on of her / now wretched, and Contemptible, the / Comons of England. // If S:[ts] in heauen can either see or heare' (fol. 76r); 'To the most heigh and myghty y[e] most pious and mercifull / the cheife Chancello[r] of heauen, and onely Iudge of Earth / the most humble petic[i]on of the poore distressed Com[m]ons / of longe afflicted England. // If bleeding soules deiected hearts finde grace' (fols 77r–78r).

British Library MS Add. 30982 (Leare MS)

Chief compiler

Daniel Leare, cousin to William Strode. Leare's inscription appears five times on the first and last leaves of this manuscript. These leaves also feature two additional inscriptions, one for Anthony Evans and the other for John Scott, suggesting that they too may have contributed to or used the volume.

Collation

8°: $1\text{–}3^8$ $4^8(-4.2)$ $5\text{–}8^8$ $9^8(-9.4,5)$ 10^8 $11^8(-11.4,5)$ $12^8(-12.7,8)$ $13\text{–}14^8$ $+23^8$ 15^8 $16^8(-16.5)$ $17^8(-17.1)$ $18\text{–}22^8$

Watermark chart

In this octavo, partial watermarks invariably appear on two leaves, either the first and fourth, or the second and third, leaves of a gathering.

1 a	2	3	4 A	5	6	7	8
9	10 A	11 a	12	13	14	15	16
17	18 A	19 a	20	21	22	23	24
25	[A]	26 a	27	28	29	30	31
32 A	33	34	35 a	36	37	38	39
40	41 A	42 a	43	44	45	46	47
48 A	49	50	51 a	52	53	54	55
56	57 A	58 a	59	60	61	62	63

64	65 a	66 A	[ ]	[ ]	67	68	69
70	71 A	72 a	73	74	75	76	77
78 A	79	80	[a]	[ ]	81	82	83
84	85 a	86 A	87	88	89	[ ]	[ ]
90 a	91	92	93 A	94	95	96	97
98 A	99	100	101 a	102	103	104	105
( ) b	( )	( )	( ) b	( )	( )	( )	( )
( ) a	[ ]	( )	106 A	107	108	109	110
111 A	112	113	114 a	[ ]	115	116	117
[a]	118	119	120 A	121	122	123	124
125	126 A	127 a	128	129	130	131	132
133	134 A	135 a	136	137	138	139	140
141 A	142	143	144 a	145	146	147	148
149	150 A	151 a	152	153	154	155	156
157 A	158	159	160 a	161	162	163	164

Paper

The paper initially used to produce this manuscript features a watermark (*a*) of two pillars with a bunch of grapes on top, with most of its distinguishing characteristics obscured by the octavo format. A second watermark appears (*b*, a pot with either the initials 'QQ' or a design of two circles with tails in the bowl), but only on blank, unpaginated leaves that could have been inserted when the book was bound in order to separate the two halves of this manuscript. (A similar mark appears in Inner Temple MS Petyt 538, vol. 43, fols 284–303.)

Hands

An apparently untrained, mixed hand transcribed most of the texts in this manuscript, including those that begin from the back of the volume in reverse and, notably, those featured in the selected contents below. This hand features secretary forms of *c*, *r*, *e*, *D*, and sometimes *H* and *C*, and a very distinctive ampersand, which looks almost like the word *is* in secretary. This hand may be Leare's, even though it does not much resemble the inscriptions of his name, in which he attempts a few different scripts. A series of additional hands added texts to a few spaces and pages that the predominant hand left blank, especially in the middle of the volume.

Selected contents

'On the D: of Buckinghame // The king loues you, you him' (fol. 7v); 'I: C: V: R: good mounseir Carr'; 'Thou Carr to 4 feirst beasts didst trust' (fol. 22r); 'An epitapht on y^e Du: of Buckinghame. // Here lyes the best & worst of fate' (fol. 45v); 'Dr Donne to his $m.^{rs}$ going to bed. // Come, madam come, all rest my powers defie' (fol. 46r–v); 'On a Maides Deniall. // Nay pish, nay pray, nay faith, & will y^u; fie' (fol. 53r); 'On a Rusticke Gallant wooing // ffayre wench I cannot court thy spirit like eyes' (fol. 73v); 'on his m^{ris} perfection. // Dearest thy tresses are not threds of gold' (fol. 78r).

British Library MS Egerton 2230
(Richard Glover MS)

Earliest known owner

According to a late-eighteenth-century inscription, the manuscript belonged in 1638 to a London pharmacist by the name of Richard Glover (Beal, *Index*, Donne Δ42).

Collation

4°: 1^{16}(−1.1) 2^{16} 3^{12}(−3.5) 4^{five} 5^{16} 6^{16}(−6.5 or 6) 7^{10}(−7.5, 7, 7.8 or 9) 8^{10}(−8.6, 8.9 or 10)

Watermark chart

In a quarto such as this, individual leaves typically feature only a portion of a watermark or countermark, divided by the sewing at the gutter. Conjugate leaves thus feature opposite sides of a given mark.

In this manuscript, even gatherings with a regular number of leaves were constructed in somewhat unorthodox ways. The second gathering, for instance, could not have been constructed by folding four full sheets together. It could have been made by folding two pairs of full sheets independently, and then fitting one gathering of eight into the middle of the other, or by folding half-sheets once. The third quire must have been made with half-sheets, in particular the middle four leaves of the gathering. The sixth gathering very well may feature another quire of four set within a similar quire (as does the second gathering). Finally, quarto gatherings of ten, like the final two quires, would have required half-sheets. (See overleaf.)

Paper

Fine, white paper of two stocks. The primary stock features a pennant or flag on the watermark (*A*) with the initials 'G 3,' resembling Heawood

[a]	1 c	2 a	3 c	4 a	5 c	6 a	7 c	8 C	9 A	10 C	11 A	12 C	13 A	14 C	15 A
16 C	17 a	18 c	19 A	20 c	21 a	22 c	23 a	24 A	25 C	26 A	27 C	28 a	29 C	30 A	31 c
		32 c	33 a	34 c	35 a	[A]	36 a	37 A	38 a	39 A	40 C	41 A	42 C		
43 a	44 a	45 A	46 c	47 C											
48 C	49 A	50 C	51 A	52 C	53 A	54 C	55 A	56 a	57 c	58 a	59 c	60 a	61 c	62 a	63 c
64 C	65 A	66 C	67 A	[C]	C	68 A	A	69 a	70 a	71 c	72 c	73 a	74 c	75 a	76 c
			77 A	78 C	79 C	80 c	[A]	81 a	[C]	[c]	82 c	83 a			
			84	85	86 b	87 b	88	[ ]	89 B	90 B	91	[ ]			

1369, and a lamb countermark (*C*) loosely resembling Heawood 2837 and surrounding. The watermark of the second stock of paper (*B*) features the very different sort of flag recorded in Heawood 1368, and has no countermark.

Hands

An early seventeenth-century script from a single hand predominates the manuscript, appearing on both stocks of paper and every gathering but the penultimate one (specifically, fols 3r–31r, 32r–35v, 45r–63r, 69r–73r, 90v–91v rev.). Later hands filled in leaves that the primary copyist left blank (fols 36r–44, 63v–67r, 68v, 73v–81v, 82v–83v, 84v rev., 85v rev., 86v–90r rev.). The best evidence that one hand produced all of the early-seventeenth-century writing comes from a design feature. Most poems conclude with a cluster and/or a linear series of symbols resembling a tilde or a sideways 's' with 2 forward slashes through it. This distinctive design element occurs throughout the manuscript's early seventeenth century sections of poems.

Selected contents

'Songe // When lying on my bed as maydes doe vse' (fol. 8r); 'Madam) soe may my verses pleasing bee' (fols 8v–9v); 'Curse // Who euer guesses, thinkes, or dreames he knows' (fols 22r–v); 'Tis painefull rowing gainst ye bigg swolne tide'; 'Ladye chang'd to venus doue' (fol. 69r); 'Were itt nott a brutish crueltye'; 'Braue worthy carter that wth thy bravado' (fol. 69v); 'The howse of the Howards' (fol. 70r); 'Heare lyeth he that once was poore'; 'A page, a knight, a viscount and an Erle' (fol. 70v); 'From Katherins dock there launcht a pinke' (fol. 71r); 'From Roberts coach to Robins carr' (fol. 71v); 'Poore Pilote thou hast lost thy Pinke' (fol. 72r); 'Ha^{d}st thou like other s^{rs}, and knights of worth' (fols 72v–73r).

British Library MS Harley 1221, Fols 65–112

Collation

2°: 1^{12} 2^{three} $3–5^{8}$ 6^{nine}

Watermark chart

In the gatherings of eight in this folio, watermarks appear throughout the first half of the quire, leaving the second half without marks. The other gatherings are not so uniform, however. Each leaf of this miscellany is now pasted onto its own stub, and several leaves are of slightly irregular size.

65	66	67 a	68	69	70 a	71	72 a	73 a	74	75 a	76 a
77 a	78 a	79 a									
		80 a	81 b	82 b	83 b	84	85	86	87		
		88 b	89 b	90 a	91 a	92	93	94	95		
		96 a	97 a	98 a	99 a	100	101	102	103		
104	105	106	107	108	109	110 a	111	112			

Paper

The first watermark (*A*) shows an elaborate single-handled pot with a crown and a small oblong, resembling a peanut shell, on top; the letter *A* in the neck; the bold initials 'RO' in the bowl (that is, letters formed with two wires in the widest part of the pot); and another letter *A* in the base.

The second watermark (*B*) is a crest or emblem with the initials 'GD' (very similar to watermarks that appear in British Library MS Stowe 962, but nevertheless from a distinct paper stock).

Hand

A fair mixed hand predominates (featuring secretary forms for the characters *c*, *e*, *r*). The scribe responsible for most of the miscellany generally reserved italic for Latin text, headings, and first lines or first words. If this scribe also copied the Latin verse on fols 102r–3r, he or she took unusual care with these texts. Later, a clearly distinct hand added a few headings and texts.

Selected contents

'Madam, so may my verses pleasinge bee' (fols 79v–80r); 'I. C. V. R' (fol. 91r); 'ffrom Katherines docke was lanched a pincke' (fol. 91v); 'Dazeled w:th the hight of place' (fol. 110r).

British Library MS Harley 6038

Collation

4°: 1^{five} $2–8^{8}$ 9^{6} $10–12^{8}$ 13^{eight}

Watermark chart

In the regular gatherings of this quarto, conjugate pairs feature either opposite ends of a watermark or no trace of a watermark.

i a1	ii a1	1 A1	2	3			
4 a2	5	6 a2	7	8	9 A2	10	11 A2
12	13 a1	14	15 A1	16 a1	17	18 A1	19
20	21	22 A2	23 A2	24 a2	25 a2	26	27
28 A1	29	30 A2	31	32	33 a2	34	35 a1
36 A2	37	38 A2	39	40	41 a2	42	43 a2
44	45	46 A2	47 A2	48 a2	49 a2	50	51
52 A1	53 A1	54	55	56	57	58 a1	59 a1
	60	61	62 a2	63 A2	64	65	
66	67 a2	68	69 a2	70 A2	71	72 A2	73
74 A1	75 a2	76	77	78	79	80 A2	81 a1
82	83	84 a1	85 a1	86 A1	87 A1	88	89
(92)	(93) A1	(94) a1	(95) A1	(96) A1	(97) a1	(98) a1	(99)

Paper

This manuscript consists of a single paper stock featuring a pair of large watermarks with a *fleur de lis* above a crest with a diagonal sash and, at the very bottom, the initials 'N' and 'M.' One of the pair of watermarks (*a1*) has a relatively straight line between the initials, possibly the letter *I*. This may have been large paper, as the watermark and resultant quarto are both quite large.

Hand

A sloppy, although occasionally ambitious, italic hand dominates through fol. 49r, after which point other hands added texts later.

Selected contents

'Madam, so may my verses pleasing bee' (fols 24r–25r); 'I: C. V. R.' (fol. 28r); 'From Katherine docke was lanch'd a Pinke' (fol. 28v); 'Dazeled with the h^{e}ight of place' (fol. 44r–v).

BRITISH LIBRARY MS SLOANE 1792

Compiler

I.A. of Christ Church, Oxford who, according to an anonymous annotation added to the manuscript in the twentieth century, may be 'Jacob Aretius (or James Martin).'

Collation

8°: (+1) 1^8(−1.1) 2–17^8 18^8(−18.6 or 7) (+1)

Watermark chart

In most of the gatherings in this octavo, small portions of the watermark appear on two non-conjugate leaves, usually the fifth and eighth or the sixth and seventh. In certain unusual gatherings, however, bits of the watermark also appear on a third or a fourth leaf (specifically, gatherings 5–8, and 16–17).

i							
[ ]	1	2	3	4 a	5	6	7 A
8	9	10	11	12 a	13	14	15 A
16	17	18	19	20	21 a	22 A	23
24	25	26	27	28 a	29	30	31 A
32	33	34	35 A	36	37	38	39 a
40	41 a	42 A	43	44	45 A	46 a	47
48 A	49	50	51	52 a	53	54	55 A
56 A	57	58	59	60 a	61	62	63 A
64	65 a	66 A	67	68	69	70	71
72	73	74	75	76 a	77	78	79 A
80	81	82	83	84	85 A	86 A	87
88	89	90	91	92 a	93	94	95 A
96	97 a	98 A	99	100	101	102	103
104	105	106	107	108	109a	110A	111
112	113	114	115	116 a	117	118	119 A
120	121 A	122	123	124	125 a	126 A	127
128 A	129	130	131 a	132 a	133	134	135
136 A	137	138	139 a	140 A	141	[ ]	142a
143							

Paper

The watermark features pillars, much of which have been trimmed away.

Hands

An unadorned, fair italic predominates, possibly but not necessarily that of I.A.

Pagination

An early modern pagination proceeds from numeral 1 (on modern fol. 2r) through 266 (on fol. 134v).

Table of contents

The volume ends with a table of contents in the main hand, which proceeds onto fol. 143. This means that this final leaf, and the similar first leaf in the manuscript, were added before the main hand finished transcription.

Ruling

Simple red rules across the top and down the left margin on each side of every leaf from fols i–143, with the exception only of fol. 1, the original cover sheet. The rules on fol. i must have been made before it was moved to its present location.

Selected contents

'S~~u~~^{i}r H. Wotton. on the Lady Elizabeth when she was first crowned / Que. of Bohemia. // yea glori^{o}us trifles of the East' (fol. 2r–v); 'Supposed to be made against the Lady / Frauncis Coun: of Somerset. // She with whom troops of bustuary slaues' (fols 2v–4r); 'On a Gentlewoman seene naked. // As I alone' (fols 7r–10r); 'Come Maddam come all rest my powers defy' (fols 27r–28r); 'All the newes that is stirring now' (fols 52v–53v); 'I: D: to his freind. // Marry and loue thy Flauia, for shee' (fols 83r–84r); 'A Song. // Haue you seen the white lilly grow?'; 'A Song. // Haue you seen a black headed Maggott' (fol. 92r); 'To his confind freind Mr Felton. // In ioy thy bondage make thy prison know' (fols 114v–15r); 'Mr Cary$^{s.}$ loues Rapture // I will enioy thee now my Celia, come' (fols 116r–19v); 'A Maides Deniall // Nay pish, nay pray, nay faith, & will you? fie' (fol. 125r–v).

British Library MS Stowe 962

Collation

4°: 1^{2} 2–10^{4}
4°: 1^{4}(−1.1) 2–12^{4} 13–18^{8} 19–26^{4} 27^{6} 28–37^{4} 38^{2} 39–40^{4} 41–43^{6} 44–46^{4}

Watermark chart

In a quarto, conjugate leaves must feature opposite ends of a watermark, unless both leaves are blank or the gathering is made of half-sheets (as were the bifolia that constituted the very first gathering and gatherings 28 and 29 in the second volume).

	i a	ii A	
1 b1	2	3	4 B1
5	6 b1	7 B1	8
9	10 b2	11 B2	12
13 B1	14	15	16 b1
17	18 b2	19 B2	20
21	22 b2	23 B2	24
25 b2	26	27	28 B2
29	30 B2	31 b2	32
33 b2	34	35	36 B2

		[c]	37	38	39 C		
		40	41 c	42 C	43		
		44	45 c	46 C	47		
		48	49 C	50 c	51		
		52 c	53	54	55 C		
		56 c	57	58	59 C		
		60 C	61	62	63 c		
		64 d	65	66	67 D		
		68	69 D	70 d	71		
		72 d	73	74	75 D		
		76 c	77	78	79 C		
		80	81 d	82 D	83		
84	85 E	86 e	87	88	89 E	90 e	91
92 e	93	94	95 E	96 e	97	98	99 E
100 e	101	102	103 E	104 e	105	106	107 E
108 e	109	110 e	111	112	113 E	114	115 E
116	117 E	118 e	119	120	121 E	122 e	123

124 e	125	126 e	127	128	129 E	130	131 E
		132	133 E	134 e	135		
		136 e	137	138	139 E		
		140 e	141	142	143 E		
		144	145 E	146 e	147		
		148 B3	149	150	151 b3		
		152	153 b4?	154 B4?	155		
		156	157 B3	158 b3	159		
		160 B3	161	162	163 b3		
	164 F	165 B4?	166	167	168 b4?	169 f	
		170 g	171 g	172 G	173 G		
		174	175	176	177		
		178 f?	179	180	181 F?		
		182	183 H	184 h	185		
		186 H	187	188	189 h		
		190 b?	191	192	193 B?		
		194	195 B	196 b	197		
		198	199 B	200 b	201		
		202	203 B	204 b	205		
		206	207 B	208 b	209		
			210	211			
		212	213 B	214 b	215		
		216	217 B	218 b	219		
220 b	221	222	223 b	224 B	225	226	227 B
228	229 B	230 b	231	232	233 B	234 b	235
236 b	237	238 b	239	240	241 B	242	243 B
		244	245 B	246 b	247		
		248	249 B	250 b	251		
		252 b	253	254	255 B		

Paper

The two distinct volumes within this manuscript feature a remarkably similar watermark (*B*): a crest with the initials 'GD,' separated by a heart atop a small *huchet.* In one of the molds, the letters appear at the same height. In the other, less symmetrical mark in the pair, the 'D' is lower and often obscured in the gutter. Both symmetrical and asymmetrical examples of the watermark, quite likely made from the same pair of molds, appear throughout the manuscript. But those instances of the mark at the front of the book differ from certain examples at the back enough to suggest that they could come from different paper stocks, and so offer little certain evidence of the unity of the entire manuscript.

The first watermark (*A*) appears only on the first two leaves of the manuscript, uncommonly divided not by the gutter but by the upper page edge. The third mark is a simple bunch of grapes (*C*). The fourth mark portrays a double-handled pot perhaps with the initials 'JT' (*D*). The fifth features a single-handled pot, with a crescent on top and initials 'GGN' or 'CCN' (*E*). Then another pot emerges, possibly with the initials 'OC' (*F*), followed by a pot with a crescent on top and the initials 'IV' (*G*), and finally a pot with the initials 'BB' (*H*).

Foliations

The manuscript features two distinct, early modern foliations, suggesting that it comprises two distinct miscellanies. The first foliation skips fol. 6 and so stays one numeral greater than the modern foliation up to fol. 36. A second early modern foliation begins with numeral 2 on fol. 37, and proceeds without error until 208 (on fol. 243r, the last page of poetic text before a first-line index).

Hands

The case for this manuscript's bibliographic unity rests on the script, specifically on the possibility that the same scribe or scribes added text to both miscellanies. The primary script of the first volume, covering fols 1r–31r, is a legible, upright secretary, which occasionally grew slanted and close, perhaps when the copyist tired. The rest of the first volume features a script with both secretary and italic characters, possibly but not necessarily from a second scribe. The primary hand of the first volume may also have begun the second miscellany in the manuscript (on fols 37r–39v). The second hand may be responsible for much of the rest of the manuscript. Regardless of the number of hands that worked on this manuscript, the consistent quality of the script leaves open the possibility of professional involvement.

Selected contents

'An Elegie•or / vndressinge of ons / mistresse. // Come madame, come, all rest my powers defie' (fols 82v–83r); 'Vppon sir Walter Rayleigh Treason wth Lo: Gray S$^{r:}$ // Watt, well I wott thy ouerweaninge witt' (fol. 84r–85v); 'Callinge to minde mine eye went longe about // Sir Walter Rawlyegh' (fol.

85v); 'Ad Comitissam Rutlandiæ // Maddam soe may my verses pleasinge be' (fol. 88r); 'Marry & loue thy fflauia for she' (fols 127v–28v); 'The fiue Sences. 1623. // Seeinge. / ffrom such a face whose excellence' (fols 144v–46r); 'Haue you seene ye white lilly growe'; 'Haue you seene but a blacke little maggot' (fol. 179v).

Cambridge University Library MS Add. 29

Collation

2°: 1^{38} (+1 +2)

Watermark chart

Due to the large size of the single folio gathering that originally constituted this manuscript, its watermark chart would require a single, prohibitively long row. Even with enough space, such a chart would have difficulty conveying the odd portions of fols 19–32 and 40 rev. that have been cut out, and the unusually tall insert and bifolium (fols 33–35) that have been added between fols 32 and 40 rev.

Paper

A pair of single-handled pot watermarks, featuring a crescent at the top and the letters 'I V,' appears throughout the original folio. The marks are distinguished by the thin handle of *a1* (at fols 2, 6, 10, 14, 38 rev.) and the very wide handle of *a2* (at fols 4, 7, 8, 17, 19, 40 rev., 36 rev.). Fol. 33 is from a unique paper stock, and shows no watermark. The watermark on fol. 35 displays another single-handled pot with crescent, but with the letters 'DH.'

Foliation

Numbers are assigned in pencil to fols 1–21, 32, 33–35, and 40–36 rev. This last set of leaves has been foliated in descending order & upside down, such that fol. 40 rev. presently follows the inserts concluding with fol. 35, and fol. 36 rev. now ends the manuscript. The foliation erroneously skips ten numbers in order to account for the eleven stubs between fols 21–32.

Main hands

A (fols 1r–16v), B (fols 16v–19v), C (fols 19v–20r).

Selected contents

'Petitio // Looke, & lament behold a face of earth' (fol. 18r); 'Responsio // Its straung to see a face so high in birth' (fol. 18r–v); 'Goe & catch a falling starr // ID' (fol. 19r).

I thank the Syndics of Cambridge University Library.

FOLGER MS V.A.103

Collation

4°: 1^{8} (−1.1 or 2 & 1.3 or possibly 4) 2^{8} 3^{6} 4^{8}(−4.5) 5^{4}(−5.1) 6^{8} 7^{8}(−7.7 or 8) 8^{8}(−8.1 or 2) 9–11^{8} 12^{four} 13^{8} 14^{8}(−14.4) 15–21^{8} 22^{6} 23^{10} 24^{two}

Watermark chart

In a quarto, conjugate pairs must feature either opposite ends of a watermark, or no watermark at all. The quires of eight leaves could have been formed by folding two full sheets together.

	[ ]?	1	[a1]?	2 A1	3 a1	4 a1	5	6
	7	8 a2	9	10 A1	11 a1	12	13 A2	14
		15	16	16 A1	18 a1	19	20	
	21	22 a	23	24 a1	[A1]	25	26 A	27
			[a]	28	29	30 A		
	31	32 a2	33	34 A2	35 a2	36	37 A2	38
	39 a2	40 a	41	42	43	44	45 A	[A2]?
	[]?	46	47 A1	48 A2	49 a2	50 a1	51	52
	53	54 a1	55	56 A1	57 a1	58	59 A1	60
	61 a1	62	63 A1	64	65	66 a1	67	68 A1
	69	70 a1	71	72 A2	73 a2	74	75 A1	76
77	78	79 A	80 A					
	81	82 a1	87	86 A2	85 a2	84	83 A1	82
	81	80 A2	79	[A2]	78 a2	77	76 a2	75
	74	73 a1	72	71 A1	70 a1	69	68 A1	67

	66 a1	65	64 A2	63	62	61 a2	60	59 A1	
	58	57	56 A2	55 A2	54 a2	53 a2	52	51	
	50 a1	49	48 a2	47	46	45 A2	44	43 A1	
	42	41 a2	40	39 A1	38 a1	37	36 A2	35	
	34 a1	33 a1	32	31	30	29	28 A1	27 A1	
	26 a1	25 a1	24	23	22	21	20 A1	19 A1	
		18 a1	17	16 A2	15 a2	14	13 A1		
12	11	10 a1	9	8 A2	7 a2	6	5 A1	4	3
2	1 a2	[ ]							

Paper

A bunch of grapes on a curved stem, similar to Heawood 2089 and 2094. The stem of *a2* slims at the bend.

Ruling

The primary verse miscellany text features ruling in brown or possibly red ink at the beginning of each generic section, and in most of these sections continuing for a few pages after the verses cease (specifically on fols 2r–17r, 20r–23r, 29r–46r, 52r–62r, 66r–80r). The ruling consists of a single line at the header, footer, and (usually) gutter, and a double line at the edge of the page (again, usually, although the double rule is at the right margin of a verso, in the gutter, in fol. 4v).

Hands

The primary verse miscellany is the work of a single scribe who worked in two major shifts and changed his ink and writing style roughly half way through most sections (specifically at fols 10v, 21r, 23r, 34r, 55r, 67r). The same scribe made University of Nottingham MS Portland PwV 37.

Generic headings

The primary text of this manuscript consists of a verse miscellany organized by poetic genre. The collector began each section of the manuscript with the name of a genre, which he repeated in running headers throughout the section: 'Laudatory Epitaphs' (fols 2r–12r); 'Epitaphs Merry & Satyricall' (fols 20r–23r); 'Love Sonnets' (fols 29r–46r); 'Panegyricks' (fols 52r–62r); 'Satyres' (fols 66r–75v), 'Miscellanea' (fols 76r–77r).

Selected contents

'Dr Donne. Going to bedd. // Come Mistresse; all rest my powers defie' (fols 40v–41r); 'Dr Dunne. The praise of an old Woman. // Marry and love thy Flavia, for shee' (fol. 54r–v); 'A Satyre entituled the Witch; supposed to bee made / against the Lady Francis Countes of Somersett. // Shee with whom troopes of Bustuary slaves' (fol. 66r–v); 'On Sr Robart Carr Earle of Som[m]-ersett. // When Carr in Court a Page at first began'; 'On the Lady Fran: Countesse of Som[m]ersett. // Lady kin to Venus dove'; 'On the same. // Plants ne're likely better prov'd' (fol. 68r); 'Against Love. / Dr Donne. // Hee is starke madd who ever saies' (fols 68v); 'A Lover against himselfe. / Dr Donne. // I am two Fooles, I know' (fol. 69r); 'On the Lady Francis Countesse of Som[m]-ersett. // At Katherins docke there launcht a Pinke' (fol. 69v).

Folger V.a.262

Collation

4°: $1^{8}(-1.1)$ 2^{8} $3^{8}(-3.6)$ 4–14^{8}

Watermark chart

The conjugate pairs in this quarto of eights feature either opposite ends of a watermark, or no watermark at all. Each gathering was most likely made by folding two full sheets together.

[A1]	(i) a2	(iii)	(v)	(vii)	(ix)	(xi) A2	(xiii) a1
(xv)	(xvii) a2	(xix)	(xxi) A1	(xxiii) a1	(xxv)	(xxvii) A2	(xxix)
(xxxi) a2	(xxxiii) a2	(xxxv)	(xxxvii)	(xxxix)	[ ]	1 A2	3 A2
5	7	9 a1	11 A2	13 a2	15 A1	17	19
21 a2	23 a2	25	27	29	31	33 A2	35 A2
37 A1	39 A1	41	43	45	47	49 a1	51 a1
53	55 a2	57	59 a1	61 A1	63	65 A2	67
69 a2	71	73 a1	75	77	79 A1	81	83 A2
85 a2	87 A1	89	91	93	95	97 a1	99 A2
101 a2	103 a2	105	107	109	111	113 A2	115 A2
117 A1	119 a2	121	123	125	127	129 A2	131 a1
133 a2	135 A1	137	139	141	143	145 a1	147 A2
149 A1	151 A1	153	155	157	159	161 a1	163 a1
165 A1	167 A1	169	171	(173)	(175)	(177) a1	(179) a1

Paper

The single stock of paper used to make this manuscript features a pair of single-handled pot watermarks, each with a crescent on top and the letters 'PR.' *A1* features a thin crescent on a lopsided clover and a simple band across the bottom of the base. *A2* has a fuller crescent and a wider band whose rounded ends extend beyond the sides of the base. Contrast Heawood 3563.

Hands

One dull, predominantly secretary hand covers the unnumbered opening leaves with generously-spaced records in Latin. Then, on the first numbered page, the verse miscellany begins in a fair, professionally-trained, mixed hand of the mid-seventeenth century. Did the verse collector begin his miscellany on the first blank page following the casual notes, or could he have left at least the better part of a gathering blank before starting work? The first verse collector is almost certainly responsible for the text on pp. 1–122, and may be responsible for 123–33 and 133–67, including the page numbers (consider the characters *w* and *A* among these groups of pages). A later hand added text from the bottom of p. 167 through p. 172, as well as the last four page numbers.

Binding

The repaired binding features early modern parchment with roughly contemporary paper pasted inside the covers.

Selected contents

'Dr Donne to a gentlewoman that gaue / him the lye. // You say I lye, I say you lye; judge whether' (p. 68); 'A Louer to his Mistris. // Come Madam, come, all rest my powers defye' (pp. 73–74); 'A Maydes denyall. // Nay pish, nay pue, nay fayth, and will you? fye!' (pp. 74–75); 'Sir Walter Ralegh to the Lady Bendbowe. // In vayne I bend the Bow, wherein to shoote I sue' (p. 81); 'On Carr. // A Page, a Knight, a vicount, and an Earle'; 'On one being Sick. // A Mayden fayre with the greene sicknes late' (p. 139).

Folger MS V.a.339

This description owes a great debt to the work that Giles Dawson did on the manuscript, the results of which he made available on modern leaves added to the back of the volume, and in 'John Payne Collier's Great Forgery,' *Studies in Bibliography*, 24 (1971), 1–26.

Earliest known owner

Joseph Hall, not the satirist and bishop of Norwich.

Collation

8°: 1^8(−1.1,5) 2–11^8 12^8(−12.6) 13–23^8 24^8(−24.8) 25^8(−25.1) 26–28^8 29^8(−29.4–6) 30–37^8 38^4(−38.4)

Watermark chart

An octavo such as this, made of paper with just one watermark, generally features that mark either at the innermost and outermost conjugate pairs of a gathering, or on leaves 2, 3, 6, and 7. While the collation lists gatherings in their original order, the chart shows the current location of quires 29 and 30, which were transposed during a 1960 Folger rebinding.

[ ]	1 a	2 a	3	[ ]	4 a	5 a	6
7	8 a	9 a	10	11	12 a	13 a	14
15	16 a	17 a	18	19	20 a	21 a	22
23 a	24	25	26 a	27 a	28	29	30 a
31 a	32	33	34 a	35 a	36	37	38 a
39 a	40	41	42 a	43 a	44	45	46 a
47	48 a	49 a	50	51	52 a	53 a	54
55	(56) a	(57) a	(58)	(59)	(60) a	(61) a	(62)
63 a	64	(65)	(66) a	67 a	68	69	(70) a
71	72 a	(73) a	74	75	76 a	77 a	(78)
79 a	80	81	82 a	83 a	84	85	86 a
87	88 a	89 a	90	91	[a]	92 a	93
94 a	95	96	97 a	98 a	99	100	101 a
102 a	103	104	105 a	106 a	107	108	109 a
110 a	111	112	113 a	114 a	115	116	117 a
118	119 a	120 a	121	122	123 a	124 a	125
126 a	127	128	129 a	130 a	131	132	133 a
134	135 a	136 a	137	138	139 a	140 a	141
142 a	143	144	145 a	146 a	147	148	149 a
150 a	151	152	153 a	154 a	155	156	157 a
158 a	159	160	161 a	162 a	163	164	165 a
166 a	167	168	169 a	170 a	171	172	173 a

174 a	175	176	177 a	178 a	179	180	181 a
182	183 a	184 a	185	186	187 a	188 a	[ ]
[ ]	189 a	190 a	191	192	193 a	194 a	195
196 a	197	198	199 a	200 a	201	202	203 a
204	205 a	206 a	207	208	209 a	210 a	211
217	218 a	219 a	220	221	222 a	223 a	224
212	213 a	214 a	[ ]	[ ]	[a]	215 a	216
225	226 a	227 a	228	229	230 a	231 a	232
233	234 a	235 a	236	237	238 a	239 a	240
241 a	242	243	244 a	245 a	246	247	248 a
249 a	250	251	252 a	253 a	254	255	256 a
257 a	258	259	260 a	261 a	262	263	264 a
265	266 a	267 a	268	269	270 a	271 a	272
273	274 a	275 a	276	277	278 a	279 a	280
281	282 a	283 a	284	285	286 a	287 a	288
		289	290	291	[ ]		

Paper

The octavo format of this book has obscured its watermarks, which seem to consist of a coat, crest, or crown with letters, possibly 'IB' or 'HB'.

Hands

The primary hand in the miscellany wrote in an exceedingly close secretary and, as Dawson noted, inscribed a few dates in the 1630s. Dawson distinguished a second hand, responsible for adding dates in the 1640s. He also suggested that Joseph Hall may not have inscribed the flyleaf before 1700, and devoted much of his work to demonstrating that, in the nineteenth century, John Payne Collier filled in the spaces that the early modern compilers left blank.

Selected contents

'Against M$^{rs:}$ / Ioseph: // Nay pish, nay pewe, nay fayth & will you? fie' (fol. 188v); 'Letchery [con]sulte wth witchery howe to cause frigidety'; 'Some ar sett on mischeife soe, that they care not w^{t} they doe' (fol. 193v); 'Sr Tho: Overbury's wife. // Each woman is a briefe of woman kinde' (fols 208v–10v); 'Poore silly wight y^{t} carkes in the night' (fol. 262v); 'ffrom such a face, whose Excellence may captivate my sou[er]aignes eye' (fol. 263r).

Folger V.a.345

Collation

$4°: +22^4\ 1^8(-1.1,5)\ 2\text{–}13^8\ 14^6(-14.4)\ 15^8\ 16^8(-16.3)\ 17\text{–}21^8$

Watermark chart

The first gathering in this book consists of very clean paper, which contrasts sharply with the dirty first leaf of the second gathering. This suggests that a modern binder moved the first gathering to its current location from a place later in the volume, probably the very end, where it was kept clean.

		( ) A1	( )	( )	( ) a1		
[A2]	i	iii	v a1	[A1]	1	3	5 a2
7 a1	9	11 a1	13	15	17 A1	19	21 A1
23	25 a2	27 a1	29	31	33 A1	35 A2	37
39	41 a2	43	45 A1	47 a1	49	51 A2	53
55	57 A1	59	61 a2	63 A2	65	67 a1	69
71	73 a2	75 A2	77	79	81 a2	83 A2	85
87 a1	89	91 a1	93	95	97 A1	99	101 A1
103 A2	105	107	109 A1	111 a1	113	116	118 a2
120 A2	122	124	126 a2	128 A2	130	132	134 a2
136 A2	138	140	142 a2	144 A2	146	148	150 a2
152 A2	154	156	158 A1	160 a1	162	164	166 a2
168 A2	170	172	174 A1	176 a1	178	180	182 a2
184	186 a2	188	190 a2	192 A2	194	196 A2	198
	200	202 a2	204 A2	[a2]	206 A2	208	
210	212 A1	214 a1	216	218	220 A1	222 a1	224
226	228 A1	[a1]	230	232	234 A1	236 a1	238
240	242 a2	244 A2	246	248	250 a2	252 A2	254
256	258 a2	260 A2	262	264	266 a2	268 A2	270
272 A2	274	276	278 A2	280 a2	282	284	286 a2
288 a1	290	292	294 a2	296 A2	298	300	302 A1
304 a1	306	308	310 a2	312 A2	314	(316)	(318) A1

Paper

The paper stock used for this manuscript features a single-handled pot watermark with a crescent on top and the initials 'QQ,' possibly under the letter 'I.'

A1 has the more slender crescent and, at the base of the handle, a curl that extends comparatively far beyond the chain-line. Contrast Heawood 3579.

Hand

An informal italic hand inscribed the entire original miscellany and numbered pages 1–244. After skipping several leaves, he added one more page number, 245, to modern p. 270 and resumed transcription.

Ruling

Every leaf recorded here features red or brown ruling, extending quite far into the gutter, suggesting that the entire volume may have been ruled before transcription began.

Selected contents

'A Coy mistres. // Nay pish, nay pu, In fayth but will you? fie' (pp. 7–8); 'A suter // ~~fayth~~ wench I loue thee but I can not sue' (p. 29); 'A Country suter to his loue // fayre wench I can not court th~~ye~~ sprightly $_{\text{eyes}}$' (p. 34); 'Of y^{e} fiue senses by Iames Iohnson 1623 / Seeing. 1 / from such a face whose excellence' (pp. 59–61); 'Dr Dunne to his m^{rs} going to bed // Come Maddam, come, al rest my powers defy' (pp. 80–81); 'Idem to his m^{rs}. // Til I haue peace wth thee, warr other men' (pp. 81–82); 'on The Lady Carr // There was at court a laydy of late' (p. 290); 'An Epitaph of ye D: of Buckingham / August 26 1628 // I that my country did betray' (p. 315).

Houghton MS Eng. 686

Collation

8°: 1–3^{8} 4^{six} 5–13^{8} 14^{8}(−14.2) 15^{8}(−15.6) 16–18^{8} 19^{8}(−19.3) 20^{8}

Watermark chart

In an octavo quire made by the standard method of folding one sheet three times, conjugate pairs consist either of two blank leaves or one blank leaf and a leaf with half of a watermark, cut off at the upper or occasionally the lower edge of a page. Gatherings 1–3, 5–13, and 17–18 show the results of this common method. In order to achieve the results evident in most of the other gatherings, however, one would have had to take the presumably unusual measure of cutting full sheets not only in halves but also in quarters before folding them into quires.

1	2 a	3 A	4	5	6	7	8
9	10 a	11 A	12	13	14	15	16
17	18 B	19 b	20	21	22	23	24
25	26 b	27	28	29	30	[ ]	
31	32 b	33 B	34	35	36	37	38
39	40 B	41 b	42	43	44	45	46
47 B	48	49	50 b	51	52	53	54
55	56 b	57 B	58	59	60	61	62
63	64 B	65 b	66	67	68	69	70
71 A	72	73	74 a	75	76	77	78
79 b	80	81	82 B	83	84	85	86
87 a	88	89	90 A	91	92	93	94
95 A	96	97	98 a	99	100	101	102
103	[b]	104 B	105	106	107	108	109
110	111	112	113	114	[?]	115	116
117	118 A	119	120 B	121	122	123	124
125 A	126	127	128 a	129	130	131	132
133	134 B	135 b	136	137	138	139	140
141 A	142 b	[ ]	143 B	144	145	146	147
148 B	149	150	151	152	153	154	155

Additional evidence for collation

In every gathering but one, the brackets in the chart above represent a visible stub without any lacunae in the text before or after. These leaves therefore must have been excised, or possibly lost, before transcription began. The exception is the odd fourth gathering, which has no stubs and ends abruptly in the middle of a text, with catchwords dangling. If the maker of this manuscript used quarter-sheets for this gathering as well, then the last two leaves are probably the ones that are missing. But if it is unlikely that he started using quarter sheets so early in the project, then one must hypothesize that 4.2 or 4.3 was excised before transcription, and that 4.8 was excised after transcription.

Paper

Two distinct watermarks appear throughout the volume. Each is a single-handled pot with a crescent on a pedestal, on a flower. But one mark (*A*) features the initials 'CR' probably under the letter 'I,' whereas the other (*B*) has the letters 'IA' over 'V.' Also, in watermark *A*, the bottom of the flower's four petals rests on the middle of five circles, which are on five ovals spread in a fan. The crown of watermark *B* lacks the circles and ovals in the other pot. Instead two pairs of leaves flank the bottom petal or stem of the flower in *B*; beside one of these pairs of leaves is the spout. The pot in watermark *B* incorporates the pedestal of Heawood 3579 and 3583 with the flower and fan of circles and ovals visible in 3585, 3587, 3590, 3593, 3604, 3605. 3627. Heawood 3591–92 have similar, but not the same, initials to those in watermark *A*. Initials similar to those of watermark *B* appear in Heawood 3552 and 3561, but the pot's distinctive crown does not.

Ruling

The manuscript was ruled in red or brown ink before leaves were excised and transcription commenced: each of the stubs features the ruling, and the text sometimes disregards the rules. These rules, which intersect at every corner, set off wide left margins, more narrow headers, and quite slender right and bottom margins.

Hands

Two distinct hands transcribed the miscellany. The first hand reserved a less embellished italic for Latin text (see fols 14r–v, 40r–41v). A second hand emerges on fol. 44v, distinguished initially by broad, sweeping tails on *h*, *y*, and *p*; a cross-stroke on *A*; a more elaborate *O*; a distinctive *I* beginning with a circular gesture at the top and ending in a cross-stroke in the middle of the letter; and greater slant throughout.

Pagination

An early pagination in light brown ink proceeds from 1 to 37 and then stops. These first page numbers correspond (although not always exactly) to those in the partial table of contents at fol. 126r.

Selected contents

'On the Spanish match. / The day was turnd to starr light & was runne' (fols 2r–4v); 'On the Spanish match. / Dr Corbet to the Duke of Buckinghame // I've read of Ilands floating & removed' (fols 5r–6r); 'Reply to the former // ffalse on his deanery, false, nay more Ile lay' (fols 6v–7r); 'On the Spanish Match. // All the newes that's stirring now' (fols 7v–8r); 'On the Princes going to Spayne. / ffrom England happy & vnequall state' (fols 8r–9v); 'The Spanish Lady // Yee meaner beauties of the night' (fols 9v–10r); 'To Buckingham• // The King loves you, you him'; 'On the Earle of Sommerset // A Page, a knight a viscount & an Earle' (fol. 10r); 'On my Lord Carr // When Carr in court at first a Page beganne' (fol. 13v); 'While thy sonnes rash vnlucky armes attempt' (fol. 17r); 'To the most high & Mighty, ye most pious, and / Mercifull, ye Chief Chancellour of Heaven, & one / ly Judge of Earth: The most humble petition of / the poore distressed Commons of long afflicted Engla / land. // If bleeding soules, dejected harts find grace' (fols 29r–30v); 'In Sommer heat & mid time of the day' (fol. 32r); 'On my L. Carr his wife. // There was at Court a Lady of late' (fol. 34r); 'Nay pish, nay phew, in faith & will you? ffye' (fol. 35r); 'Come Madam come, all rest my powers defye' (fols 35v–36v); 'vppon a woman who the Author taught / to love & Complement. // Natures Lay Ideot, I taught thee to love' (fol. 37r–v); 'On the blasinge starre: // A starre of late appeared in Virgoes traine'; 'On the Duke of Buckinghames goinge to / sea, the 24th day of June: 1627 // And wilt thou goe? Greate Duke' (fol. 52r); 'Rex and grex are of a sounde' (fol. 53r); 'ffrom such a face whose excellence' (fols 59v–60v); 'Let other beautys have ye powr' (fol. 88r–v); 'Let other Arses have ye power' (fol. 88v).

Huntington MS HM 198, Part I

Earliest known owner

Edward Denny, who signed his name 'EDWDenny' on a stub bound with the miscellany.

Collation

2°: 1^6(−1.1) 2^4 $3–4^{10}$ $5–8^8$ 9^6 10^{10}(−10.10) 11^{five} 12^4 13^{12}(−13.5) 14^8(−14.1,8) 15^{two}

Watermark chart

In a folio such as this, of course, conjugate pairs feature a watermark on only one leaf.

		[a]	1 a	3	5 a	7	9		
			11 a	13 a	15	17			
19 a	21 a	23	25	27	29 a	31 a	33 a	35	37
39	41 a	43	45 a	47	49 a	51	53 a	55	57 a

		59 a	61	63 a	65	67 a	69	71 a	73		
		75	77 a	79 a	81 a	83	85	87	89 a		
		91 a	93	95	97	99 a	101 a	103 a	105		
		107 a	109 a	111 a	113	115 a	117	119	121		
			123 a	125	127	129 a	131 a	133			
	135 a	137 a	139 a	141 a	143 a	145	147	149	151	[ ]	
153	155	[?]	157	159 a	161						
				163 a	165 a	167	169				
171 a	173 a	175	177 a	[ ]	179	181 a	183 a	185	187 a	189	191
		[?]	193 a	195 a	197 a	199	201	203	[?]		
205	[?]	207 A									

Textual evidence for collation

Leaves must be missing where the text abruptly stops or starts, such as between pp. 152–53, 178–79, 192–93, 204–5, possibly 156–57, and probably at the end of p. 206.

Modern evidence

On an interleaf before p. 161, the manuscript's nineteenth-century owner Henry Huth added a 'Memorandum' explaining in convoluted prose that he found the following leaves 'severred' from the preceding ones, 'as if the entries, or transcripts, were intended to form a distinct collection.' Indeed a second seventeenth-century pagination begins briefly right after his insert. Nevertheless, Huth must have been right to combine these leaves, given the unity of the paper and script throughout the first part of the composite manuscript. I thank Mary Robertson of the Huntington for identifying Huth and for confirming my understanding of his note.

Paper

The only watermark in this part of the composite manuscript depicts a bunch of grapes on a stand atop an H-shaped structure, consisting of two pillars; a crossbar made of circles; four circles of varying sizes beneath the crossbar; and the initials 'R' and 'G' on either side of the stand holding the grapes.

Ruling

This miscellany features single-line ruling throughout: at the header and both margins, and at the ends of many poems. Rules at the edge of the page often intersect, whereas the header rule hardly ever crosses the margin rule at the gutter. Likewise, lines separating texts usually do not cross margin rules.

Hand

I concur with Beal's assessment that 'a single hand' transcribed the manuscript (*Index*, 1:1:253).

Pagination

Page numbers begin in the same ink and hand as the text and ruling, proceeding 1–5, 7–146; p. [6], a verso, is blank. Pages 163–65 feature a second seventeenth-century pagination.

Selected contents

'The description of A woman // whose head befringed with bescattered tresses' (pp. 8–10); 'On the Countess of Sommersett, // from Cathernes docke theer launch't A pritty Pinke' (pp. 19–21); 'The fiue Sences / Seing // From such A face whose excellence' (pp. 30–32); 'If shaddoues be A pictures excellence' (pp. 32–33); 'verses made on the Cou: of Somersett: // She that with Troupes of Bustuary Slaues' (pp. 33–34); 'Duns Curse upon him that knew his m:^{rs} // whoesoeuer ghesses, thinkes, or dreames he knowes' (pp. 34–35); 'upon the loss of A Braclett: // Not that in cullour it was like thy Haire' (pp. 35–37); 'verses made upon S^{r} francis Bacon / viscount verulam: // when you A wake dull Brittons and behould' (pp. 37–40); 'why faire uow breaker haue thy sins thought fitt' (pp. 40–42); 'Dedicated to the la: I: B: // Hide not thy loue and mine shalbe' (pp. 42–43); 'Come Madame come all rest my powers defye' (pp. 43–44); 'And art return'd againe with all thy faults' (pp. 44–46); 'vpon A faire woeman: // when last wee mett (Praising your beauty) you' (pp. 51–53); 'To ower blessed S:^{t} Eliz: of famous memory ye Humble Petition of / her now most wretched & most Contemptable ye Comons of England: // If Saints in Heauen can eyther see or heare' (pp. 62–63); 'Geo: D: Buckinghame: // Twas fatall unto the that in thy race' (p. 96); 'A rapture: // I will enioye the now my Celia come' (p. 117); 'To ffelton in Prison // Enioy thy bondage make thy prison know' (p. 152); 'on the Duke of Buckinghams Tombe: // Theis are the solem obsequyes' (p. 156); 'The Coppy of A Rodomantatho sent by the Duke to the house of Comons 28: In: 1628: / by the lord Grimes: his graces seruant: // Auaunt y^{u} giddy headed Multitude' (pp. 157–58); 'on felton: // Imortall man of glory whose braue hand' (pp. 158–59); 'And art thou who whilom thoughts thy state' (p. 159); 'The hayre A forrest is of Ambushes' (pp. 193–94); 'fletcher: to y^e^ Countes of Rutland. // Maddam soe may my uerses pleasing bee' (pp. 205–6).

Leicestershire Record Office MS DG9/2796

Collation

Long 4°: 1^{three} $2^{8}(-2.7)$ 3–5^{8} $6^{8}(-6.7,8)$ 7^{three} 8^{12} 9^{three}

Watermark chart

Most of the gatherings in this wide, short quarto were probably made by folding two sheets together, first longways. The two sheets used for the fourth quire, however, must have been folded separately, as were the outermost leaves of the gathering of twelve. In this format, watermarks are cut at the bottom edge of a leaf, and so are conjugate with leaves without any trace of a watermark.

1 a	3	5 a									
		7 A	9	11	13 a	15	17 A	[a]	19		
		21 A	23	25	27 a	29	31 A	33 a	35		
		37 A	39 a	41	43	45 a	47 A	49	51		
		53	55	57	59	61 A	63 A	65 a	67 a		
		69	71 A	73 a	75	77 A	79	[ ]	[a]		
81	83	85 A									
87 A	89 a	91 A	93	95	97 a	99	101 A	103 a	105	107	109
111 A	113 A	115 a									

Paper

Single-handled pot with a crescent on top and bold initials, possibly 'OO.'

Hand

The primary hand is an ambitious mixed italic, with pure italic reserved for headings and emphasis. This hand is responsible for virtually all of the text on pp. 1–78. Other hands added text later.

Selected contents

'Io. Felton's ffreindes. // Yo:[w] braueing spiritts (not braue) enflamd from hell' (pp. 1–4); 'A contemplac[i]on vpon the Dukes Graue // Heere lyes thy vrne. Oh. what a simple blowe' (pp. 5–6); 'vpon the Duke of Buckingham. // Yet weere bridentals sacred, & y[e] place' (pp. 7–10); 'Felton's Epitaph // Heere vninterr'd suspendes, though not to saue' (pp. 10–11); 'In commendation of declining Beawtie. // Noe spring, or som[r] beawtie hath such grace' (pp. 12–14); 'A l[ett]ere to the Countesse of Rutland. // Madam: soe maie my verses pleasing be' (pp. 24–28); 'An Elegie of loues progresse. // Who ev:[r] loues, if he doe not p[r]pose' (pp. 68–72).

MORGAN MS MA 1057 (HOLGATE MISCELLANY)

Compiler

Michael Denbo has, with qualification, identified the compiler as William Holgate of Great Bardfield (*b.* 1590, *fl.* 1634).

Collation

4°: $1^8(-1.5)$ $2–15^8$ $16^8(-16.4–6)$ $17^8(-17.7)$ $18^8(-18.1–2)$ 19^8 $20^8(-20.2)$ 21^8 $22^6(-22.4)$

Watermark chart

Each gathering of eight in this quarto could have been, and so probably was, made by folding two sheets of paper together. In this format, conjugate leaves feature either complementary portions of a watermark, or no watermark. As Denbo explains in his dissertation edition of this manuscript, the first leaf was originally attached to the cover, and the first three leaves are now glued together. So their watermarks are presently obscured, as indicated in the chart, even though the leaves are not missing, as noted in the collation.

[ ]	[a1]	[ ]	1 A1	3 [a1]	5	7 A1	9
11	13 A2	15	17 a2	19 A2	21	23 a2	25
27	29 A2	31	33 A1	35 a1	37	39 a2	41
43	45	47 A1	49 a2	51 A2	53 a1	55	57
59	61	63 A1	65 A1	67 a1	69 a1	71	73
75	77	79 a2	81 a2	83 A2	85 A2	87	89

91 a1	93	95 a2	97	99	101 A2	103	105 A1
107	109 A2	111	113 A1	115 a1	117	119 a2	121
123 a1	125	127 a2	129	131	133 A2	135	137 A1
139 a1	141 a1	143	145	147	149	151 A1	1153 A1
155 a1	157	159 a2	161	163	165 A2	167	169 A1
171 A2	173 a1	175	177	179	181	183 A1	185 a2
187	189	191 a2	193 A1	195 a1	197 A2	199	201
203 A2	205	207 a2	209	211	213 A2	215	217 a2
219	221 a1	223	225 a2	227 A2	229	231 A1	233
235 a1	237	239 a2	[ ]	[ ]	[A2]	241	243 A1
245	247	249 a2	251 a2	253 A2	255 A2	[ ]	257
[a1]	[ ]	259 a2	261	263	265 A2	267	269 A1
271	273 a1	275	277 A1	279 a1	281	283 A1	285
287	[ ]	299 A1	301 A1	303 a1	305 a1	307	309
311 a1	313 A2	315	317	319	321	323 a2	325 A1
	327	329	331 A1	[a1]	331/3	(335)	

Paper

Probably a pair of nevertheless quite distinct pot watermarks appears throughout this manuscript. Each pot features the letters 'OO,' 'CO,' or two circles across its broadest part. Yet *A1* lacks the crescent that tops *A2*. Also, *A1* is lopsided compared to the more symmetrical *A2*. Denbo refers to Heawood 3579.

Hands

Denbo identifies the earliest hand (α), which predominates pp. 1–216, 227–29, and 303–29, as that of Holgate; and the second two scripts (β, γ) as the dull mixed, hand and the clear italic, respectively, of Holgate's late-seventeenth and early eighteenth-century descendant John Wale.

Binding

Denbo describes 'a limp vellum binding sewed on four alum-tawed thongs. The ends of the alum-tawed thongs are laced through the cover at the joints. It never had headbands' (1).

Selected contents

'goinge to Bedd: // defie, / Thers no pennance due to innocence' (pp. 4–5); 'Good Madam Fowler doe not trouble mee' (p. 64); 'Seeinge // From such a face whose excellence' (pp. 80–81); 'Seeinge: // From a Gypsie in the morninge' (pp. 82–83); 'Marry and Loue thy Flauia for shee' (pp. 86–87); 'To the Countess of Rutland: // Maddame, soe my verses pleasinge bee' (pp. 105–6); 'By Ld Carr: Earle of Som[er]sett: his owne verses: // If euer woe possest a stubern heart' (pp. 190–91).

Rosenbach MS 239/27

Collation

8°: $1^{8}(-1.1,2)$ $2\text{–}3^{8}$ 4^{three} $5\text{–}25^{8}$ 26^{four} $27\text{–}28^{8}$ $29^{8}(-29.5,6)$ 30^{three}

Watermark chart

Most of the gatherings in this octavo were made with a single, full sheet of paper. Those sheets that feature a small watermark display portions of it on just two leaves: the first and fourth leaf of a gathering; or the second and third; or the fifth and eighth; or the sixth and seventh. Those sheets with a large watermark show segments of it on four leaves: usually the first, fourth, fifth, and last leaves of a gathering; or the second, third, sixth, and seventh.

[ ]	[A]	1 a	3	5	7	9	11
13	15	17	19	21	23 a	25 A	27
29	31 a	33 A	35	37	39	41	43
45	47	49					
51	53 B	55 b	57	49	51 b	53 B	55
57 B	59	61	63 b	65 b	67	69	71 B
73	75 B	77 b	79	81	83 b	85 B	87
89	91	93	95	97 c	99 c	101 c	103 c
105 b	107	109	111 B	113 B	115	117	119 b
121	123 b	125 B	127	129	131 B	133 b	135
137 B	139	141	143 b	145 b	147	149	151 B
153	155 b	157 B	159	161	163 B	165 b	167
169	171 B	173 b	175	177	179 b	181 B	183
185	187 B	189 b	191	193	195 b	197 B	199
201 B	203	205	207 b	209 b	211	213	215 B
217	219 B	221 b	223	226	228 b	230 B	232
234	236 B	238 b	240	242	244 b	246 B	248
250 b	252	254	256 B	258 B	260	262	264 b

266	268	270	272	274 a	276	278	280 A
282	284	286	288	290	292 a	294 A	296
298	300	302	304	306 a	308	310	312 A
314	316	318	320	322	324 a	326 A	328
330	332	334	336	338 a	340	342	344 A
346	348	350	352	354	356 A	358 a	360
362 b	364	366	368 B	370 B	372	374	376 b
378	380	382 d	384 D				
386 e	388	390	392 E	394	396	398	400
402 e	404	406	408 E	410	412	414	416
418 e	420	422	424 E	[ ]	[ ]	430	432
(434)	(436) f	(437)					

Paper

This manuscript features several distinct paper stocks, yet two watermarks predominate and appear interchangeably. The first watermark (*A*) features a flag on a pole and the number *3* under the flag. The flagpole has a wide base at the bottom, a pointy cap at the top, and a chain line right down its middle. The flag has two points, rather like two pennants joined together. The second discernible watermark (*B*) features a pair of pillars or columns (or possibly an unusual pair of scales) with rounded tops flanking a third, taller shape that is also rounded at the top. As is often but not always the case in octavos, no more than a quarter of this mark is apparent on a single leaf. In addition to these two paper stocks, at least three others appear in this manuscript. The eighth gathering features a paper that is much thicker than the rest of the paper in the manuscript. Its watermark (*C*), however, is illegible. The twenty-sixth gathering, which contains just four leaves (possibly, although not necessarily, made with a half-sheet), shows portions of yet another watermark (*D*): a *huchet* or, possibly, an anchor unlike any of Briquet's. The final three gatherings of eight display an elaborate crest or crown with a long top including a cross and three medium-sized circles (*E*). In addition, the three leaves immediately following the third gathering seem to be inserts and very well may be on a distinct paper stock. Although page 45 is quite loose, these leaves seem to have been pasted to the first leaf of the next gathering before the second hand indexed the entire volume. The last three leaves in the volume are also paste-downs, and may be on yet another paper stock (*F*). Although the variety of papers in this manuscript may suggest that it is a composite volume, the fact that the two predominant paper stocks repeat interchangeably suggests otherwise.

Hands

If a single hand transcribed this manuscript, as others have claimed, that hand was capable of two remarkably distinct scripts. The first script appears on pp. 1–17 and 29–44. This italic is in general the more elaborate of the manuscript's two scripts, especially after the first nine pages when it introduces some quite bold strokes to the characters *h*, *k*, *b*, *l*, *S*, and *C*. On these pages, the scribe reserved the left margin for the first capital letter of each line of verse. Yet he filled in these letters on only a few pages (specifically, on pp. 1–10 and through the first few lines of pp. 11 and 13). As a result, most of the poetry on pp. 11–17 and 29–44 lacks the first letter of each line. On p. 29, and on certain poems on pp. 31–35 and 43–44, the missing characters have been added in modern pencil. The second distinct script, and possibly the second hand, fills up the bottom of p. 17 and the rest of the second gathering. Then, at p. 45, it effectively takes over the transcription. Among the letterforms that most dramatically distinguish this script or hand from the first in the MS is its highly unusual ampersand. I hypothesize, then, that one copyist first transcribed gatherings 1–2 and 3, and that, after he had given up his ambitious task, a second hand filled in the blank leaves of gathering 2 as well as the rest of the manuscript, including the index.

Ruling

The entire manuscript, including even the leaves that are now pasted to the inside covers, is ruled in red or brown ink, with two vertical lines down the left margin. These rules strengthen the case for this manuscript's bibliographic unity.

Selected contents

'Verses vpon the Princes returne from / Spaine. // The day was turn'd to starlight, & was runne' (pp. 1–6); 'Another on the same. // Oh for an Ovid or a Homer now' (pp. 6–10); 'To his confined freind M^{r} ffelton. // Enjoy thy bondage make thy prison knowe' (pp. 45–46); 'Verses one the state // Our states a game att cardes, the counsell deale' (p. 46); 'Iustice of late hath lost her witts' (pp. 46–47); 'A thing gott by candle light' (p. 47); 'Vpon on goeinge to bed to his mistresse. // Come madam come, all rest my powers defye' (pp. 47–48); 'Loues voyage into the Netherlands. // The haire a forrest is of ambushes' (pp. 49–50); 'Sr Walter Rawleigh to his M^{ris}. // Passions are likened to floods & streames' (p. 50); 'Wronge not deare empresse of my heart' (pp. 50–51); 'On his mistresse risinge. // Lye still my deare why dost thou rise' (pp. 51–52); 'On the Lord Carr. // When Carr att first in court a page beganne' (p. 57); 'On the Duke // And art return'd againe with all thy faults' (pp. 54^{b}–57^{b}); 'The Dukes ffarewell. // And wilt thou goe great Duke & leaue vs heare' (p. 57^b); 'Anagram [m]a: // Georgius Villerus. Regis, vulgi elusor' (p. 57^b); 'On the fiue senses. / 1 Seeinge. // ffrom such a face whose excellence' (pp. 58^b–60); 'Another to K. Iames. // ffrom a gipsy in the morninge' (pp. 60–62); 'The Letany: // ffrom Mahomett & Paganisme' (pp. 62–64); 'A songe. // When Charles hath gott the spanish girle' (pp. 66–68); 'A songe. // Arme, arme. / In heauen there is a factio [n]' (pp. 82–84); 'A maides denyall. // Nay pish, nay pheu, nay faith but will you, fy' (p. 157); 'The rusticke gallants wooinge. // ffaire wench I cannot court thy spritelike eyes' (p. 182); 'To the Duke of Buckingham. // The kinge loues you, you him, both loue ye same' (p. 194); 'On a Lady. // There was att Court a Lady of late' (p. 194); 'On a downright suitor // Faith wench I loue thee, but I cannot sue' (p. 206); 'On the Dukes death. // Some say the Duke was vertuous gracious, good' (p. 318); 'The Dukes Ghoast // I that my Country did betray' (pp. 318–19); 'Another on the Duke // Loe in this marble I entombed am'; 'On Felton suspended. // Heere unterr'd suspends (though not to saue' (p. 319); 'On the Duke of Buck[ingham]s: death // when Poetts vse to write, men vse to saye' (pp. 384–86).

Rosenbach MS 1083/15

Collation

4°: $1^8(-1.1)$ 2^8 $3^8(-3.3)$ $4–9^8$ $10^8(-10.8)$ $11–12^8$

Watermark chart

In this quarto in eights, conjugate pairs feature either complementary portions of a watermark, or no watermark on either leaf. The arrangement of watermarks demonstrates that each gathering was most likely made by folding two sheets twice each. The sheets must have been folded separately in gatherings 2, 8–9, and 11.

[ ]	1 a1	3	5 A2	7 a2	9	11 A1	13
15	17 A2	19 a2	21	23	25 A2	27 a2	29
31 a2	33	[a2]	35	37	39 A2	41	43 A2
45	47 a1	49	51 a1	53 A1	55	57 A1	59
61 a2	63	65 a2	67	69	71 A2	73	75 A2
77	79 a1	81	83 A2	85 a2	87	89 A1	91
93 A1	95	97 A1	99	101	103 a1	105	107 a1
109	111 A2	113 a2	115	117	119 A2	121 a2	123

125 a2	127	129	131 a1	133 A1	135	137	139 A2
141	143 a1	145	147 a1	149 A1	151	153 A1	[ ]
155	157 a1	159 a2	161	163	165 A2	167 A1	169
171 a2	173	175 a2	177	179	181 A2	183	185 A2

Paper

The paper used throughout the volume features a pair of single-handled pots with the letters 'AH' and, on the top, a four-petaled flower with a stem made of a single wire, standing on a conventional crown. In *A1*, the handle is relatively thin, and the crown extends beyond the laid line opposite the handle and does not reach the laid line near the handle. Watermark *A2* has a broader handle and a crown that stretches from one laid line to the other.

Hands

In his dissertation edition of the manuscript, James Sanderson distinguished three or four hands: the first a secretary, which predominates the first 37 folios; the second a mixed hand that alternates with the first from fol. 38r on; a third an italic that appears on fol. 69v; and a fourth script that concludes, beginning at fol. 77v, and may be from the first hand (Sanderson, lx).

Binding

A rudimentary, early modern parchment binding survives, with three cords at the spine and only the tops and bottoms (not the sides) of the covers folded.

Selected contents

'Nay pish: nay pue: nay fayth [*torn*] will you fie' (p. 3); 'ffaire was the morne & brightsome was the day' (pp. 18–22); 'In som[m]ers heat at midtyme of the day' (p. 43); 'A Lady faire two suiters had' (p. 44); 'Of Sr Robert Carr Earl of Somerset / & ye diuorced Lady of ye E. of Essex y^t^ / went for a mayd still his present wife. // Lady chaynd to Venus Doue'; 'plants enow thence may ensue' (p. 139); 'On the late Earle of Somersett / ICVR, good monseir Carr' (p. 140).

ROSENBACH MS 1083/16

Compiler

In his dissertation edition of the manuscript, David Redding identified the compiler as Robert Bishop.

Collation

4°: $1^8(-1.1)$ $2–8^8$ $9^8(-9.1)$ $10–16^8$ 17^{12} 18^8 $19^8(-19.8)$

Watermark chart

In some of this manuscript's conjugate pairs, the watermark is split between two leaves, such as in 3.1 and 3.8 (fols 31 and 45). But in other pairs, the entire watermark appears on just one leaf as in 3.3 (fol. 35), which I record in the chart by including signs for both the upper and lower portion of the watermark within the same cell (as in *Aa2*). (See overleaf.)

Paper

This manuscript is made of paper with a pair of watermarks displaying a bunch of grapes supporting three letters (possibly 'MAL') and, above the letters, a crown. The crown distinguishes the two marks, and typically consists of: a horizontal line across the top of the letters; a circle directly above each letter; tall leaves atop each circle; and arcs that join the leaves and touch the circles below, curling inward. The crown of *a1* is the more symmetrical of the two, with less clear arcs that do not reach the circles below; a misformed center leaf; and a lopsided middle circle. The comparatively symmetrical crown of *A2* features distinct leaf forms. *A2* must have been placed to one side of the full sheet, accounting for its appearance in full in so many leaves.

Hand

Redding describes the hand as mixed, favoring secretary *e* and italic *r*, and alternating between both forms of *h* (xlv–xlvi).

Selected contents

'Carre & Carter // ffrom Car a Carter surely tooke his name'; 'ffrom Robins Coach to Robins Carr'; 'Old Venus with her borrowed light' (p. 13); 'In praise

		[A1]	1	3 Aa2	5	7	9	11	13 a1		
		15	17	19 Aa2	21 Aa2	23	25	27	29		
		31 a1	33	35 Aa2	37	39	41	43	45 A1		
		47	49 A1	51	53	55	57	59 a1	61 Aa2		
		63	65	67	69	71	73	75 Aa2	77 Aa2		
		79	81 A1	83	85 Aa2	87	89	91 a1	93		
		95	97	99 Aa2	101 a1	103 A1	105	107	109		
		111	113	115 Aa2	117 a	119 A	121	123	125		
		[A1]	127	129 Aa2	131	133	135	137	139 a1		
		141 a1	143	145 Aa2	147	149	151	153	155 A1		
		157	159	161 Aa2	163 a1	165 A1	167	169	171		
		173	175	177 a1	179	181	183 A1	185	187 Aa2		
		189	191 A1	193	195	197	199	201 a1	203 Aa2		
		205 A1	207	209 Aa2	211	213	215	217	219 a1		
		221	223	225 Aa2	227 Aa	229	231	233	235		
		237 A1	239 A1	241	243	245	247	249 a1	251 a1		
253	255	257	259 Aa2	261 Aa2	263 Aa2	265	267	269	271	273	275
		277 A1	279	281 a1	283	285	287 A1	289	291 a1		
		293	295 A1	287	299 Aa2	301	303	305 a1	[ ]		

of a Gentlewoman: // Her haire but thin, in all they are but three' (p. 32); 'We Maddame y[t] doe Fucus vse' (p. 33); 'A wooer // ffayre wench I can not court thy sprightly eyes' (pp. 47–48); 'The 5 senses p[r]sented / to K. Iames: / Seeing: // ffrom such a face whose Excellence' (pp. 84–87); 'On the late Earle of Sommersett. // ICVR Good Mounsieur Carr' (p. 172); 'On the Duke // Rex & Grex are both of a sound' (p. 181); 'A prayer for the Duke: // Come heere me braue Muses & helpe me to sing' (pp. 196–98); 'On the D. of Buckingham: // The king loues you, you him, both loue the same' (p. 246); 'A sonnet: one the spanish match; // Poore silly wight' (pp. 248–50); 'Another: // All the news y[ts] stirring now' (pp. 250–51); 'Madam Fowler: // Good Madam Fowler doe not trouble mee' (pp. 275–76).

University of Nottingham MS Portland PwV 37

Collation

4°: $1\text{–}2^8$ $3^8(-3.7)$ $4\text{–}9^8$ $10^8(-10.3)$ 11^8 $12^8(-12.7)$ 13^8 $14^8(-14.5)$ $15\text{–}16^8$ $17^8(-17.2)$ $18\text{–}20^8$ $21^8(-21.5)$ $22\text{–}24^8$ $25^8(-25.7)$

Watermark chart

In a quarto, a conjugate pair must feature opposite ends of a watermark, or no watermark at all. Most of the quires in this manuscript must have been made by folding two full sheets separately and then fitting one gathering of four within another (this is the case, specifically, in quires 1–4, 8, 10–11, 15–17, 20–22, 25).

iii	iv a	1 A	3	5	7a	9 A	11
13 a	15	17	19 A	21 a	23	25	27 A
29	31 a	33 a	35	37	39 A	[A]	41
43 a	45	47	49 a	51 A	53	55	57 A
59	61 a	63	65 A	67 a	69	71 A	73
75 A	77	79 a	81	83	85 A	87	89 a
91 a	93	95 a	97	99	101 A	103	105 A
107	109 a	111 a	113	115	117 A	119 A	121
123	125 a	127	129 a	131 A	133	135 A	137
139 a?	141	[ ]	143 a	145 A	147	149	151 A?
153	155 a	157 a	159	161	163 A	165 A	167
169	171 a	173	175 a	177 A	179	[A]	181
183	185 a	187	189 a	191 A	193	195 A	197

199 a	201	203 a	205	[ ]	207 A	209	211 A
213 a	215	217	219 a	221 A	223	225	227 A
229 a	231	233	235 a	237 A	239	241	243 A
245 a	[ ]	247	249 a	251 A	253	255	257 A
259	261 a	263	265 a	267 A	269	271 A	273
275	277 a	279	281 a	283 A	285	287 A	289
291 a	293	295	297 a	299 A	301	303	305 A
307	309 a	311 a	313	[ ]	315 A	317 A	319
321 a	323	325	327 a	329 A	331	333	335 A
337	339 a	341	343 A	345 a	347	349 A	351
353	355 a	357	359 a	361 A	363	365 A	367
(369) a	371	373	375 a	377 A	379	[ ]	381 A

Paper

With the exception of the first and last two leaves, which were taken from printed works and which I have omitted from the chart, all of the paper in this volume features the same watermark, with a bunch of grapes on one end and, on the other, something of a crown consisting of five rounded, elongated shapes.

Ruling

Rules in red, one to mark each of the four margins, appear on both sides of every leaf (with the exception of the printed fly-leafs).

Hands

The early modern miscellany is entirely in one fair, close, upright italic hand, with occasional bold capitals mimicking print. This possibly professional scribe is also responsible for Folger MS V.a.103.

Generic headings

'Laudatory Epitaphs' (pp. 1–32); 'Epitaphs Merry & Satyricall' (pp. 37–46); 'Love Sonnets' (pp. 59–79); 'Panegyricks' (pp. 107–17); 'Satyres' (pp. 135–57); 'Miscellanea' (pp. 169–206); 'Serious Poemes' (pp. 225–54); 'Merry Poems' (pp. 307–23); 'Verses on Christ=Church Play' (pp. 363–73).

Selected contents

'Dr Dunne. The praise of an old Woman. // Marry and love thy Flavia, for Shee' (pp. 112–13); 'A Satyre entituled the Witch; supposed to bee made / against the

Lady Francis Countes of Somersett. // Shee with whom troopes of Bustuary slaves' (pp. 135–36); 'On Sr Rob: Carr Earle of Sommersett. // When Carr in court a Page at first began'; 'On the Lady Francis Countesse of Sommersett. // Lady kin to Venus dove'; 'On the same. // Plants ne're likely better prov'd'; 'On the same. // At Katherins docke there launcht a Pinke' (p. 142).

University of Wales, Bangor MS 422

Collation

8°: 1^{4} $2\text{–}3^{8}$ $4^{8}(-4.2,3)$ $5^{8}(-5.1)$ 6^{8} $7^{8}(-7.6 \text{ or } 7)$ 8^{four} 9^{three}

Watermark chart

The chart proposes the original order of the pages in the Bangor manuscript, which were bound in the wrong order before being paginated. As in most octavos, originally conjugate leaves feature either bits of a watermark on both leaves, or no trace of a watermark.

		1	3 a	5 a	7		
15 a	17	19	21 a	23 a	25	27	29 a
39 a	31	33	35 a	9 a	11	13	37 a
95 a	[ ]	[ ]	97 a	99 a	101	103	93 a
[ ]	41 a	43 a	45	47	49 a	51 a	53
55	57	59	61 A	63 a	65	67	69
71 a	73	75	77 a	79 a	81	[ ]	83 A
85 a	87	89 a	91				
105 a	107 a	109					

Textual evidence

The text indicates that the third gathering was substantially rearranged before the volume was paginated. The text ending the second gathering on p. 30 continues on p. 39; the poem ending abruptly on p. 36 resumes on p. 9; and the verses on p. 14 conclude on p. 37. After folding and transcription, then, this third gathering was separated into three parts, each of which was placed in a new position before foliation: 3.2–4; 3.5–7; and 3.1,8. This outermost conjugate pair was folded backwards and inserted as a bifolium. The William Strode poem that ends abruptly at the end of the third gathering on p. 38 continues on p. 95, originally

4.1. And the incomplete poem beginning p. 97 (the recto of 4.4, I figure) indicates that it originally followed at least one leaf that is now missing.

Paper

The single paper stock used in this manuscript features a crest with a crown on top, made indecipherable by the octavo format.

Hands

Most of the miscellany is in two distinct, interchanging scripts: a large, sloppy italic with a distinctive *I* and a fair, close mixed hand with secretary forms of *e, c, r, v.* The italic script gives way to the mixed hand in the middle of poems on pp. 16, 19, 104. Either these are the two writing styles of one copyist, or two hands worked quite closely on this manuscript. The first script appears on pp. 15–16, 18–19, 20–22, 28, 41–70, 93–104. The second script shows up on pp. 9–14, 16–18, 19–20, 23–30, 31–36, 37–38, 39. A third hand may be responsible for the text on pp. 83–85, 91–92, 106–9 which includes writing in Welsh. Other text was probably added quite late.

Selected contents

'To his mistres as shee was comming / to bed // Come madame, come, all rests my powers defy' (pp. 43–44); 'A contention beetwixt a gentleman / and a gentlewoman // Nay pish, nay phew, infaith but will you, fye' (p. 50); 'A libell made on ye earle of / Sommerset // A page, a knight, a vicount and an earle' (p. 59); 'On ye duke Buck: memory // he y^{t} can reade a sigh, or spell a teare' (pp. 60–61); 'Vppon the dukes name // The bucke grew tall and striueing for to runne' (p. 65); 'On ye duke // Adew faire duke, whome fauour of a kinge'; 'On a cornet which appeared / before Q: Anes death / and the prince / his goinge to Spaine // A starre of late arose in virgoes traine' (p. 67); 'Let Charles & George doe what'; '1628 / Since with this yeare thy' (p. 91); 'On y^{e} D: of B: kild by F: // The Bucking^{game} lutes musike loued' (p. 97).

Victoria and Albert Museum (National Art Library) MS Dyce 44 (25.F.39)

Collation

8°: 1^{four} $2^{8}(-2.8)$ $3–5^{8}$ $6^{8}(-6.2)$ $7^{8}(-7.8)$ 8^{8} 9^{five} 10^{8} 11^{one} $12^{8}(-12.4)$ 13–15^{8} 16^{8} $17^{8}(-17.4?)$

Watermark chart

In this octavo in eights, halves of watermarks appear on one of the following pairs of (non-conjugate) leaves: 1 and 4; 2 and 3; 6 and 7; or 5 and 8.

1	2	3	4				
5	6	7	8	9 a	10	11	[A]
12	13 a	14 A	15	16	17	18	19
20	21 B	22 b	23	24	25	26	27
28	29	30	31	32 a	33	34	35 A
36	[B]	37 b	38	39	40	41	42
43	44	45	46	47	48 A	49 a	[ ]
50	51	52	53	54 b	55	56	57 B
58	59	60	61 b	62			
63	64	65	66	67 b	68	69	70 B
71 B							
72	73	74	[ ]	75	76 B	77 b	78
79	80	81	82	83	84 B	85 b	86
87	88	89	90	91 b	92	93	94 B
95	96	97	98	99 b	100	101	102 B
103 b	104	105	106 B	107	108	109	110
111	112	113	[ ]	114 b	115	116	117 B

Paper

The first watermark (*A*) shows a single-handled pot with crescent on top, and possibly a series of letters ending in 'A.' The second mark (*B*) displays another single-handled pot with a clover on top and the initials 'IB' or perhaps 'IBI' with the final 'I' on the bottom.

Hands

Despite Robert Krueger's claim to the contrary, a single, highly distinctive hand copied texts throughout this manuscript and certainly transcribed Davies' anti-courtly love poems on fol. 57r–v (*Poems of Sir John Davies*, 439). This hand features an unusual *h* that concludes by sweeping down and to the left; a hooking ascender on the left side of *v*; and huge descenders on *s*, *f*, *g*, *I*, and *A*.

Selected contents

'Pardon sweet flower of matchlesse poetry' (short version of Nashe's 'The choise of valentines' written partly in code, fols 2r–4r); 'I loue thee not for sacred chastity' (fol.

57r); 'Fayth wench I cannot courte thy piercing eyes' (fol. 57r–v); 'Sweet wench I loue thee yet I will not sue' (fol. 57v); 'Admire all weakenesse wrongeth right' (fol. 81r); 'From Katharens docke was lanch'd a pinke'; 'I C V R good Mounsier Car' (fol. 97r); 'A p[ro]per & pleasant new ballad to ye tune of / Whoope doe me no harme good man or y^e^ / cleane contrarie way wth wch youre / stomacke & ye tune can best agree. // There was an olde lad ridde in an olde pad' (fols 97v–98r); 'Poore pilot thow are like to loose thy pinke'; 'From Roberts coach to Robins carre' (fol. 98v); 'Epitaph // Heere lyes one, y^t^ once was poore' (fol. 99r).

Reproduced with the kind permission of the Trustees of the Victoria and Albert Museum.

West Yorkshire Archive Service, Leeds MS WYL156/237

Earliest known owner

Sir John Reresby, based on a loose fragment kept with the volume which reads in secretary, 'To my euer honored good / Cosen Sr Iohn Reresby.'

Collation

2°: 1^{18}(−1.1,2) 2^{14} 3^{20} 4^{14} 5^{18}(−5.9–13) +6^{12}(−6.1) 7^{16}(−7.10–14)

The sixth gathering was inserted after the transcription and pagination of the other gatherings, but was transcribed in the main hand, or one of the main hands.

Watermark chart

In a folio, conjugate pairs consist of one leaf with a watermark and another leaf with no mark. (See facing page.)

Paper

The numbered leaves are all on one paper stock, featuring a symmetrical watermark (*a*) of two pillars, each topped with leaves or flowers, wrapped loosely in a thin flag. The unnumbered leaves have different watermarks: a large bunch of grapes (*b*), and a single-handled pot with a crescent on top and the initials 'RO' in the bowl, possibly under the letter, 'G' (*c*).

Pagination

The early modern pagination may be in the main hand, and certainly predates the insertion of the sixth gathering.

	[ ]	[a]	1 a	2	3 a	4	5	6	7	8 a	9 a	10 a	11 a	12	13 a	14	15	16 a	
			17 a	18	19 a	20	21 a	22 a	23	24 a	25	26	27 a	28	29 a	30			
31	32 a	33 a	34 a	35	36	37 a	38 a	39	40 a	41	42 a	43	44	45 a	46 a	47	48	49	50 a
			51 a	52	53 a	54 a	55	56 a	57 a	58	59	60 a	61	62	63 a	64			
	65	66	67 a	68 a	69 a	70 a	71	72 a	73 a	[ ]	[ ]	[a]	[ ]	[ ]	79	80	81 a	82 a	
				[ ]	( ) b	( )	( ) b	( )	( ) c	( )	( ) b	( )	( ) b	( )	( ) b				
		83 a	[?]	85 a	86 a	87	88	89	90	91 a	92 a	[a]	[a]	[ ]	[ ]	[?]	[ ]		

Hands

The manuscript features either the work of two hands or two styles from the same hand. All of the script is in a fair italic. Although it features two alternating writing styles, these scripts lose many of their distinguishing characteristics as the volume proceeds. On fols 44v–45r and 50r, for instance, the two scripts become quite difficult to decipher. The first script, a fair italic with an epsilon *e*, covers fols 1r–16v, 21v–36r, 38v–40r, 40v–41r, 42r–v, 43r, 45r–47v, 48r–v, 49r–50r, 50v–58r, 59r–61v, 62v, 64r–65v, 66v–73v, 79r (bottom), 80v–81r, 82v, the whole of gathering 6, and fols 83r–92v. A second, neater italic script begins with the secretary character *e* and develops first the italic and then the epsilon forms of that letter on fols 17r–21r, 36r–38r, 40r–v, 41v–42r, 42v–43r, 43v–44v, 47v–48r, 50r–v, 58v–59r, 61v–62v, 63r–64r, 66r–v, 79r (top), 79v–80r, 81v–82r. A secretary hand, featuring all three forms for *e*, appears briefly on 49r, but does not necessarily indicate a new scribe.

Binding

The manuscript is bound in possibly original, seventeenth-century parchment, with four cords poking through the cover on each side of the spine.

Selected contents

'A maides deniall // Nay pish, nay pue, nay faith and will you? fy' (fol. 6r); 'Madame so may my uerses pleasing bee' (fol. 9r–v); 'A Maydes dreame // As I aloane lay slumbringe in my bedd' (fol. 18r); 'Caries Rapture. // I will enioy thee, now (my Cælia) come' (fols 19r–21r); 'On Sr Walter Raleighes death // Great hart, who taught the so to dye' (fols 30v); 'An Epitaph on the Duke of Buckingham // Long let this word hang on thy lipps' Hee's dead' (fol. 31r–v); 'Caron At Porchmouth (Duke) I can no longer staye' (fols 31v–32r); 'Yet war Bydentales sacred, and the place' (fol. 32r–v); 'Mr Cooe hauing writt some verses which hee / intituled, An Apologie for the Duke, / this answer was sent him . . . // So earst did the Plutonian Cart-wheele creake' (fols 32v–33r); 'Som say the Duke was gratious ~~good~~ vertuous good' (fol. 33r); 'An Epitaph on the Duke / of Buckingham // Reade, stand still and looke. Loe heere I am' (fol. 33r); 'Verses directed to Felton the / Murderer of the Duke // Immortall man of glory, whose braue hand' (fol. 33v); 'Feltons Epitaph // ~~Heren~~^{Herein} interd,^{suspends} (though not to saue' (fol. 34r); 'Vppon the dead body of Queene Elizabeth / brought from Richmond to White Hall // The Queene is come from Richmond to White Hall' (fol. 35v); 'A louer to his m^{rs} // Come Madam come, all rest my powers defy' (fols 59v–60v); 'On A sonne of the Duk of Buckingham

// Made of course and churlish clay' (fol. 79r); 'On the Duke of Buckinghame // I (that my countrey did betray' (fol. 80v); 'On the Duke of Buckinggame // Sooner may I a fixed Statue bee' (fols 82v–83r); 'A Letter to his M[rs] // Lett others sweare theire mistrisses bee fayre' (fols 82^{i}v–82^{k}r); 'Her Answer // S[r] you say some prayse ther M[rs] for her face' (fol. 82^{k}r–v); 'An other To Felton // Enioy thy bondage; make thy prison knowe' (fol. 83v).

Westminster Abbey Library MS 41 (Morley MS)

Owner, and possible co-compiler

George Morley, later Bishop of Winchester (1598–1684).

Collation

8°: $1^{8}(+1)$ $2\text{–}4^{8}$ $5^{8}(-5.7,8)$ $6\text{–}13^{8}$ 14^{four}

Watermark chart

As usual in an octavo in eights, the watermark appears on two leaves per gathering: the first and fourth; the second and third; the fifth and eighth; or the sixth and seventh. The second leaf in the first gathering (fol. 2) is an insert, pasted on to the first leaf.

1 +2 a	3 A	4 a	5	6	7	8	9
10	11	12	13	14	15 A	16 a	17
18 A	19	20	21 a	22	23	24	25
26	27 A	28 a	29	30	31	32	33
34	35	36	37	38 A	39	[ ]	[a]
40 A	41	42	43 a	44	45	46	47
48	49 A	50 a	51	52	53	54	55
56	57 A	58 a	59	60	61	62	63
64	65	66	67	68	69 A	70 a	71
72 A	73	74	75 a	76	77	78	79
80	81	82	83	84	85 A	86 a	87
88 A	89	90	91 a	92	93	94	95
96	97	98	99	100	101 A	102 a	103
104 A	105	106	107				

Paper

The paper in this manuscript features a single-handled pot with the initials 'CN' or 'GN' and a crescent on top.

Hands

Several hands appear in the manuscript.

Selected contents in the first hand

'Marry & loue thy Flauia for shee' (fol. 14r–v); 'Come, Madam come, all rest my powers defy' (fol. 14v–15r); 'All the newes that is stirring now' (fol. 18r–v); '5 Senses. / i Seeing. // from such a face whose excellence' (fols 21r–22r); 'B.I. 5 senses. i seeing. // From a Gypsy in the Morninge' (fols 27v–28v).

Selected contents in other hands

'As the sweet sweate of roses in a still' (fols 67v–68r); 'haue y^{u} seene the white lilly grow' (fol. 88v); 'Haue you seen a blackheaded maggott' (fol. 89r).

Index of Manuscripts Cited

All Souls College, Oxford University
155 17

Arundel Castle (The Duke of Norfolk)
Arundel Harington MS 10–11

Beinecke Rare Book and Manuscript Library, Yale University
Osborn b54 200
Osborn b62 62 n.77, 63 n. 78, 127 n.73, 174, 182, 204, 205, 209–10
Osborn b197 191, 195, 197, 205
Osborn b200 138 n.7, 174, 175, 204, 205, 211–14
Osborn b205 175
Osborn b208 62 n.77
Osborn b356 144 n.21, 197, 200, 204
Osborn c152 62 n.77
Osborn Poetry Box VI 205

Bodleian Library, Oxford University
Add. A. 368 62 n.77
Add. B. 97 71 n.7
Ashmole 36, 37 124 n.67, 138 n.6–7, 191
Ashmole 38 60 n.74, 63 n.78, 69 n.5, 72 n.9, 156–61, 174, 181, 183, 205, 214–17
Ashmole 47 127 n.73, 174, 202, 205, 217–19
Don. b. 8 197, 204
Don. b. 9 177
Don. c. 54 181, 182, 183
Don. d. 58 60 n.74, 174, 178, 181
Douce f. 5 175, 182
Eng. poet. c. 50 60 n.74, 61 n.75, 71 n.6, 110 n.37, 123 n.64, 130, 138 n.7, 191, 195, 200, 204
Eng. poet. c. 53 177, 205
Eng. poet. e. 14 71 n.6, 104–5, 135 n.5, 147, 175, 182, 195, 204, 205, 219–22
Eng. poet. e. 37 200
Eng. poet. e. 40 60 n.74, 62–3 n.77–9
Eng. poet. e. 97 138 n.7, 153–5, 174, 175, 204, 222–5
Eng. poet. f. 10 191, 195
Eng. poet. f. 16 202
Eng. poet. f. 27 62 n.77, 174, 175, 205
Firth d. 7 182, 183
Malone 19 12 n.26, 71 n.7, 72 n.9, 73, 100–1, 127 n.71, 127 n.73, 174, 181, 182, 183, 191, 197, 225–7
Malone 21 175, 204, 205, 227–8
Malone 23 22 n.44, 71 n.7, 95–100, 138 n.6, 180, 181, 191, 195, 200, 204, 205
Rawl. D. 398 191, 195
Rawl. D. 1048 69, 72, 100 n.19, 181, 182, 183, 197
Rawl. poet. 26 60 n.74, 114 n.46, 129, 153 n.45, 183, 197, 200, 204
Rawl. poet. 31 18, 71 n.6, 177
Rawl. poet. 84 183, 205
Rawl. poet. 85 1–4, 8, 11, 15–17, 19, 21–4, 173–4
Rawl. poet. 117 62 n.77, 123 n.64, 200
Rawl. poet. 142 204
Rawl. poet. 147 205
Rawl. poet. 153 62–3 n.77–9, 204
Rawl. poet. 160 48–52, 106–8, 122, 123, 139–43, 181, 182–3, 185–97, 200, 205, 228–32
Rawl. poet. 172 42 n.32
Rawl. poet. 199 174, 175, 178, 204, 205
Rawl. poet. 212 42
Rawl. poet. 214 174
Sancroft 53 182
Tanner 75 38
Tanner 465 72 n.9, 181, 200, 205
Top. Cheshire c. 7 191, 195

British Library, London
Add. 5832 191, 197
Add. 10308 48

British Library (*cont.*)
Add. 15226 205
Add. 15227 62 n.77, 182
Add. 15476 182
Add. 18647 82 n.37
Add. 19268 178
Add. 22582 174
Add. 22602 48 n.51, 122, 138 n.7, 174
Add. 22603 174
Add. 23229 85–6, 200
Add. 25303 177, 200
Add. 25707 21, 85, 102–3, 176–7, 191, 207, 233–5
Add. 27406 62 n.77
Add. 28622 48
Add. 28640 118, 200
Add. 29492 197, 205
Add. 29879 71 n.7
Add. 30982 12 n.25, 62 n.77, 174, 175, 182, 202, 205, 235–7
Add. 33998 17, 62 n.77, 205
Add. 34217 191
Add. 34218 183
Add. 37719 138 n.7
Add. 44963 181, 205
Add. 47111 62 n.77, 128 n.73, 205
Add. 61683 197
Add. 61944 183
Add. 63742 39 n.18
Egerton 923 60 n.74, 62–3 n.77–8, 128 n.73, 174, 200, 205
Egerton 1160 205
Egerton 1994 17 n.33
Egerton 2026 20
Egerton 2230 87, 89, 177, 181, 183, 213, 237–9
Egerton 2421 62 n.77, 174
Egerton 2725 60 n.74, 138 n.7
Egerton 2877 62 n.77
Harley 367 200
Harley 907 197
Harley 1221 86–7, 177, 182–3, 239–40
Harley 1836 181
Harley 3511 205
Harley 3910 177, 180
Harley 4064 71 n.6, 177
Harley 4955 20, 182
Harley 6038 86–7, 135 n.5, 177, 182, 183, 240–1
Harley 6057 47, 174, 183, 205
Harley 6383 138 n.6, 205
Harley 6931 175, 205
Harley 6947 138 n.7
Harley 7316 182, 183
Harley 7319 205
Harley 7392 1
Lansdowne 740 74, 82 n.37, 177
Lansdowne 777 12
Printed Books, E.1617.(1.) 169 n.20
Printed Books, C.39.a.37 178, 182
Sloane 363 191, 195
Sloane 542 128 n.73, 174
Sloane 826 129–31, 138 n.6, 205
Sloane 1199 205
Sloane 1446 177
Sloane 1479 191
Sloane 1489 62 n.77, 181, 182
Sloane 1792 62 n.77, 174, 178, 180, 197, 202, 205, 242–3
Sloane 2023 183
Sloane 4178 205
Stowe 962 33–6, 42, 46–7, 48 n.49, 63 n.78, 114 n.46, 123 n.64, 178, 200, 240, 244–7

Brotherton Collection, Leeds University Library
Lt 28 191, 195
Lt q 11 128 n.73
Lt q 44 144 n. 21, 191, 195, 200

Cambridge University Library
Add. 29 86, 247–8
Add. 4138 182
Add. 7196 62 n.77
Dd.5.75 20
Ee.5.23 135 n.5
Gg.4.13* 197

Cheshire Archives and Local Studies
ZCR 63/2/19 69, 134, 181, 182, 195, 197

Chetham's Library, Manchester
Mun. A 3.47 200
Mun. A 4.15 183
Mun. A 4.16 181, 182

William Andrews Clark Memorial Library, University of California, Los Angeles
S4975M1 60 n.74

Corpus Christi College, Oxford University
176 62 n.77
309 128 n.73
328 62–3 n.77–8, 128 n.73, 163 n.2, 174, 205

Derbyshire Record Office
D258/34/26/1 (Gell collection) 177

Downing College, Cambridge University
Bowtell MS, "Wickstede's Thesaurus," Part 2 200

Durham Cathedral Library
Hunter 27 200

Folger Shakespeare Library, Washington D.C.
V.a.89 1
V.a.97 62 n.77, 174, 205
V.a.103 55–66, 90–1, 103, 178–80, 181–2, 183, 248–50, 272
V.a.124 174
V.a.125 202, 205
V.a.162 12, 62 n.77, 70 n.6, 72 n.9, 128 n.73, 181, 182, 197
V.a.170 12 n.25, 156 n.51, 178, 202
V.a.245 12 n.25, 175, 202
V.a.262 60–1 n.74–5, 62 n.77, 72 n.9, 174, 181, 250–1
V.a.275 95, 191, 195, 200
V.a.276 138 n.6, 200
V.a.319 62 n.77, 174, 205
V.a.322 62 n.77, 174, 205
V.a.339 27–9, 174, 200, 251–3
V.a.345 60 n.74, 62–3 n.77–8, 110 n.37, 114 n.46, 123 n.64, 174, 175, 200, 254–5
V.b.43 205
V.b.110 138 n.6
X.d.235 200
X.d.241 33 n.2
Printed books, STC 17876 17 n.33

Hatfield House, Hatfield, Hertfordshire
206/100 200

Houghton Library, Harvard University
Eng. 686 12 n.26, 56 n.66, 72 n.9, 123 n.64, 127–8, 174, 181, 182, 191, 197, 200, 207–8, 255–8
Eng. 966.2 56 n.66
fMS Eng. 966.3 82 n.37, 177
Eng. 966.5 56 n.66
Eng. 966.7 177
Eng. 1278 205

Huntington Library, San Marino CA
EL 6232 135 n.5
EL 6893 56 n.66
HM 116 62 n.77, 156 n.51
HM 198, Part 1 88–9, 105–6, 123 n.64, 148–51, 177, 180, 183–4, 191, 200, 205, 207, 258–61
HM 198, Part 2 71 n.6, 177, 207
HM 46323 100 n.19, 178, 197, 202
Rare Books 9769 169

Inner Temple, London
Petyt 538, vol. 10 39 n.18
Petyt 538, vol. 43 236

Leicestershire Record Office (now The Record Office for Leicestershire, Leicester, and Rutland)
DG7/Lit.2 123 n.64, 181, 200, 205, 206
DG9/2796 177, 206, 261–2

London Metropolitan Archives
ACC/1360/528 205

Marsh's Library, Dublin
Z3.5.21 39

Meisei University, Tokyo
Crewe MS 62 n.77

National Archives, Kew (formerly the London Public Record Office)
SP 16/111/51 118 n.51
SP 16/114/32 133 n.2

National Library of Scotland, Edinburgh
Advocates' 19.3.8 138 n.7, 200

National Library of Wales, Aberystwyth
Dolau Cothi 6748 82 n.37
NLW 5390D 174
NLW 12443A, Part 2 62 n.77, 128 n.73, 200, 206

New York Public Library, Astor, Lenox, and Tilden foundations
Arents S288 128 n.73, 174, 181
The Henry W. and Albert A. Berg Collection of English and American Literature, Westmoreland MS 20

The Pierpont Morgan Library, New York
MA 1057 62 n.77, 123 n.64, 177, 200, 202, 262–4

Princeton University Library, Department of Rare Books and Manuscripts, Manuscripts Division
Overton, Robert, *Gospell Observations*, General Manuscripts (Bound) C0199 (no. 812) 13 n.27

Private hands
Kinzers, Pennsylvania, The Family Album, Edwin Wolf II MS 175
Mount Stuart, Bute MS 104 200
New York, Robert S. Pirie MS 68–9
Duke of Rutland, Belvoir Castle, *Letters and Papers*, Verses, Vol. XXV 182

Rosenbach Museum & Library, Philadelphia PA
239/18 62 n.77, 174
239/27 52–5, 62–3 n.77–9, 123–5, 128n.73, 143–7, 174, 175, 182, 198–204, 205, 206, 264–7
240/2 205
240/7 175, 206
243/4 175
1083/15 23–7, 71 n.7, 174, 182, 267–8
1083/16 60 n.74, 63 n.79, 71 n.6, 175, 182, 197, 200, 269–71
1083/17 175

St. John's College, Cambridge University
K.56, no. 59 191
K.56, no. 60 191
K.56, no. 61 195
K.56, no. 62 195
K.56, no. 72 197
S.32 123 n.64, 175, 200, 202, 205, 206
U.26 181, 195

Senate House Library, University of London (formerly University of London Library)
313 68–9, 135 n.5, 180, 181, 183

Shakespeare Birthplace Trust Record Office, Stratford upon Avon
ER 93/2 62 n.77

Shakespeare Centre Library and Archive ER93/2

Somerset Record Office, Taunton
DD/SF C/2635, Box 1 182, 200

Texas Tech University
PR 1171 D14 82 n.37, 177
PR 1171 S4 82 n.37, 177

Trinity College, Cambridge University
R.3.12 82 n.37

Trinity College Dublin
412 178
652 174, 175
806 138 n.7
877 60 n.74, 82 n.37, 174, 177, 200, 205

University of Aberdeen
29 202

University of Edinburgh (now Edinburgh University Library, Special Collections Department)
H.-P. Coll. 401 60 n.74, 62 n.77, 72 n.9, 113–17, 181
Laing.III.493 177

University of Kansas
4A:1 177

University of Newcastle (now Special Collections, Robinson Library, Newcastle University)
Bell/White 25 174, 175

The University of Nottingham, Manuscripts and Special Collections
Cl LM 43 202
Portland PwV 37 55–66, 90–1, 103–4, 178, 180, 182, 183, 191, 195, 200, 202, 249, 271–3

The University of Texas at Austin, Harry Ransom Humanities Research Center
HRC 79 88 n.50, 181, 183, 184, 191, 195, 197, 200

University of Wales, Bangor (now Archives and Special Collections, Bangor University)
422 69 n.5, 72 n.9, 138 n.7, 174, 180–1, 273–4

Victoria and Albert Museum, National Art Library, Westminster
Dyce 44, 25.F.39 63 n.78, 89–90, 174–5, 182, 183, 274–6
F48.G.2/1 205

West Yorkshire Archive Service, Bradford
SpSt 9/1a 60 n.74, 62 n.77
32D86/17 12 n.24, 175
32D86/34 100 n.19, 181, 191, 195, 197, 200, 202

West Yorkshire Archive Service, Leeds, Sheepscar
WYL156/237 (formerly MX 237) 62 n.77, 135 n.5, 151–3, 174, 177, 205, 206, 276–9

Westminster Abbey
41 123 n.64, 126–7, 178, 197–8, 200, 202, 279–80

Worcester College, Oxford University
Printed books, Plays.2.5 17 n.33

Printed Works Cited

Abraham, Gerald, letter, *TLS* (30 May 1968), 553.

Adams, Simon, 'Davison, William (*d.* 1608),' *ODNB*.

Anderson, Randall, '"The Merit of a Manuscript Poem": The Case for Bodleian MS Rawlinson Poet. 85,' in Arthur F. Marotti and Michael D. Bristol, eds., *Print, Manuscript & Performance: The Changing Relations of Media in Early Modern England* (Columbus: Ohio State University Press, 2000), 127–71.

Andreasen, N. J. C., *John Donne: Conservative Revolutionary* (Princeton: Princeton University Press, 1967).

Anglo, Sydney, *Spectacle, Pageantry, and Early Tudor Policy* (Oxford: Clarendon, 1969; rpt. 1997).

Arber, Edward, ed., *A Transcript of the Registers of the Company of Stationers, 1554–1640*, 5 vols. (Gloucester MA: P. Smith, 1967).

Bald, R. C., *John Donne: A Life*, ed. Wesley Milgate (Oxford: Oxford University Press, 1970).

Baron, S. A., 'Gainsford, Thomas (*bap.* 1566, *d.* 1624),' *ODNB*.

B[asse?], W[illiam], and E[dward] P[hillips, or Edward Pond?], *A Helpe to Discovrse* (London: Bernard Alsop for Leonard Becket, 1619; STC 1547).

Bastard, Thomas, *Chrestoleros. Seuen Bookes of Epigrames written by T B* (London: Richard Bradocke for I.B., 1598; STC 1559).

Beal, Peter, 'The Folger Manuscript Collection: A Personal View,' ed. Heather Wolfe, *'The Pen's Excellencie': Treasures from the Manuscript Collection of the Folger Shakespeare Library* (Washington DC: Folger, 2002), 16–19.

——, ed., *Index of English Literary Manuscripts*, 2 vols. (London: Mansell, 1980–93).

——, *In Praise of Scribes: Manuscripts and Their Makers in Seventeenth-Century England* (Oxford: Clarendon, 1998).

Bellany, Alastair, 'Felton, John (*d.* 1628),' *ODNB*.

——, 'Libels in Action: Ritual, Subversion and the English Literary Underground, 1603–42,' in Tim Harris, ed., *The Politics of the Excluded* (Basingbroke: Palgrave, 2001), 99–124.

——, 'A Poem on the Archbishop's Hearse: Puritanism, Libel, and Sedition after the Hampton Court Conference,' *Journal of British Studies*, 34/2 (1995), 137–64.

Bellany, Alastair, *The Politics of Court Scandal in Early Modern England: News Culture and the Overbury Affair, 1603–1660* (Cambridge: Cambridge University Press, 2002).

——, '"Rayling Rymes and Vaunting Verse": Libellous Politics in Early Stuart England,' in Kevin Sharpe and Peter Lake, eds., *Culture and Politics in Early Stuart England* (Stanford: Stanford University Press, 1993), 285–310.

—— and Andrew McRae, eds., 'Early Stuart Libels: An edition of poetry from manuscript sources,' *Early Modern Literary Studies*, Text Series 1 (2005). http://purl.oclc.org/emls/texts/libels/ accessed 22 June 2005.

Bishop, Carolyn, 'Raleigh Satirized by Harington and Davies,' *Review of English Studies*, 23/89 (February 1972), 52–56.

Black, L. G., 'A Lost Poem by Queen Elizabeth I,' *TLS* (23 May 1968), 535.

Bly, Mary, *Queer Virgins and Virgin Queans on the Early Modern Stage* (Oxford: Oxford University Press, 2000).

Bowers, Fredson, 'The Early Editions of Marlowe's *Ovid's Elegies*,' *Studies in Bibliography*, 25 (1972), 150–73.

Bray, Alan, *The Friend* (Chicago: University of Chicgao Press, 2003).

——, *Homosexuality in Renaissance England* (London: Gay Men's Press, 1982; rev. rpt. New York: Columbia University Press, 1995).

Bredbeck, Gregory W., *Sodomy and Interpretation: Marlowe to Milton* (Ithaca: Cornell University Press, 1991).

Briquet, Charles, *Les Filigranes* (Leipzig: K. W. Hiersemann, 1923).

Brooks, Christopher W., 'Chute, Chaloner (c. 1595–1659),' *ODNB*.

Camden, William, *Remaines Concerning Britaine* (London: By Iohn Legatt for Simon Waterson, 1614; STC 4522).

——, *Remaines Concerning Britaine* (London: Nicholas Okes, for Simon Waterson . . . at the signe of the Crowne in Pauls Churchyard, 1623; STC 4523).

——, *Remaines Concerning Brittaine* (London: A.I. for Symon Waterson . . . at the signe of the Crowne in Pauls Churchyard, 1629; STC 4524).

——, *Remaines Concerning Britaine. . . . The fift Impression* (London: Thomas Harper, for John Waterson, 1636; STC 4525).

Campion, Thomas, *The Description of a Maske: Presented in the Banqueting Roome at Whitehall, on Saint Stephens Night Last, at the Mariage of the Right Honourable the Earle of Somerset: and the Right Noble the Lady Frances Howard* (London: by E. A. for Laurence Li'sle, dwelling in Paules Church-yard, at the signe of the Tygers head, 1614; STC 4539).

Carey, John, 'The Ovidian Love Elegy in England,' DPhil diss., Oxford University, 1960.

Casas, Bartolomé de las, *The Tears of the Indians*, trans. John Phillips (London: by J.C. for Nath. Brook, 1656; Wing C799).

Chamberlain, John, *The Letters of John Chamberlain*, ed. Norman Egbert McClure, 2 vols. (Philadelphia: American Philosophical Society, 1939).

C[hamberlain], R[obert], ed., *The Harmony of the Muses* (London: by T.W. for William Gilbertson, 1654; Wing C105).

——, *The Harmony of the Muses by Robert Chamberlain, 1654*, ed. Ernest W. Sullivan, II (Aldershot, Hants: Scholar Press, 1990).

Chapman, George, *A Free and Offenceles Iustification, of a Lately Pvblisht and Most Maliciously Misinterpreted Poeme: Entitvled Andromeda Liberata* (London: for Laurence L'Isle and are to be sold at his shop in Pauls church-yard at the signe of the Tigers-head, 1614; STC 4977).

——, *Andromeda Liberata. Or The Nvptials of Persevs and Andromeda* (London: for Lavrence L'isle and are to be sold at his shop in St, Paules-Church-yard, at the signe of the Tigers-head, 1614; STC 4964).

——, *The Conspiracie, and Tragedie of Charles Duke of Byron, Marshall of France* (London: by G. Eld for Thomas Thorppe, and are to be sold at the Tygers head in Paules Church-yard, 1608; STC 4968).

Chappell, William, and Joseph W. Ebsworth, eds., *The Roxburghe Ballads*, 10 vols. (Hertford: Ballad Society, 1871–99).

Clayton, Roderick, 'Finet, Sir John (1570/71–1641),' *ODNB*.

Cleveland, John, *The Poems of John Cleveland*, eds. Brian Morris and Eleanor Withington (Oxford: Clarendon, 1967).

Cogswell, Thomas, *The Blessed Revolution: English Politics and the Coming of War, 1621–1624* (Cambridge: Cambridge University Press, 1989).

——, 'John Felton, Popular Political Culture, and the Assassination of the Duke of Buckingham,' *The Historical Journal*, 49/2 (2006), 357–85.

——, 'Underground Verse and the Transformation of Early Stuart Political Culture,' in Susan D. Amussen and Mark A. Kishlansky, eds., *Political Culture and Cultural Politics in Early Modern England: Essays Presented to David Underdown* (Manchester: Manchester University Press, 1995), 277–300.

Coiro, Ann Baynes, 'Milton and Class Identity: The Publication of *Areopagitica* and the 1645 *Poems*,' *Journal of Medieval and Renaissance Studies*, 22 (1992), 261–89.

Colclough, David, *Freedom of speech in Early Stuart England* (Cambridge: Cambridge University Press, 2005).

Considine, John, 'The Humanist Antecedents of the First English Character-Books,' DPhil diss., Oxford University, 1994.

Craig, John, 'Rogers, Thomas (c. 1553–1616),' *ODNB*.

Croft, P. J., 'Errata in "Poems from a Seventeenth-Century Manuscript with the Hand of Robert Herrick. Edited, with Introduction and Facing Transcriptions, by Norman K. Farmer, Jr.,"' *Texas Quarterly*, 19/1 (Spring 1976), 160–73.

Croft, Pauline, 'Libels, Popular Literacy and Public Opinion in Early Modern England,' *Historical Research*, 68/167 (October 1995), 266–85.

——, 'The Reputation of Robert Cecil: Libels, Political Opinion and Popular Awareness in the Early Seventeenth Century,' *Transactions of the Royal Historical Society*, 6th ser., 1 (1991), 43–69.

Cummings, Laurence, 'John Finet's Miscellany,' PhD diss., Washington University, 1960.

Davies, Sir John, *The Poems of Sir John Davies*, ed. Robert Krueger (Oxford: Clarendon, 1975).

—— and Christopher Marlowe, *Epigrammes and Elegies. By I.D. and C.M.* (Middleborough[?]: n.p., n.d.[1599?]; STC 6350).

Dawson, Giles, 'John Payne Collier's Great Forgery,' *Studies in Bibliography*, 24 (1971), 1–26.

Day, Angel, *The English Secretary*, ed. Robert O. Evans (Gainesville FL: Scholars', 1967).

Dekker, Thomas, *The Wonderfull Yeare. 1603* (London: by Thomas Creede, n.d.; STC 6535.3).

Denbo, Michael, 'The Holgate Miscellany (The Pierpont Morgan Library—MA 1057): A Diplomatic Edition,' PhD diss., The City University of New York, 1997.

Devereux, Walter Bouchier, *Lives and Letters of the Devereux, Earls of Essex, in the Reigins of Elizabeth, James I., and Charles I. 1540–1646*, 2 vols. (London: J. Murray, 1853).

D'Ewes, Simonds, *The Diary of Sir Simonds D'Ewes, 1622–1624*, ed. Elisabeth Bourcier (Paris: Didier, 1974).

DiGangi, Mario, *The Homoerotics of Early Modern Drama* (Cambridge: Cambridge University Press, 1997).

Doelman, James, 'Epigrams and Political Satire in Early Stuart England,' *Huntington Library Quarterly*, 69/1 (March 2006), 31–45.

Donne, John, *The Complete Poetry of John Donne*, ed. John T. Shawcross (Garden City NY: Anchor, 1967).

——, *The Divine Poems*, ed. Helen Gardner (Oxford: Clarendon, 1952).

——, *The Elegies and the Songs and Sonnets*, ed. Helen Gardner (Oxford: Clarendon, 1965).

——, *The Epithalamions, Anniversaries and Epicedes*, ed. Wesley Milgate (Oxford: Clarendon, 1978).

——, *Letters to Severall Persons of Honour* (London: J. Flesher for Richard Marriot, 1651; Wing D1864).

——, *Poems* (London: by M.F. for Iohn Marriott, 1633; STC 7045).

——, *Poems by J.D.* (London: M.F. for John Marriot, 1635; STC 7046).

——, *Poems* (London: T.N. for Henry Herringman, 1669; Wing D1871).

——, *The Poems of John Donne,* ed. Herbert J. C. Grierson, 2 vols. (Oxford: Clarendon, 1912).

——, *The Satires, Epigrams and Verse Letters*, ed. Wesley Milgate (Oxford: Clarendon, 1967).

——, *The Variorum Edition of the Poetry of John Donne*, gen ed. Gary A. Stringer (Bloomington: University of Indiana Press, 1995–).

Dubrow, Heather, *Echoes of Desire: English Petrarchism and its Counterdiscourses* (Ithaca: Cornell University Press, 1995).

Duncan-Jones, Katherine, '"Preserved Dainties": Late Elizabethan Poems by Sir Robert Cecil and the Earl of Clanricarde,' *Bodleian Library Record*, 14/2 (April 1992), 136–44.

Durston, Christopher, *Cromwell's Major Generals: Godly Government During the English Revolution* (Manchester: Manchester University Press, 2001).

Eckhardt, Joshua, '"From a Seruant of Diana" to the Libellers of Robert Cecil: the Transmission of Songs Written for Queen Elizabeth I,' in Peter Beal and Grace Ioppol, eds., *Elizabeth I and the Culture of Writing* (London: British Library, 2007), 115–31.

Elizabeth I, *Queen Elizabeth I: Selected Works*, ed. Steven W. May (New York: Washington Square Press, 2004).

Ellis, Sir Henry, ed., *Original Letters of Eminent Literary Men of the Sixteenth, Seventeenth, and Eighteenth Centuries* (London: Camden Society, 1843).

Fairholt, Frederick W., ed., *Poems and Songs Relating to George Villiers, Duke of Buckingham; and his Assassination by John Felton* (London: Percy Society, 1850).

Farmer, Jr., Norman K., 'Poems from a Seventeenth-Century Manuscript with the Hand of Robert Herrick,' *Texas Quarterly*, 16/4 (Winter 1973), supplement.

Felton, John, *The Prayer and Confession of Mr. Felton* ([London]: n.p., 1628; STC 10762).

Finet, John, *Ceremonies of Charles I: The Note Books of John Finet, 1628–1641*, ed. A. J. Loomie (New York: Fordham University Press, 1987).

Flynn, Dennis, 'Donne, Henry Wotton, and the Earl of Essex,' *John Donne Journal*, 14 (1995), 185–218.

——, *John Donne and the Ancient Catholic Nobility* (Bloomington: Indiana University Press, 1995).

Foucault, Michel, *The History of Sexuality*, trans. Robert Hurley, 3 vols. (New York: Random House, 1978–86; rpt. 1988–90).

Gaunt, Peter, *Oliver Cromwell* (Oxford: Blackwell, 1996).

Goddard, William, *A Neaste of Waspes* (Dort: n.p., 1615; STC 11929).

Goldberg, Jonathan, ed., *Queering the Renaissance* (Durham: Duke University Press, 1994).

Goldberg, Jonathan, *Sodometries: Renaissance Texts, Modern Sexualities* (Stanford: Stanford University Press, 1992).

Grafton, Anthony, '"Discitur ut agatur": How Gabriel Harvey Read His Livy,' in Stephen A. Barney, ed., *Annotation and Its Texts* (New York: Oxford University Press, 1991), 108–29.

——, 'Gabriel Harvey's Marginalia: New Light on the Cultural History of Elizabethan England,' *Princeton University Library Chronicle*, 52/1 (Autumn 1990), 21–24.

Gray, Catharine Emma, 'Forward Writers/Critical Readers: Women and Counterpublic Spheres in Seventeenth-Century England,' PhD diss., State University of New York at Buffalo, 2001.

——, *Women Writers and Public Debate in 17th-Century Britain* (New York: Palgrave, 2007).

Greene, Jody, ed., 'The Work of Friendship: In Memoriam Alan Bray,' spec. issue of *GLQ: A Journal of Gay and Lesbian Studies*, 10/3 (2004), 319–541.

Greg, W. W., *Dramatic Documents from the Elizabethan Playhouses* (Oxford: Clarendon, 1931).

——, *Bibliography of the English Printed Drama to the Restoration*, 4 vols. (London: Bibliographical Society at the University Press, Oxford, 1939–59).

——, *The Shakespeare First Folio, Its Bibliographical and Textual History* (Oxford: Clarendon, 1955).

Guibbory, Achsah, '"Oh, Let Me Not Serve So": The Politics of Love in Donne's *Elegies*,' *ELH*, 57 (1990), 811–33.

Hammer, Paul E. J., 'Latewar, Richard (1559/60–1601),' *ODNB*.

——, *The Polarisation of Elizabethan Politics: The Political Career of Robert Devereux, 2nd Earl of Essex, 1585–1597* (Cambridge: Cambridge University Press, 1999).

Hammond, Paul, *Figuring Sex between Men from Shakespeare to Rochester* (Oxford: Clarendon, 2002).

Harington, Sir John, *The Letters and Epigrams of Sir John Harington*, ed. Norman Egbert McClure (New York: Octagon, 1977).

Harlow, V. T., 'Harington's Epigrams,' *Times Literary Supplement* (14 July 1927), 488.

Harvey, Gabriel, *The Trimming of Thomas Nashe Gentleman* (London: for Philip Scarlet, 1597; STC 12906).

Heawood, Edward, *Watermarks, Mainly of the 17th and 18th Centuries* (Hilversum, Holland: Paper Publications Society, 1950).

Hester, M. Thomas, 'Donne's Epigrams: A Little World Made Cunningly,' in Ted-Larry Pebworth and Claude Summers, eds., *The Eagle and the Dove: Reassessing John Donne* (Columbia: University of Missouri Press, 1986), 80–91.

——, 'Donne's (Re)Annunciation of the Virgin(ia Colony) in *Elegy XIX*,' *South Central Review*, 4/2 (Summer 1987), 49–64.

Hobbs, Mary, *Early Seventeenth Century Verse Miscellany Manuscripts* (Aldershot: Scolar, 1992).

The Honorable Entertainement gieuen to the Queenes Maiestie in Progresse, at Eluetham in Hampshire (London: Iohn Wolfe, 1591; STC 7583).

Hughey, Ruth, ed., *The Arundel Harington Manuscript of Tudor Poetry*, 2 vols. (Columbus: Ohio State University Press, 1960).

The Hvsband. A Poeme Expressed In a Compleat Man (London: for Lawrence L'isle, dwelling at the Tygres head in Pauls Church-yard, 1614; STC 14008).

Jardine, Lisa and Anthony Grafton, '"Studied for Action": How Gabriel Harvey Read His Livy,' *Past and Present*, 129 (November 1990), 30–78.

Jonson, Ben, *Ben Jonson*, eds. C. H. Herford and Percy and Evelyn Simpson, 11 vols. (Oxford: Clarendon, 1925–52).

——, *The Characters of Two Royall Masques* (London: for Thomas Thorp, and are to be sold at the signe of the Tigers head in Paules Church-yard, [1608]; STC 14761).

——, *The Complete Poetry of Ben Jonson*, ed. William B. Hunter, Jr. (Garden City NY: Anchor, 1963).

——, *Conversations with William Drummond of Hawthornden*, ed. R.F. Patterson (London: Blackie, 1923).

Kelliher, Hilton, 'Donne, Jonson, Richard Andrews and The Newcastle Manuscript,' *English Manuscript Studies, 1100–1700*, 4 (1993), 134–73.

——, 'Unrecorded Extracts from Shakespeare, Sidney and Dyer,' *English Manuscript Studies 1100–1700*, 2 (1990), 163–87.

Kelsey, Sean, 'Scott, Thomas (*d.* 1626),' *ODNB*.

Knowles, James, 'Marston, John (bap. 1576, d. 1634),' *ODNB*.

——, 'To "scourge the arse/Jove's marrow so had wasted": Scurrility and the Subversion of Sodomy,' in Dermot Cavanagh and Tim Kirk, eds., *Subversion and Scurrility: Popular Discourse in Europe from 1500 to the Present* (Aldershot: Ashgate, 2000), 74–92.

Leishman, J. B., '"You Meaner Beauties of the Night": A Study in Transmission and Transmogrification,' *The Library*, 4th ser., 26/2–3 (September, December 1945), 99–121.

Lesser, Zachary, *Renaissance Drama and the Politics of Publication* (Cambridge: Cambridge University Press, 2004).

Lindley, David, *The Trials of Frances Howard: Fact and Fiction at the Court of King James* (London: Routledge, 1993).

Lithgow, William, *The Totall Discourse, of the Rare Aduentures, and Painefull Peregrinations of Long Nineteene Yeares Trauayles* (London: Nicholas Okes, and are to be sold by Nicholas Fussell and Humphrey Mosley, 1632; STC 15713).

Lockyer, Roger, *Buckingham: The Life and Political Career of George Villiers, First Duke of Buckingham 1592–1628* (New York: Longman, 1981).

——, 'Villiers, George, first duke of Buckingham (1592–1628),' *ODNB*.

Love, Harold, *Scribal Publication in Seventeenth-Century England* (Oxford: Clarendon, 1993).

MacCulloch, Diarmaid, *Reformation: Europe's House Divided 1490–1700* (London: Penguin, 2003).

Main, C. F., 'Ben Jonson and an Unknown Poet on the King's Senses,' *Modern Language Notes*, 74/5 (1959), 389–93.

——, 'Wotton's "The Character of a Happy Life,"' *The Library: Transactions of the Bibliographical Society*, 5th ser., 10/4 (1955), 270–74.

Marlowe, Christopher, *The Complete Works of Christopher Marlowe*, ed. Fredson Bowers, 2nd edn, 2 vols. (Cambridge: Cambridge University Press, 1973, 1981).

Marotti, Arthur F., *John Donne: Coterie Poet* (Madison: University of Wisconsin Press, 1986).

——, *Manuscript, Print, and the English Renaissance Lyric* (Ithaca: Cornell University Press, 1995).

Marquis, Paul A., 'Politics and print: The curious revisions to Tottel's *Songes and Sonettes*,' *Studies in Philology*, 97/2 (Spring 2000), 145–64.

Masten, Jeffrey, *Textual Intercourse: Collaboration, Authorship, and Sexualities in Renaissance Drama* (Cambridge: Cambridge University Press, 1997).

May, Steven W., 'Companion Poems in the Ralegh Canon,' *English Literary Renaissance*, 13/3 (1983), 260–73.

——, *The Elizabethan Courtier Poets: The Poems and Their Contexts* (The University of North Carolina at Asheville: Pegasus, 1999).

——, *Henry Stanford's Anthology: An Edition of Cambridge University Library Manuscript Dd.5.75* (New York: Garland, 1988).

McMillin, Scott and Sally-Beth MacLean, *The Queen's Men and Their Plays* (Cambridge: Cambridge University Press, 1998).

McRae, Andrew, *Literature, Satire and the Early Stuart State* (Cambridge: Cambridge University Press, 2004).

Merritt, J. F., 'Price, Theodore (*c*.1570–1631),' *ODNB*.

Milton, John, *Joannis Miltoni Angli defensio pro populo Anglicano* (Londini: Typis Du Gardianis, 1651; Wing M2168).

Morrill, John, 'Cromwell, Oliver (1599–1658),' *ODNB*.

Morillon, Claude, *The Fvnerall Pompe and Obsequies of the Most Mighty and Puissant Henry the Fourth, King of France and Nauarre* (London: by Nicholas

Okes, and are to be sold in Pauls Church-yard, at the signe of the Tygers head, 1610; STC 13136).

Mosser, Daniel W. and Ernest W. Sullivan, II., *The Thomas L. Gravell Watermark Archive* http://wiz2.cath.vt.edu:8200/ accessed 27 August 2007.

Moulton, Ian Frederick, *Before Pornography: Erotic Writing in Early Modern England* (Oxford: Oxford University Press, 2000).

N., W., et al. *Merry Drollery... The First Part* (London: J.W. for P.H., 1661; Wing M1860).

——, *Merry Drollery, Complete* (London: Simon Miller, 1670; Wing M1861).

——, *Merry Drollery Compleat* (London: William Miller, 1691; Wing M1862).

Norbrook, David, '"This blushing tribute of a borrowed muse": Robert Overton and his overturning of the poetic canon,' *English Manuscript Studies, 1100–1700*, 4 (1993), 220–66.

—— and H. R. Woudhuysen, eds., *The Penguin Book of Renaissance Verse, 1509–1659* (London: Penguin, 1992).

O'Callaghan, Michelle, 'Performing Politics: The Circulation of the "Parliament Fart,"' *Huntington Library Quarterly*, 69/1 (March 2006), 121–38.

Orders of His Highness The Lord Protector... against Printing Unlicensed and Scandalous Books and Pamphlets (London: by Henry Hills and John Field, Printers to His Highness, 1655; Wing C7151).

Overbury, Sir Thomas, *Characters*, ed. Donald Beecher (Ottawa: Dovehouse, 2003).

——, *A Wife now the Widdow of Sir Thomas Overbury* (London: T.C. for Laurence Lisle, 1614; STC 18907).

——, *Sir Thomas Ouerbury his Wife* (London: for Laurence Lisle, and are to be sold by Henry Seile at the Tigers-head in Pauls Church-yard, 1622; STC 18913).

Patterson, Annabel, *Reading Between the Lines* (Madison: University of Wisconsin Press, 1993).

Pebworth, Ted-Larry, 'First-Line Index to HH1 (The Bridgewater ms., Huntington Library ms. EL 6893),' http://donnevariorum.com/fli/hh1fli.htm accessed 22 June 2005.

——, 'John Donne, Coterie Poetry, and the Text as Performance,' *Studies in English Literature, 1500–1900*, 29/1 (Winter 1989), 61–75.

——, 'Sir Henry Wotton's "Dazel'd Thus, with Height of Place" and the Appropriation of Political Poetry in the Earlier Seventeenth Century,' *Papers of the Bibliographical Society of America*, 71 (1977), 151–69.

Perry, Curtis, *Literature and Favoritism in Early Modern England* (Cambridge: Cambridge University Press, 2006).

Phillips, John, *Responsio ad apologiam anonymi* (Londini: Typis De-gardianis, 1652; Wing P2098).

Phillips, John, *A Satyr against Hypocrites* (London: for N.B., 1655; Wing P2101).
——, ed., *Sportive Wit* (London: for Nath: Brook, 1656; Wing P2113).
——, ed., *Wit and Drollery* (London: for Nath: Brook, 1656; Wing W3131).
——, ed., *Wit and Drollery* (London: Obadiah Blagrave, 1682; Wing W3133).
Pitcher, John, *Samuel Daniel: The Brotherton Manuscript: A Study in Authorship*, Leeds Texts and Monographs, new ser., 7 (Leeds: University of Leeds, School of English, 1981).
Pollard, Alfred W., *Shakespeare Folios and Quartos: A Study in the Bibliography of Shakespeare's Plays, 1594–1685* (London: Methuen, 1909).
——, *Shakespeare's Fight with the Pirates and the Problems of the Transmission of his Text* (London: A. Moring, 1917).
Puttenham, George, *The Arte of English Poesie* (London: by Richard Field, 1589; STC 20519.5).
Ralegh, Sir Walter, *The Poems of Sir Walter Ralegh: A Historical Edition*, ed. Michael Rudick (Tempe: Arizona Center for Medieval and Renaissance Studies, 1999).
Raylor, Timothy, *Cavaliers, Clubs, and Literary Culture: Sir John Mennes, James Smith, and the Order of the Fancy* (Newark: University of Delaware Press, 1994).
Redding, David Coleman, 'Robert Bishop's Commonplace Book: An Edition of a Seventeenth-Century Miscellany,' PhD diss., University of Pennsylvania, 1960.
Riddell, James A. and Stanley Stewart, *Jonson's Spenser: Evidence and Historical Criticism* (Pittsburgh: Duquesne University Press, 1995).
Rogers, Thomas, *Leicester's Ghost*, ed. Franklin B. Williams, Jr. (Chicago: University of Chicago Press, 1972).
Rollins, Hyder Edward, *An Analytical Index to the Ballad-Entries (1557–1709) in the Registers of the Company of Stationers of London* (University of North Carolina Press, 1924; repr. Hatboro PA: Tradition, 1967).
——, ed., *Tottel's Miscellany* (Cambridge: Harvard University Press, 1928).
Rousseau, George S. and Neil L. Rudenstine, eds., *English Poetic Satire: Wyatt to Byron* (New York: Holt, Rinehart and Winston, 1972).
Sanderson, James L., 'An Edition of an Early Seventeenth-Century Manuscript Collection of Poems,' PhD diss., University of Pennsylvania, 1960.
Saslow, James M., *Ganymede in the Renaissance: Homosexuality in Art and Society* (New Haven: Yale University Press, 1986).
Scott, Thomas, *Robert Earle of Essex His Ghost* (Printed in Paradise [London: by J. Beale?], 1624; STC 22084).
——, *Sir Walter Rawleighs Ghost, or Englands Forewarner* (Vtricht: by Iohn Schellem, 1626; STC 22085).

——, *Vox Popvli. Or Newes from Spayne* ([London?]: n.p., 1620; STC 22098.5).

Shakespeare, William, *The Complete Sonnets and Poems*, ed. Colin Burrow (Oxford: Oxford University Press, 2002).

——, *The Norton Shakespeare*, gen. ed. Stephen Greenblatt (New York: Norton, 1997).

——, *Venus and Adonis* (London: by Richard Field, 1594; STC 22355).

Sharpe, Kevin, *Criticism and Compliment: The Politics of Literature in the England of Charles I* (Cambridge: Cambridge University Press, 1987).

——, *Reading Revolutions: The Politics of Reading in Early Modern England* (New Haven: Yale University Press, 2000).

Shawcross, John T., *The Arms of the Family: The Significance of John Milton's Relatives and Associates* (Lexington: University Press of Kentucky, 2004).

Sherman, William H., *John Dee: The Politics of Reading and Writing in the English Renaissance* (Amherst: University of Massachusetts Press, 1995).

Simmons, J. L., 'Diabolical Realism in Middleton's and Rowley's *The Changeling*,' *Renaissance Drama*, new ser., 11 (1980), 135–70.

Smith, Bruce R., *Homosexual Desire in Shakespeare's England: a Cultural Poetics* (Chicago: University of Chicago Press, 1991).

Smyth, Adam, 'An Index of Poetry in Printed Miscellanies, 1640–1682,' www.adamsmyth.clara.net/ accessed 19 August 2007.

——, '*Profit and Delight*': *Printed Miscellanies in England, 1640–1682* (Detroit: Wayne State University Press, 2004).

Songes and Sonettes (London: Apud Richardum Tottel, 1557; STC 13861).

Songes and Sonettes (London: Apud Richardum Tottel, 1557; STC 13862).

Sowernam, Esther [pseudonym], *Ester Hath Hang'd Haman: or An Answere to a Lewd Pamphlet, entituled, The Arraignment of Women. With the Arraignment of Lewd, Idle, Froward, and Vnconstant Men, and Husbands* (London: for Nicholas Bourne, 1617; STC 22974).

Stater, Victor, 'Herbert, William, third earl of Pembroke (1580–1630),' *ODNB*.

Straznicky, Marta, *Privacy, Playreading, and Women's Closet Drama, 1550–1700* (Cambridge: Cambridge University Press, 2004).

——, ed., *The Book of the Play: Playwrights, Stationers, and Readers in Early Modern England* (Amherst: University of Massachusetts Press, 2006).

Sullivan, Ernest W., II, ed., *The First and Second Dalhousie Manuscripts: Poems and Prose by John Donne and others* (Columbia: University of Missouri Press, 1988).

——, 'The Renaissance Manuscript Verse Miscellany: Private Party, Private Text,' in W. Speed Hill, ed., *New Ways of Looking at Old Texts: Papers of the Renaissance English Text Society, 1985–1991* (Binghamton NY: Medieval and Renaissance Texts and Studies, 1993), 289–97.

Swetnam, Joseph, *The Araignment of Lewde, Idle, Froward, and Vnconstant Women: or the Vanitie of them, choose you whether* (London: Edw: Allde for Thomas Archer, 1615; STC 23533).

Tennenhouse, Leonard, 'Sir Walter Ralegh and the Literature of Clientage' in Guy Fitch Lytle and Stephen Orgel, eds., *Patronage in the Renaissance* (Princeton: Princeton University Press, 1981), 235–58.

Thurloe, John, *A Collection of the State Papers of John Thurloe, Esq.*, 7 vols. (London: Printed for the executor of F. Gyles, 1742).

Traub, Valerie, *The Renaissance of Lesbianism in Early Modern England* (Cambridge: Cambridge University Press, 2002).

Tricomi, Albert H., 'John Marston's Manuscripts,' *Huntington Library Quarterly*, 43 (1979–1980), 87–102.

——, 'Philip, Earl of Pembroke, and the Analogical Way of Reading Political Tragedy,' *JEGP*, 85 (1986), 332–45.

Weldon, Anthony, *The Court and Character of King James* (London: by R.I. and are to be sold by John Wright, 1650; Wing W1273).

West, Richard, *Wits A.B.C. or a Centurie of Epigrams* (London: for Thomas Thorp, and are to be sould at the signe of the Tigers head in Paules Churchyard, [1608]; STC 25262).

White, Beatrice, *Cast of Ravens: The Strange Case of Sir Thomas Overbury* (New York: Braziller, 1965).

White, Paul Whitfield and Suzanne R. Westfall, eds., *Shakespeare and Theatrical Patronage in Early Modern England* (Cambridge: Cambridge University Press, 2002).

Wilcher, Robert, *The Writing of Royalism, 1628–1660* (Cambridge: Cambridge University Press, 2001).

Wilson, F. P., 'Shakespeare and the "New Bibliography,"' *The Bibliographical Society, 1892–1942: Studies in Retrospect* (London: Bibliographical Society, 1954), 76–135.

Witts Recreations (London: Printed for Humph: Blunden at ye Castle in Cornhill, 1640; STC 25870).

'Wonderful, a.,' *The Oxford English Dictionary*, 2nd edn (Oxford: Oxford University Press, 1989). http://dictionary.oed.com/cgi/entry/50286815 accessed 19 August 2007.

Woodbridge, Linda, *Women and the English Renaissance: Literature and the Nature of Womankind, 1540–1620* (Urbana: University of Illinois Press, 1984).

Woudhuysen, H. R., *Sir Philip Sidney and the Circulation of Manuscripts* (Oxford: Clarendon, 1996).

Yachnin, Paul, 'Scandalous Trades: Middleton's *The Witch*, the "Populuxe" Market and the Politics of Theater,' *Medieval and Renaissance Drama in England*, 12 (1999), 218–35.
Young, R. V., '"O my America, my new-found-land": Pornography and Imperial Politics in Donne's *Elegies*,' *South Central Review*, 4/2 (Summer 1987), 35–48.

General Index

Abbot, George, archbishop of Canterbury 81, 83 n.40, 109
Abraham, Gerald 39 n.19–20
Adams, Simon 12 n.24
Adolphus, Gustavus, King of Sweden 142
Allde, Edward 70 n.6
Alsop, Bernard 73 n.11
Amussen, Susan D. 9 n.18
Anderson, Randall 17 n.30
Andrews, Richard 20
Anne, queen of England, Scotland, and Ireland 12
Arber, Edward 39 n.19, 162 n.1
Arbiter, Petronius 157 n.51
Archer, Thomas 70 n.6
Ashmole, Elias 156, 218
Ayton, Sir Robert 47–9, 52, 55, 122–3, 143, 145, 147

Bacon, Sir Francis 12, 156
Bald, R. C. 80 n.29
Ball, Peter 167
Barker-Benfield, B. C. 228–31
Barkstead, Sir John 171
Baron, S. A. 141 n.14
Bashe, Edward 8, 11, 26 n.59
Basse, William 73 n.11, 157 n.51
Bastard, Thomas 72–3, 89, 181
Beal, Peter 6 n.9–10, 17–18, 69 n.3, 80 n.31, 88 n.49, 148 n.35, 260
Beaumont, Francis 7, 21, 31–2, 76–9, 81, 85–7, 89, 91, 176–7
Becket, Leonard 73 n.11
Beecher, John 74 n.13
Bellany, Alastair 8 n.16, 9 n.18, 15 n.28, 22 n.44, 33–4 n.2–3, 60 n.72–3, 64 n.80, 69–70 n.4–5, 74–5, 81 n.35, 83 n.40, 92 n.60, 93 n.1, 97, 110 n.37, 118 n.50, 129–33, 135 n.5, 138 n.6, 144 n.23–4, 160 n.59
Bishop, Carolyn 42 n.34
Bishop, Robert 269
Black, L. G. 39 n.19
Blagrave, Obadiah 171 n.28
Blount, Charles, eighth Baron Mountjoy and earl of Devonshire 42
Blunden, Humphrey 60 n.74
Bly, Mary 5 n.8
Bourne, Nicholas 70 n.6
Bowers, Fredson 23 n.50
Bradocke, Richard 73 n.11
Bray, Alan 118–19
Bredbeck, Gregory W. 117 n.48
Breton, Nicholas 1–2
Briquet, Charles 208 n.1, 212
Bristol, Mark D. 17 n.30
Brook, Nathaniel 32, 168–72
Brooke, Christopher 11
Brooks, Christopher 17 n. 33
Buckingham, George Villiers, first duke of 12, 31–2, 83, 92–7, 101, 109–11, 113, 116–25, 127–61, 203–6
Burghe, Nicholas 60 n.74, 155–61, 163, 166, 215
Byrd, William 39

Cambridge University 22–3
Camden, William 60–3
Campion, Thomas 74–5
Carew, Thomas 32, 47–9, 52, 55, 122–3, 143, 145, 147, 150–1, 164–6, 170
Carey, John 22 n.48
Carr, Robert, *see* Somerset
Cavanagh, Dermot 118 n.49
Cecil, Sir Robert, earl of Salisbury 28–9, 41 n.30, 43 n.36, 60
Chamberlain, John 22 n.44
Chamberlain, Robert 32, 163–8, 170
Chapman, George 17 n.33, 74–5
Chappell, William 39 n.19
Charles I, King 12, 31, 92–3, 96–8, 101, 107, 109, 116, 121–2, 129–31, 133, 137–8, 140, 158, 160, 165, 167, 170
Christ Church, Oxford 126, 153, 167, 211, 242

Chute, Chaloner 17–19
Clayton, Roderick 17 n.30, 25 n.58
Cleveland, John 160 n.57, 164
Coiro, Ann Baynes 98 n.11
Cogswell, Thomas 9 n.18, 97 n.9, 107 n.33, 129 n.76, 132–3 n.1–2, 134
Coke, Edward 26
Colclough, David 68 n.1
Collier, John Payne 27 n.62, 253
Coloma, Don Carlos 130 n.78
Considine, John 74 n.13
Conway, Edward, first viscount Conway 85–6
Corbett, Richard 89 n.53, 152, 154
Craig, John 33 n.2
Croft, Pauline 9 n.18
Croft, P. J. 88 n.50
Cromwell, Richard 17 n.33
Cromwell, Oliver 32, 164, 167–9, 171–2
Cummings, Laurence 1–4, 8, 17, 22 n.47

Dalton, Roger 215
Daniel, Samuel 84
Davenport, William 69, 134
Davies, Sir John 7, 23–6, 32, 42, 70–2 , 81, 89, 104–5, 146, 154–5, 174–5, 275
Davison, William 11
Dawson, Giles 27 n.62, 251–3
Day, Angel 20 n.42
Dekker, Thomas 17 n.33, 61–2
de las Casas, Bartolomé 169
Denbo, Michael 262–3
Denny, Edward 88, 105, 148–51, 258
Devereux, Robert, *see* Essex
Devereux, Walter Bouchier 37 n.10, 38 n.17
D'Ewes, Simonds 118 n.49
DiGangi, Mario 119 n.58
Digby, Sir Kenelm 164
Doelman, James 10 n.19
Donne, John 6–9, 11–15, 20–1, 23, 25 n.58, 28–33, 35–6, 43–7, 49–59, 65–6, 75–6, 78–92, 102–8, 121–8, 132, 136–7, 143, 145–6, 148–53, 155–67, 170
Drummond, William 74 n.13, 78–9, 110 n.37, 114, 198
Dubrow, Heather 4
Duncan-Jones, Katherine 41 n.30
Durston, Christopher 168 n.15
Dyer, Sir Edward 22 n.46, 38

Ebsworth, Joseph W. 39 n.19
Eld, G. 74 n.15
Eliot, John 151–3
Elizabeth I, Queen 1–3, 34–49, 52, 60–4, 77–8, 91, 95–108, 121–2, 128, 145, 151, 156–8, 165
Elizabeth, Princess, queen of Bohemia 12, 48, 65 n.83, 96–7, 142
Elvetham 1
Elwes, Sir Gervase 68 n.2
Erskine, Thomas, first earl of Kellie 83 n.40
Essex, Robert Devereux, second earl of 37–43, 59–60, 68–9 n.2, 82, 141
Essex, Robert Devereux, third earl of 30, 67–70, 74, 70
Evans, Anthony 235
Evans, Robert O. 20 n.42
Exeter College, Oxford 167

Fairholt, Frederick W. 117 n.48
Fane, Francis, first earl of Westmoreland 19–20
Farmer, Jr, Norman K. 88 n.50
Feathery scribe 18
Felltham, Owen 152
Felton, John 117, 132–6, 138–40, 144, 147, 149–54, 157–60
Field, John 168 n.16
Field, Richard 39 n.18, 153 n.43
Feilde, Henry 68–9
Finet, Sir John 16–17, 22
Flesher, J. 29 n.64
Fletcher, John 105 n.27, 151 n.38, 261
Fletcher, Richard 26
Flynn, Dennis 43 n.36
Ford, Alun 69
Foucault, Michel 118, 120
Fox, Adam 9 n.18
Franklin, James 68 n.2
Frederick V 12, 96–7
Freeman, Arthur and Janet Ing Freeman 27 n.62

Gainsford, Thomas 141
Gardner, Helen 9 n.17, 80
Gaunt, Peter 168 n.15
Gifford, Mary 26
Gil, Jr, Alexander 118
Gilbertson, William 163 n.3
Giuliano, Greg 23 n.51
Glover, Richard 89, 237
Goddard, William 8 n.15
Goldberg, Jonathan 118
Gondomar, Don Diego Sarmiento, Count of 141
Goodyer, Sir Henry 21, 28–9, 80, 82–5, 91
Grafton, Anthony 5 n.8
Gravell, Thomas L. 208 n.1, 210
Gray, Catharine 98
Greenblatt, Stephen 70 n.6
Greene, Jody 119 n.57
Greg, W. W. 5 n.7
Gresham, Sir Thomas 8
Grey, Thomas, fifteenth Baron Grey of Wilton 34
Greyhound Inn 133
Grierson, Herbert J. C. 9 n.17, 56 n.66
Grimald, Nicholas 11
Guibbory, Achsah 44–5, 91

Hall, Joseph 27, 29, 252–3
Hammer, Paul E. J. 37 n.10, 42 n.32
Hammond, Paul 110 n.36, 118 n.54
Hare, Sir Nicholas 21
Harington, Sir John 10–11, 20, 42–6, 70 n.6, 81
Harlow, V. T. 42 n.34
Harper, Thomas 60 n.74
Harris, Tim 9 n.18
Harvey, John 127
Harvey, Gabriel 5 n.8, 22 n.47
Harwood, Richard 133
Hatton, Sir Christopher 36
Hay, James, first earl of Carlisle 80 n.29
Heawood, Edward 208 n.1, 210, 212, 215, 218, 220, 223, 229–31, 233, 237–9, 249, 251, 255, 257, 263
Heneage, Sir Thomas 36–7, 41
Henrietta Maria, Queen 137–8, 167
Henry, Prince 74 n.13
Herbert, Philip, fourth earl of Pembroke 5 n.8
Herbert, William, third earl of Pembroke 83, 109–10
Herrick, Robert 88 n.50
Herringman, Henry 162
Hester, M. Thomas 43–4, 47, 91, 121
Heywood, Thomas 17 n.33
Hills, Henry 168 n.16
Hobbs, Mary 6 n.9
Hodgson, William 142 n.20
Holgate, William 263–4
Holland, Hugh 63
Hopkinson, John 12 n.24
Hoskyns, Sir John 11, 80
Howard, Frances, *see* Somerset
Howard, Thomas, fourteenth earl of Arundel 83 n.40
Hunter, Jr, William B. 76 n.19
Hurley, Robert 118 n.52
Hurtado, Juan, de Mendoza, Marquis of Inijosa 130 n.78
Huth, Henry 259

Ioppolo, Grace 17 n.31

James VI and I, King 11–13, 22, 30–1, 33, 48, 59, 67, 80 n.29, 81, 83, 92–7, 109–25, 127, 130–1, 135, 152, 172
Jardine, Lisa 5 n.8
Johnson, James 110 n.37, 123 n.64
Jones, Edward 11
Jonson, Ben 5 n.8, 20, 31, 73 n.11, 74 n.13, 74 n.15, 76, 78–9, 95, 111–15, 117, 124, 126, 157 n.51, 178, 200–2
Joseph, Mrs 27

Kavanagh, Bernard J. 71 n.8
Kelliher, Hilton 20, 22 n.46
Kelsey, Sean 140 n.12
King, Henry 142 n.20
Kirk, Tim 118 n.49
Kishlansky, Mark A. 9 n.18
Knowles, James 112 n.42, 118, 158 n.55
Krueger, Robert 24 n.52, 71 n.7, 275

Lake, Peter 9 n.18
Lake, Sir Thomas 83 n.40
Lambe, Dr John 133

Latewar, Richard 42, 64
Lawson, Henry 104–5, 147, 219
Leare, Daniel 235
Leicester, Robert Dudley, earl of 37
Leishman, J. B. 12 n.26
Lesser, Zachary 10 n.20
Lindley, David 69 n.5
Lisle, Lawrence 74–5, 85
Lockyer, Roger 83 n.40, 110 n.36, 117 n.48
Loomie, A. J. 17 n.30
Love, Harold 6 n.9, 17 n.32, 18
Ludlow, Henry 11
Lytle, Guy Fitch 38 n. 13

MacCulloch, Diarmaid 97
MacLean, Sally-Beth 5 n.8, 10 n.20
Main, C. F. 12 n.26, 73 n.11
Marriot, John 43 n.36, 162–3
Marriot, Richard 29 n.64
Marston, John 158
Martin, Richard 11
Maria, Spanish Infanta 12, 31, 92–102, 106–9, 116, 120–2, 127–9, 137
Mary I 11
Marlowe, Christopher 7, 22–4, 28, 89
Marotti, Arthur F. 6 n.9, 8 n.13, 9 n.17, 17 n.30, 19 n.37, 69 n.5, 70 n.28
Masten, Jeffrey 118
Matthews, Sir Toby 170 n.24
May, Steven W. 1, 20 n.42, 34, 36 n.8, 37–41
McClure, Norman Egbert 22 n.44, 42–3 n.34–5, 70 n.6
McMillin, Scott 5 n.8, 10 n.20
McRae, Andrew 8 n.13, 8 n. 15, 22 n.44, 28–9, 33–4 n.2–3, 60 n.72–3, 64 n.80, 68 n.1, 97, 110 n.37, 113–15, 117–18, 129–31, 133 n.2, 138 n.6, 144 n.23–4, 160 n.59
Mennes, Sir John 169–70
Merritt, J. F. 143 n.20
Middle Temple 25
Middleton, Thomas 17 n.33, 74 n.14
Milgate, Wesley 9 n.17
Miller, Simon 124 n.67
Miller, William 124 n.67
Mills, Robert 22
Milton, John 32, 118, 168, 172
Monson, Sir Thomas 68 n.2
Morillon, Claude 74–5 n.15
Morley, George 126, 279
Morrill, John 168 n.14
Morris, Brian 160 n.57
Mosser, Daniel W. 208 n.1
Moulton, Ian Frederick 8 n.13

Nashe, Thomas 7, 22–4, 71 n.7, 89
Naylor, Lawrence 132–3
Newcastle, William Cavendish, duke of 20
New College, Oxford 127
Norbrook, David 13 n.27, 71 n.7

O'Callaghan, Michelle 12 n.23
Okes, Nicholas 75 n.15
Orgel, Stephen 38 n.13
Overbury, Sir Thomas 30–1, 67–0, 73–82, 85, 91–4, 102, 110
Overton, Robert 13
Ovidian poetry 4 n.5, 22–4, 26, 30, 46, 89
Owen, John 74 n.13
Oxford, Edward de Vere, seventeenth earl of 1 n.1, 40 n.21
Oxford University 8, 11, 126–8, 153, 166–7

Patterson, Annabel 80 n.29
Patterson, R. F 74 n.13
Pebworth, Ted-Larry 12 n.24, 43 n.36, 56 n.66, 81 n.33
Percy, Henry, ninth earl of Northumberland 43 n.36
Perry, Curtis 8 n.16, 119 n.56
Petrarch 40
Petrarchan poetry 4, 7, 36, 46, 57, 66, 152
Philips, Katherine 13
Phillips, Edward 73 n.11
Phillips, John 32, 168–72
Pitcher, John 84
Pollard, Alfred W. 5 n.7
Pond, Edward 73 n.11
Price, Dr, Theodore 142–3
Puttenham, George 39 n.18

Ralegh, Sir Walter 7, 12, 30–66, 68 n.2, 76, 91, 104, 121–2, 124–5, 128, 135–7, 139, 141–3, 145–7, 151

Ramsay, John, earl of Holdernesse 81 n.36
Raylor, Timothy 169–70
Redding, David Coleman 71 n.6, 269
Reid, Julian 128 n.73
Reresby, Sir John 151–3, 276
Reshoulde, James 22
Rich, Penelope Devereux, Lady Rich 82
Riddell, James A. 5 n.8
Robertson, Mary 259
Roe, Sir John 80
Roe, Sir Thomas 25 n.58, 142 n.20
Rogers, Thomas 33–5, 42, 46–7
Rolleston, John 20
Rollins, Hyder, Edward 39 n.19
Rudick, William 12 n.24, 47
Rudyard, Sir Benjamin 25 n.58
Russell, Lucy Harington, countess of Bedford 83–4
Rutland, Elizabeth Sidney Manners, countess of 74 n.13, 76–9

Sanderson, James L. 23–6, 71 n.7
Saslow, James M. 117 n.48
Scarlet, Philip 22 n.47
Schellem, John 141 n.16
Scott, John 235
Scott, Thomas 140–2, 145
Seile, Henry 75–7, 79, 85
Shakespeare, William 7, 22 n.46, 23, 70, 152–3
Sharpe, Kevin 5 n.8, 9 n.18, 165 n.6
Shawcross, John 9 n.17, 81 n.33, 168 n.16, 169 n.18, 172
Sherbourne 135
Sherman, William H. 5 n.8
Sidney, Sir Philip 22 n.46, 40 n.21, 76, 78
Simmons, J. L. 74 n.14
Skipwith family 21, 85, 102–4, 207, 233
Smith, Bruce R. 118
Smith, G. C. Moore 42 n.34
Smith, James 160–1, 169–70
Smyth, Adam 164, 170 n.24
Somerset, Frances Howard, countess of 27–8, 30–1, 66–94, 101–3, 108, 136, 178–84
Somerset, Robert Carr, earl of 12, 27–8, 30–1, 66–94, 102, 109–10, 135–6, 145–8, 179–84
Sowernam, Esther 70 n.6
Spenser, Edmund 5 n.8, 39–40
St John's College, Cambridge 1–4, 8, 11, 15–16, 19, 21, 24
Stanford, Henry 20
Stater, Victor 83 n. 40, 110 n.36
Stephens, John 70 n.6
Stewart, Stanley 5 n.8
Straznicky, Marta 10 n. 20
Stringer, Gary A. 6 n.10, 81 n.33
Strode, William 235, 273
Stuart, Lady Arabella 33
Suckling, Sir John 165 n.6, 170
Sullivan, II, Ernest W. 81–2, 163, 208 n.1
Summers, Claude 43 n.36
Swetnam, Joseph 70 n.6

Temple, Richard 135 n.5
Tennenhouse, Leonard 37–8
Theobald's 22 n.44
Thomason, George 169 n.20
Thorp, Thomas 74 n.15
Thurloe, John 169 n.20, 171 n.27
Tottel, Richard 10–11
Townley, Zouch 152, 154, 203–4
Traub, Valerie 118
Tricomi, A. H. 5 n.8, 158 n.54
Turner, Anne 68 n.2

Urban VIII, Pope 143 n.20

Wale, John 263
Waterson, John 60 n.74
Weldon, Anthony 22 n.44
Wentworth, Thomas, earl of Strafford 138
West, Richard 74 n.15
Westfall, Suzanne R. 10 n.20
Weston, Richard 68 n.2
White, Beatrice 69 n.5
White, Paul Whitfield 10 n.20
Wilcher, Richard 160 n.57
Williams, Franklin B. 33 n.2
Willoughby, George 132–3
Wilson, F. P. 5 n.7
Windmill tavern 132–3
Winwood, Sir Ralph 83 n.40
Withington, Eleanor 160 n.57
Woodbridge, Linda 70 n.6

Woodward, Rowland 19–20
Wolfe, Heather 17 n.33
Woodward, Rowland 19, 91
Wotton, Sir Henry 12, 21, 65 n.83, 80, 156
Woudhuysen, H. R. 6 n.9, 19 n.37, 22 n.46, 71 n.7
Wright, John 22 n.44
Wright, William 39
Wriothesley, Henry, third earl of Southampton 69 n.2, 83 n.40
Wyatt, Sir Thomas 11

Yachnin, Paul 74 n.14
Yelverton, Sir Christopher 17, 19
Young, R. V. 43–4, 47, 91, 121

Zouche, Sir Edward 22 n.44